WOMEN AND WORK, PAID AND UNPAID

GARLAND REFERENCE LIBRARY
OF SOCIAL SCIENCE
(Vol. 315)

WOMEN AND WORK, PAID AND UNPAID

A Selected, Annotated Bibliography

Marianne A. Ferber

GARLAND PUBLISHING, INC. • NEW YORK & LONDON
1987

Library of Congress Cataloging-in-Publication Data

Ferber, Marianne A., 1923–
Women and work, paid and unpaid.

(Garland reference library of social science ; v. 315)
Includes index.
1. Women—Employment—Bibliography. I. Title.
II. Series.
Z7963.E7F47 1987 [HD6053] 016.3314 87-8652
ISBN 0-8240-8690-2 (alk. paper)

Printed on acid-free, 250-year-life paper
Manufactured in the United States of America

To those in Women's Studies who are concerned with efficiency, to those in Economics who are concerned with equity, and to the memory of Bob Ferber who was concerned with both.

CONTENTS

INTRODUCTION

Prior to the nineteen sixties and the beginning of the most recent feminist movement, economists had paid scant attention to the role of women in the labor market, to their economic value in the home or the relation between the two. The trickle of research on these topics which began during that period has since turned into a vast stream of publications that is increasingly difficult to encompass. The time therefore seems right to summarize the numerous contributions to this literature in a format readily accessible to researchers and students alike. By the same token, however, the task has become a formidable one. To make it more manageable, it was necessary to set limits on what is to be included, and to organize the material that is to be covered.

The first question that arose was with respect to other disciplines. Concern with issues relevant to the economic status of women is not confined to economists, but is to a greater or lesser extent shared by scholars in the other social sciences. To provide thorough coverage of material from all these fields would have made this project entirely unwieldy. To exclude all of it would be a great loss because of the direct relevance of some of the work to research done by economists. Both of these problems were avoided by focusing primarily on the economics literature but providing some references from other fields, to the extent that they have made important contributions particularly relevant to economics.

The second question was whether to include items published before the 1960's, and those dealing with developments before that time. Again, it seemed best to compromise. Actually, not much relevant work was done earlier, but several "classics" appeared of sufficient interest to be included, and a few historic curiosities were thrown in, as much for amusement as for edification. Material concerned only with the more distant past was omitted, unless it is particularly relevant to recent events.

Next, a determination had to be made whether to choose from all the literature available in English, or focus only on U.S. publications, and those concerned with the situation in the U.S. The latter perspective seemed too narrow. A great deal can be learned by comparing and contrasting the position of women in other countries with various economic systems, political structures, and cultures. Therefore the intent has been to make this bibliography as all-inclusive as possible, within the constraint of the availability of material in accessible libraries.

Last, and most difficult, was the decision to what extent only important, original, scholarly work should be included. What seems trivial to one person is likely to be of considerable interest to someone else. No research is entirely original, for everyone builds on the knowledge and ideas of predecessors. At the same time, virtually all research, even replications with different data sets, at a different time or place, adds to our knowledge base. There is even merit to "popularizing" scholarly work and thus making it available to persons who could not, or would not, struggle with a more rigorous, but also more difficult exposition. But this is not the audience addressed here. Hence, brief references are provided to many items that may be regarded as minor, and largely derivative, but only to those that go beyond mere simplification of the work of others.

In many, but by no means all cases, editorial comments, either of a laudatory, explanatory or critical nature, are appended to the summaries. They are often argumentative in tone, and speculative in nature, intended more to raise questions than to answer them.

It is hoped readers will find this volume a useful research tool and guide to further reading. Clearly, anyone who wants to pursue a topic in depth needs to turn to the originals.

ORGANIZATION

This bibliography is divided into nine major sections. Many individual items are, however, relevant to more than one of these. The summaries are included in the segment where their primary concern lies, but are cross-referenced elsewhere, as appropriate. Those that are of general interest, and do not fit neatly into any of the categories, are included in the "general" section.

For each entry there is an indication whether the emphasis is primarily on theory (1), on methodology (2), empirical evidence (3), or policy issues (4). In some cases more than one is appropriate. Items that are particularly difficult to read without considerable background in econometrics or mathematics are identified (Q).

In instances where the authors wrote very similar papers on the same topic, they are generally summarized under one heading. Similarly, when comments were written by others, these comments and the rebuttal by the author(s) are added to the summary of the original paper. References to investigations that obtained similar or conflicting results are frequently included, but are not exhaustive.

Entries, within each section, are arranged alphabetically, by the last name of the first author; co-authored items follow those written by the first author only, arranged alphabetically by last name of the second author; for the same (set of) author(s) they are arranged chronologically.

TIPS TO THE READER

It is impossible, in some instances, to provide any idea of what a paper or a monograph is about without using concepts that require some technical knowledge on the part of the reader. The most important and most frequently encountered of these are briefly defined in the introductions to the various sections. Those with no knowledge of economics and statistics, and no inclination to acquire even the rudiments, will do best simply to assume that in those instances where the summaries are difficult for them to grasp, they would find the original even more inaccessible. Such readers will, nonetheless, frequently be able to glean some useful information about the substantive conclusions made by the authors. The emphasis in the summaries is, in any case, on these rather than on methodology, or the finer points of theory.

ABBREVIATIONS OF NAMES OF JOURNALS

Academe (formerly AAUPB)	A
Academy of Management Journal	AMJ
Agricultural Finance Review	AFR
American Association of University Professors Bulletin (later A)	AAUPB
American Economic Review	AER
American Economist	AE
American Journal of Agricultural Economics	AJAE
American Journal of Economics and Sociology	AJES
American Journal of Sociology	AJS
American Psychologist	AP
American Sociological Review	ASR
American Statistical Association, Papers and Proceedings	ASAPP
American Statistician	AS
Annals of the American Academy of Political and Social Sciences	AAAPSS
Annals of Economic and Social Measurement	AESM
Annals of the New York Academy of Sciences	ANYAS
Annual Review of Sociology	ARS
Applied Economics	Appl.E
Atlantic Economic Journal	AEJ
Australian Bulletin of Labour	ABL
Australian Economic Papers	AEP
Australian Economic Review	AuER
Bell Journal of Economics	BJE
British Journal of Industrial Relations	BJIR
Brookings Papers on Economic Activity	BPEA
California Management Review	CMR
Cambridge Journal of Economics	CJE
Canadian Journal of Economics	CanJE
Canadian Public Policy	CPP
Canadian Review of Sociology and Anthropology	CRSA
Canadian Slavonic Papers	CSP
Challenge	Ch
Child Development	CD

Columbia Journal of World Business	CJWB
Columbia Law Review	CLR
Czechoslovak Economic Digest	CED
Daedalus	Daed.
De Economist	DE
Demography	Dem.
Developmental Psychology	DP
Eastern Economic Journal	EEJ
Econometrica	Economet.
Economic Development and Cultural Change	EDCC
Economic Affairs	EA
Economic Forum	EF
Economic Inquiry (formerly WEJ)	EI
Economic Journal	EJ
Economics of Education Review	EER
Economic Record	ER
Economica	Economica
Economics Letters	EL
Empirical Economics	EE
European Economic Review	EurER
Family Economics Review	FER
Finance and Development	FD
Fortune	F
Group and Organizational Studies	GOS
Growth and Change	GC
Harvard Business Review	HBR
Harvard Law Review	HLR
Illinois Research	IllR
Industrial and Labor Relations Review	ILRR
Industrial Organization Review	IOR
Industrial Relations	IR
Industrial Relations Journal	IRJ
Inquiry	I
International Economic Review	IER
International Journal of Social Economics	IJSE
International Labour Review	ILR
International Social Science Journal	ISSJ
Journal of the American Statistical Association	JASA
Journal of Applied Psychology	JAP
Journal of Behavioral Economics	JBE
Journal of Business and Economic Statistics	JBES
Journal of Business Research	JBR
Journal of Child Psychology	JCP
Journal of Comparative Economics	JCE
Journal of Consumer Research	JCR
Journal of Contemporary Business	JCB
Journal of Developing Areas	JDA
Journal of Development Economics	JDE

Journal of Development Studies	JDS
Journal of Economic Development	JED
Journal of Economic Issues	JEI
Journal of Economic Psychology	JEP
Journal of Economics and Business	JEB
Journal of Educational Sociology	JES
Journal of Health Economics	JHE
Journal of Higher Educaton	JHEd
Journal of Human Resources	JHR
Journal of Labor Economics	JLE
Journal of Labor Research	JLR
Journal of Law and Economics	JLawE
Journal of Marketing Research	JMR
Journal of Marriage and Family (formerly MFL)	JMF
Journal of Modern African Studies	MJAS
Journal of Policy Analysis and Management	JPAM
Journal of Political Economy	JPE
Journal of Post Keynesian Economics	JPKE
Journal of Public Economics	JPubE
Journal of Regional Sciences	JRS
Journal of the Royal Statistical Society	JRSS
Journal of Urban Economics	JUE
Kyklos	K
Land Economics	LE
Law and Contemporary Problems	LCP
Malaysian Economic Review	MER
Management Accounting	MA
Manchester School of Economic and Social Studies	MSESS
Marriage and Family Living (later JMF)	MFL
Monthly Labor Review	MLR
Nebraska Journal of Economics and Business (later QJBE)	NJEB
New York University Law Review	NYULR
Oxford Bulletin of Economics	OBE
Oxford Economic Papers	OEP
Pakistan Development Review	PakDR
Personnel Management	PM
Personnel Review	PR
Philippine Economic Journal	PEJ
Population and Development Review	PDR
Population Review	PopR
Population Studies	PS
Problems of Economics	PE
Psychology Today	PT
Public Finance	PF
Public Finance Quarterly	PFQ
Public Interest	PI
Public Policy	PP

Quarterly Journal of Business and Economics (formerly NJEB)	QJBE
Quarterly Journal of Economics	QJE
Quarterly Review of Economics and Business	QREB
Regional Studies	RS
Research in Labor Economics	RLE
Review of Black Political Economy	RBPE
Review of Business and Economic Research	RBER
Review of Economic Studies	REStud.
Review of Economics and Statistics	RES
Review of Income and Wealth	RIW
Review of Radical Political Economics	RRPE
Review of Social Economy	RSE
Revue Economique	RE
Science	Science
Science and Society	SS
Scientific American	SA
Scottish Journal of Political Economy	SJPE
Sex Roles	SR
Signs. Journal of Women in Culture and Society	SJWCS
Sloan Management Review	SMR
Social Concept	SC
Social and Economic Studies	SES
Social Forces	SF
Social Indicators Research	SIR
Social Problems	SP
Social Science Quarterly	SSQ
Social Security Bulletin	SSB
Sociological Methods and Research	SMR
Sociology of Education	SE
Sociology and Social Research	SSR
Sociology of Work and Occupations (later WO)	SWO
Sociometrica	Sociom.
Southern Economic Journal	SEJ
Studies in Comparative Communism	SSC
Urban Studies	US
Western Economic Journal (later EI)	WEJ
Women and Work	WW
Women's Studies	WS
Work and Occupations (formerly SWO)	WO
World Development	WD
Yale Law Journal	YLJ

Women and Work, Paid and Unpaid

Chapter 1

GENERAL WORKS

Most of the works included in this bibliography have a rather specific focus and belong into one or another of the sections dealing with particular topics. A relatively few, however, are too broad, or deal with a subject that does not quite fit any of them. These are the ones found in this "general" section. A reader interested in gaining a broad overview, rather than examining a particular topic in greater depth, might look to some of the references here.

1. Baker, Elizabeth F. Technology and Women's Work, New York: Columbia University Press, 1964.

The tone of this book is set in the preface, when the author writes that women's course through more than 160 years has been "a zigzag road in man's domain, beset by obstacles--social, economic, physical, and psychological. For women have been contending not only with the difficulties of the new work itself, but also with the problems of establishing their right to have it, particularly when jobs have been scarce during economic depressions." We are then led through history from "Alexander Hamilton and the Eighteenth Century," to women's role in the labor market in the post WWII era.

Barrett (1973) See item 838.
Behrman and Wolfe (1984) See item 840.

2. Bergmann, Barbara R. "Women's Plight: Bad and Getting Worse." Ch 26, 1 (Mar./Apr. 1983): 22-26.

The main thrust of this paper is that the Reagan Administration has hit hard at women, whose income level and job opportunities are far below those of men, and many of whom are single parents. It is further argued that as more women crowd into the labor market, persistent occupational segregation will be all the more harmful, and that substantial aid to single parents, including reform of archaic and poorly functioning child support enforcement is urgently needed. Last, but not least, the author urges help for the many older women who have inadequate resources and whose only hope is federal aid.

3. Bergmann, Barbara R. and Irma Adelman. "The 1973 Report of the President's Council of Economic Advisors: The Economic Role of Women." AER, 63, 4 (Sept. 1973): 509-14.

This is a review from a feminist perspective of the chapter on women's issues that was included for the first time in the 1973 Report of the President's Council of Economic Advisors. It gives full credit for a competent presentation of the facts, appropriate concern for problems, and interest in finding solutions. There is also criticism, however, of the unquestioning acceptance of much of the conventional wisdom--such as ascribing higher female unemployment rates to a larger proportion of new entrants and lower wages in large part to less experience--and traditional attitudes--such as the need for women to drop out for child care and our inability to measure the value of nonmarket work.

4. Bianchi, Suzanne and Daphne Spain. "American Women: Three Decades of Change." U.S. Department of Commerce, Bureau of the Census, Special Demographic Analysis, Aug. 1983a.

This is a thorough review of data from 1950 to 1980 on various aspects of women's lives, from marital status, fertility and household living arrangements, to education, labor force participation, earnings and occupations. There is a brief concluding section on women's poverty problems.

Boserup (1970) See item 851.

5. Chapman, Janet R. <u>Economic Independence for Women: The Foundation for Equal Rights</u>. Sage Yearbooks in Women's Policy Studies VI, Beverly Hills, CA: Sage 1976.

This was the first volume of the Sage Yearbooks in Women's Policy Studies. The contributors include Martha W. Griffiths, a former member of the U.S. House of Representatives, a number of eminent academic economists and sociologists, and representatives from a variety of organizations concerned with improving the economic status of women. Some of the papers deal with general issues; others focus on particular problem areas such as blue collar jobs and poverty. Emphasis is placed on policies that would help to improve conditions for women.

Darling (1975) See item 870.
Devi and Ravindra (1983) See item 876.
DeVries (1971) See item 877.

6. England, Paula and George Farkas. <u>Households, Employment, and Gender</u>, NY: Aldine Publishing Company, 1986. (1,3)

This informative book uses economic, sociological and demographical analysis to examine persistence and change in the roles of men and women in the household and labor market. The authors display a thorough knowledge of the literature in these disciplines, evaluate it critically, and often weave the most worthwhile contributions from each into a more realistic model than any previously available. One need not agree with all their interpretations to appreciate the contribution such a synthesis can make in breaking down barriers between fields that have, in the past, tended to hamper cross-fertilization.

7. Feinstein, Karen W., ed. Working Women and Families, Beverly Hills, CA: Sage Publications, 1979.

Though some of the papers in this book are inevitably somewhat dated, there is a great deal of material that remains relevant. For the most part, the focus is on the effect a woman's labor force participation has on the family, and the impact her family role has on her status in the labor market. More than most, these authors show awareness of the inevitability of problems as long as it is mainly wives who have "family responsibilities." One of the most interesting chapters explores the possibility of flexible work arrangements for both men and women.

8. Fogarty, Michael P., Rhona Rapoport and Robert N. Rapoport. Sex, Career, and Marriage, London: George Allen and Unwin Ltd., 1971.

This comprehensive book deals with the problems of and prospects for women who combine having a family with a career, as opposed to merely a job. The approaches and experiences in both Eastern Europe and Western countries, with emphasis on Great Britain, are examined and evaluated. Surprisingly, and perhaps sadly, much of the material is still timely.

Galenson (1973) See item 888.

9. Greenberger, Ellen and Lawrence D. Steinberg. "Sex Differences in Early Labor Force Experience: Harbinger of Things to Come." <u>SF</u> 62, 2 (Dec. 1983): 467-87. (3)

This study of 3,101 suburban 10th and 11th graders finds that many of the well-known differences among adult workers already hold for these teenagers. Jobs are segregated, male jobs pay better, girls earn lower hourly wages and tend to work fewer hours. In general, these differences continued over the early work histories of these young people.

Heitlinger (1979) See item 909.
Henry and Wilson P. (1975) See item 910.
Horna (1978) See item 913.

10. Husby, Ralph D. "Day Care for Families on Public Assistance: Workfare versus Welfare." <u>ILRR</u>, 27, 4 (July 1974): 503-10.

This study estimates that the short run costs of a program to promote self-sufficiency among women who head welfare families would be greater than the cost of income maintenance, even under very optimistic assumptions. The author also points out, however that his study did not take into account various potential long run effects, including favorable psychological effects on the mother and her children, and the benefits of high quality day care. Thus, one may well conclude that calculating only short run effects is likely to be short sighted.

11. James, Estelle. "Income and Employment Effects of Women's Liberation," in Cynthia B. Lloyd, ed., <u>Sex, Discrimination and the Division of Labor</u>, NY: Columbia University Press, 1975, pp. 379-400.

This paper explores the intriguing question what the world will look like after women have achieved economic equality with men. A model is set forth that helps to analyze occupational integration, its impact on output and income, as well as the distribution of gains and losses. Further, the impact on female labor supply is also explored.

12. Kreps, Juanita M. Sex in the Marketplace: American Women at Work. Baltimore: Johns Hopkins Press, 1971.

The title of this book suggests the liveliness of this small volume which provides an overview, albeit a somewhat superficial one, of the main economic issues related to the movement of women into the labor market. Some of the material seems rather dated now, and gives a good idea of how much the lives of women have changed, and how much more we have learned about them meanwhile.

13. Kreps, Juanita M., ed. Women and the American Economy: A Look to the 1980's. Englewood Cliffs, NJ: Prentice-Hall, 1976.

This small book provides a useful overview of the changes in women's world of work and their relation to "women's revolution of rising expectations." Contributions by various authors deal with history, economic and legal developments, and the interdependence between women's role in the labor market and the home. Much of the content of these papers, including the last chapter which asks, "Will women have different roles?", is still relevant 10 years later.

Kurian and Ghosh (1981) See item 928.
Lapidus (1978)(1981) See items 932, 933.
Leijon (1975) See item 937.

14. Lloyd, Cynthia B., Emily S. Andrews, and Curtis L. Gilroy. Women in the Labor Market, NY: Columbia University Press, 1979.

This is a collection of important papers, for the most part similar to articles previously published elsewhere. Bargaining analysis is applied to household decisions, as the authors did in Manser and Brown, M. (1978). Women's labor supply is examined, as it was by Smith, R. E. (1979) and Heckman (1978). Occupational segregation is discussed, much as in Polachek (1976), wage differentials are considered as in Corcoran (1978) and Chiplin (1976). Some of the other chapters, especially those on the role of government policy, however, present new work, and many of the comments, at the end of each section, are perceptive and interesting. In any case, this book has the virtue of bringing a good deal of research together under one cover.

15. Lloyd, Cynthia B. and Beth T. Niemi. The Economics of Sex Differentials, New York: Columbia University Press, 1979.

This book, relying on neoclassical analysis, and drawing mainly on research done by others within the same framework, examines the performance and rewards of women in the labor market. At the same time the authors provide information about the institutional framework, and confront the reality that discrimination appears to be an important factor that helps to determine women's occupations and earnings. Further, this book is written at a level making it accessible to the diligent non-specialist.

16. Lopata, Helena Z. and Kathleen F. Norr. "Changing Commitments of American Women to Work and Family Roles." SSB 43, 6 (June 1980): 3-14.

This study explores women's attitudes toward social security and retirement, focusing on differences by level of education, training and employment status. Secondarily, cohort changes in life patterns, employment, and family roles are also examined.

17. Madden, Janice F. "The Development of Economic Thought on the 'Woman Problem'." RRPE 4, 3 (July 1972): 21-39.

Early thought about the economic role of women is reviewed, including that of Marxist economists, such as Engels, Bebel and Zetkin, classical economists, such as Mill and Edgeworth, and feminists such as Gilman and Wollstonecraft. This is followed by a brief consideration of the work of some of the best known more recent contributors to this subject, again chosen from individuals representative of a wide variety of points of view.

18. Medoff, Marshall H. "Christian Politics and the Economic Status of Women." JBE 13, 1 (Summer 1984): 23-40.

This study uses data from the U.S. Bureau of Census, State Reports, Detailed Characteristics, 1970, and United States Summary, 1970, as well as from Churches and Church Membership in the United States, 1971, to investigate the relationship between evangelical groups and the economic status of women. No impact on relative wages or occupational status was found, but there was evidence that fundamentalists tended to translate their belief that women needed protection into restrictive labor laws, which caused the female unemployment rate to be higher relative to male unemployment. Further, these religions had an unmistakeable positive effect on the proportion of women who married.

19. Mill, John Stuart. The Subjection of Women, ed., Sue Mansfield, Arlington Heights, IL: AHM Publishing Company, 1980.

This book was written in 1861, published in 1896. Two quotes give a good idea of how timely it still is more than a hundred years later. "Every restraint on the freedom of conduct of any of their human fellow-creatures...leaves the species less rich...in all that makes life valuable to the individual human being." Or again, the author questions whether there is "really any distinction between the highest masculine and highest feminine character? ... The women ... who possess the highest measure of what are considered feminine qualities, have combined with them more of the highest masculine qualities than I have ever seen in any but one or two men, and those one or two were also in many respects almost women."

Mincer (1985) See item 949.

20. Mott, Frank L., ed. The Employment Revolution: Young American Women in the 1970s, Cambridge, MA: The MIT Press, 1982a.

The papers in this book are all based on data for the cohort of young women of the National Longitudinal

Surveys for 1968 to 1975. Collectively, they show that a real revolution has taken place not only in women's labor force participation, but in their attachment to the labor force, and in attitudes toward women's employment. They also show, however, that considerable obstacles remain in the way of achievement of full equality, from attitudes of families toward sons and daughters, to the effect of children on the labor force attachment of mothers, even though the impact of these inhibiting factors is declining.

Myrdal and Klein (1986) See item 954.
Nash (1970) See item 957.
OECD (1985) See item 961.

21. Owen, John D. "Flexitime: Some Management and Labor Problems of the New Flexible Hour Scheduling Practices." ILRR 30, 2 (Jan. 1977): 152-61.

This paper suggests that in the U.S. flexitime has been well received by employers, while it is unions that are skeptical. So far, this practice has not been around long enough, or wide-spread enough, to draw firm conclusions. But where it has been successfully maintained, it is popular with the employees as well as employers. The author urges that it is crucial for productivity to be maintained and that gains, if any, be shared with workers. Also, he believes we need assurance that no bogus coercive flexitime be used. Many success stories are found in Europe.

Pavlátová (1978) See item 966.
Powell (1984) See item 970.

22. Pujol, Michele A. "Gender and Class in Marshall's Principles of Economics." CJE 8, 3 (Sep. 1984): 217-34.

The author argues that Marshall's embryonic human capital theory is based on a conception of capitalist social reproduction in which women are entirely defined by Victorian bourgeois values. Working class women particularly are expected to look after their families and raise healthy children of good character, with no direct return for their contribution to male human capital. Hence Marshall favored low wages for women, so that they would be induced to stay home and not "neglect their duties."

Ratner (1980) See item 972.

23. Roderick, Roger D. and Andrew I. Kohen. Year for Decision, A Longitudinal Study of the Educational and Labor Market Experience of Young Women, Vol. 3, Washington, DC: U.S. Department of Labor, Employment and Training Administration, Road D Monograph 24, 1976.

This is an update of Shea et al. (1971) five years later, describing the changes in educational and occupational aspirations, as well as the employment status of the young women's cohort of the National Longitudinal Surveys.

24. Root, Norman and Judy R. Daley. "Are Women Safer Workers? A New Look at the Data." MLR 103, 9 (Sept. 1980): 3-10.

Women workers do have a better safety record than men, but this may reflect that relatively few are in hazardous jobs. Data from 26 states suggest that men and women doing the same kind of work incur similar injuries with about the same frequency.

Ruggie (1984) See item 980.
Safilios-Rothschild (1970b) See item 981.
Schmid and Wetzel (1984) See item 982.
Scott, H. (1974) See item 984.
Seguret (1983) See item 986.

25. Shea, John R., Roger D. Roderick, Frederick A. Zeller, Andrew I. Kohen and Associates. Years for Decision: A Longitudinal Study of the Educational and Labor Market Experience of Young Women, Vol. 1, 1971, Columbus, OH: Center for Human Resource Research, Ohio State University.

This volume uses the National Longitudinal Survey on Young Women, begun in 1965, to provide evidence on marital and family status, schooling, employment and unemployment of this cohort. The information, interesting in itself, is also useful background for the numerous studies by other researchers that utilize this data set.

Sloane (1980) See item 993.

26. Smith, Ralph E., ed. The Subtle Revolution, Women at Work. Washington, D.C.: The Urban Institute, 1979.

This volume is one of the best reference works on the causes, nature, and consequences of women's increased labor force participation. The individual chapters review the literature on topics ranging from women's movement into the labor market, occupations, earnings and unemployment to the relation between their market activities and their role in the family.

27. Stromberg, Ann H. and Shirley Harkess, eds. Women Working, Palo Alto, CA: Mayfield Publishing Company, 1978.

This volume is composed primarily of review papers, mainly written by economists and sociologists, which provide information on women in the labor market, but also includes chapters on workers in particular occupational groups, and some on women's role in the family. All are written at a level readily accessible to nonspecialists, and would be useful for assignment to undergraduates.

Taylor (1985) See item 1013.

28. Vogel, Elaine. "Some Suggestions for Advancement of Working Women." ILR 112, 1 (July 1975): 29-43.

The author sees conditioning to sex roles passed on from generation to generation at the root of discrimination, which must be ended if women are to achieve equality. She therefore urges a thorough reform of society's values, as well as "the introduction of dynamic vocational training and employment policies, the adoption of legislation and regulations that will effectively promote equality of work, and the institution of comprehensive family welfare programms designed to lighten the burdens currently assumed by women...." Now if we can only find a way of doing all this, the millenium will be just around the corner.

29. Waite, Linda J. "U.S. Women at Work." PB 36, 2 (May 1981): 1-43.

A useful survey article, this provides an overview of changes in women's labor force participation and family roles with references to relevant research, as well as a brief discussion of related policy issues.

30. Yanz, Lynda and David Smith. "Women as a Reserve Army of Labor: A Critique." RRPE 15, 1 (Spring 1983): 92-106.

The authors claim that among "Marxists, Marxist Feminists, and in the working class and women's movement in general" there is a notion of women as a "reserve army of labor" in capitalist systems. They then proceed to refute the argument, mainly by pointing out that women are so large a segment of the labor force, and they are so segregated in female occupations, that they cannot be a "reserve army." This downplays the fact that historically great efforts were made to attract women into the labor force in war times, that laws were passed to keep them out during depressions, and that women have tended to enter the labor force most rapidly during prosperous times. Nonetheless, much of the criticism in this paper is well taken.

Chapter 2

ECONOMICS OF THE FAMILY: TRADITION AND CHANGE

Most people live most of their adult lives as members of families (defined as units consisting of two or more persons living together, related by blood, marriage, or adoption), where income and consumption are to some extent shared, and satisfaction of individuals is more or less interdependent. It is therefore of particular interest to examine the allocation of time of men and women living in such households between market work and housework.

The facts are clear and generally agreed upon. There has been a sustained and rapid increase in the labor force participation of women, and the largest increases have been among groups who were previously least likely to work for pay, namely wives with husbands present, and most of all mothers with young children. But women also continue to do the bulk of the housework, whether or not they work outside the home. Men tend to do no more of it when the woman is employed than when she is a full-time homemaker. The increasing proportion of women who have part-time jobs appear to solve the overload problem by working shorter hours in the labor market. Women who accept the lion's share of household responsibilities also tend to opt for more flexible and less demanding jobs. It is the interpretation of these facts that creates much disagreement.

The widely accepted human capital explanation assumes that women continue to have a relative advantage in housework, men in market work. That is to say, they can produce household services with a smaller sacrifice of market earnings, either because they are more efficient than men in performing these services at home, or because they earn less when employed. This is so in spite of the fact that women's real wages in the labor market have been increasing relative to the value of their contribution in the household, so that it is worthwhile for more and more of them to spend some time working for pay. The differences in relative efficiency between the sexes are explained to a greater or lesser extent by biological factors, and by the cumulative experience in one kind of work resulting from specialization itself. In any case the conclusion is that in order to maximize the well-being of the family at least one person must specialize entirely in one type of work, though the partner need not do so.

This line of reasoning not only explains the present situation--women either specializing in housework or, increasingly, dividing their time between household and market, while men largely specialize in market work--but also endorses it as being efficient, the result of rational decision making, and presumably good for everyone in the family.

Feminists take quite a different view of the situation. They question that biological differences account for much of the existing specialization of men and women, and point to the circular reasoning involved in the claim that women spend more time on housework because men have a relative advantage in the market, and that men have a relative advantage in the market because women spend more time on housework. They also point to the problems the traditional division of labor causes, especially for women, whether or not it is efficient in maximizing income for the family.

Doing long hours of one kind of work or the other is likely to be more tedious than doing some of both kinds, and while men at least initially have some choice among a variety of different types of jobs in the labor market, there is far less scope for variation within the household. Specializing in unpaid housework tends to be devalued in a society which puts great emphasis on money income, and does, in fact, make the woman dependent on the man's earnings. Her position becomes increasingly precarious over the life-cycle, since her value at home declines as the children grow up and at the same time her labor market skills depreciate. This is likely to effect her status within the family unfavorably and to have disastrous results in case she needs to support herself, and possibly her children. The man who has acquired no facility with housework at all will also be at a disadvantage if he should need to take care of a home.

These are the main issues addressed in this section: How do men and women allocate their time between household and labor market? To what extent do they make a rational, informed decision rather than simply following tradition? What are the long run effects of choices made on the family and its various members? We leave for the next chapter studies that specifically address the closely related issue of women's labor force participation.

31. Adler, Hans J. and Oli Hawrylyshyn. "Estimates of the Value of Household Work, Canada 1961 and 1971." RIW 24, 4 (Dec. 1978): 333-55. (3)

Like Murphy (1978) this study, using Canadian data, finds that estimates of value of housework based on the cost of hiring workers for different tasks, and estimates based on the cost of wages foregone by the homemaker, do not give very different results. In either case the value of household work equals about 40 percent of GNP. While studies for the United States suggest that this percentage appears to be declining, no evidence of this is found in Canada.

32. Anderson, Kathryn H., Robert L. Clark and Thomas Johnson, "Retirement in Dual Career Families," in Robert L. Clark, ed., Retirement Policy in an Aging Society, Durham, N.C.: Duke University Press, 1980: 109-27. (3)

Research based on data from the Retirement History Study of the Social Security Administration Survey, 1969-1971, and using a simultaneous decision model, produced evidence that for women married to older men, their own and their husband's labor force participation rate is positively related to their own wages. This suggests that non-market time of husbands and wives may be complements among the elderly. Since wages are related to experience, these findings also suggest later retirement for dual career couples. It may be that eligibility for pension benefits works in the opposite direction, but data for woemn have only recently become available, and have not been incorporated.

33. Angrist, Shirley S., Judith R. Lave and Richard Michelson. "How Working Mothers Manage: Socioeconomic Differences in Work, Child Care and Household Tasks." SSQ 56, 4 (Mar. 1976): 631-37. (3)

This study finds major differences in ways employed women assume their roles as worker, mother, and housekeeper. Professional-managerial work tends to be associated with high family income, and a shorter work day. Accordingly, these women purchase more child care, but also spend more time on child care themselves. Women in clerical-technical occupations rely more frequently on relatives and friends. The amount of help a woman receives from other family members with household chores is positively related to hours worked. The authors conclude the differences are only partly explained by economic factors, and point to the importance of sociological ones as well.

34. Axelson, Leland J. "The Marital Adjustment and Marital Role Definitions of Husbands of Working and Non-working Wives." JMF 25, 2 (May 1963): 189-95. (3)

Data collected by mail questionnaire for this study show that husbands of employed women had more liberal views not only toward wives working outside the home, but toward other issues concerning women, than did husbands of full-time homemakers. Nonetheless, similar to Burke and Weir (1976), poorer marital adjustment was found in families where the wife was employed, and the author suggests this is the cost of the new arrangements, even when the husband has relatively egalitarian attitudes. Some later studies, such as Boath (1977) and Orden and Bradburn (1969) did not obtain the same results. Further, Axelson does not consider there may be a bias to the extent that women who are in unsatisfactory marriages are more likely to work outside the home. This would reverse the cause and effect relationship.

35. Bartlett, Robin L. and Charles Poulton-Callahan. "Changing Family Structures and the Distribution of Family Income: 1951 to 1976." SSQ 63, 1 (Mar. 1982): 28-37. (3)

Data from Current Population Reports confirm that the increase in recent decades of two-earner families has tended to decrease the inequality of money income among male-headed families. At the same time, however, the increase in female-headed families has had the opposite effect on income distribution for all families. The net result is an apparent stability overall.

36. Becker, Gary S. "A Theory of Marriage." JPE 81, 4 (July/Aug. 1973): 813-46; 82, 2 (Mar./Apr. 1974): S11-S26. (1)

As in his other work, the author here applies micro-analytic economic maximizing principles to his analysis of family relationships. The contributions and flaws of this paper are essentially the same as those in Becker (1981).

37. Becker, Gary S. A Treatise on the Family, Cambridge, MA: Harvard University Press, 1981. (1)

This book is a compendium of the voluminous work on the family of the acknowledged father of the "New Home Economics." His stated purpose is to analyze marriage, births, divorce, division of labor in households, prestige, and other nonmaterial behavior with the tools and framework developed for material behavior. The major contributions of Becker's work are that it applies the powerful tools of economic analysis in areas which economists had either abandoned or never before entered, and that its scope is broad enough to encompass societies throughout the world and throughout history.

Unfortunately the limitations of this body of thought are as serious as its insights are brilliant. The most jarring are: 1. A tendency to cite indiscriminately those who support the proposed views as though they were authorities (the most extreme case is a reference to the Ayatollah Khomeini), while virtually ignoring the fairly substantial body of critical literature. 2. Unwarranted conclusions drawn from well-established facts. A good example is using the incontrovertible fact that only women bear children to support the contention that they are peculiarly suited to rearing the young, and even to do all forms of housework. 3. Sweeping generalizations made in face of conflicting evidence. Asserting that women have traditionally relied on men for provision of food and shelter is a case to the point. 4. Selective use of facts, such as citing recent experience in evidence of the negative relation between income and fertility, while ignoring the declining number of children during the great depression and the baby boom of the fifties. 5. Constructing unnecessarily elaborate models to explain simple relationships, such as the obvious affinity of individuals with similar backgrounds. 6. Hedging bets so thoroughly that no conceivable outcome would be inconsistent with the proposed theories. How could one possibly falsify the contention that "mating of likes (or unlikes) takes place when such pairings maximimize aggregate commodity output..."?

Anyone seriously interested in studying the family can not afford to ignore this book, for it has had an enormous impact in a variety of disciplines, and provides a great deal of food for thought. It should not, however, be read uncritically, or heedlessly used as a basis for policy.

38. Becker, Gary S., Elizabeth M. Landes and Robert T. Michael. "An Economic Analysis of Marital Instability," JPE 85, 6 (Dec. 1977): 1141-87. (1)

Though this theory of divorce relies on uncertainty, an imperfection that is not permitted to mar other aspects of family behavior (Becker 1981), we are still in a Beckerian world. One person may, for instance, want a divorce when unexpected good fortune makes a better match possible or, when, say, undesired fertility makes the present match less so, but we must never believe that this person walked out, or the other was abandoned. The partner who would rather remain married can always do so by accepting a less favorable division of benefits, or has to be placated by a generous divorce settlement. Further, this supposedly holds independent of existing divorce laws, and uncertainty does not appear to extend to divorce settlements.

39. Bell, Carolyn S. "Working Women's Contributions to Family Income." EEJ 1, 1-2 (Apr.-July 1974): 185-201. (3)

The author points out that looking only at the average share of family income earned by employed wives underestimates the importance of their contribution. Their income frequently makes the difference between poverty and an adequate standard of living, and most of the time provides a safety cushion in the case of financial emergencies. Also, while the proportion of families where the woman earns half or more of the income is small, their absolute number is quite large.

40. Beneria, Lourdes. "Reproduction, Production and the Sexual Division of Labour." CJE 3, 3 (Sept. 1979): 203-25. (1),(3)

Though the author places great emphasis on women's role in biological and social reproduction, she also contends that the sexual division of labor in the family and the inequality between men and women based on it are not a given and could be changed. On the contrary, she argues that it is the division of labor in the market sector that causes the existing family arrangements. To make her argument she draws upon evidence from Third World countries. Her views are diametrically opposed to the usual contention that the causal relation is in the opposite direction. The truth may well lie in between.

Berent (1970) See item 844.

41. Bergmann, Barbara R. "The Economic Risks of Being a Housewife," AER 71, 2 (May 1981): 81-86. (1)

Being a housewife is quite different from other occupations, and it has peculiar risks. Mutual attraction of spouses may decline, the value of the homemaker's contribution will decline as children grow up. For these reasons, the risk of "losing the job" is substantial. If that happens she will have to change occupations, at least for a time, though she will be ill prepared for it. She may also have to move out. With all these problems, termination of a marriage presents serious risks to the homemaker, which in large part explains why increasingly fewer women are willing to choose this occupation, except perhaps for brief periods of time.

42. Berk, Richard A. and Sarah F. Berk, "A Simultaneous Equation Model for the Division of Household Labor." SMR 6, 4 (May 1978): 431-68. (3)

A three-equation nonrecursive model in the tradition of the New Home Economics is estimated with data from a sample of 184 households, in order to examine the division of labor. The unique feature of this research is that direct measures of household efforts of husband and children are employed. Allocation of work is found to respond to economic variables, but many anomalies also surface. The wife tends to do most of the household work, no matter what the circumstances.

43. Bianchi, Suzanne M. and Daphne Spain. "Wives Who Earn More Than Their Husbands." U.S. Department of Commerce, Bureau of the Census, Special Demographic Analysis, Nov. 1983b. (3)

Contrary to the popular image, wives who earn more than their husbands are not generally "superstars." Most are not college educated and not in professional or managerial jobs, but rather women married to men who have labor market difficulties. Since these problems are often temporary, and require major adjustments, such couples do not provide a useful sample for testing the widely-held hypothesis that income superiority on part of a wife is detrimental to marital happiness.

44. Blau, David M. "Family Earnings and Wage Inequality Early in the Life Cycle." RES 66, 2 (May 1984): 200-207. (3)

This research, using data on white, married, spouse present couples from 1968 to 1975 from the National Longitudinal Survey of Young Women, confirms findings of other studies (e.g., Bartlett and Poulton Callahan 1982) that wives contribute to equalizing the distribution of family earnings. The main reason for this is wives' labor supply behavior. It is also the case, however, that the dispersion of wives' wage rates, at least in the early stages of the life cycle, is lower than that of husbands.

45. Blood, Robert O., Jr. and Robert L. Hamblin. "The Effect of the Wife's Employment on the Family's Power Structure." SF 36, 4 (May 1958): 347-52. (3)

The authors used a sample consisting of 80 couples with an employed wife, and the same number with a full-time homemaker, to determine whether "working wives have more influence in decision making." Unlike some studies, such as Heer (1958) and Weller (1968), they found that support for this hypothesis was not "reliable," though their research showed that husbands do somewhat more housework. Had they stipulated a longer period than one year for the wife to have been in her present employment status, this difference might well have been greater.

46. Boath, Alan. "Wife's Employment and Husband's Stress: A Replication and Refutation." JMF 39, 4 (Nov. 1977): 645-50. (3)

In order to re-examine the question whether husbands of employed wives were in poorer health and less contented with their marriage as Burke and Weir (1976) claimed, this study employed improved methods of sampling, measurement and analysis. The author found no evidence to support the earlier conclusions. There was also little difference in well-being between wives who had, for some time, been in or out of the labor market. The women who did show more signs of stress than others were those who had recently experienced a transition from one employment status to the other. This suggests that there may be short-run difficulties of adjustment in either direction.

47. Brown, Clair. "An Institutional Model of Wives' Work Decisions." IR, 24, 2 (Spring 1985): 182-204. (1)

The author, dissatisfied with neoclassical models of household behavior, which have tended to underpredict women's labor force participation and are, in any case, unrealistic, proposes an institutional alternative. She suggests that women have sought employment not because they are able to purchase goods and services they used to produce at home, but in order to be able to buy commodities produced by a modern economy, previously nonexistent. This model has quite different implications than the neoclassical one. Women cannot always buy substitutes for home production, outputs are not necessarily optimal, and when a woman becomes unemployed she cannot to any great extent substitute home production for earnings. But Brown's views may be somewhat extreme. Hunt, J. C. and Kiker (1981) as well as Nickols and Fox, K. D. (1983), for instance, find evidence of possibilities for substitution of purchased goods and services for time.

48. Brown, Lisa J. "Neoclassical Economics and the Sexual Division of Labor." EEJ 10, 4 (Oct.-Dec. 1984): 367-79. (1)

This paper examines the neoclassical research program from an explicitly feminist point of view. Both the explanation that specialization within the family is based on the greater relative efficiency of women in housework and an alternative approach which treats men and women symmetrically are considered. The feminist perspective is based on the assumption that the existing division of society into separate realms is a social rather than a natural construction. To illustrate this, the author points out that in some ways the labor supply response of black women is more like that of black men than that of white women.

49. Burke, Ronald J. and Tamara Weir. "Relationship of Wives' Employment Status to Husband, Wife and Pair Satisfaction and Performance." JMF 38, 2 (May 1976): 279-87. (3)

Data were collected by having 189 husband and wife pairs complete separate questionnaires. In general, employed wives were found to be more satisfied, as was true for such other studies as Ferree (1976) and Orden and Bradburn (1969), and to perform more effectively than full-time homemakers. Like Axelson (1963) and Pleck (1980) they found, however, that husbands of employed compared to nonemployed wives had more adjustment problems. The authors, plausibly, suggest that this may be because husbands are less prepared for, and see less advantage in, more egalitarian arrangements in the marriage. Nonetheless, Boath (1977) was unable to replicate these findings.

50. Chiswick, Carmel U. "The Value of a Housewife's Time." JHR 17, 3 (Summer 1982): 413-25. (1)

The author argues that the opportunity cost of an hour spent at the margin in home production determines the rate at which the homemaker's time should be valued. The cost is the higher of her potential wage rate, or the value of her output if she sold it. The latter, in fact, is not different from using the cost of hiring someone to do the work in the home. The problems with estimating and using the former are discussed at some length in Ferber and Birnbaum, B. G. (1980).

51. Cohen, Malcolm S. and Frank P. Stafford. "A Life Cycle Model of Household's Time Allocation." <u>AESM</u> 3, 3 (July 1974): 447-62. (1,Q)

A model is developed to explain simultaneously the number of children born, the level of expenditures, the spacing of children and husband's and wife's time devoted to them, as well as labor force participation. A computer simulation is then performed to illustrate how a husband-wife family would behave if it tried to optimize lifetime utility. The main virtue of this model is that it demonstrates interdependencies in various aspects of life cycle planning.

Concepcion (1974) See item 867.

52. Coverman, Shelley. "Gender, Domestic Labor Time and Wage Inequality." <u>ASR</u> 48, 5 (Oct. 1983): 623-36. (3)

Regression analysis using data for employed, married women and men shows that time spent on housework, including child care, is significantly negatively related to earnings for working class people as well as others. It should be noted, however, that this does not establish definitely that the former causes the latter, rather than vice versa.

53. Cramer, James C. "Fertility and Female Employment: Problems of Causal Direction." <u>ASR</u> 45, 2 (Apr. 1980): 167-90. (3)

The author concludes on the basis of available evidence that the dominant effects are from fertility to employment in the short run, but vice versa in the long run.

54. Darity, William, Jr. and Samuel L. Myers, Jr. "Changes in Black Family Structure: Implications for Welfare Dependency," <u>AER</u> 73, 2 (May 1983): 59-64. (4)

The proportion of female-headed families has been historically higher among blacks than among other ethnic groups in the U.S. It has risen even further in recent years. The authors construct an economic model to test the hypothesis that the availability of welfare payments is an important determinant of the behavior of black women. The data used are for the years 1955 to 1980. The results suggest that there is no such causal relationship and that alterations in the welfare system would not reverse the current trend.

55. Davies, Margery and Michael Reich. "On the Relationship Between Sexism and Capitalism" in Richard C. Edwards, Michael Reich and Thomas E. Weisskoff, eds. The Capitalist System, Englewood Cliffs, NJ: Prentice-Hall, 1972: 348-561. (1)

The authors, writing from a Marxist point of view, suggest on the one hand that capitalism is undermining the traditional family, but also argue that capitalism benefits from the sexist character of the usual husband-wife relationship.

56. Davis, Kingsley and Pietronella van dan Oever. "Demographic Foundation of New Sex Roles." PDR 8, 3 (Sept. 1982): 495-512. (1)

This paper discusses to what extent all ascription of status on the basis of sex is likely to disappear in advanced societies. The effect of important demographic changes, such as increased longevity, widening sex differences in mortality, and low fertility on sex roles is examined. The authors conclude that the tendency of modern women to emphasize market work and to fail to achieve replacement fertility will, in the long run, be self-defeating. They do not even consider the possibility that men might make a greater contribution to child-rearing but assume women will be pushed, or enticed back into the home.

Devaney (1983) See item 209.

57. Duncan, Greg J. "Educational Attainment," in James N. Morgan, Katherine Dickinson, Jonathan Dickinson, Jacob Benns and Greg J. Duncan, eds., Five Thousand American Families--Patterns of Economic Progress, Vol. 1, Institute for Social Research, University of Michigan, 1974: 305-31. (3)

The data show that the mother's educational attainment is much more important than the father's in influencing the educational achievement of daughters. The second interesting finding is that family size has twice the negative impact on daughters as on sons. This suggests that when resources are scarce, girls are more likely to get short-changed.

58. Duncan, Greg J. "Unmarried Heads of Households and Marriage," in Greg J. Duncan and James N. Morgan, eds., Five Thousand American Families--Patterns of Economic Progress, Vol. 4, Institute for Social Research, University of Michigan, 1976: 78-115. (3)

According to this study women, but not men, who married or remarried tended to improve their economic status relative to need. This conclusion is, however, based on money income only, ignoring the value of non-market work. Welfare payments had no significant effect on rate of remarriage of women, but income, age, and being black had a negative effect. The last two factors had the same influence on men.

59. Duncan, Greg J. and James N. Morgan. "Persistence and Change in Economic Status and the Role of Changing Family Composition," in Martha S. Hill, Daniel H. Hill and James N. Morgan, eds., Five Thousand American Families--Patterns of Economic Progress, Vol. 9, Institute for Social Research, University of Michigan, 1981: 1-44. (3)

In families with male heads the chances of keeping up with inflation were reduced by 34 percent if the head quit work, by 19 percent if the wife did. In families with female heads, chances were improved by 23 percent if she got married, 22 percent if she started work, but deteriorated 19 percent if she quit work. These numbers give an idea of the relative importance of work status and marital status for the economic status of men and women.

60. Ellis, Charles M. "Divorce, Sexual Autonomy, and the Economic Status of Women," JBE 11, 1 (Summer 1982): 38-60. (3)

The author successfully tests the hypothesis that the interaction of sexual autonomy and female employment help to explain much of the variation in the divorce rate during the period since WWII. His expressed concern that this will be seen as a chauvinistic view seems ill founded, for few today would question such a relationship. Further, his opinion that a higher divorce rate is likely to have benefits as well as costs reduces the likelihood that he would be considered unduly biased on this issue.

Farkas (1976) See item 471.

61. Ferber, Marianne A. and Bonnie G. Birnbaum. "The New Home Economics: Retrospects and Prospects." JCR 4, 1 (June 1977): 19-28. (1)

This paper offers a number of fundamental criticisms of the "New Home Economics," which considers specialization by the husband in market work and the wife in household work to be a rational way to maximize family well-being. 1. While claiming tasks are rationally allocated between husbands and wives, authors routinely refer to women's household "responsibilities" and child-rearing "duties." 2. Neoclassical models ignore the high risk, especially for the housewife, when spouses each specialize in the "appropriate" sphere. 3. It is important to remember that (dis)satisfaction associated with work or leisure is derived only by the individual involved, and that there is likely to be diminishing marginal utility for both. 4. Since husbands and wives are likely to have different tastes, to a greater or lesser extent, it is unrealistic to assume a single utility function for a family. Similar questions were raised by Sawhill (1977).

62. Ferber, Marianne A. and Bonnie G. Birnbaum. "Housework: Priceless or Valueless?" RIW 28, 4 (Dec. 1980): 387-400. (2,3)

Two ways of estimating the value of housework are explored. One is the opportunity cost approach, which sets the value of nonmarket work equal to the income the person could earn in the labor market. The other is the market cost approach, which uses the cost of hiring someone to do the housework to determine its value. Relying on data of earnings of female clerical workers to obtain estimates of their opportunity cost, the results are not found acceptable. The authors reach the conclusion, as did Rosen, H. S. (1974), that using the wages of general household workers is a preferable, though not perfect, alternative. It should be noted, however, that Adler and Hawrylyshyn (1978) as well as Murphy (1978) found that the two approaches do not necessarily produce very different results.

63. Ferree, Myra M. "Working Class Jobs: Housework and Paid Work as Sources of Satisfaction." SP, 23, 4 (April 1976): 431-41. (3)

Interviews with 135 women living in a working-class community whose youngest child was in school found that of the slightly more than half who were employed a considerably smaller proportion expressed dissatisfaction than did those who were full-time homemakers. Further, the latter wanted their daughters to be "mostly different." It appeared to be mainly social isolation and a lack of feeling of competence that troubled homemakers. The author acknowledges, however, that this is by no means true for all, and that employed wives have problems as well. The same material is presented in abbreviated form in "The Confused American Housewife," (PT 70, 4 Sept. 1976: 76). Not all other studies confirm these findings (e.g., Wright 1978).

Finch (1985) See item 885.

64. Fleisher, Belton M. and George F. Rhodes, Jr. "Fertility, Women's Wage Rates, and Labor Supply." AER 69, 1 (Mar. 1979): 14-24. (3)

This research shows a negative relation between women's earning power and desired family size, but not between the number of children and mother's lifetime labor supply. The former suggests that increased opportunity cost has a negative effect on the demand for children. The latter may be explained by young children increasing demand for home time, while older children increase demand for money income. Another interesting finding of this study is that, contrary to Becker, G. S. (1981), income elasticity of demand does not appear to be greater for quality than for quantity of children.

65. Folbre, Nancy. "Exploitation Comes Home: A Critique of the Marxian Theory of Family Labour." CJE 6, 4 (Dec. 1982): 317-29. (1)

The author points out that the economic consequences of patriarchy within the family have generally been overlooked. The neoclassical view that there can be no exploitation when there is a voluntary exchange has contributed to this, but she focuses particularly on the Marxist view that there can be no exploitation within the family. A theory based on the concept of socially-necessary labor time is used to describe intra-household allocation in value terms, and to distinguish between voluntary and exploitative forms of unequal exchange. This analysis should be of interest to anyone concerned with the effects of power relationships within the family, whether or not they accept the Marxist framework.

66. Folbre, Nancy. "The Pauperization of Motherhood: Patriarchy and Public Policy in the United States." RRPE 16, 4 (Winter 1984): 72-88. (1)

This paper makes the interesting point that children no longer provide significant economic benefits to parents, but do so to the older generation as a whole. Hence, it is argued, mothers and especially single mothers, who carry a disproportionate share of the cost of child rearing are essentially subsidizing non-parents, including absent fathers, who do not contribute adequately either through public assistance or through child support.

67. Geerken, Michael and Walter R. Gove. At Home and at Work: The Family's Allocation of Labor, Beverly Hills, Sage Publications, CA: 1983. (1,3)

This book attempts to use functionalism, stripped of some of its shortcomings, and combined with some microeconomic perspectives, minus rigid utility maximization assumptions, to explain, among other things, the division of household work between spouses. The authors conclude that the work-housework allocation is a rational adaptation to economic circumstances, but also that this is only partly true. They further recognize that even though opposition to the work role for wives and mothers is crumbling rapidly, traditions concerning housework are changing far more slowly.

68. Gianopulous, Artie and Howard E. Mitchell. "Marital Disagreement in Working Wife Marriages as a Function of Husband's Attitude Towards Wife's Employment." JMF 19, 4 (Nov. 1957): 373-78. (3)

This study involved couples that had sought help from the Marriage Council of Philadelphia between 1949 and 1953. No information on sample size is provided. More conflict was found among couples where the husband disapproved of the wife working than among those where the husband had no objection to her employment, or where the wife did not work. No consideration is given to the possibility that when a husband objects to the wife making her own decision in such matters, he may be a difficult man to get along with, especially for a wife who has a mind of her own.

69. Gilbert, Lucia A. Men in Dual-Career Families: Current Realities and Future Prospects, Hillsdale, NJ: Lawrence Erlbaum Associates, Publishers, 1985. (3)

This book deals with the effects of dual-career families on the personal and professional lives of husbands. The work is thoroughly researched, and the conclusions are based on the best available evidence in the recent literature.

70. Gilbert, Neil. "In Support of Domesticity: A Neglected Family Policy Option." JPAM 2, 4 (Summer 1983): 628-32. (4)

This author complains that the full-time homemakers and the traditional family division of labor are held in low esteem, and that policies to make this arrangement more attractive are not getting adequate attention. So far from recognizing that tax policies which do not count the value of home production and permit income splitting for couples, as well as a social security system which provides some coverage for homemakers, already discriminate substantially in favor of the single earner family, he proposes going further in this direction.

71. Gillespie, Dair. "Who Has the Power? The Marital Struggle." JMF 33, 3 (Aug. 1971): 445-58. (3)

The author investigates and confirms the importance of socialization, the marriage contract, income, occupational prestige, organizational participation, education and physical coercion in determining power within a marriage. She further argues that, in general, men tend to have the advantage in all of these, not because of differences in individual resources or personal competence, but because of discrimination against women in society. She concludes that husbands gain power in marriage as a class, and that this is true in white-collar as well as blue collar, black as well as white families. This paper shows how complicated the issue is, and helps us to understand why earlier and simpler approaches, such as Blood and Hamblin (1958) and Heer (1958) did not reach consistent conclusions.

72. Goldschmidt-Clermont, Luisella. Unpaid Work in the Household: A Review of Economic Evaluation Methods, Geneva: International Labor Office, 1982. (1,3)

A careful summary and evaluation of different approaches to the valuation of nonmarket work, including an extensive international bibliography of publications on this subject.

73. Gover, David A. "Socioeconomic Differential in the Relationship Between Marital Adjustment and Wife's Employment Status." MFL 25, 4 (Nov. 1963): 452-56. (3)

Finding that earlier studies provided conflicting evidence about the relationship between a wife's employment and her marital satisfaction, this author undertook his own study based on a sample of 361 white married women living with their husbands in Greensboro, NC. Because most of these women indicated that they believed, at least to some extent, that woman's place is in the home, the author suggests that those who conform to this belief are also more likely to conform to generally accepted beliefs that they should not express dissatisfaction in their statements about marital adjustment. He further conjectures that a wife's satisfaction is likely to be influenced by the extent to which her employment is considered to be nonconforming behavior.

74. Gramm, Wendy L. "The Demand for Wife's Non-Market Time." SEJ 41, 1 (July 1974): 124-33. (3)

A model is developed to explain the allocation of the wife's time between market work and different types of housework. Its implications are tested using a sample of 400 women who either are or have been teachers. As would be expected, number of children and wages of both husband and wife influence the amount of time spent on various activities. Additional findings are reported in Gramm (1975).

75. Greene, William H. and Aline O. Quester. "Divorce Risk and Wives' Labor Supply Behavior." SSQ 63, 1 (Mar. 1982): 16-27. (1)

The hypothesis is offered that wives subject to high probability of marital dissolution will be more likely to work for pay, and hence accumulate more on-the-job experience than other wives. This suggests that labor force participation of married women may, at least in part, be the result of the high divorce rate, rather than merely its cause.

76. Greenwood, Daphne. "The Economic Significance of Women's Place in Society: A Neo-Institutionalist View." JEI 18, 3 (Sept. 1984): 663-80. (1)

The author suggests that women's low status in the labor market is closely related to the low status accorded to their nonmarket production.

77. Gronau, Reuben. "The Effect of Children on the Housewife's Value of Time." JPE 81, 2 (Mar./Apr. 1973a, Part 2): S168-S199. (3)

The only statistically significant result of this study, which uses the 1960 Census 1/1000 sample, is that the effect of a child on the value of the mother's time declines with the child's age. Such other differences as are found suggest the effect of young children on the value of the mother's time may be somewhat greater, and decline somewhat more slowly, for women with more education.

78. Gronau, Reuben. "The Intrafamily Allocation of Time: The Value of Housewives' Time." AER 63, 4 (Sept. 1973b): 634-51. (3)

This paper attempts to explain allocation of each family member's time between market work, housework, and leisure, relying on the usual neoclassical analysis with its emphasis on relative advantage. The price of non-market time is assumed to exceed the value of the foregone market earnings. The actual value is estimated to lie between the limits of 20 percent more or less than average wages of working women. The results are, of course, only as reliable as is the model.

79. Grossbard-Shechtman, Amyra. "A Theory of Allocation of Time in Markets for Labor and Marriage." EJ 94, 376 (Dec. 1984): 863-82. (1)

This paper presents a theory of interrelated labor and marriage markets. As in her other work, the author emphasizes the importance of the ratio of men to women, and suggests that when it is higher, the labor force participation rate of wives is likely to be lower. She also concludes, as many others have, that changes in income have a greater influence on labor force participation of wives than of husbands. The proposition that a positive correlation between achievement in the labor market and in the household may help to explain a backward bending labor supply of wives is more novel. Few studies have, so far, found any evidence that the supply for women is anything but upward sloping, but this may change as women's earnings increase.

80. Grossman, Allyson S. and Howard Hayghe. "Labor Force Activity of Women Receiving Child Support or Alimony." MLR 105, 11 (Nov. 1982): 39-41. (3)

A special survey in 1979 showed that about 35 percent of 7.1 million mothers living with children from absent fathers had received any child support in 1978. It was also found that those who received such support were more likely to be in the labor market than others, as were those receiving alimony. This may well be because they were not on welfare, and hence did not lose income from every dollar they earned. It was further found that mothers not receiving support were more likely to be black, less educated, and young, and also had higher unemployment rates. The paper does not use the more sophisticated statistical methods required to sort out the effect of each individual factor.

81. Hand, Horace B. "Working Mothers and Maladjusted Children." JES 30 (Jan. 1957): 245-46. (3)

This brief note, written 40 years ago, contains a remarkably candid admission by the author that he had "long cherished the opinion that the employment of mothers ... is a patent factor in producing maladjustment among the children... ." He then goes on to report evidence that among a small sample of children the proportion of those who were maladjusted was the same for those whose mothers did and did not work outside the home. Interestingly, he found that the proportion was higher among sons and lower among daughters of employed women, foreshadowing the results of far more extensive and sophisticated recent studies which show that if there are any difficulties, it is more likely to be for boys.

82. Happel, S. K., J. K. Hill and Stuart A. Low. "An Economic Analysis of the Timing of Childbirth." PS 38, 2 (July 1984): 299-311. (3)

Economic variables that may be relevant to the timing of childbirth are: the rate of the wife's job skill depreciation during periods of non-employment, her premarital work experience, her potential earnings, the mean and dispersion of the husband's earnings profile. It would be expected that the length of the first birth interval would be inversely related to the depreciation rate of the wife's skills, and possibly to the husband's lifetime earnings, unless they have a strong effect on demand for quality of children, while the other variables would exert a positive influence. The results are consistent with these expectations, and show that economic factors play a significant role.

83. Hartmann, Heidi I. "The Family as the Locus of Gender, Class and Political Struggle: The Example of Housework." SJWCS 6, 3 (Spring 1981): 366-94. (1)

A radical analysis of the family as the instrument of patriarchy and capitalism, which helps to perpetuate both the subordinate role of women and the existing economic system.

84. Hayghe, Howard. "Families and the Rise of Working Wives." MLR 99, 5 (May 1976): 12-19. (3)

This paper points out that multi-worker families increased from 36 percent in 1950 to 49 percent in 1975 and goes on to discuss briefly various factors that influenced this development.

85. Hayghe, Howard. "Husbands and Wives as Earners: An Analysis of Family Data." MLR 104, 2 (Feb. 1981): 46-53. (3)

As of 1978 it was found that most working wives held full-time jobs, were, on average, younger, better educated, and were less likely to have preschool children than those not in the labor market. Not surprisingly, dual earner families had about 20 percent higher incomes than traditional families, and close to one-third of them placed in the upper fifth of the income distribution. At the same time only 1.8 percent were in poverty, as compared to 5.5 percent of traditional families.

86. Hedges, Janice N. and Jeanne K. Barnett. "Working Women and the Division of Household Tasks." MLR, 95, 4 (Apr. 1972): 9-14. (3)

This paper, written in the early 1970's, already comments on the substantial influx into the labor market not only of married women, but of mothers. At the same time, it reports on several surveys which show that women with jobs continue to do the bulk of household work.

87. Heer, David M. "Dominance and the Working Wife." SF 36, 4 (May 1958): 341-47. (3)

This study of Irish Roman-Catholic families with at least one child of elementary school age found that, whether working class and middle class, the employed wife exerted more influence in decision making than did full-time homemakers. At the same time it was also the case that working class women, whether or not employed, exerted more influence than their middle class counterparts, and that husbands gained more influence with additional children.

88. Heer, David M. "The Measurement and Bases of Family Power: An Overview." JMF 25, 2 (May 1963): 133-39. (1)

The author proposes that the power of the wife vis-a-vis the husband is determined by the difference between the value to the wife of the resources contributed by her husband and the value to her of the resources she might earn outside the existing marriage. This view explicitly assumes that each partner considers separation as a possibility. The author suggests that his theory is consistent with the findings of earlier studies, but this is not necessarily the case (e.g., Blood and Hamblinn, 1958). Certainly later studies do not all lend support to this view (e.g., Gillespie, 1971).

89. Hofferth, Sandra L. "Long-Term Economic Consequences for Women of Delayed Child-Bearing and Reduced Family Size." Dem. 21, 2 (May 1984): 141-56. (3)

This study, based on data from the Panel Study of Income Dynamics, found that women over 60 years of age who had their first child at age 30 or more are significantly better off than those who had children when they were younger, and those who had no children. The latter is surprising, especially since it was also found that among delayed childbearers those with fewer children were better off.

90. Hofferth, Sandra L. and Kristin A. Moore. "Early Childbearing and Later Economic Well-Being." ASR 44, 5 (Oct. 1979): 784-815. (3)

This was one of the first studies to firmly support the widely held belief that early child bearing results in less education, large families and more incidence of poverty. National Longitudinal Surveys data were used to trace the causal and cumulative effect on women who had children before the age of 27. The impact was, however, found to be somewhat less detrimental for black than for white women.

Hoffman, E. P. (1985) See item 241.

91. Hoffman, Lois W. "Effects of the Employment of Mothers on Parental Power Relations and the Division of Household Tasks." MFL 22, 1 (Feb. 1960): 27-35. (3)

Data obtained from 324 Detroit in-tact families with at least one child showed that, even when other factors such as wife's attitude toward sex roles, husband's occupation and number of young children, were held constant, employed mothers did a lesser share of housework, and made fewer decisions about routine household matters than full-time homemakers. There was no difference in the husband-wife power allocation when the other characteristics were held constant, but, in fact, employed wives did have more power than those who did not work outside the home. This suggests it is not employment per se that influences the power relationship and is consistent with Gillespie's (1971) findings that this issue is one of considerable complexity.

92. Hoffman, Lois W. "Effects of Maternal Employment on the Child." CD 32, 1 (Mar. 1961): 187-97. (3)

This study examines the effect of the mother's employment on children, while controlling for other factors. Mothers who like their work are found to use mild discipline and avoid inconveniencing their children. The children are characterized as nonassertive and ineffective. Mothers who do not like their work seem less involved with and more demanding of their children. The children are deemed to be assertive and hostile. The author suggests that these results are consistent with the hypothesis that the difficulties are caused by the mother's feeling of guilt. Therefore, the real problem may be with a society that makes an employed mother feel guilty. Further, a careful reading of the evidence suggests that the interpretation may be unduly negative, as is also suggested by the absence of similar findings in a good deal of other research (see particularly the excellent review by Urie Bronfenbrenner and Ann C. Crouter, "Work and Family Through Time and Space" in Sheila B. Kamerman and Cheryl D. Hayes, eds. Families That Work: Children in a Changing World, Washington, DC: National Academy Press, 1982, pp. 39-83).

93. Hoffman, Lois W. and Francis I. Nye. Working Mothers, San Francisco, CA: Jossey-Bass Publishing, 1975. (3)

The stated aim of this book was "to pull together research findings on the effects of maternal employment on the family from the fields of psychology and sociology." It was very successful in achieving this goal, and did much to dispell the widespread impression that there were likely to be serious negative effects, especially on children.

94. Hoffman, Saul D. "Marital Instability and the Economic Status of Women." Dem 14, 1 (Feb. 1977): 67-76. (3)

This paper investigates the relationship between changes in the marital status and economic status of women and men, black and white, using Panel Study of Income Dynamics data. The most important finding is that, after adjusting for changes in family size, the economic status of divorced or separated men improves while that of women declines. The effects are greater for whites than nonwhites. The calculations on which these conclusions are based take into consideration money income only, and ignore the value of household time. Therefore they undoubtedly overstate the difference. But there is no reason to question the direction of the changes.

95. Hoffman, Saul D. and John Holmes. "Husbands, Wives and Divorce," in Greg J. Duncan and James N. Morgan, eds., Five Thousand American Families--Patterns of

Economic Progress, Vol. 4., Institute for Social Research, University of Michigan, 1976: 23-75. (3)

The economic status of husbands, relative to need, was shown to improve, while that of wives deteriorates as a result of divorce. Correlates of divorce were also investigated: positive relations were found with wife's hours of work, husband's previous marriage, and among the poor, higher welfare payments. On the other hand, presence of children under two years of age, church attendance and residence in a small community had the opposite effect. Interestingly, other things held constant, black marriages appeared to be more stable. These empirical findings are useful, even though the model the authors construct, based on the notion that divorce or separation is inherently a joint decision, is most questionable in the light of their own findings that only husbands tend to gain as a result of divorce, at least when only money income is taken into account.

96. Hudis, Paula M. "Commitment to Work and to Family: Marital-Status Differences in Women's Earnings." JMF 38, 2 (May 1976): 267-78. (3)

Using information from the 1967 Survey of Economic Opportunity, this study found support for the conclusion that married women receive lower returns to education and occupational status as compared to men, mainly because of work interruptions. It was also discovered, however, that formerly married women manage to overcome some of this disadvantage. The author suggests this may be because of their greater need, but this is conjectural, and other interpretations are at least equally plausible. For instance, it may be women with higher earnings potentials who are more likely to terminate a marriage.

97. Hunt, Janet C. and B. F. Kiker. "The Effect of Fertility on the Time Use of Working Wives." JCR 7, 4 (Mar. 1981): 380-87. (3)

By applying data from the Panel Study of Income Dynamics to a household utility maximization model, it was found that number and young age of children tend to increase the time wives devote to household production, including child care. Surprisingly, "child quality," defined as investment in skills and abilities of children, has a negative relationship with such time. The suggested explanation is that higher income of the parents makes possible substitution of purchased goods and services for time, mainly in other housework, but to an extent even in child care.

98. Hunt, Janet C. and B. F. Kiker. "Parental Time Devoted to Children in Two- and One-Wage-Earner Families." EER 3, 1 (Winter 1984): 75-83. (3)

This study finds, on the basis of indirect evidence from the Panel Survey of Income Dynamics data, that parents in two-earner families spent virtually the same amount of time with pre-schoolers as parents from one-earner families did, but less time with older children, particularly teenagers. The authors suggest the possibility that this may deprive the older groups of needed attention, but do not consider the possibility that it might help them to grow up to be more independent and responsible.

99. Hunt, Joseph W. and Eleanor D. Craig. "Should We Provide More Government Funding for Day Care?" PP 20, 4 (Fall 1972): 565-76. (4)

This paper develops a cost-benefit framework for making policy decisions with respect to day care. Most of the discussion is very general, and raises issues well-informed individuals would already be aware of. Perhaps the only surprising question raised is the authors' concern that day care centers might be used by the government for purposes of indoctrination. To the extent this is a problem, it is unlikely to be more serious than in public schools.

100. Hutchens, Robert M. "Welfare, Remarriage, and Marital Search." AER 69, 3 (June 1979): 369-79. (3)

This paper examines the effect of AFDC transfers on the probability of remarriage of female household heads with children using Panel of Income Dynamics data. The results show that an increase in such payments increases the time before a woman remarries, and reduces the likelihood she will remarry. The author points out, however, that the marriages that do take place after a longer search may be more stable.

101. Johnson, Shirley B. "The Impact of Women's Liberation on Marriage, Divorce, and Family Life Style," in Cynthia B. Lloyd, ed. Sex, Discrimination and the Division of Labor, NY: Columbia University Press, 1975, pp. 401-26. (3)

This author defines the effect of the "Women's Movement" in economic terms as a change in the preference functions of women in favor of more activities outside the household. This is in contrast to the analysis of many economists, and even sociologists (e.g., Oppenheimer, 1970) who view the changes in women's behavior merely as a response to changing economic conditions. The main conclusion of this paper is that the immediate impact of "Women's Liberation" was to lower the economic returns to marriage, but that after a transitional period this may, once again, change. Continued vitality for the women's movement was also predicted.

102. Jones, Elise F. "Ways in Which Childbearing Affects Women's Employment: Evidence from the U.S. 1975 National Fertility Study." PS 36, 1 (Mar. 1982): 5-14. (3)

This study, using longitudinal data, found that the intention to have another child has an independent negative effect on labor force participation. It also found, however, that mothers often claimed to be working because of the financial needs related to children, and that childless women worked in anticipation of needing the money later when they planned to have children.

Jonung (1978) See item 918.

103. Juster, F. Thomas. "A Note on Recent Changes in Time Use" in F. Thomas Juster and Frank P. Stafford, eds., Time, Goods and Well-Being, Ann Arbor: Institute of Social Research, University of Michigan, 1985. (3)

Analysis of admittedly limited data collected in 1981-82 on time use shows that men spent about 1 hour per week less on market work in 1981 than in 1975, and over 1 hour more on housework, while women spent almost 2 hours more on market work, and 1/2 hour less on housework. The changes were substantially greater for younger men and women, though even in this younger 25 to 44 years of age group men did almost twice as much market work as women, and women did slightly more than twice as much housework as men. The more rapid pace among younger cohorts suggests that the rate of change may continue to accelerate.

Kelley and deSilva (1980) See item 921.

104. Kessler-Harris, Alice. "The Debate Over Equality for Women in the Work Place. Recognizing Differences." WW, 1 (1985): 141-161. (1)

The author suggests that women historically remained a "special" group in the labor force because of their primary role in the family, which caused them to act differently from male workers. She further argues that this leaves them with the dilemma of either depending on the family, or rejecting it in order to achieve equality in the labor market. The solution suggested is that women proudly acknowledge their nurturant, family-oriented values and that men come to share them as they come to share family responsibilities. This will presumably enable women to attain equality in the labor market without adopting the male competitive, achievement-oriented orientation. It is not clear, however, how this is to be accomplished.

105. Kimmelman, Barry. "Executives' Wives--The Need for a Positive Company-Sponsored Approach." CMR 11, 3 (Spring 1969): 7-10. (3)

This paper is concerned with the wife purely because of her effect on the efficiency of her executive husband. Among her characteristics that may cause problems are listed not only "prone to drink too much," but also "mentally underdeveloped compared to her husband" and "excessively interested in her own career or activities." One suspects it may be difficult to tread the fine line between the last two, especially without resorting to the first.

106. Kolko, Gabriel. "Working Wives: Their Effect on the Structure of the Working Class." SS 42, 3 (Fall 1978): 257-77. (1)

The author concludes that the rise of the working wife created a fundamental change in the structure of the working class, making it both larger and more prosperous. He also believes, however, that this has now reached a plateau, and that, in the end, it has only increased the insecurity of the labor force. His pessimistic conclusions are based on the premise that capitalism cannot produce sufficient new employment, an argument more people tended to believe in the 1930's. His view that the two-earner family has twice the risk of being hit by unemployment can be challenged because it underestimates the importance of spreading the risks.

107. Krashinsky, Michael. "Subsidies to Child Care, Public Policy and Optimality." PFQ 9, 3 (July 1981): 243-69. (4)

The author argues that family utility will be maximized through tax deductions for child care, and that these deductions, rather than subsidies, will provide maximum efficiency. He goes on to argue that deductions can even be justified in terms of equity, a conclusion that will surprise anyone who is aware that deductibility is irrelevant to the really poor who pay no income tax, and becomes increasingly valuable to families in higher tax brackets. Further, even this author admits that concern for the well being of children can justify higher subsidies, restricted to employed parents, but not only directed to day care centers.

Kumiansky (1983) See item 927.

108. Kushman, John E. and Richard M. Scheffler. "Family Power Structure and Family Labor Supply." SSQ 56, (Sept. 1975): 239-51. (3)

Sociologists have generally found that in Western cultures husbands and wives appear to make separate decisions with respect to labor supply, but that the decision of the male is prior and is accepted as a constraint by the female. The results of this study, using 1966-67 Survey of Economic Opportunity data, restricted to couples where both worked, did find evidence supporting the attachment of men to the bread-winner role, but found that the indirect evidence from labor supply functions does not support the hypothesis of male dominance in the woman's supply decision. The authors rightly suggest, however, that the analysis should be extended to one-earner couples, for it is here that men may be more dominant.

Kyriazis and Henripin (1982) See item 930.

109. Lazear, Edward P. and Robert T. Michael. "Real Income Equivalence Among One-Earner and Two-Earner Families." AER 70, 2 (May 1980): 203-208. (3)

We are offered the conclusion that two-earner families on the average have 20 percent more money income than comparable one-earner families, but also require about 30 percent more money income to achieve the same standard of living. The authors themselves, however, acknowledge that they have looked at only one particular type of family, have examined only a subset of expenditures, and have ignored savings, as well as psychological and sociological advantages of one family structure over the other. These constraints are serious enough to make their conclusions virtually meaningless.

110. Leibowitz, Arlene. "Education and Home Production." AER 64, 2 (May 1974): 243-50. (3)

The author used time budget data collected by Kathryn Walker and Census data to investigate the effect of education on the amount of time mothers spend with children. This paper received much attention because it offered evidence that in spite of the higher opportunity cost of their time, more highly educated mothers tend to spend more time on child care. The increase need not be at the expense of market work, but rather may be achieved by a sharp reduction in other housework. Whether education causes a greater increase in value of time spent in the labor market, or time spent in child care, there can be little doubt that it will have the least effect on the value of time spent on other housework. Much the same material is presented in "Education and the Allocation of Women's Time" in Thomas F. Juster, ed., Education Income, and Human Behavior, NY: McGraw-Hill Book Co., 1975, pp. 171-97.

Leppel (1982) See item 938.

111. Leppel, Karen. "Market and Household Sectors: Is Dual Participation Optimal?" AEJ 11, 4 (Dec. 1983): 81-82. (1)

In this brief note, the author points out that, contrary to the dictum of Becker, G. S. (1981), that at most one member of an efficient household would allocate time to both the household and the market sector, increasing numbers of husbands and wives actually do so. This puzzle is solved by introducing diminishing marginal productivity and constraints on hours per week to be spent in the market. Other factors, not mentioned by this author, are that each spouse might have a relative advantage in some type of housework, which consists of many varied activities, and that they might enjoy doing some work together.

112. Leppel, Karen. "Income Effects on Marriage and Household Formation: A Paradox Resolved." AEJ 13, 2 (July 1985): 89. (1)

This very brief note suggests that both the probability of marriage and of living in a one-person household are positively related to income, because both are more expensive than living with one or more persons, other than one's spouse or one's children. Surprisingly, the author does not mention the fact that two-earner couples may have to pay higher taxes when they are married as one of the deterrents to marriage. Even more surprisingly, she does not consider the possibility that the effect of higher income on the probability of marriage may be different for men and women.

113. Leuthold, Jane H. "Home Production and the Tax System." JEP 3, 1 (Mar. 1983): 145-57. (3)

A study using data from the Survey of Income Dynamics for 1976 shows that taxation tends to encourage home production of wives, but to discourage that of husbands. These findings suggest that husband's and wife's time are, at least to some extent, substitutes. The author also concludes that husbands and wives may have different preference systems. This would not be surpising in a society where sex stereotyping, especially with respect to housework, is still widely prevalent.

114. Levitan, Sar A. and Richard S. Belons. "Working Wives and Mothers. What Happens to Family Life?" MLR 104, 9 (Sep. 1981): 26-30. (3)

In the 1960's and early 1970's employed wives averaged about 65 hours per week of work in the home and in the labor force, about 8 hours more than their husbands. Like Juster (1985) these researchers also found that this differential had disappeared. Married women and men both worked a total of about 60 hours, though men continued to do far less housework. The authors conclude that most women were managing to combine market and housework successfully, and that the family was changing, but surviving.

115. Locke, Harvey J. and Muriel Mackeprang. "Marital Adjustment and the Employed Wife." AJS 54,6 (May 1949): 536-38. (3)

This pioneering paper, based on two studies, one of "happily married" and one of divorced couples, concluded that there was no significant difference between the marital adjustment of wives who were employed full-time, and those who were not employed. Nor was any difference found in the marital adjustment of the husbands of the two groups. The authors acknowledge that the samples were small, consisted entirely of college graduates, and were not matched for other characteristics. Later studies generally did find differences, but these were by no means consistent (e.g., Axelson 1963; Boath 1977; Burke and Weir 1976; Ferree 1976).

116. Madden, Janice F. and Michelle J. White. "Spatial Implications of Increases in the Female Labor Force: A Theoretical and Empirical Synthesis." LE 56, 4 (Nov. 1980): 432-46. (3)

This paper offers a synthesis of existing knowledge about sex differences in workplace-residence separation and concludes that a more general "urban/labor economic" model is needed. It is further pointed out that there are formidable problems for empirical studies of these questions, in part because both husbands' and wives' commuting decisions are usually involved.

117. Manser, Marilyn and Murray Brown. "Marriage and Household Decision Making: A Bargaining Analysis." IER 2, 1 (Feb. 1978): 31-44. (3,Q)

The relatively new game-theoretic approach permits the inclusion of phenomena that traditional theory has difficulty handling. It explicitly allows for differences in tastes among family members and provides a means by which such differences can be reconciled. While the empirical findings of this study nonetheless confirm the conclusions of much of the traditional literature, that female labor supply is much more responsive to wage and income changes than is male labor supply, they also show that absolute and relative earnings of men and women have different effects on marriage decisions.

118. Martin, Jack K. and Sandra L. Hanson. "Sex, Family Wage Earning Status, and Satisfaction with Work." WO, 12, 1 (Feb. 1985): 91-110. (3)

Quality of Employment data show that men and women respond differently to some conditions of employment. This is true especially of women who are not head of households. They are more likely to place emphasis on convenience and comfort.

119. Matthaei, Julie A. "Consequences of the Rise of the Two-Earner Family: The Breakdown of the Sexual Division of Labor." AER 70, 2 (May 1980): 198-202. (3,1)

The author argues that the entry of increasing numbers of married women into the labor force represents a breakdown of the sexual division of labor. She goes on to suggest that neoclassical economic theory erroneously derives existing specialization from differences in tastes of men and women, while her own analysis is based on the premise that it is the sexual division of labor that is the source of masculine/feminine differences. Hence, she concludes, the rise of the two-earner family and the emergence of companionate marriage, will bring about fundamental change.

120. Matthaei, Julie A. "Capitalism and the Sexual Division of Labor: An Essay in U.S. Economic History." SC 1, 2 (Fall 1983): 13-35. (1,3)

According to this author, the traditional Marxist explanation of the inequality between men and women fails because it does not take account of their roles in the home. This paper extends the approach, incorporating the view that the sexual division of labor is inevitably related to the socially determined concepts of manhood and womanhood, as well as their interaction and polarization in marriage. This theory is then applied to American economic history, analyzing the development of male-female relationships during the three historic stages of the family economy in colonial times, industrialization in the 19th century, and the breakdown of the sexual division of labor in the 20th century.

Meissner, Humphreys, Scott, M. M. and Scheu (1975). See item 944.

121. Michael, Robert T. "Education in Non-Market Production." JPE 81, 2, (Mar./Apr. 1973, Part 1): 306-27. (1,3)

The author suggests that investment in human capital is likely to increase productivity not only in the labor market, but also in other activities. In this paper a model is developed and tested to determine the nonmarket rate of return to education, which essentially relies on expenditures for luxuries and necessities as evidence. Data from the Bureau of Labor

Statistics' Consumer Expenditure Survey 1960-61 are used to provide empirical evidence. The conclusion is reached that education increases money income more than household productivity, but that, nonetheless, it has a positive effect on the latter as well.

122. Michael, Robert T. "Consequences of the Rise in Female Labor Force Participation Rates: Questions and Probes." JLE 3, 1 (Jan. 1985, Suppl.): S117-S146. (13)

Evidence is provided of the extent to which increased labor force participation of women has resulted in (1) an increase in career-oriented schooling and acquisition of market skills; (2) a shift away from female time-intensive household production; (3) a decline in differences in time allocation between men and women. The author, however, also acknowledges in the introduction that "the more profound consequences may very well be psychological (an increased sense of self-sufficiency, self-reliance, and self-respect) or social (a change in both men's and women's expectations about sex roles...)."

123. Miller, Joanne and Howard H. Garrison. "Sex Roles: The Division of Labor at Home and in the Workplace." ARS 8 (1982): 237-62. (3)

The main purpose of this paper is to add to our understanding of the processes by which sex roles influence the system of social stratification and to identify critical theoretical questions that remain, as well as effective research strategies for answering them. In a review of recent literature the authors are especially concerned with sex roles as channeling and integrative mechanisms, and the way they influence the division of labor in the family and in the labor market.

124. Moffitt, Robert A. "Profiles of Fertility, Labor Supply and Wages of Married Women: A Complete Life Cycle Model." REStud. 51, 2 (Apr. 1984): 263-78. (3,Q)

A life cycle model, based upon utility maximizing choice, is developed and estimated. The results provide support for the notion that shifts in the level of the lifetime wage profile are associated with shifts in lifetime fertility rates and employment rates of women. On the other hand, birth cohort and education appear to have little independent effect.

125. Mooney, Marta. "Wife's Permanent Employment and Husband's Hours of Work." IR 20, 2 (Spring 1981): 205-11. (3)

Earlier studies had suggested that husbands are not likely to reduce time worked to any great extent in response to increasing labor force participation of wives, first, because of institutionalized constraints on hours of work, second, because the wife's income may not be viewed as permanent. The author nonetheless concludes on the basis of her research that the dramatic increase in labor force participation of married women in the 1970's may be reinforcing the trend towards a more leisure-oriented male work force. She obviously gives no thought to the possibility that men may be increasing their participation in housework.

Mott (1982b) See item 280.
Mott and Shapiro (1983) See item 281.

126. Murphy, Martin. "The Value of Time Spent in Home Production." AJES 35, 2 (Apr. 1976): 191-97. (2)

For a variety of reasons, the value of home production is of interest to many social scientists, as well as, for instance, lawyers. The author points out the shortcomings of the replacement cost approach, where a task is valued according to how much it would cost to hire someone to do it (e.g., Rosen, H. S. 1974). He erroneously suggests that this is the method most commonly used by economists. This issue is discussed at greater length, and more objectively in Goldschmidt-Clermont (1982).

127. Murphy, Martin. "The Value of Nonmarket Household Production: Opportunity Cost Versus Market Cost Estimates." RIW 24, 3 (Sept. 1978): 243-55. (2)

This study examines estimates of the value of household production in the United States based on the assumption that the value of time spent on housework must be at least equal to the market earnings foregone by staying at home, and those based on hiring someone to do the housework. The first set of estimates was found to be only slightly higher. These results, similar to those of Adler and Hawrylyshyn (1978), may be interpreted to show that women's wages in other jobs are, in general, not much higher than those paid for household help. The author emphasizes that this shows there is little upward bias in using the opportunity cost approach.

128. Nickols, Sharon Y. and Karen D. Fox. "Buying Time and Saving Time: Strategies for Managing Household Production." <u>JCR</u> 10, 2 (Sept. 1983): 197-208. (3)

This study, based on a survey of 1,639 two-parent, two-child families from a number of states, found that the main time-buying strategies used by two-earner families as compared to those with a full-time homemaker were mainly more purchases of child care, meals away from home, and disposable diapers; time-saving strategies correspondingly consisted of fewer meals prepared and less household production. Nonetheless, the wives also had substantially less leisure.

129. Nieva, Veronica F. "Work and the Family Linkages." <u>WW</u> 1 (1985): 162-90. (3,4)

This essay deals with the impact of family responsibilities on labor market performance, and of labor force participation on the family, with special emphasis on policy issues.

130. North, Gary. "A Note on the Opportunity Cost of Marriage." <u>JPE</u> 76, 2 (Mar.-Apr. 1968): 321-23. (1)

This note, and the responses to it by George J. Stigler and Robert M. Berardo (<u>JPE</u>, 75, 5 Sept.-Oct. 1969: 862, 863), might be disregarded, except for the light they shed on the views of the prominent economists who wrote them and the editors of a prestigious journal who chose to publish them. North argues that a male historian would make a great mistake in marrying a physicist who could earn a large salary, because the opportunity cost of her staying at home to look after her family would be very high. Stigler, responds that if the "girl physicist" stays at home, her value there must be even greater. Berardo avoids offensive language, and extolls various potential virtues of an educated wife. But none of the authors consider the possibility that she might spend most or all of her life in the labor market, and certainly not that the husband, whose opportunity cost is far lower, might become the homemaker. So much for economic rationality.

131. Nye, Francis I. and Lois W. Hoffman, eds., The Employed Mother in America, Chicago: Rand McNally, 1963. (3)

This book deals briefly with the causes of the employment of married women, and at considerably greater length with the effect of such employment on the children, the marriage, and the woman herself, all from the perspective of psychologists. Hence this work constitutes a very useful supplement to the work of economists, and some other social scientists, so steeped in their own discipline that they tend to overlook the importance of the factors emphasized here.

Oppenheimer (1973) See item 288.

132. Orden, Susan R. and Norman M. Bradburn. "Working Wives and Marriage Happiness." AJS 74, 4 (Jan. 1969): 392-407. (3)

This study of 781 husbands and 957 wives shows that not the wife's work status, but her freedom to choose is an important predictor of happiness in marriage of both husband and wife. On the other hand, the wife's choice to be in the labor market is generally related to both more satisfactions and more tensions for both spouses. These findings are contrary to conclusions by other researchers, such as Axelson (1963), and Burke and Weir (1976) who found poorer marital adjustment in families with employed wives.

133. Peterson, Evan T. "The Impact of Maternal Employment on the Mother-Daughter Relationship." MFL 23, 4 (Nov. 1961): 355-61. (3)

The study finds that, controlling for such variables as social class and broken homes, the employment of mothers appears to have no effect on their maternal role or on the relationship with their daughters.

134. Pleck, Joseph H., Graham L. Staines, and Linda Lang. "Conflicts Between Work and Family Life." MLR 103, 3 (Mar. 1980): 29-32. (3)

This study used the Quality Employment Survey of the Department of Labor to examine possible conflicts between paid work and family life. A substantial proportion of the families, especially among those with children, reported excessive work time, inconvenient schedules, fatigue, and irritability, but this was no more true for women than for men. Not surprisingly, those who experienced such conflicts were likely to be less satisfied with their jobs, their family life, and life in general. The findings of numerous other studies were considerably less negative.

135. Pollak, Robert A. and Michael L. Wachter. "The Relevance of the Household Production Function and its Implications for the Allocation of Time." JPE 83, 2 (Apr. 1975): 255-77. (1,Q)

This paper points out that many applications of the household production function model require that the technology exhibit constant returns, and no joint production. The latter condition is rarely satisfied in situations involving the allocation of time. Alternative approaches are also suggested.

136. Preston, Samuel H. and Alan T. Richards. "The Influence of Women's Work Opportunities on Marriage Rates." Dem. 12, 2 (May 1975): 209-22. (3)

This paper sheds light on the question whether, on balance, improved employment opportunties for women tend to reduce the proportion married, and finds this to be the case. Other variables operating in the same direction are a lower ratio of men to women, a higher proportion of Catholics and, perhaps surprisingly, a larger number of inhabitants.

137. Pyun, C. S. "The Monetary Value of Housework." <u>AJES</u> 28, 3 (July 1969): 271-84. (2)

This author suggests a methodology for estimating the value of the home time of housewives which is basically a variation on the opportunity cost approach. It begins with the assumption that the value of work at home must be at least equal to the potential earnings of the worker in the labor market. Some of the general flaws in this method are discussed in Ferber and Birnbaum, B. G. (1980), the specific flaws in this paper are pointed out by Rosen, H. S. (1974).

Quinlan (1980) See item 295.

138. Rapoport, Robert N. and Rhona Rapoport. <u>Dual-Career Families</u>. London: Penguin, 1976. (3)

This is the second edition of a book on dual career families, first published in 1969. It is concerned with couples where both have jobs requiring a high degree of commitment and involving a continuous developmental character. The first three chapters deal with general issues, including who such families are, and why they are becoming more common. The next five chapters tell us about five such couples. The last three chapters elaborate further on the changing situation of dual career couples and consider policy issues that deserve further attention.

139. Reid, Margaret G. <u>Economics of Household Production</u>, New York: J. Wiley and Sons, Inc., 1934. (1,3)

This author was a pioneer in applying economic analysis to the household, and has not been adequately recognized as the "foremother" of the "New Home Economics." Her book, now more than 50 years old, still makes interesting reading for anyone concerned with the economics of household production.

140. Rein, Martin. "Women and Work--The Incomplete Revolution." AuER 51 (3rd Quarter 1980): 11-17. (3)

The author makes a clear distinction between women who merely enter the labor force to supplement family income and those who make a full commitment to employment, and also have a job that pays as much as men's jobs do. He argues that so far few fall into the latter category and that this is the reason why the traditional division of household responsibilities continues. The problem with the author's analysis of the situation is that he puts the onus of change entirely on women--they must develop more attachment to the labor market. He largely ignores the possibility that equal opportunity in the labor market, and more participation by husbands in the household could help to break the vicious circle.

141. Ridley, Carl A. "Exploring the Impact of Work Satisfaction and Involvement on Marital Interaction When Both Partners Are Employed." JMF 35, 2 (May 1973): 229-37. (3)

This study of teachers showed that for men job satisfaction had a positive relationship with marital satisfaction, but that this was not necessarily the case for women. The author suggests this may be because the work role is secondary for women. Clearly, other interpretations are possible. For instance, husbands may resent the wife being too involved in her work.

142. Robinson, John. Changes in America's Use of Time: 1965-1975, Cleveland: Communicatins Research Center, Cleveland State University, 1977. (3)

This update of the author's America's Use of Time: A Social-Psychological Analysis of Everyday Behavior, NY: Praeger Publishers, 1977, uses more recent survey data to show that there have been substantial changes in the allocation of time of married men and women. The number of hours of work for pay per week declined from 51.3 to 47.4 for husbands, from 38.4 to 30.1 for wives. Hours spent on all household work rose slightly from 9.0 to 9.7 for husbands, declined from 28.8 to 24.9 for employed wives, and from 50.0 to 44.3 for homemakers. These decreases were mainly in housework other than childcare.

143. Rosen, Harvey S. "The Monetary Value of a Housewife: A Replacement Cost Approach." AJES 33, 1 (Jan. 1974): 65-73. (2)

The exposition and some of the conclusions of Pyun (1969) with respect to estimating the value of household time by the opportunity cost method is criticized. The author prefers using the cost of hiring someone to do the work, and specifically favors the cost of hiring a substitute for the homemaker, rather than a number of workers each doing a specialized task. Essentially the same conclusions were reached by Ferber and Birnbaum, B. G. (1980).

Rosenzweig and Schultz (1982) See item 979.

144. Ross, Heather L. and Isabel V. Sawhill. Time of Transition. The Growth of Families Headed by Women. Washington, DC: The Urban Institute, 1975. (3,4)

This book, now more than 10 years old, is still an excellent source of information about the causes and the results of the rapid increase in families headed by women. There is a wealth of descriptive material, a very useful review of relevant research, and thoughtful discussion of policies that have been, or might be, employed to mitigate the serious problems many of these families face.

145. Safilios-Rothschild, Constantina. "The Study of Family Power Structure: A Review, 1960-69." JMF, 32, 4 (Nov. 1970a): 539-52. (1,3)

In this paper the author critically evaluates the methodologies, and the underlying theories of various studies of marital power. She concludes that more, and more sophisticated work is needed before we can get a better understanding of the issues involved.

146. Salkever, David S. "Children's Health Problems and Maternal Work Status." JHR 17, 1 (Winter 1982): 94-109. (3)

Not very surprisingly, this study finds that children's health problems have a negative impact on the labor force participation of the mother, especially in low income families. This is, however, considerably less so in non-white and female-headed households. The data used were from the 1972 Health Interview Survey.

147. Sander, William H. "Women, Work and Divorce." AER 75, 3 (June 1985): 519-23. (3)

Data drawn from the U.S. farm sector are used to confirm that when farm women acquire more human capital and hence increase their earning ability, there is a substantial increase in the divorce rate. These findings are consistent with lower rural than urban divorce rates, since rural women are more likely to specialize in nonmarket work. On the other hand, ownership of farm assets was not found to have the inhibiting affect on divorce that might have been expected.

148. Santos, Fredericka B. "The Economics of Marital Status" in Cynthia B. Lloyd ed., Sex, Discrimination and the Division of Labor, NY: Columbia University Press, 1975. (3)

The author points to the rise in women's market work as one of the main causes for the long run decline in the proportion of women married. There can be no doubt that earning her own income enables a woman to delay marriage, or to terminate an unsatisfactory one. It is not clear, however, that it makes marriage less attractive, for there are other economic and non-economic benefits besides specialization and exchange. Hence it is not surprising that by far most people continue to marry. In fact, the proportion of men and women never married in their life time has not increased to date, though it may in the future.

149. Sawhill, Isabel V. "Economic Perspectives of the Family." Daed. 106, 2 (Spring 1977): 115-25. (1)

This critical review of the "New Home Economics" argues that the "traditional" family with the male breadwinner and female homemaker may have evolved in response to historic circumstances, but does not necessarily represent rational maximizing behavior today. With smaller families, the great increase in the availability of market goods and services, and the dramatic increase in life expectancy, homemaking can no longer plausibly be regarded as a full-time job over most of the life cycle. Further, arguing that the traditional allocation of responsibilities is the result of women's greater efficiency in the home and their lower wages in the market, and then ascribing their lower earnings to the fact that they have household responsibilities is flagrant circular reasoning. Similar views were expressed in Ferber and Birnbaum, B. G. (1977).

Schultz (1985) See item 983.

150. Seguret, Marie-Clair. "Child-Care Services for Working Parents." ILR 120, 6 (Nov.-Dec. 1981): 711-25. (3)

Even though the author begins by pointing out a trend toward egalitarian attitudes about men's and women's roles in the family, she goes on to consider the child care problem as related to women's increased labor force participation. Drawing broadly, but superficially, on the experinces in many countries, she concludes by urging that local, non-governmental organizations should provide such services. While this might be helpful to some families, it is difficult to believe that it could make anything more than a minor dent in this enormous problem.

151. Sen, Gita. "The Sexual Division of Labor and the Working Class Family: Towards A Conceptual Synthesis of Class Relations and the Subordination of Women." RRPE 12, 2 (Summer 1980): 76-86. (1)

This paper argues that there is a tendency within capitalism to create a division of labor based on marital and life cycle status as well as race, ethnicity, and gender. The conclusion is reached that families are, on the one hand, important for the survival of members of the working class and, on the other hand, subordinate women within them.

152. Siegel, Alberta E., Lois M. Stolz, Ethel A. Hitchcock and Jean Adamson. "Dependence and Independence in the Children of Working Mothers." CD 30, 4 (Dec. 1959): 533-46. (3)

This study attempts to improve upon earlier ones which tended to confound the effect of a working mother with those of other family characteristics often associated with the mother's work status. The main conclusion reached is that maternal employment per se does not appear to be a very influential factor in determining the degree of independence of children, at least for children of kindergarten age, the age group that was studied. This is also the opinion of Urie Bronfenbrenner and Ann C. Crouter, "Work and Family Through Time and Space" in Sheila B. Kamerman and Cheryl D. Hayes, eds., Families That Work: Children in a Changing World, Washington, DC: National Academy Press, pp. 39-83.

153. Smith, A. Wade. "Old Fashioned Families as an Endangered Species." SIR 13, 1 (July 1983): 17-38. (3)

The author focuses on the importance of studying the family rather than the individual, a view one might question at a time when marital dissolution is extremely high. Relying on 1969-78 data from the Panel Study of Income Dynamics this study finds (1) a decline in family size, regardless of the mother's work status; (2) a slight increase in labor force participation of older women; (3) rather surprisingly, an increase in the number of nonworking mothers in small families.

Smith, S. K. (1981) See item 994.

154. Smith, Tom W. "Working Wives and Women's Rights: The Connection Between the Employment Status of Wives and the Feminist Attitudes of Husbands." SR 12, 5-6 (Mar. 1985): 501-08. (3)

To determine whether there is a connection between the feminist attitudes of husbands and the employment status of their wives, items on women's rights from the General Social Surveys conducted by the National

Opinion Research Center were examined. A significant positive relationship was found. It was greater on attitudes relating to employment and traditional roles in the home and family than on those dealing with political rights and general equality between men and women, but significant in all cases. The author fails to consider the possibility that the wife's attitude and her labor force participation may influence the husband, as is suggested by Ferber (1982).

155. Sokoloff, Natalie J. Between Money and Love. The Dialectics of Women's Home and Market Work. N.Y.: Praeger, 1980. (1)

Since the focus of this study is on the "recalcitrant social relations of patriarchy and capitalism, which reinforce women's subordination in both home and the market," a more appropraite title would be "Neither Love Nor Money." In the author's view, only internal contradictions in the existing system which provide sources of change give more hope for the future. Chapter 7 offers an interesting analysis of the role of women in the U.S. in the dynamic context of the institutions prevalent in this country. Regrettably, however, no consideration is given to the interaction of non-capitalist systems with patriarchy. This is all the more serious because the author claims to be concerned about broad implications for other societies.

156. Stafford, Frank P. "Women's Use of Time Converging With Men's." MLR 103, 12 (Dec. 1980): 57-59. (3)

This paper shows that between 1965 and 1975 the amount of time spent in paid work declined for both married men and women, but more so for men. At the same time married men very slightly increased the amount of time spent on housework and women decreased theirs. Nonetheless, wives spent almost 6 times as many hours on housework as did husbands. Total working time, however, had been somewhat higher for women in 1965, and was very slightly lower in 1975. It should be noted that these data are only for men and women who are in the labor market, and that the proportion of married women working for pay substantially increased over this decade.

157. Stafford, Rebecca, Elaine Backman and Pamela Dibono. "The Division of Labor Among Cohabiting and Married Couples." JMF 39, 1 (Feb. 1977): 43-54. (3)

Using a matched sample of 25 cohabiting and 30 married college student couples, the authors found that women took most of the responsibility for housework to the same extent in both cases. On the other hand, women did more of the work among married couples. Upon more careful examination of the evidence the authors conclude that this is not caused by differences in the amount of time available, or by a power struggle, but rather by different attitudes toward the proper roles of men and women.

158. Staines, Graham L. and Pamela O'Connor. "Conflicts Among Work, Leisure and Family Roles." MLR 103, 8 (Aug. 1980): 35-39. (3)

According to this report complaints about too much time spent on "work" were more common among men than women, married rather than unmarried people, and parents rather than persons without children. Oddly, only conflict between "work," presumably paid work, and "leisure" is discussed, ignoring household work, which continues to occupy a very large share of women's time.

159. Stanfield, Jacqueline B. "Research on Wife/Mother Role Strain in Dual Career Families." JES 44, 3 (July 1985): 355-63. (1)

A review of studies of the determinants of wife/mother role strain of career women leads the author to conclude that they have gone no further than providing useful hypotheses, and setting the stage for the empirical research needed to gain understanding of the problems such strains create and of the possible solutions available.

Stokes and Hsieh (1983) See item 1003.

160. Strober, Myra H. "Formal Extrafamily Child Care--Some Economic Observations," in Cynthia B. Lloyd ed., Sex, Discrimination and the Division of Labor, NY: Columbia University Press, 1975b, pp. 346-75. (4)

This paper, while fully recognizing the importance of other issues involved in making decisions about provision of and subsidies for extra-family child care, focuses on the economic questions involved. The author concludes that much additional research will be required before we have all the answers, but makes a useful beginning here in clarifying the various costs and benefits that need to be considered, and the variety of forms child care may take.

161. Strober, Myra H. and Charles B. Weinberg. "Working Wives and Major Family Expenditures." JCR 4, 3 (Dec. 1977): 141-47. (3)

Wife's labor force status was not found to be significant in purchase decisions on a variety of time-saving and other durables, hobby and recreation items, or children's college educations, once other economic variables have been accounted for. Size of total family income and whether the family had recently moved to a different house were found to be important variables. Data for this research were from the 1967-70 Panel Survey of Consumer Finances. Nickols and Fox, K. D. (1983) investigated a different set of expenditures and obtained different results.

Szabady (1969) See item 1007.
Szalai (1972) See item 1008.
Szinavacz (1977) See item 1009.

162. Udry, J. Richard. "Marital Instability by Race, Sex, Education, and Occupation Using 1960 Census Data." AJS 72, 21 (Sept. 1966): 203-209. (3)

Analysis of 1960 Census data shows that there is an inverse relationship between marital disruption and the level of education for men and women, black and white. For men there is also a clear inverse relationship with occupational status. But neither of these relationships adeqately explains the far higher rate of marital disruption among non-whites. The author provides some interesting suggestions that might explain this difference by race, but gives no evidence of real interest in the differences of the effect of occupations on men and women.

163. Vanek, Joann. "Time Spent in Housework." SA 231.5 (Nov. 1974): 16-20. (3)

This paper was the first to bring to general attention the surprising fact that at that time women who were not in the labor force were spending as much time on housework as their grandmothers had 50 years earlier, though the nature of the work had changed. As might be expected, employed women devoted considerably less time to homemaking.

164. Vickery, Clair. "The Time-Poor: A New Look at Poverty." JHR 12, 1 (Winter 1977a): 27-48. (1)

Since the minimal non-poor level of consumption requires household production as well as money, the author suggests that the official poverty standard, which ignores the former, does not correctly measure household needs. She further points out that any income support program using this measure will discriminate against families with only one adult, and recommends a more useful two-dimensional definition of poverty.

165. Waite, Linda J. and Ross M. Stolzenberg. "Intended Childbearing and Labor Force Participation of Young Women: Insights from Nonrecursive Models." ASR 41, 2 (Apr. 1976): 235-52. (3)

The results of simultaneous equation models using National Longitudinal Surveys data for young women show that the number of children they intend to bear has only a small effect on their plans for labor force participation. But their intention to be employed at the age of 35 has a substantial effect on the number of children they plan to have in their lifetime. These findings are not inconsistent with the conclusion reached by Cramer (1980).

166. Wales, Thomas J. and A. D. Woodland. "Estimation of the Allocation of Time for Work, Leisure and Housework." Economet. 45, 1 (Jan. 1977): 115-32. (2,Q)

This paper, using Panel Study of Income Dynamics data, shows that estimates of labor supply responses are substantially different when a distinction is made between time spent on leisure and on housework. It also shows that including estimated equations explaining hours of housework produces further improvements as compared to assuming them to be exogenous. Interestingly, while this study finds that the division of housework hours between husband and wife is responsive to the ratio of their wage rates, the effect is not statistically significant.

167. Walker, Kathryn and William Gauger. "Time and Its Dollar Value in Household Work." FER 62, 5 (Fall 1973): 8-13. (1,3)

This paper suggests that the value of housework can be considered equivalent to the cost of hiring someone to do it. Actual estimates are provided using the allocation of time of a large sample of upstate New York families, broken down by number and ages of children, as well as employment status of the wife.

168. Wallston, Barbara. "The Effects of Maternal Employment on Children." JCP 14, 2 (June 1973): 81-95. (3)

This review attempts to integrate research specifically concerned with the impact of the mother's employment on children, from infants to preschoolers, school children and adolescents, and also to take into account sex and class. Among the most important factors that were found to influence the outcomes are quality of substitute care, and how satisfied the mother is with her situation, whether or not she is employed. The author further suggests that various processes are likely to mediate maternal employment, such as social milieu.

169. Weatherly, V. G. "How Does the Access of Women to Industrial Occupations React on the Family?" AJS 14, 6 (May 1909): 740-65. (3)

This author was well ahead of his time in objecting to housework being considered as unproductive and "not gainful." He was equally farsighted in concluding that the "proprietary family" will persist until the wife becomes independent through her own paid labor. Last, he was discerning, in viewing the lock-step demands of employment, with little flexibility or possibility of adjustment to family needs as one of the main obstacles to progress.

170. Weinberg, Charles B. and Russell S. Winer. "Working Wives and Major Family Expenditures: Replication and Extension." JCR 10, 2 (Sept. 1983): 259-63. (3)

This paper updates an earlier study by Strober and Weinberg (1977), which compared purchases of time-saving and other durable goods, as well as hobby and recreation items by wives who did and wives who did not work for pay. In 1977, as was true a decade earlier, no significant difference was found between the two groups once income, stage of life cycle, and other situational variables were held constant.

171. Weller, Robert H. "The Employment and Cumulative Family Size in the United States, 1970 and 1960." Dem. 14, 1 (Feb. 1977): 43-65. (3)

This study, using the Bureau of the Census Public Use Samples, shows that the negative relationship between wife's employment and cumulative family size is stronger for whites than nonwhites, and is greater for those with 12 or more years of schooling, with higher incomes, and with no relatives living in the family. Interestingly, the relationship was, however, somewhat less pronounced in 1970 than in 1960, consistent with the view that working and having young children is becoming more acceptable.

Weller (1969) See item 1021.

172. Weller, Robert H. "The Employment of Wives, Dominance and Fertility." JMF 30, 3 (Aug. 1968): 437-42. (3)

A survey conducted in lower- and middle-class neighborhoods in San Juan, Puerto Rico yielded results consistent with the propositions that (1) the wife has more influence in family decision making when she is in the labor force, (2) this greater influence results in lower fertility, and (3) the negative influence on fertility is strongest in wife-dominant or egalitarian families. The possibility that preferences for family size may vary among men and women who have different attitudes toward women's role is not considered.

173. White, Michelle J. "Sex Differences in Urban Commuting." AER 76, 2 (May 1986): 368-72. (3)

This study draws upon methodology from both labor economics and urban economics to investigate the differences between men and women in commuting patterns, which are found to be considerable. Mainly, children have a positive effect on the distance a male worker commutes, but less so if there is a second worker in the household. For female workers, on the other hand, only the presence of young children matters, and it reduces the distance travelled to work.

Winegarden (1984) See item 1023.

174. Wolfe, Barbara and Robert Haveman. "Time Allocation, Market Work and Changes in Female Health." AER 73, 2 (May 1983): 134-139. (3)

The authors used Panel Study of Income Dynamics data to investigate the effect of time allocation on women's health status. They found a definite relationship, not between market work and health, but between the dual role of working and having young children, and health deterioration. Beyond that, the nature of the market work and its environment also made a difference.

175. Wright, James D. "Are Working Women Really More Satisfied? Evidence fom Several National Surveys." JMF 40, 2 (May 1978): 301-13. (3)

Relying on data from six national surveys, the author examines whether "working women" are more satisfied than homemakers, as suggested, for instance, by Ferree (1976). He fails to confirm this conclusion, but rather finds that there are benefits and costs in each case, with no significant differences in overall life satisfaction between the two. The author fails to consider that this may be, to a considerable extent, the result of self-selection. Presumably, wives who least like being homemakers are most likely to enter the labor market--as they have been doing in increasing numbers.

176. Yarrow, Marian R., Phyllis Scott, Louise de Leeuw, and Christine Heinig. "Child Rearing in Families of Working and Nonworking Mothers." <u>Sociom.</u> 25, 2 (June 1962): 122-40. (3)

Like a number of investigations (e.g., Peterson, E.T. 1961, Siegel 1959, and Wallston 1973), this study of intact, white, economically stable families found that childrearing practices were not directly related to mother's work status. They were, however, related to mother's education and motivation. Most problems were found when the mother stayed home because of a sense of obligation, even though she would have preferred to be employed. When the mother had a high school education children were treated more firmly and were given more responsibility if she worked for pay. There was no such difference for college educated mothers.

Chapter 3

LABOR FORCE PARTICIPATION AND HOURS OF WORK

The most visible change in the economic status of women during the second half of the twentieth century has been the large increase in their labor force participation. (The labor force includes all those individuals 16 years of age and over who work for pay or profit or are actively seeking such employment.) It is not surprising therefore that this subject has received a great deal of attention in the economics literature. Much has been learned about the factors associated with this phenomenon, from industrialization and more recently the growing importance of the clerical and service sectors of the economy, the labor shortage during WWII, and the higher level of education, to declining family size, the increasing divorce rate and the feminist movement of the last 25 years. But a great deal of uncertainty remains about the relative importance of each of these factors, and even, in some cases, to what extent they may have been the result rather than the cause of increased labor force participation.

The greater availability of market produced goods and services increased the ability and willingness of women to give up full-time homemaking, and greater market production was in part a response to the growing demand as more and more women entered the labor market. The expansion of the sectors of the economy which rely heavily on female workers attracted women into paid work and the increasing availability of women who were willing to work for low wages also precipated the growth of these sectors. Women are more inclined to enter the labor market because they have more education and fewer children; they spend more years in school and fewer on childrearing because they want to work for pay. The increased labor force participation rate causes more divorces; actual and anticipated divorces cause women to enter the labor market.

Learning more about the interaction among these factors is important not only for understanding how the present situation evolved but also will help us to predict what is likely to happen in the future and to determine how different policies may, purposefully or inadvertently, influence such developments. Particularly important is the question to what extent higher wages for women will cause them to devote more time to paid work and spend less time in the home (substitution effect), and to what extent these higher wages, as well as more other family income, will have the opposite result (income effect) because the need for additional earnings is less urgent.

The determinants of how many hours a day, how many weeks a year, and how many years in a lifetime a woman spends in the labor market constitute the primary subject of this section. Such related topics as the energy devoted to work, absenteeism, quit rates, and others are also included. What kind of work women do, and how they are rewarded for it, however, are subjects covered in the next two chapters.

177. Ahking, F. W. "A Study of the Labor Force Participation Rate of Single Women." AE 23-2 (Fall, 1979): 50-55. (3,4)

This research investigates the question whether the labor supply of single women is backward bending. The results indicate this is not the case. It is not clear, however, that this necessarily suggests single women are secondary workers as the author claims. Other reasons for the upward sloping supply of labor are possible. It is even more difficult to understand how these findings are supposed to be related to disguised unemployment, or to the conclusion that efforts should be directed mainly towards expanding employment opportunities for the primary work force.

178. Alban, Edward and Mark Jackson. "The Job Vacancy - Unemployed Ratio and Labor Force Participation." ILRR 29, 3 (Apr. 1976): 412-19. (3)

The authors suggest that the ratio of job vacancies to the number of unemployed is a better indicator of the state of the labor market than the unemployment rate alone. They also find that this ratio is a significant determinant of labor force participation of secondary wage earners.

Anderson, K. H., Clark and Johnson, T. (1980) See item 32.

179. Andrews, Howard F. "Journey to Work Considerations in the Labor Force Participation of Married Women." RS 12, 1 (1978): 11-20. (3)

The data on which this study is based came from a 1968 survey of married women in five urban areas. It was found that an increase in distance of travel to work, everything else remaining the same, reduced the probability of labor force participation. The impact differed, however, as between full-time and part-time workers, as well as by region. Other variables, such as income of the wife, and of the husband, clearly also played a part.

Anker (1983) See item 835.

180. Applebaum, Eileen. Back to Work. Determinants of Women's Successful Re-Entry. Boston, MA: Auburn House Publishing Company, 1981. (3)

This small book offers a thorough analysis of the consequences of work intermittency for the National Longitudinal Surveys cohort of 5,000 women 30 to 44 years old. It is found that the economic cost of extended interruptions is substantial, and that the major determinants of ease of re-entry are years of schooling, choice of college major, and participation in post-school training. It is also pointed out that, though working part-time instead of dropping out reduces some problems, it is by no means a panacea.

181. Ashenfelter, Orley and James J. Heckman, "The Estimation of Income and Substitution Effects in a Model of Family Labor Supply." Economet. 42, 1 (Jan. 1974): 73-85. (2,Q)

The authors have formulated the theoretical restrictions arising from the application of the classical theory of consumer behavior to the household demand for leisure in a way that makes them readily amenable to being tested. The tests, when applied to one data set, tended to support the classical restrictions and, in at least one instance, resulted in a significant improvement in the precision of all parameter estimates.

182. Baker, Laura N. Wanted: Women in War Industry. NY: E. P. Dutton and Company, Inc., 1943. (4)

This book, a straightforward appeal to women to do their patriotic duty by working, particularly in war industries, is included here as a historic curiosity. It is particularly interesting to note that there is much discussion how women can best succeed in the labor market, including a whole chapter on "What the Well Dressed Worker Wears," but no mention is made at all of the need for mothers to stay home to look after their children, which we hear so much about in times when women are not urgently needed in the labor market.

183. Barnes, William F. and Ethel B. Jones. "Differences in Male and Female Quitting," JHR 9, 4 (Fall 1974): 439-51. (3)

Establishment and household data are used to distinguish between male and female labor turnover. Women quit more often to leave the labor force, men quit more often to move to another job. Total female quitting is larger, male quitting more variable. For both sexes, however, quits decrease with higher earnings. Hence these results are not inconsistent with Blau, F. D. and Kahn (1981) who found that, other things equal, there is no significant difference between male and female quit rates.

184. Bell, Duran. "Why Participation Rates of Black and White Wives Differ." JHR 9, 4 (Fall 1974): 465-79. (3)

Analysis of data from the 1967 Survey of Economic Opportunity shows that in 1966 fully 61.4 percent of black wives as compared with 46.7 percent of white wives were in the labor force. Interestingly, full-time work was more common in better educated, more stable black families, but the opposite was true for whites. The author concludes that black women were entering the white collar jobs that opened up to them, while upper middle class white wives found barriers to high status employment they might have been attracted to.

Beneria (1981) See item 842.
Ben Porath and Gronau (1985) See item 843.

185. Berger, Mark C. "Labor Supply and Spouse's Health: The Effects of Illness, Disability and Mortality." SSQ 64, 3 (Sep. 1983): 494-509. (3)

This study, like Henretta and O'Rand (1980) showed that, in general, wives tend to increase their market work when a spouse's health deteriorates, or he dies, while husbands are likely to reduce their market work under comparable circumstances. Berger and Fleisher (1984) shed further light on this issue.

186. Berger, Mark C. and Belton M. Fleisher. "Husband's Health and the Wife's Labor Supply." JHE 3, 1 (Apr. 1984): 63-75. (3)

Data from the National Longitudinal Surveys show that when no transfers are available, wives tend to do more market work when the husband is in ill health, presumably to compensate for lost earnings. Wives, however, reduce their market work, presumably to spend more time with the husband, as transfer payments become more attractive.

187. Bergmann, Barbara R. "The Effect of Wives' Labor Force Participation on Inequality in the Distribution of Family Income." JHR 15, 3 (Summer 1980a): 452-55. (3)

Much concern has been expressed at times by persons not noted for their preoccupation with income inequality about the possibility that women's increasing labor force participation may lead to a more unequal distribution of income. The results of two simulations in this note show that initially inequality will decrease if women mainly enter from families with low income, but will increase if the opposite is true. In any case there will be little effect on inequality once most women are in the labor force.

Berliner (1983) See item 845.
Bilsborrow (1977) See item 846.
Blau, F. D. (1978) See item 694.
Blau, F. D. and Jusenius (1976) See item 353.

188. Blau, Francine D. and Lawrence M. Kahn. "Race and Sex Differences in Quits by Young Workers." ILRR 38, 4 (July 1981): 563-77. (3)

Using data for young men and women from the National Longitudinal Surveys, it was discovered that, all else equal, white and black women were no more likely to quit their jobs than men of the same race. The authors concluded that the reason for the observed sex differential in quitting is the difference in jobs rather than in personal characteristics. Similar results were obtained by a British study (Shorey, 1983).

189. Boskin, Michael J. "The Economics of Labor Supply," in Glen G. Cain and Harold W. Watts, eds., Income Maintenance and Labor Supply, Institute of Research on Povery Monograph Series. Chicago: Rand McNally College Publishing Co., 1964, pp. 163-81. (3)

Using data from the Survey of Economic Opportunity, 1967, the author examines elasticity of supply of labor for subgroups distinguished by sex, race, age and marital status. Positive wage elasticities were found only for wives, female teenagers, and white husbands at or near retirement age. Modest negative income elasticities, manifested entirely through reduction in annual hours (not labor force participation) were also found for white husbands and wives. Caveats offered are that preferences are assumed to be constant across workers within subgroup, and marital status is assumed to be exogenous.

190. Boskin, Michael J. "The Effect of Government Expenditures and Taxes on Female Labor." AER 64, 2 (May 1974): 251-56. (3)

In this overview of the main effects of government taxes and expenditures on male and female labor supply, it is noted that many of these effects are not the same for both sexes. As is true in most studies, the elasticity of supply of labor of wives is found to be positive and considerably greater than that of husbands. This is assumed to be the case in part because for women market work is to a considerable extent a substitute for housework, but also because lower returns tend to particularly depress women's investment in human capital. Since taxes reduce take home pay, their effect is similar to a reduction in pay rate, as is also shown by Leuthold (1978).

Brown, C. (1985) See item 47.
Brown, L. J. (1984) See item 48.

191. Bowen, William G. and T. Aldrich Finegan. The Economics of Labor Force Participation, Princeton, N.J.: Princeton University Press, 1969. (1,3)

This massive work builds upon but extends and improves previous research using regression analysis to quantify factors that determine, or are at any rate associated with labor force participation among various age-sex-race-marital status population groups. Data from the 1960 Census, and some earlier Census years, as well as later Current Population surveys, are used. The underlying model assumes that the household is the decision making unit. The quality of the data used was not up to the level of the relatively sophisticated methodology used, and cross-section data are not ideal for this purpose in any case. Hence it is not surprising that few firm answers were obtained, and later studies, such as Cohen, M. S., Lerman, and Rea (1971) and Fields (1976) tended to get different results.

192. Burggraf, Shirley P. "Women Youth and Minorities and the Case of the Missing Productivity." AER 74, 2 (May 1984): 254-59. (3)

The author takes issue with the use of the influx of women, youth, and minorities into the labor force as the explanation for declining productivity experienced in the U.S. She suggests the main reason was that the increase in the labor force outstripped the growth of capital during the 1970's. On the other hand, she concedes that the productivity of white men may be higher, if only because of the support network which has been produced for them by women and minorities.

193. Cain, Glen G. Married Women in the Labor Force: An Economic Analysis. Chicago: University of Chicago Press, 1966. (3)

This study of black and white women is based on Census data for 1940 to 1960. It shows that at times the income effect, which causes higher wages to have a negative impact on the amount of market work, is stronger than the substitution effect, which causes the amount of market work to increase. Therefore, unlike Mincer (1962), the author concludes that higher wages do not fully explain the rising labor force participation during that period.

194. Cain, Glen G. and Martin D. Dooley. "Estimation of a Model of Labor Supply, Fertility, and Wages of

Married Women." JPE 84, 4 (Aug. 1976, Part 2): S179-99. (2,3)

The units of observation in this study are standard metropolitan statistical areas at the time of the 1970 Census. These data were used on the assumption that for purposes of prediction and of policy it is the behavior of groups that is of particular interest. The model developed corresponds closely to the neoclassical theory of household decision making, and the variables used correspond to its requirements. Strong support is derived for the prevailing hypothesis that the wage effect on labor supply is positive, but the income effect negative. Hypotheses about wages and fertility, on the other hand, were not much illuminated. The authors, nonetheless, believe there is good reason to continue to use simultaneous-equation models.

195. Cain, Glen G., Walter Nicholson, Charles B. Mallar, and Judith Wooldridge. "The Labor-Supply Response of Married Women, Husband Present." JHR 9, 2 (Spring 1974): 201-22. (4)

This study focuses on the effects the negative income tax experiment in New Jersey and Pennsylvania had on the labor supply of married women. The authors chose this group because they are thought to have relatively flexible work choices. They found that over three years the amount of work increased for the control group. Among those in the treatment group, there was an initial decline in hours, earnings, and labor force participation only for white wives, small in absolute terms, and that was reversed in the third year. The work reduction was somewhat greater for plans that carried higher income guarantees, but again, not significantly so.

Canlas and Razak (1979) See item 853.

196. Carliner, Geoffrey. "Female Labor Force Participation Rates for Nine Ethnic Groups," JHR 16, 2 (Spring 1981): 286-93. (3)

The regressions in this paper show that the same factors which influence the labor force participation decisions of black and white wives are generally also important for other groups. It is also shown, however, that there are even greater differences in the effects these factors have on blacks and whites than had generally been previously noted.

Carliner, Robinson and Tomes (1980) See item 854.

197. Chenoweth, Lillian and Elizabeth G. Maret-Havens. "Women's Labor Force Participation - A Look at Some Residential Patterns." MLR 101, 3 (Mar. 1978): 38-41. (3)

Rural women have a much lower labor force participation rate than their urban counterparts. One explanation is that this is the result of fewer opportunities another views traditional attitudes as the cause. Using data from the National Longitudinal Surveys, this study examines the effect of different location and of differences in the characteristics of the people. The results clearly show that attitudes of rural residents are not more conservative than those of the rest of the population, so that job opportunities seem to be the main factor behind variations in labor force participation. This conclusion would be supported by Andrews, H. F. (1978), who found that increased distance of travel to work had a negative effect on women's labor force participation.

198. Clark, Robert L., Thomas Johnson and A. A. McDermed. "Allocation of Time and Resources by Married Couples Approaching Retirement." SSB 43, 4 (Apr. 1980): 3-16. (3)

This research, based on data from the Retirement History Study for 1969-73, shows that the behavior of husbands and wives in this age group is mutually interdependent. Both spouses respond positively to increases in their own wages, but negatively to the wages of their partner. Further, the probability that one will be in the labor force is greater when the spouse is unemployed.

199. Clogg, Clifford C. "Cohort Analysis of Recent Trends in Labor Force Participation." Dem. 19, 4 (Nov. 1982): 459-79. (3)

A model with a special type of age-period interaction and data from the March Current Population Survey are used to investigate labor force participation during the interval 1969-1979. Findings are that younger cohorts of nonblack men, nonblack women and black women have greater "intrinsic" tendencies to participate than older cohorts, but the opposite is true for black men.

200. Cogan, John F. "Fixed Costs and Labor Supply." Economet. 49, 4 (July 1981): 945-63. (3,2,Q)

A model is developed which assumes that if a woman is to be in the labor market, the minimum number of hours she is willing to supply to the market may be considerably higher than zero. This is so because of fixed costs of working, estimated here to be about 28 percent of a married woman's average earnings. The relationships derived differ considerably from those obtained by conventional methods.

201. Cohen, Malcolm S., Robert I. Lerman and Samuel A. Rea, Jr. "Area Employment Conditions and Labor Force Participation: A Microstudy." JPE 79, 5 (Sep.-Oct. 1971): 1151-60. (3)

This study compared the results of the authors' research with those of Bowen and Finegan (1969) on the importance of the discouraged worker and additional worker effects. Using the Current Population Survey data for March 1967, and a model that employed a family-utility function, they found that a rise of one percentage point in the unemployment rate induced, at most, a fall in adult women's participation rate of slightly more than one percentage point. Further, no significant additional worker effect was found when the husband was unemployed. They ascribe the fact that they found smaller effects in both respects partly to their improved methods, partly to the difference in time period studied.

Cohen, M. S. and Stafford (1974) See item 51.
Colombino (1985) See item 866.
Concepcion (1974) See item 867.

202. Cooney, Rosemary S. "Changing Labor Force Participation of Mexican American Wives: A Comparison with Anglos and Blacks." SSQ 56, 2 (Sep. 1975): 252-61. (3)

This study focuses on the socioeconomic factors that help to explain the relatively low labor force participation rate of Mexican American women as opposed to Anglo and black women. Such factors as education, number of children and residence account for some of the difference, but leave part--a large part in the case of blacks--unexplained. Thus one may conclude that cultural factors play a significant role as well. The results also show, however, that this was less true by 1970 than in 1960.

203. Cooney, Rosemary S. "Changing Patterns of Female Labor Force Participaton." IR 16, 3 (Oct. 1977): 355-62. (3)

This paper challenges the primary emphasis in the social science literature on general processes of economic growth and urbanization as causes of the rise in non-agricultural labor force participation of women. This author focuses attention on a number of facts which raise questions about this simple relationship. She points first to the loose relationship between urbanization and female labor force participation and second, to national variations in female labor force participation as related to industry variations. Last, she shows there were many cases where it was not new industries that attracted women, but where previously male industries became feminized.

Cooney (1978) See item 868.

204. Cooney, Rosemary S. "Intercity Variations in Puerto Rican Female Participation." JHR 14, 2 (Spring 1979): 222-35. (3)

Among eight major ethnic/racial groups of women, the labor force participation declined only for Puerto Ricans between 1950 and 1970. This research shows that the labor market conditions in particular locations played a major part, as evidenced by the fact that labor force participation for Puerto Rican women increased in Chicago, though it declined in New York.

205. Cooney, Rosemary S. and Vilmar Ortiz. "Nativity, National Origin, and Hispanic Female Participation in the Labor Force." SSQ 6, 4, 3 (Sept. 1983): 510-23. (3)

This research examines the relationship of education, English language proficiency, and household headship with labor force participation among Hispanic females, native and foreign born, and with varying national origin. The process of integration into the workforce appears to be more influenced by whether a woman was born in the U.S. or elsewhere, than by differences in national origin, which are important only for the foreign born. Data were obtained from the 1976 Survey of Income and Education.

Cox, D. (1984) See item 458.

206. Corcoran, Mary E. "The Structure of Female Wages." AER 68, 2 (May 1978a): 165-70. (3)

This paper explores the process by which women's "household responsibilities" affect their labor market behavior and wages. The two issues considered are the effects of women's intermittent labor force participation and their adjustment of paid work to demands of homemaking while they are in the labor force. Using data from the Panel Study of Income Dynamics it was found that interruptions had almost no effect on wages, though delays in starting work after school did. Similarly, self-imposed restrictions on job hours or location had no significant impact. In fact, differences in work history, labor force attachment and formal schooling together accounted for less than half of the earnings gap between white men and white women, less than one-third between white men and black women. This work raises serious doubts about the possibility of explaining most, let alone all, of the male-female earnings gap in terms of differences in human capital.

207. Cramer, James C. "Employment Trends of Young Mothers and the Opportunity Cost of Babies in the United States." Dem. 16, 2 (May 1979): 177-97. (3)

This paper develops a model of opportunity cost in terms of time lost. Using Panel Study of Income Dynamics data, the average loss of employment attributable to a second- or higher-order birth is found to be over 400 hours per year when calculated for a child about 2 years old. This time cost does not appear to depend either on wife's education, her potential wage rate, or wage rate of the husband, which is contrary to what microeconomic theory would suggest. The author concludes that economic models are far too simple for what is, in reality, a very complex situation. Specifically, he argues, babies consume home time, which is not directly related to price of time.

Cramer (1980) See item 53.

208. Darian, Jean C. "Factors Influencing the Rising Labor Force Participation Rate of Married Women with Pre-School Children." SSQ 56, 4 (Mar. 1976): 614-30. (3)

Using data from the 1960 and 1970 Census the author concludes that the large increase in the labor force participation rate of mothers with young children has been caused to a greater extent by factors related to the relatively young age of the mothers than to a reduction in constraints, though both played a part. The most important single influence is the higher labor force participation of younger as compared to older women. It is suggested that better contraceptive techniques, changing attitudes toward fertility and women's roles, as well as rising income aspirations may all have contributed to this.

Dauffenbach and El Hun (1980) See item 871.
Denti (1978) See item 874.

209. Devaney, Barbara. "An Analysis of Variations in U.S. Fertility and Female Labor Force Participation Trends." Dem. 20, 2 (May 1983): 147-61. (3)

This study covers the years 1947-1977. It appears that male income relative to that of earlier cohorts has a significant positive effect on fertility, and a negative effect on female work effort, but that the opposite effect of female wage rates is dominant.

210. Diamond, Irma. "The Liberation of Women in a Full Employment Society." AAAPSS 418 (Mar. 1975): 138-46. (4)

This paper argues for a full employment act in part because women's entry into and progress within the labor market would be far easier in a full employment economy, but also points out the important role of support services.

211. Dickinson, Jonathan. "Labor Supply of Family Members," in James N. Morgan, Katherine Dickinson, Jonathan Dickinson, Jacob Benns and Greg J. Duncan, eds., Five Thousand American Families--Patterns of Economic Progress, Vol. 1, Institute for Social Research, University of Michigan, 1974: 177-250. (3)

This research finds evidence of a strong positive response to higher wages in hours of work supplied by married women, but also provides evidence that the individual has far less choice with respect to hours than most standard models assume. Labor force participation and hours are both found to be negatively related to the husband's wage rate, but are not influenced by the likelihood of his becoming unemployed.

Dixon (1982) See item 878.

212. Dooley, Martin D. "Labor Supply and Fertility of Married Women: An Analysis with Grouped and Individual Data from the 1970 U.S. Census." JHR, 17, 4 (Fall 1982): 499-531. (2)

This study uses 1970 Census data to estimate a model of fertility and labor supply of married women. Using data sets at different levels of aggregation leads to quite different supply estimates. Since estimates based on individual observations show results similar to those found in other apparently reliable studies, the author concludes that it is the grouped published data which indicate little association between labor force participation and mean hourly wages that are likely to be biased.

213. Duggan, James E. "The Labor Force Participation of Older Workers." ILRR 37, 3 (Apr. 1984): 416-30. (3)

The author's research shows that labor force participation of older men and older women has been responsive to economic and demographic factors. Supplemental Security Income and Social Security have contributed to earlier retirement for both groups. The author also claims that older women increased their labor force participation in response to the labor-supply shift of younger persons that led to a decline in relative wages for both groups. This explanation seems rather forced and unconvincing.

214. Duncan, Beverly. "Change in Worker/Nonworker Ratios for Women." Dem. 16, 4 (Nov. 1979): 535-47. (3)

Effects of age, birth year, and observation year on work behavior are estimated by regression, using data from the Current Population Surveys. It is found that economic climate, as well as the other factors, has a substantial effect, and that the effect is different for various age groups.

Durand (1975) See item 882.

215. Durban, Elizabeth. "The Vicious Cycle of Welfare: Problems of the Female-Headed Household in New York City," in Cynthia B. Lloyd, ed., Sex Discrimination and the Division of Labor, NY: Columbia University Press, 1975, pp. 313-45. (4)

It was found in this study that the labor force participation of women at the higher end of the income scale had been increasing, but that of women at the other end of the scale had declined. The author suggests that the latter could do better on AFDC than on the low earnings they could hope to achieve. The fundamental dilemma, not directly addressed in this chapter, is that a society not ready to fully accept the legitimacy of mothers of young children working, will be ambivalent about policies that would help such women become self-sufficient.

Elizaga (1974) See item 883.
Eyland (1982) See item 884.

216. Fair, Ray C. "Labor Force Participation, Wage Rates and Money Illusion." RES 53, 2 (May 1971): 164-68. (3)

The author noted that up to that time studies had tended to rely on cross-section rather than time-series data, and pointed out that two problems the latter would have to face were the choice of an appropriate wage rate variable, as well as the appropriate lag distribution of wage rates. These issues are related to the possible existence of "money illusion," meaning that people would not take into account changes in prices, as well as changes in the money wage. The study found little evidence of such money illusion, not even in the short run. This conclusion is supported by Wachter (1972) who finds it is real wage rates that are important for the labor supply of secondary workers.

217. Farkas, George. "Cohort, Age, and Period Effects Upon the Employment of White Females: Evidence for 1957-68." Dem. 14, 1 (Feb. 1977): 33-42. (3)

The net effects of birth cohort, age, and economic conditions upon the employment of white women is examined, using data from the Social Security Administration's continuous work history file. The long-run, or cohort effect of increasing employment is found to be stronger than the short run or cyclical effect, though both are significant.

218. Felmlee, Diane H. "A Dynamic Analysis of Women's Employment Exits." Dem. 21, 2 (May 1984): 171-83. (3,2)

This research examines women's rates of leaving a job without entering other employment, using data from the National Longitudinal Survey of Young Women (1968-1973). Several findings are different from the relationships suggested in much of the current literature. For instance, education appears to increase leaving rates, and high income of a spouse appears to decrease them. No explanations are offered for these puzzling relationships. Not as surprising is the discovery that the longer a woman has had a job, the less likely she is to leave it. The author points out that none of these conclusions would be reached if only cross-section data were used.

219. Ferber, Marianne A. "Labor Market Participation of Young Married Women: Causes and Effects." JMF 44, 2 (May 1982): 457-68. (3,1)

This paper explores the complex interrelationships of changing economic and social conditions, attitudes and married women's labor force participation. In general, evidence is found to support the view that women's changing attitude toward labor force participation and consequent changes in their behavior tend to influence other variables, not just vice versa. For instance, the extent to which a husband approves of a wife's employment appears to change in response to her labor force status. This conclusion is consistent with the findings reported by T. W. Smith (1985), but not with his interpretation.

220. Fields, Judith M. "A Comparison of Intercity Differences in the Labor Force Participation Rates of Married Women in 1970, 1960, 1950 and 1860." JHR 11, 4 (Fall 1976): 568-77. (3)

This paper compares earlier regressions for Standard Metropolitan Statistical Areas reported by Bowen and Finegan (1969) with those obtained for a similar model applied to 1970 data. The results show that by 1970 the model had lost much of its explanatory power, explaining at most somewhat over half of the variation between wives' labor force participation in different areas. Only unemployment showed increased explanatory significance, while other variables are apparently dwarfed by the growing trend toward greater labor force attachment, especially among younger cohorts.

221. Finegan, T. Aldrich. "Participation of Married Women in the Labor Force," in Cynthia B. Lloyd, ed., Sex, Discrimination, and the Division of Labor, NY: Columbia University Press, 1975, pp. 27-60. (3)

This chapter presents an overview of the labor force participation of married women in the U.S. since 1945, and the extent to which it was influenced by labor market conditions, as well as by characteristics of individuals and their families. The author concludes, as did many other researchers, that rising real wages, development of labor-saving devices, changes in the occupational and industrial mix, the shorter work week, lower fertility, earlier school attendance of children and greater educational attainment of women all played an important part in causing the increase in labor force participation. Inadequate consideration is given to the extent the causal connection for some of these developments may also have been in the opposite direction.

Fleisher and Rhodes (1979) See item 64.
Franz and Kawasaki (1981) See item 887.

222. Fullerton, Howard N., Jr. "How Accurate Were the Projections of the Labor Force?" MLR 105, 7 (July 1982): 15-21. (3)

This paper makes the very interesting observation that four projections, the last from as late as 1976, all substantially underestimated the 1980 labor force. It may be noted further that the male labor force was overestimated in the earlier projections, as was true in all four cases for older women. Thus it was the increase in participation of young women that considerably exceeded expectations.

223. Fullerton, Howard N., Jr. "The 1995 Labor Force: BLS' Latest Projections." MLR 108, 11 (Nov. 1985), 17-25. (3)

This paper offers projections of the labor force which include a continued, though slightly slower rise in labor force participation of women, and a very modest and slightly slower decline in the labor force participation of men. Previous projections for women were generally too low, but one may assume that the experts have learned from their past mistakes.

224. Fullerton, Howard N., Jr. and James J. Byrne. "Length of Working Life for Men and Women, 1970." MLR 99, 2 (Feb. 1976): 31-35. (3)

The work life expectancy of women rose from 20.1 to 22.9 years from 1960 to 1970. The change was caused entirely by increases in labor force participation of married women. During the same period work life expectancy of men declined from 41.4 to 40.1.

Geerken and Gove (1983) See item 67.

225. Goodwin, Leonard. "Welfare Mothers and the Work Ethic." MLR 95, 8 (Aug. 1972): 35-37. (4)

Based on a study for the Brookings Institution, the author reports that both mothers on long-term welfare and their sons continue to have a strong work ethic, and tend to identify their self-esteem with work. Hence, he concludes, the concern about welfare payments doing damage in this respect is misplaced. Though, interestingly, nothing is mentioned here about daughters, there is no reason to assume that their attitudes would not be similar.

Gramm (1973)(1974) See items 767, 74.

226. Gramm, Wendy L. "Household Utility Maximization and the Working Wife." AER 65, 1 (Mar. 1975): 90-100. (2,3)

This paper develops a model of the wife's labor supply which incorporates children into the decision making process. The results show that the wife's productivity is largest in households with young children, and that the arrival of the first child is very important in explaining her labor supply. More surprising is the finding that mothers of one child are slower to return to the labor market than those with more children, presumably because the latter are in more urgent need of earnings. It was also determined that the labor supply of women without children is the least responsive to wage changes.

Greenhalgh (1977)(1980) See items 893, 894.
Gregory, P. R. (1982) See item 897.
Gregory, R. G., McMahon, P. and Wittingham (1985) See item 899.
Gronau (1973a)(1973b)(1976) See items 77, 78, 900.

227. Gronau, Reuben. "Leisure, Home Production and Work: The Theory of the Allocation of Time Revisited." JPE 85, 6 (Dec. 1977): 1099-23. (1,3)

This paper clearly distinguishes among three uses of time rather than merely two, recognizing that both housework and leisure are alternatives to use of time for market work. An increase in wages may be expected to reduce work at home, but the effect on leisure is indeterminate because higher income tends to increase demand for the latter. Empirical tests, based on data from the Panel Study on Income Dynamics, tend to support these conclusions.

Grossbard-Schechtman (1984) See item 79.

228. Grossman, Allyson S. "The Labor Force Patterns of Divorced and Separated Women." MLR 100, 1 (Jan. 1977): 48-53.

Divorced women have had the highest labor force participation rate of any marital group of women--more than 7 out of 10 worked for pay in 1975. Separated women were younger, less educated, less likely to be employed, and more likely to have children. Hence they had an income level even below the relatively low level of divorced women.

229. Grossman, Allyson S. "Labor Force Patterns of Single Women." MLR 102, 8 (Aug. 1979): 46-49. (3)

Single women have a long history of labor market activity, but they used to mainly view their jobs as temporary. As women married increasingly later, and tended to stay in or reenter the labor market after marriage, this changed. Nonetheless, they continue to be concentrated in clerical and service work.

Since many are young, they share in the high unemployment rate of that group.

Gustafsson and Jacobsson (1985) See item 902.

230. Hafstrom, Jean L. and Marilyn M. Dunsing. "Socioeconomic and Social-Psychological Influences on Reasons Wives Work." JCR 5, 3 (Dec. 1978): 169-75. (3)

This study relied on a survey conducted in the Champaign-Urbana area in 1970-71 of women under 65 with children in the home. It was found that sociopsychological as well as socioeconomic factors play a part in the work decision.

Haig and Wood (1976) See item 90.
Hartog and Theeuwes (1985) See item 905.

231. Hausman, Jerry A. "The Effect of Wages, Taxes and Fixed Cost on Women's Labor Force Participation." JPE 14, 2 (Oct. 1980): 161-94. (3,Q)

This paper estimates a structural model of labor force participation, chiefly in order to evaluate the disincentive effects of taxes and transfer payments. As expected a higher marginal tax rate lowers the probability of participation, as do higher transfer payments. Thus the effect of shifting from welfare payments to a negative income tax could have a positive or negative effect on labor force participation, depending on marginal tax rates implicit in the two policies.

232. Hausman, Leonard J. and Hirshel Kasper. "The Work Effort Response of Women to Income Maintenance," in Larry L. Orr, Robinson G. Hollister, and Myron J. Lefcowitz, Income Maintenance - Interdisciplinary Approaches to Research, Chicago: Markham, 1971, pp. 89-104. (4)

This work, like a number of others, makes clear that a great many variables, such as earnings potential, marital and family status, earnings of spouse, level of education and health status all play a part in determining women's labor force participation. This study also shows that the availability and level of welfare assistance plays an important part.

Hayghe (1976) See item 84.

233. Heckman, James J. "Effects of Child Care Programs on Women's Work Effort," JPE 82, 2 (Mar.-Apr. 1974a): S136-63. (3,2,Q)

The separation of preferences from constraints allowed the author to estimate the labor-supply parameters of individuals. The estimates suggest that wage rates are strongly correlated with preferences for work, but a special procedure employed avoids the bias this might cause. The main conclusions offered are that "If formal sources provide higher quality day care, the decision to work, the length of the work week, and the choice of the mode of child care are jointly determined and mutually dependent on the wage rate and on the prices of formal and informal care," and that this "is an approach that might prove fruitful in future research on the economics of child care."

234. Heckman, James J. "Shadow Prices, Market Wages and Labor Supply." Economet. 42, 4 (July 1974b): 679-94. (2,3,Q)

This paper demonstrates an econometric methodology that permits researchers to combine observations on working and nonworking women to estimate labor force participation functions. The results of the empirical application support the value of this approach. It has been widely used in other studies since then.

235. Heckman, James J. "A Partial Survey of Recent Research on the Labor Supply of Women." AER 68, 2 (May 1978): 200-207. (3,Q)

The author reviews and evaluates much of the best known research on the labor supply of married women done up to that point. He distinguishes between those studies that are concerned with the amount of labor supplied either at one time or over the life cycle as opposed to those that examine the decision whether or not to be in the labor market as a discrete choice, but also attempts to merge the two approaches.

236. Heckman, James J. and Thomas E. MaCurdy. "A Life Cycle Model of Female Labor Supply." RE Stud. 47, 1 (Jan. 1980): 47-74. (1,3,Q)

This paper first presents a life cycle model of labor supply decisions of married women, then uses Panel Survey of Income Dynamics data to obtain empirical estimates. Unlike some earlier studies, the researchers do not assume that non-market time at one age is a perfect substitute for that at any other age. They do, however, maintain the unrealistic assumptions of perfect certainty and no credit constraints. Some of their results, such as lifetime labor supply being influenced by children, are no doubt sound. Others, such as evidence supporting the permanent income hypothesis, are actually disavowed in a later "Corrigendum" (RE Stud. 49, 158, Oct. 1982: 659-60).

237. Heckman, James J. and Robert J. Willis. "A Beta-Logistic Model for the Analysis of Sequential Labor Force Participation by Married Women." JPE 85, 1 (Feb. 1977): 27-58. (2,Q)

The authors apply this sophisticated methodology to the treatment of panel data on labor force participation of married women. Their main substantive conclusion is that "the distribution of participation probabilities is U shaped, indicating that most women have participation probabilities near zero or near one." This is challenged by Mincer and Ofek ("Comment," JPE 87, 1, Feb. 1979: 197-201) who pointed out, among others, that there are no qualifications concerning the length of time for which this conclusion is to hold. Actual retrospective data in fact show that the proportion of women who worked 30-50 percent of their lives exceeds the proportion of those who worked less than 20 percent or more than 80 percent of the time. While Heckman and Willis in their response (203-11) provide some technical explanations and objections, they cannot refute this fact.

238. Henretta, J. C. and A. M. O'Rand. "Labor Force Participation of Older Married Women." SSB 43, 8 (Aug. 1980): 10-16. (3)

The two main factors influencing the labor force participation of older married women are first, the need to support children or parents, which has a positive effect, and second, the availability of a pension, which has a negative effect. The latter may be enhanced by the frequent mandatory retirement rules associated with pensions. A third factor, one that also appears to reduce an older wife's labor force participation, is ill health of her husband. See, however, Berger and Fleisher (1983) for modifications of this conclusion.

239. Hill, Daniel H. "Labor Force Participation Decisions of Wives," in Greg J. Duncan and James N. Morgan, eds., Five Thousand American Families--Patterns of Economic Progress, Vol. V, Ann Arbor: Institute for Social Research, University of Michigan, 1977. (3)

Empirical tests using Panel Study of Income Dynamics data showed that life cycle, human capital, and family characteristics variables had the expected effect on the labor force participation rate of wives. Approaching retirement age had a negative effect, as did presence of young children and higher family income. Ownership of a house and level of education (whether or not there were young children) had a positive effect. Race also had a significant effect, presumed by the author to be related to tastes for goods and market work. Unemployment rate in the country, on the other hand, had little effect.

Hill, M. A. (1983) See item 911.

240. Hoffman, Emily P. "Comparative Labor Supply of Black and White Women." RBPE 11, 4 (Summer 1982): 429-39. (3)

The main focus of this research is on the question why black women have a higher labor force participation rate than white women. A neoclassical model of labor supply is constructed using National Longitudinal Surveys data for mature women in 1969, 1971, and

1974 in order to examine the sensitivity of black and white women's labor supply to unearned income, as well as their own and their husband's earnings. The results show that for white women hours of work have a significantly negative relationship to husband's income, but this is not the case for black women. The author suggests that these results are open to the interpretation that black women do not rely on their husband's earnings to as great an extent as white women do.

241. Hoffman, Emily P. "Fertility and Female Employment." QREB 25, 1 (Spring 1985), 85-95. (3)

This investigation, relying on data from the National Longitudinal Surveys Data for Mature Women, found a significant negative relationship between labor force participation and the presence of children under 5 years old. Fertility was also a significant determinant of hours of work per year, but not vice versa.

242. Honig, Marjorie. "AFDC Income, Recipient Rates, and Family Dissolution." JHR, 9, 3 (Summer 1974): 303-22. (4)

The increasing female headship during the 1960's is here linked to rising Aid to Families with Dependent Children payments. This relationship is tested and verified using cross section data at the SMSA level. William Darity, Jr. and Samuel L. Myers, Jr. ("Changes in Black Family Structure: Implications for Welfare Dependency." AER, 73, 2 (May 1983: 59-64), however, question the relevance of this study for black families. Among others, they point out that AFDC payments no longer rose relative to wages in the 1970's, but female headship continued to grow explosively, and that the problem of the sheer unavailability of men is ignored. Darity and Myers themselves find, on the other hand, that demographic variables are particularly important.

243. Honig, Marjorie. "Partial Retirement Among Women." JHR, 20, 4 (Fall 1985): 613-21. (3)

This study uses data for white unmarried women from the first three panels of the Retirement History Survey (1969-73), in part because the majority of older female workers in the U.S. fall into the categories of never-married or, more frequently, widowed. The results show that partial retirement constitutes a significant and structurally distinct state, and does not merely lie on a continuum between full employment and full retirement. A previous study had shown this was also true of men. It appears, however, that for women more clearly than men the critical issue is that of labor force participation, with hours of work being determined conditionally.

244. Hughes, Barry. "Direct Income and Substitution Effects in Participation Decisions." JPE 80, 4 (July-Aug. 1972): 793-95. (1)

This brief note rejects the view generally accepted since Mincer (1962) that the substitution effect dominates in women's labor force participation decision, but the income effect dominates for men, as an oversimplification. Further, it is pointed out that some historic developments do not fit this pattern, e.g., the decline over time of hours of participation of women who are in the labor force, and a positive relationship for some groups of men. He offers the plausible explanation that the size of the income effect depends on the number of hours the person is already working, or planning to work.

Humphrey (1984) See item 915.

245. Hunt, Janet C., Charles D. DeLorne, Jr. and R. Carter Hill. "Taxation and the Wife's Use of Time." ILRR 34, 3 (Apr. 1981): 426-32. (4)

Relying on data from the Panel Study of Income Dynamics, this research determines how much time husbands and wives devote to market work and housework. Like Gronau (1977), this is an improvement on studies which assume all time not spent in the market is leisure time. Higher tax rates are found to cause wives to reduce market work and increase housework. Hence, the authors conclude, there is little decline in production. They recognize, however, that wives lose through depreciation of market skills.

Iglesias and Riboud (1985) See item 916.

246. Inglehart, Alfreda P. Married Women and Work: 1957 and 1976, Lexington, MA: D. C. Heath, Lexington Books, 1979. (1,3)

A thoughtful study of the causes and effects of the change from the traditional 1950's, when women were expected to be housewives, to the 1970's, when working wives were becoming the norm. Relying on surveys done by the Survey Research Center at the University of Michigan in 1957 and 1976 the author examines the factors that pushed and pulled women into the labor market, but explicitly recognizes that the very assumption that we need to explain why women do work outside the home, rather than why they do not, represents a biased view. She also emphasizes to what extent societal expectations influence women's own views of their situation.

247. Johnson, Terry R. and John H. Pencavel. "Forecasting the Effects of a Negative Income Tax Program." ILRR 35, 2 (Jan. 1982): 221-34. (4)

The authors estimate labor supply functions for married men, married women, and single women who were participants in the Seattle-Denver Income Maintenance Experiments. On the basis of their findings they conclude that changes in the wage rate of an individual covered by the negative income tax (where the person is compensated for a short-fall in income below a stipulated amount) causes substantial changes in the hours of work of that person's spouse, as well as of that person.

248. Johnson, Terry R. and John H. Pencavel. "Dynamic Hours of Work Functions for Husbands, Wives, and Single Females." Economet. 52, 2 (Mar. 1984): 363-89. (3,Q)

One more sophisticated econometric study which finds men's own-wage elasticity of supply of hours of work to be extremely low, but that of both single and married women to be considerably higher.

Jones, E. F. (1982) See item 102.
Joshi (1985) See item 920.

249. Kahne, Hilda. Reconceiving Part-Time Work, New Perspectives for Older Workers and Women. Totowa, NJ: Rowman and Allanheld, 1985. (3)

This book emphasizes the growing importance of part time work because of the growing proportion of employed women and of the elderly in the population, two groups particularly interested in the alternative to full time jobs. It also explores the reasons why some people prefer to work part time, how the availability of such arrangements is influenced by attitudes of employees and unions, economic conditions, and government policies. Finally, there is a concluding chapter which considers possible changes for the future.

Kelley and deSilva (1980) See item 921.
Kessler-Harris (1985) See item 104.

250. Kim, Sookon. "Cross-Substitution Between Husband and Wife as One of the Factors Determining Married Women's Labor Supply." JED 2, 1 (July 1977): 131-45. (3)

The purpose of this paper is to investigate cross-substitution between husband and wife in addition to variables that have been used by other researchers to estimate women's labor supply. Husband's expected earnings are found to be an important determinant for white, but not for black women.

251. King, Allan G. "Industrial Structure, the Flexibility of Working Hours, and Women's Labor Force Participation." RES 60, 3 (Aug. 1978): 399-407. (3)

This paper tests the hypothesis that the array of hours of work from which women can choose is an important factor influencing their labor force participation. This is, of course, based on the premise that, for the most part women adjust their labor force participation to their "household responsibilities," rather than vice versa. The author's empirical findings support his hypothesis for mothers with pre-school children.

Kleinman (1976) See item 705.

252. Kraft, Arthur. "Preference Orderings as Determinants of the Labor Force Behavior of Married Women." WEJ 11, 3 (Sept. 1973): 270-84. (3,Q)

The author develops a model for the labor supply of married women derived from family utility functions and examines the degree of participation, rather than merely whether or not they are in the labor force. Like many other studies, this one finds that the husband's labor supply is backward bending, but the wife's is not. This presumably shows that the former have a greater preference for leisure, the latter for market work. One may speculate, however, that the real reason is that the wife spends much of her non-market time on housework.

Kushman and Scheffler (1975) See item 108.
Kyriazis and Henripin (1982) See item 930.
Layard, Barton and Zabalza (1980) See item 936.

253. Leon, Carol and Robert W. Bednarzik. "A Profile of Women on Part-Time Schedules." MLR 101, 10 (Oct. 1978): 3-12. (3)

During 1977 fully 20 percent of adult women in the labor force worked part-time by choice. The average part-timer was a married woman with school age children, working nearly 20 hours per week in a clerical or sales job.

254. Leonard, Jonathan S. "The Effect of Unions on the Employment of Blacks, Hispanics and Women." ILRR 39, 1 (Oct. 1985): 115-32. (4)

An investigation of 1,273 California manufacturing plants during the period 1974-80 showed that, in general, minorities and women increased their share of union employment. Further, black men's employment increased significantly faster in union than in nonunion plants.

255. Leuthold, Jane H. "The Effect of Taxation on the Probability of Labor Force Participation by Married Women." PF 33, 3 (1978a): 289-94. (3,4)

Like Boskin (1974) evidence based on data from the National Longitudinal Survey of women ages 30-44 shows that taxes tend to discourage female labor force participation, and that the effect is stronger for black than for white wives.

256. Leuthold, Jane H. "The Effect of Taxation on the Hours Worked by Married Women." ILRR 31, 4 (July 1978b): 520-26. (3,4)

In this companion piece to Leuthold (1978a), the author uses the same data from the National Longitudinal Survey of women 30-44 years of age, and similar methods, this time to investigate the effect of taxes on hours of work. Again, the impact is negative.

257. Leuthold, Jane H. "Taxes and the Two-Earner Family: Impact on the Work Decision." PFQ 7, 2 (Apr. 1979): 147-61. (3)

Data from the 1970 National Longitudinal Survey are used to provide estimates of the effect of changes in the marginal rates of income and payroll taxes on hours worked by men and women in two-earner families. The results suggest that these effects of the tax structure are substantial, and do have an impact on the allocation of responsibilities within the family.

258. Leuthold, Jane H. "Income Splitting and Women's Labor Force Participation." ILRR 38, 1 (Oct. 1984): 98-105. (3)

This study investigates the probable effect of abolishing the option of married couples splitting their income as though each partner had earned half of it. The results lead the author to conclude that labor force participation of women would increase substantially. This hypothesis is supported by evidence from Sweden (Gustafsson and Jacobsson 1985).

259. Leuthold, Jane H. "Work Incentives and the Two-Earner Deductions." PFQ 13, 1 (Jan. 1985): 63-73. (4)

As of 1983, two earner families were able to claim a deduction equal to 10 percent of the earnings of the lesser earning spouse up to a maximum of $3,000. Using Survey of Income Dynamics data, it is determined that this increases the probability of a married woman working for pay. The increase is likely to be modest for most women but rises with the deduction rate along with the husband's earnings.

260. Levy, Frank. "The Labor Supply of Female Household Heads, or AFDC Incentives Don't Work Too Well." JHR 14, 1 (Winter 1979): 76-97. (4,3)

This study estimates that any change in Aid to Families with Dependent Children which increases the breakeven point will reduce expected hours of work of female heads of such households. Liberalized work incentives may encourage current recipients to work more, but former nonrecipients who will be attracted to the program will more than offset this by working less. This analysis implies such a change is therefore not worthwhile, ignoring that both types of families will be better off.

261. Lewis, H. Greg. "Economics of Time and Labor Supply." AER 65, 2 (May 1975): 29-34. (4)

This paper begins by pointing out the vastness of the existing literature on labor force participation, and the diversity of findings. It then goes on to focus on the results of the negative income tax experiments, which for white married couples point toward only small reductions in the labor supply of husbands, though they become greater as their wage decreases, and considerably larger reductions for wives. These findings are consistent with others that show male labor supply to be relatively inelastic at low wages (and backward bending at high levels, not reached by participants in this experiment), but female supply to be far more elastic. The author acknowledges that results for nonwhite and Hispanic families were puzzling, and need more study.

Lillydahl and Singell (1985) See item 707.

262. Link, Charles R. and Russell F. Settle. "A Simultaneous-Equation Model of Labour Supply, Fertility and Earnings of Married Women: The Case of Registered Nurses." SEJ 47, 4 (Apr. 1981): 977-89. (3)

A simultaneous-equation model of labor supply, fertility and earnings is estimated for married registered nurses. The results show a negative relation between fertility, on the one hand, and earnings and hours worked, on the other. On this basis the authors draw the doubtful conclusion that higher wages would not have a substantial effect on the labor supply. For one, they overlook that in the long run new entrants could be attracted if pay were increased.

263. Lloyd, Cynthia B. and Beth T. Niemi. "Sex Differences in Labor Supply Elasticity: The Implications of Sectoral Shifts in Demand." AER 68, 2 (May 1978): 78-83. (3)

Using data from the Bureau of Labor Statistics, the authors compare men's and women's cyclical labor supply responses in the 1960's and 1970's. They conclude that women's response has become less positive as wages increase, and men's response less backward bending, so that the distinction between primary and secondary earners is becoming less sharp. Nonetheless, the authors conclude that further progress for women in the labor market would be difficult in a stagnant labor market, and without broader opportunities for women within that market.

264. Long, Clarence D. The Labor Force Under Changing Income and Employment, Princeton, NJ: Princeton University Press, 1958. (3)

This massive early work considers the labor force participation of women, as well as men, white and nonwhite. The data used were rather crude as compared with those generally used now, and some variables are available only for men. Even so, such findings as the negative relation of wives' labor force participation to husbands' earnings, the higher labor force participation of black as compared to white women, all else equal, and the positive effect of education on labor force participation have withstood the test of time.

265. Long, James E. and Ethel B. Jones. "Labor Force Entry and Exit by Married Women: A Longitudinal Analysis." RES 62, 1 (Feb. 1980b): 1-6.

National Longitudinal Survey data are employed to determine how various factors influence the labor force participation of married women. As in other studies, their own wage has a positive effect, but husband's earnings, the birth of a child, and a low-status occupation have a negative effect. Interestingly, however, the relationships are not always symmetrical for determinants of entry into and exit from the labor force.

266. Long, James E. and Ethel B. Jones. "Married Women in Part-Time Employment." ILRR 34, 3 (Apr. 1981): 413-25. (3)

The authors, using multivariate analysis, find that husband's income, family size, the wife's health, previous work experience and race are among the variables that influence whether a married woman will work part-time. They also find that wages and returns to some investments in human capital tend to be lower for part-time workers, even though the earnings structure is generally similar to that of full-time workers. Last, they suggest that the opportunity to work part-time appears to increase the length of the working life of wives.

267. Lundberg, Shelly J. "The Added Worker Effect." JLE 3, 1 (Jan. 1985, Part 1): 11-37. (3)

Estimates based on employment probabilities are used to simulate changes in wives' labor force participation following an increase in unemployment among their husbands. The results show a small but significant added worker effect, at least for white families.

268. Madden, Janice F. "Why Women Work Closer to Home." US 18, 2 (June 1981): 181-94. (3)

Data from the 1976 Panel Survey of Income Dynamics are used to examine the extent to which differences in labor force status, household composition and household roles account for sex differences in workplace-residence separation. The results suggest that women select jobs closer to home because lower wage rates and shorter hours reduce the returns to commuting, and also because "their household responsibilities" increase the cost of commuting. Interestingly, according to the findings in this study, changing either the situation in the market or in the household would be enough to make women's work trips as long or longer than men's.

269. Mahoney, Thomas A. "Factors Determining Labor Force Participation of Married Women." ILRR, 14, 4 (July 1961): 563-77. (3)

This study used a sample of married women in St. Paul, MN to examine interrelationships among variables presumed to influence the labor force participation of such women, which are not usually available for the general population. Previous labor force experience was found to be the best predictor, though modified by such other factors as age and the presence of young children. Of course, this does not tell us anything about the determinants of the previous labor force participation.

270. Mallan, Lucy B. "Women Born in the Early 1900's: Employment, Earnings and Benefit Levels." SSB 37, 3 (Mar. 1974): 3-25. (3)

This study uses data from the Continuous Work History Sample maintained by the Social Security Administration to provide evidence about women's labor force participation patterns. On the basis of the available evidence the author offered one of the early predictions that labor force interruptions by mothers of young children would tend to diminish.

271. Maret, Elizabeth G. "How Women's Health Affects Labor Force Attachment." MLR 105, 4 (Apr. 1982): 56-58. (3)

Preliminary findings from the National Longitudinal Surveys suggested that health is an important determinant of the labor force participation of women and particularly black women, fewer of whom tend to be in good or excellent health. This study, using the NLS mature cohort data, confirms these results.

272. Maret, Elizabeth G. Women's Career Patterns. Influences on Work Stability. Lanham, MD: University Press of America, Inc., 1983. (3)

This book reports on a study of career patterns of 5,000 mature women, using data from the National Longitudinal Surveys. A great diversity in their market work experiences was found. The main characteristics that distinguished the about 15 percent who worked full time, year round, and continuously since leaving school were (1) a mother who was employed; (2) high investment in human capital; (3) residence in an urban area; (4) being single, or having a liberal spouse and a small family; (5) low commitment to traditional sex roles; and (6) economically rewarding jobs.

Mason, K. O. and Palan (1981) See item 940.
Matthaei (1980)(1983) See item 119, 120.

273. McLaughlin, Steven D. "Differentials in Female Labor Force Participation Surrounding the First Birth." JMF 44, 2 (May 1982): 407-20. (3)

Five years of panel data from the National Longitudinal Surveys on women aged 14 to 24 are examined. They support the hypothesis that declines in labor force participation prior to the birth of the first child, and increases in participation following it, vary by education, economic well-being, and previous work experience. The author recognizes, of course, that other variables are likely to play a part as well.

McMahon, P. J. (1986) See item 942.
McNabb (1977) See item 943.

274. Meyer, Jack A. "The Impact of Welfare Benefit Levels and Tax Rates on the Labor Supply of Poor Women: Note." RES 57, 2 (May 1975): 236-38. (3)

Data for this study related to women 30 to 44 years of age who were employed, were poor and had at least one child in the household during the survey year of 1967, were obtained from the Bureau of the Census. Hours worked were not found to be significantly related to the market wage rate. The author interprets this to show that the income effect and the substitution effect roughly offset each other. Potential other income, however, is negatively related to hours worked, and especially so when potential welfare benefits are included.

Michael (1985) See item 122.
Miller, B. D. (1982) See item 946.
Miller, J. and Garrison (1982) See item 123.

275. Mincer, Jacob. "Labor Force Participation of Married Women: A Study of Labor Supply," in National Bureau of Economic Research, Aspects of Labor Economics, Princeton, NJ: Princeton University Press, 1962, pp. 63-105. (1,3)

Using Census data on white women for 1950 the author concludes that women do not primarily substitute paid work for leisure, but rather for housework. Hence higher wages tend to result in more market work, because this substitution effect is likely to be more important than the income effect which causes increased demand for leisure. This would seem to explain the substantial increase in women's labor force participation, but has been challenged by other researchers, such as Cain (1966) and Hughes (1972). They point out that the situation will vary according to the labor force status of the woman, as well as by number of hours she is working and how much she is earning.

276. Mincer, Jacob. "Labor Force Participation and Unemployment: A Review of Recent Evidence," in Robert A. Gordon and Margaret S. Gordon, eds. Prosperity and Unemployment, NY: John Wiley and Sons, 1966, pp. 73-112. (3)

Among the main findings of this study is the trend toward growing responsiveness of the labor force participation to changes in unemployment. The author explains this mainly in terms of the growth of discretionary labor force participaton, and the weakening of the income effect, and hence of incentives for added-worker behavior. Both these factors are closely related to the rise in women's labor force participation.

Mitchell, J. B. (1984) See item 795.

277. Moffitt, Robert A. "The Labor Supply Response in the Gary Experiment." JHR 14, 4 (Fall 1979): 477-87. (3,4)

In this paper a significant work disincentive was found as a result of the Gary Negative Income Tax Experiment for husbands and, to a greater extent, for female heads of households. No such effect was, however, discovered for wives. The author suggests this may be because the Gary labor market offers few opportunities for part-time work.

Moffitt (1984) See item 124.
Mooney, J. D. (1967) See item 711.

278. Morgenstern, Richard D. and William Hamovitch. "Labor Supply of Married Women in Part-Time and Full-Time Occupations." ILRR 30, 1 (Oct. 1976): 59-67. (3)

In this study separate supply functions are estimated for married women working part-time and those working full-time, and they are found to be substantially different. Young children are less of a deterrent to part-time work, the income elasticity is smaller, and wage elasticity greater for them than for full-time workers.

279. Morris, Jeffrey. "Some Simple Tests of the Direct Effect of Education on Preferences and on Nonmarket Productivity." RES 58, 1 (Feb. 1976): 112-17. (3)

This study concludes that education has a substantial effect on tastes and hence on life-styles, but very little effect on non-market productivity. Such findings help to explain why higher education, which does tend to increase earnings in the labor market, is related to higher labor force participation of women.

Moskoff (1982) See item 953.

280. Mott, Frank L., ed. The Employment Revolution: Young American Women in the 1970's, Cambridge, MA: The MIT Press, 1982b. (3)

This book examines the reasons for the rapid increase in the labor force participation of young women, but supplements the standard economic analysis by also considering the more complex socio-psychological and demographic aspects of women's motivation to work. The transition from traditional pressures keeping women in the home, and at a disadvantage in the labor market, is also considered.

281. Mott, Frank L. and David M. Shapiro. "Complementarity of Work and Fertility Among Young American Mothers." PS 37, 2 (July 1983): 239-52. (3)

Using data from the National Longitudinal Surveys of Labor Market Experience of Young Women, the authors find no link between early work behavior and later fertility, contrary to the negative relation suggested by cross-section data. On the other hand, a strong link is found between early employment and later attachment to work. These findings, like those of Shapiro and Mott (1979), may be interpreted to show that even women who plan to have children are increasingly less likely to drop out of the labor force for extensive periods of time.

Nakamura, A. O. and Nakamura, M. (1981) See item 955.

282. Nakamura, Alice O. and Masao Nakamura. "Dynamic Models of the Labor Force Behavior of Married Women Which Can Be Estimated Using Limited Amounts of Past Information." JE 27, 3 (Mar. 1985): 273-98. (2)

The usual models using cross-section data do not tend to provide good predictions of work behavior of wives. The authors offer a way of using limited recall data to make better forecasts of employment, hours of work, and earnings of wives.

283. Nakamura, Masao, Alice O. Nakamura and David Cullen. "Job Opportunities, the Offered Wage, and the Labor Supply of Married Women." AER 69, 5 (Dec. 1979): 1787-805. (3)

The two main findings of this study are that local job opportunities have a significant effect on women's labor force participation, and that employed wives work fewer hours as wages increase. The latter results are unlike those most other researchers have found for married women, but are similar to those reported for men.

284. Niemi, Beth T. and Cynthia B. Lloyd. "Female Labor Supply in the Context of Inflation." AER 71, 2 (May 1981): 70-75. (3)

The authors point out that throughout the inflationary years of the late 1960s and 1970s women's labor force participation continued to rise. They further suggest that this increase, particularly among women with young children, was the result of a trend toward long-term career commitment rather than simply an influx of marginal workers. Less convincing is their view that inflation had an independent positive effect on female labor force participation, presumably because of the "money illusion." Fair (1971), for instance, found no evidence that rising wages accompanied by similarly rising prices have any effect on labor force participation.

Ofer and Vinakur (1983) See item 962.
Officer and Anderson, P. R. (1969) See item 963.

285. Olmsted, Barney. "Job Sharing: An Emerging Work-Style." ILR 118, 3 (May-June 1979): 283-97. (4)

The increase in job sharing in the U.S., and to a lesser extent in Canada, has caused growing interest in this new approach to arranging working time. The problems as well as the advantages of this way of providing flexibility to workers are discussed. The author's evaluation of prospects for a great expansion in job sharing is appropriately cautious, even though he concludes that "it would appear that the time is ripe for developing a wider range of choice."

286. O'Neill, June A. "A Time-Series Analysis of Women's Labor Force Participation." AER 71, 2 (May 1981): 76-80. (3)

The author questions the general interpretation of cross-section data as showing the responsiveness of women's labor supply to higher wages, because of the rapid influx of women into the labor force in the 1970's, a period of unusually slow growth in earnings. She concludes, nonetheless, that time series data also show a positive effect of the wage rate on women's allocation of time to the market, but points out the substantial slowdown in husbands' incomes was also a major contributing factor.

287. Oppenheimer, Valerie K. The Female Labor Force in the United States: Demographic and Economic Factors Concerning its Growth and Changing Composition. Population Monograph Series, No. 5, Berkeley, CA: University of California, 1970. (3)

Unlike most earlier researchers, this author emphasizes increasing demand rather than supply as the basic explanation for the rapid increase in women's labor force participation rate. Specifically, she points to industrial and occupational trends as the basic causes. There is no reason to disagree with her conclusion that demand for women workers increased. But this does not exclude the possibility that supply increased as well, or that there was a feedback effect between the two.

288. Oppenheimer, Valerie K. "Demographic Influence on Female Employment and the Status of Women." AJS, 78, 4 (Jan. 1973): 946-61. (1,3)

The author recognizes the well-established relationship between fertility and women's labor force participation, but is primarily concerned about the extent to which each is cause and effect. Since she believes that the growth in female market opportunities was the primary cause of increased numbers of women working for pay, and that this in turn influenced the birth rate, she is concerned about potential limits on the expansion of female occupations. She appears to have been very pessimistic about possible reductions in occupational segregation, as well as the growth of new occupations for women.

289. Ortiz, Vilma and Rosemary S. Cooney. "Sex-Role Attitudes and Labor Force Participation Among Young Hispanic Females and Non-Hispanic White Females." SSQ 65, 2 (June 1984): 392-400. (3)

The hypothesis that sex-role attitudes have an especially strong influence on the labor force participation of Hispanic females is examined, using data on the youth cohort of the National Longitudinal Survey. It was found that first-generation Hispanic women were more likely to have traditional views than those whose family had been in the U.S. longer, and that first and second generation Hispanic women were less likely to be in the labor force. Even so, the main reason for lower labor force participation was less education. The author fails to consider, however, that traditional attitudes may influence years of schooling.

Palmer, I. (1977) See item 965.

290. Paringer, Lynn. "Women and Absenteeism: Health or Economics?" AER 73, 2 (May 1983): 123-27. (3)

This study finds that not only health status but age are major determinants of work absences, though their effect differs somewhat for men and women, and also varies by occupation. On the other hand, little evidence is found of the impact of economic variables, such as the availability of sick leave, for either men or women.

Pittin (1984) See item 968.
Powell (1976) See item 969.

291. Power, Marilyn. "From Home Production to Wage Labor: Women as a Reserve Army of Labor." RRPE 15, 1 (Spring 1983): 71-91. (1)

The tone of this paper is set when the author in the first sentence refers to the "proletarization" of married women in the twentieth century. While fundamentally she presents the rather standard explanations for the influx of women into the labor force, she refers to the changes that took place in the household with "the invasion of their traditional production for use and exchange in the home by capitalist production," and views the increased demand for women workers as taking advantage of the female "reserve army of labor." Nonetheless, she concludes that by making women into wage workers, capitalism has eroded the material basis of patriarchy.

292. Presser, Harriet B. "Job Characteristics of Spouses and Their Work Shifts." Dem. 21, 4 (Nov. 1984): 575-89. (3)

This study, using data from the May 1980 Current Population Survey, finds that the wife's doing shift work is contingent upon both her occupation and industry and that of her husband, but the husband's is contingent only upon his occupation and industry. The stated conclusion, that it is important to take a "couple" perspective on shift work among married persons, is therefore only half true.

293. Quester, Aline O. "The Effect of the Tax Structure on the Market Behavior of Wives." JEB 29, 3 (Spring/Summer 1977): 171-80. (3)

The author questions whether previous studies which found a negative relationship between wife's labor supply and "other family income" were correct in assuming that women did less market work because of the higher income. She points out that the income effect could also cause her to do less housework. Her own empirical work, using 1970 Census data, shows that the independent explanatory effect of husband's income on wife's labor force participation is very small if wife's wage is measured net of taxes and baby sitting expenses. It appears that wives respond to spendable wages, which decline as the tax rate increases with husband's earnings. Rosen, H. S. (1976) also found that women tend to respond to net rather than gross wages.

294. Quester, Aline O. and Janice Olson. "Sex, Schooling, and Hours of Work." SSQ 58, 4 (Mar. 1978): 566-82. (3)

This paper examines important differences in schooling, time spent in the labor market, and returns received between men and women in professional and technical occupations. Among the most interesting findings is that, other things constant, there is a positive relation for women between wage and hours worked, while the opposite is true for men. Education, on the other hand, though it had a positive effect on wages of both women and men, had a negative effect on hours spent by women. The authors conclude that choice of occupation mainly enables men to vary their earnings, but makes it possible for women to vary their hours. This is presumably important for women because of the demands on their non-market time.

295. Quinlan, Daniel C. and Jean A. Shackleford. "Labor Force Participation Rates of Women and the Rise of the Two-Earner Family." AER, 70, 2 (May 1980): 209-12. (3)

This paper explores the role of demand in increasing labor force participation of women to the point where by 1978 the typical husband-wife family consisted of two wage earners. Using Census reports by state, the authors examine the effect of occupational and sectoral changes on demand for female labor. They find little evidence to support the importance of these factors, but admit that their results are not conclusive. Maryann O'Keating (p. 213), in her comments on this paper, suggests that the model they employ, where demand for female labor is derived from demand for male labor, which is derived from expanding industries, may be deficient. Nonetheless research such as this raises question about the great emphasis on demand ever since Oppenheimer (1970).

Rea (1974) See item 716.

296. Reimers, Cordelia W. "Cultural Differences in Labor Force Participation Among Married Women." AER 75, 2 (May 1985): 251-55. (3)

This study analyzes the differences in labor force participation between various U.S. born and foreign born ethnic groups, using data from the Bureau of the Census 1976 Survey of Income and Education. The results show that the lower participation of those born abroad, including Hispanics, can be largely or entirely accounted for by differences in language, family size and age structure, and education. Hence, the author concludes that if culture is a factor, it only plays a part indirectly through these variables. On the other hand, the higher participation rates of U.S. born Asian and black wives, as opposed to U.S. born white wives, were not explained by these other factors, hence should be ascribed to cultural differences.

Rein (1980) See item 140.
Renaud and Siegers (1984) See item 973.
Riboud (1985) See item 974.
Robertson and Roy (1982) See item 976.

297. Robins, Philip K. "A Comparison of the Labor Supply Findings from the Four Negative Income Tax Experiments." JHR 20, 4 (Fall 1985): 567-82. (3)

This paper points out that the labor supply responses from the four U.S. Government-sponsored negative income tax experiments conducted between 1968 and 1982 show fairly consistent results, in spite of widely different treatments and methodologies. On average, husbands reduced labor supply by about the equivalent of two weeks, wives and single women by about three weeks, youths by about four weeks. These findings confirm those of most other studies in showing greater responsiveness of female as compared to male labor supply.

Robinson, C. and Tomes (1985) See item 977.
Robinson, J. (1977) See item 142.

298. Rohrlich, Lara T. and Ethel L. Vatter. "Women in the World of Work: Past, Present, and Future." WS 1, 3 (1973): 263-77. (3)

A readable, albeit somewhat superficial review of the reasons for women's increasing labor force participation, followed by some suggestions for futher facilitating progress in the future.

299. Rosen, Harvey S. "Tax Illusion and the Labor Supply of Married Women." RES 58, 2 (May 1976): 167-72. (3)

The results of this study strongly support the hypothesis that married women in their decision on whether to work and how much to work respond to net wages rather than to gross wages. This is consistent with the findings by Quester (1977).

Rosenzweig and Schultz (1982) See item 979.

300. Rothschild, Kurt W. "A Note on Female Labor Supply." K 33, 2 (1980): 246-60. (1)

The author develops a model to explain the rapid increase in female labor force participation, common to virtually all West European and North American countries. He concludes that it was primarily smaller families, reinforced by changing attitudes toward the role of women, rather than relative movements of men's and women's wages that brought about the observed changes. He does not confront the question of what caused the reduced number of children and the more emancipated views.

301. Ryscavage, Paul M. "More Wives in the Labor Force Have Husbands with 'Above Average' Incomes," MLR 102, 6 (June 1979): 40-42. (3)

This paper points out that, in spite of the negative relation between husband's income and wife's labor force participation, all else constant, other factors more than offset this. The author also expresses concern about the possible effect this might have in increasing the inequality of income distribution among families. A cynic may wonder why so much attention is given to this issue, often by individuals not noted for their concern with the many factors that are far more important in creating inequality in our economy.

302. Salkever, David S. "Effects of Children's Health on Maternal Hours of Work: A Preliminary Analysis." SEJ 47, 1 (July 1980): 156-66. (3)

Data from the 1972 Panel Study of Income Dynamics provide evidence that ill health or disability of children have a significant negative effect on labor force participation only for women in one-parent families. They have a negative effect on hours worked, by women, and especially white women, as well as two-parent families.

Salkever (1982) See item 146.

303. Sandell, Steven H. "Attitudes Toward Market Work and the Effect of Wage Rates on the Lifetime Labor Supply of Married Women." JHR 12, 3 (Summer 1977a): 379-86. (3)

The author uses a model of lifetime labor force participation of married women to show that the frequent omission of attitude variables in empirical estimates of the labor supply does not provide accurate results. His data suggest that these estimates have a significant upward bias relative to own-wage elasticity, but also show that test itself is likely to be affected considerably by the respondent's wage and previous employment. He concludes therefore, regretfully, that it is not clear which estimates are likely to be more accurate.

304. Sanderson, Warren C. "A Nonutilitarian Economic Model of Fertility and Female Labor Force Participation," RE 3, 6 (Nov. 1980): 1045-1080. (1)

The main aim of the author is to show that interesting economic models need not be confined to those that assume utility maximizing behavior of the family, or separate constant returns to scale production functions. He expects this to make the models more acceptable to scholars in other disciplines. Dispensing with some of the most unrealistic assumptions of the standard neoclassical models does seem a step in the right direction.

Santos (1975) See item 148.

305. Sekscenski, Edward S. "Women's Share of Moonlighting Nearly Doubles During 1969-1979." MLR 103, 5 (May 1980): 36-39. (3)

In 1979 nearly 1 in 20 workers held more than one job, a ratio which had remained the same for a decade. During this period, however, the proportions of those workers who were women rose from 16 percent to 30 percent. The increase was almost entirely confined to white women. Only 26 percent of women "moonlighters" held at least one full time job, while this was true of 72 percent of the men.

306. Shapiro, David and Frank L. Mott. "Labor Supply Behavior of Prospective and New Mothers." Dem. 16, 2 (May 1979): 199-208. (3)

Using data from the National Longitudinal Surveys of Young Women, labor supply behavior just before and just after the birth of a child is examined in great detail, with particular emphasis on first birth. It is found that young women, especially black women, are likely to retain labor market ties during their early childbearing years. This has obvious long-run implications of far greater lifetime labor force attachment for these women than older cohorts tended to have. The authors therefore conclude that these women may be expected to invest more in both education and training. Apparently they attach little importance to barriers that may continue to exist.

307. Shapiro, David and Frank L. Mott. "Effects of Selected Variables on Work Hours of Young Women." MLR 106, 7 (July 1983): 31-34. (3)

This study uses data from the National Longitudinal Data on Young Women to learn more about the determinants of the number of hours worked during the years 1968-73 and 1973-78. Hours of work were greater for the later cohort, among both blacks and whites, and so were levels of education. Further, the 1973-78 cohort was less likely to be married or have children. But there was also evidence of changing behavior for women with the same socioeconomic and demographic characteristics. For instance, being married and husband's income had a far less negative effect, and education had a far more positive effect on mothers, though not on women without children. The results were similar for blacks and whites.

308. Shapiro, David and Lois B. Shaw. "Growth in the Labor Force Attachment of Married Women: Accounting for Changes in the 1970s." SEJ 50, 2 (Oct. 1973): 461-73. (3)

In this study, which employs probit and tobit analysis to analyze data from the National Longitudinal Surveys, after making appropriate adjustment for sample selection bias, it is found that wages and schooling are positively related to women's work activity, while the relation to husband's wages and unemployment is negative. Evidence is also found that changing attitudes toward women working encouraged growth attachment to the labor force.

309. Shaw, Lois B., ed. Unplanned Careers: The Working Lives of Middle-Aged Women, Lexington, MA: Heath, Lexington Books, 1983. (3)

This book is based on information collected between 1967 and 1977 on women who were between 30 and 44 years of age at the beginning of that period. This group was chosen because many among them were likely to return to the labor force, including some of those who may not have originally planned to do so. Various papers examine how these women managed their reentry, how they fared in the labor market, how they were affected by adverse health and family developments.

310. Shaw, Lois B. "Determinants of Increasing Work Attachment of Married Women." SWO, 12, 1 (Feb. 1985): 41-58. (3)

Among the factors that helped to increase labor force attachment between 1966 and 1976 for white women were primarily declining family responsibilities, increased work experience, and changing attitudes towards women roles; for black women, lessening family responsibilities, higher educational attainments, and improved health. On the other hand, rising unemployment was an inhibiting factor for both groups. This study was based on data from the National Longitudinal Surveys of Labor Market Experience.

311. Shea, John R. "Welfare Mothers: Barriers to Labor Force Entry." JHR 8 (Suppl. 1973): 90-102. (4)

Data used for this study were from a national sample of women 30 to 44 years old who were out of the labor force in 1967. They were questioned about a hypothetical job offer. Blacks more often indicated willingness to accept a job than did whites, and particularly more of them gave an unqualified yes. There was, however, no difference among the poor and the nonpoor, though the latter generally required a higher wage if they were to take a job, as did women who were potentially eligible for AFDC.

Shimada and Higuchi (1985) See item 988.
Shorey (1983) See item 989.
Siegers and Zandanel (1981) See item 991.

312. Smirlock, Michael L. "Working Women in America: Factors Which Influence Their Participation and Attachment to the Labor Force." AE 24, 2 (Fall 1980): 47-52. (3)

This paper argues that the long-run trend toward increased labor force participation of women, and especially married women, means that they should no longer be viewed as secondary workers. It is suggested the lingering belief that they are is responsible for viewing them as inferior workers when they are employed, and for being less concerned when they are unemployed. He argues for accepting women on an equal basis, and for policies that would bring that about.

313. Smith, Georgina. Help Wanted Female: A Study of Demand and Supply in a Local Labor Market for Women. New Brunswick, NJ: Institute for Management and Labor Relations, Rutgers - The State University, 1964. (3)

This study used data collected on women workers in one small area in New Jersey in 1962. Though the author recognized that her sample was not representative, she believed the following conclusions were warranted: (1) The large supply of women workers for the relatively few types of occupations they could enter, in part caused their low wages. (2) In time they became the beneficiaries of shifts in demand favoring them. (3) Women may not reap the full benefits of these changes because, especially in the absence of high and stable general economic growth men may move into the newly higher paying jobs. This concern proved to be justified, for Blau and Hendricks (1979) found that between 1960 and 1970, there was some movement of men into traditionally female occupations.

314. Smith, James P., ed. Female Labor Supply: Theory and Estimation, Princeton, NJ: Princeton University Press, 1980. (1,2,3,Q)

The authors use sophisticated econometric techniques to examine determinants of women's market wages the value of home time, and factors affecting supply of market work. Many issues nonetheless remain unresolved, and numerous disagreements remain even among the essays in this volume. An acknowledged limitation of the work is that the researchers failed to use longitudinal data. Conclusive answers to many questions, for instance about labor market entry vs. hours of work, about short run vs. lifetime behavior, have yet to be found.

315. Smith, James P. and Michael P. Ward. Women's Wages and Work in the Twentieth Century, Santa Monica, CA: Rand, 1984. (1,3)

A thorough examination of changes in women's labor force participation in the U.S. during the 20th century. The extensive discussion of the causes and effects of these developments offers much food for thought. The analysis is marred, however, by its single-minded adherence to the view that women's progress, or the lack thereof, can be entirely explained in terms of their human capital. How much human capital they acquire is, in turn, entirely explained without any concern for such factors as changing attitudes or equal opportunity laws.

316. Smith, James P. and Michael P. Ward. "Time Series Growth in the Female Labor Force." JLE 3, 1 (Jan. 1985 Suppl.) S59-S90. (3)

A thorough investigation, quite similar to that in Smith and Ward (1984), suggests that 58 percent of the long-term increase in female labor force participation in the United States since 1900 can be explained by an increase in women's real wages, directly, and indirectly by reducing fertility. Of course, this leaves fully 42 percent to be explained by other factors.

317. Smith, Ralph E. "Sources of Growth of the Female Labor Force, 1971-75." MLR 100, 8 (Aug. 1977): 27-29. (3)

This study finds that 75 percent of the female labor force participation rate changes occurred among married women, especially among those under age 35, and that women with children under 6 contributed the largest part of the labor force growth. Thus, a simple demographic explanation would account for less than one third of the increase. The remainder is the result of women behaving differently than they did under similar circumstances only 4 years earlier.

Smith, S. K. (1985) See item 994.

318. Smith, Shirley J. "New Worklife Estimates Reflect Changing Profiles of Labor Force," MLR 105, 3 (Mar. 1982): 15-20. (3)

Based on labor force patterns observed in 1977, the Bureau of Labor Statistics estimated that the average man 16 years of age can expect to spend 38.5 years in the labor force, the average woman 27.7 years. These figures have been converging at least since WWII, and did so at an accelerating rate in the 1970's. This was mainly because the rate of withdrawals of women from the labor force dropped, even though it continues to be substantially higher than that of men.

Smith, T. W. (1985) See item 154.

319. Sobol, Martin G. "A Dynamic Analysis of Labor Force Participation of Married Women of Childbearing Age." JHR 8, 4 (Fall 1973): 497-505. (3)

This study relates labor force behavior of a panel of married women of childbearing age to economic and other variables. Labor force attachment is measured not only by current work behavior, but also by labor force participation over a decade, and work plans. Expected family size and the woman's education are found to be the main determinants of her labor supply.

Soherer (1978) See item 995.

320. Solberg, Eric J. "The Supply of Labor Time for Mature Females." AEJ 9, 3 (Sept. 1981): 20-33. (3)

While this study, based on data for the 1972 National Longitudinal Surveys of mature women finds that most women remain on the part of their labor supply curve that is positive, and hence work more hours at higher wages, some women, particularly those with no spouse present, seem to be moving toward the backward bending segment of the curve, where, just like men, they increase their leisure as their earnings rise.

Sorrentino (1983) See item 997.

321. Spitze, Glenna D. and Linda J. Waite. "Labor Force and Work Attitudes: Young Women's Early Experiences." SWO 7, 1 (Feb. 1980): 3-32. (3)

The relations between work-related attitudes and early labor force experiences are examined, using data from the National Longitudinal Surveys of Young Women. In general the evidence suggests that sex-role attitudes are the effect rather than the cause of different early work experiences. The authors also conclude, however, that strong tastes for market work may create early patterns of behavior which maximize long-term rather than short-term benefits.

Stafford (1980) See item 156.
Standing (1976) (1981) See items 998, 999.
Steel (1981) See item 1000.

322. Stein, Barry A., Allan Cohen and Herman Gadon. "Flex Time: Work When You Want To." PT 10, 1 (June 1976): 40-43, 80. (3)

This paper reports on 1,000 companies and government agencies that had introduced what is termed "this European idea." The authors conclude that lower absenteeism and higher productivity was experienced in these establishments. From the point of view of women, who still tend to bear the main share of household responsibilities, the advantages of a more flexible schedule are obvious, and its availability might encourage men to take on a larger share of housework.

Stelcner (1985) See item 1001.

323. Stephan, Paula E. and Larry D. Schroeder. "Career Decisions and Labor Force Participation of Married Women," in Cynthia B. Lloyd, Emily S. Andrews and Curtis L. Gilroy, eds. Women in the Labor Market, NY: Columbia University Press, 1979, pp. 119-36. (3)

The authors argue that the view of the wife working only to supplement family income when the husband's earnings are inadequate is not appropriate in all cases. There are substantial differences between women's attitudes, and those with high labor force commitment will respond quite differently to variations in wages, unemployment, number and spacing of children, level of education, race and husband's earnings than do women with a lesser commitment. Evidence is provided using data from the National Longitudinal Surveys for 1967.

Stevens, Register and Grimes (1985) See item 718.

324. Stewart, James B. "Some Factors Determining the Work Effort of Single Black Women." RSE 40, 1 (Apr. 1982): 30-44. (3)

This study, using data from the one-in-a-hundred public use sample, confirms the great complexity of the relationship of receipt of public assistance to household configuration and work effort. Among the results found were that for young never-married black females the presence in the household of relatives ameliorates the negative impact of children on labor force participation, and that there is a positive relationship between work and school attendance.

Stokes, C. S. and Hsieh (1983) See item 1003.

325. Stolzenberg, Ross M. and Linda J. Waite. "Local Labor Markets, Children and Labor Force Participation of Wives." Dem. 21, 2 (May 1984): 157-70. (3)

This study seeks to determine how characteristics of geographic areas structure the relationship between properties of individual women and the probability of their labor force participation. The data used are for 409 areas from the 1970 Census. The results tend to support the authors' hypotheses that the effect of children on their mother's labor force participation is a function of the cost and availability of child care, and of the "convenience" of the jobs available in the area.

Strober (1975) See item 160.

326. Sum, Andrew F. "Female Labor Force Participation: Why Projections Have Been Too Low." MLR 100, 7 (July 1977) 18-24. (3)

This paper was written at a time when it became increasingly obvious that experts had consistently underestimated the extent to which women's labor force participation would increase. The author points out that this was in part because projections underestimated the extent to which women would be working year-round, rather than only six or nine months of the year.

327. Sweet, James A. Women in the Labor Force. NY: Seminar Press, 1973. (3)

The author focuses on the relationship between family composition and the labor force participation and earnings of women. He found that presence of young children reduced the positive effect of education and the negative effect of other income on the likelihood of working for pay. Low level of education, however, generally had a negative effect.

Takahashi (1968) See item 1011.

328. Tella, Alfred J. "The Relation of Labor Force to Employment." ILRR 17, 3 (Apr. 1964): 454-69. (3)

An investigation of total labor force experience shows that the short-run labor supply of women is especially responsive to variations in employment.

Turchaninova (1975) See item 1015.
Verma (1975) See item 1020.

329. Viscusi, W. Kip. "Sex Differences in Worker Quitting." RES, 6, 3 (Aug. 1980): 388-98. (3)

Analysis of a sample of almost 6000 workers suggests that female quit behavior differs from that of males not by a constant amount, but differentially depending on characteristics of both the workers and the type of work. It is suggested this may be because of differences in uncertainties associated with jobs traditionally held by men. The main conclusion offered, however, is that the higher quit rates of women, both overall and within major occupational groups is not particularly informative, and that sex differences in quitting have been overdrawn in many previous discussions. It is also likely that, had the author investigated quits within more detailed occupational categories male-female differences would have been even smaller. (See Blau, F. D. and Kahn 1981.)

330. Wachter, Michael L. "A Labor Supply Model for Secondary Workers." RES 54, 2 (May 1972): 141-51. (3)

This study shows that four variables are of primary importance in determining the labor supply for secondary workers: current real wage, a distributed lag real wage, the aggregate unemployment rate, and an inflation variable. Most interesting are the implication that relative wage effect, rather than permanent wage effect, appears to be important, and the author's suggestion that the inflation variable may serve as a proxy for labor market conditions.

331. Wachter, Michael L. "Intermediate Swings in Labor Force Participation." BPEA 2 (1977): 545-74. (3)

The author argues that the usual emphasis on short run fluctuations associated with discouraged workers, and on trend in explaining labor force participation, ignores the importance of intermediate swings, which represent a kind of relative income effect. He illustrates this point by the influx of the baby boom generation, which depressed family income, represented by earnings of prime-age men, compared to that of previous cohorts. This, he claims, explains the decline in fertility and the increase in labor force participation of young women, as a result of their effort to maintain the desired standard of living. This reasoning needs to be considered in light of the fact that it led him to predict a decline in the labor force participation of young women, which has failed to materialize to date.

332. Waite, Linda J. "Working Wives and the Family Life-Cycle." AJS 86, 2 (Sept. 1980): 272-94. (3)

Data from the National Longitudinal Survey of Young Women are used to test the hypothesis that the labor force participation of married women varies with stages of the life cycle. Beyond the obvious results, the researcher found that wives who considered their families complete were more responsive to their financial circumstances and to the characteristics of the labor market than either childless women, or mothers who expected to have more children. On the other hand, employment history was most important for this last group.

Waite and Stolzenberg (1976) See item 165.

333. Waldman, Elizabeth K. "Changes in the Labor Force Activity of Women." MLR 93, 6 (June 1970): 10-18. (3)

This paper reviews the changes in women's labor force participation between 1920 and 1970, then goes on to examine the situation in 1970 with respect to employment by age, marital and parental status, as well as occupational distribution. Last, the determinants of earnings, on the one hand, and the effect of women's incomes on the well-being of their families, are discussed.

Wales and Woodland (1977) See item 166.

334. Wallace, Phyllis A. with Linda Datcher and Julianne Malveaux. Black Women in the Labor Force, Cambridge, MA: MIT Press, 1980. (3,4)

An examination of existing research revealed that the use of macro-analysis leads to many unresolved paradoxes. The authors try to resolve these by using more critical microanalysis, and find that there are significant differences in the labor market activity of black and white women. This is not surprising, given conditions that are more or less specific to black women, such as racial discrimination, inadequacy in their husband's earnings, the structure of black families, and so forth. One of the main conclusions of this work is that much further research is needed.

335. Ward, Kathryn B. and Fred C. Pampel. "Structural Determinants of Female Labor Force Participation in Developed Nations, 1955-75." SSQ, 66, 3 (Sept. 1985): 654-67. (3)

This study is unusual in that it examines both cross-sectional and longitudinal data for 16 developed nations over five time points from 1955 to 1975. The results show that determinants of labor force participation are complex. They provide support for several of the standard explanations, particularly demand for female workers, but find the effects of the population sex ratio--a variable often ignored--to be strongest. Andrea Tyree (same issue, pp. 668-78) challenges not the main conclusions, but the assumption of the authors that it is competition between men and women that causes this outcome, but Ward and Pampel (pp. 675-79) defend their approach.

336. Weil, Mildred W. "An Analysis of the Factors Influencing Married Women's Actual or Planned Work Force Participation." ASR 26, 1 (Feb. 1961): 91-96. (3)

Unlike many studies which emphasize conflicts faced by women combining homemaking and careers, this note focuses on factors which were found to permit a woman to succeed in doing so. Among these are, first and foremost, the wife's career orientation, and the husband's favorable attitude and willingness to do a larger share of child care. Not surprisingly, it is also easier for the mother when children are at least school age. This study was based on a sample of 200 mothers in a housing development in a New Jersey town, but its findings may be broadly representative even so.

337. Weiss, Yoram and Reuben Gronau. "Expected Interruptions in Labour Force Participation and Sex-Related Differences in Earnings Growth," REStud. 58, 5, (Oct. 1981): 607-19. (1)

A model is constructed in which partipication in the labor force and investment in job-related skills and training are jointly determined. With appropriate assumptions the model yields results which suggest that discrimination causes longer withdrawals and lower earnings growth.

Werneke (1978) See item 1022.

338. Yatchew, Adonis J. "Labor Supply in the Presence of Taxes: An Alternative Specification." RES 67, 1 (Feb. 1985): 27-33. (3,Q)

This paper estimates the effect of progressive taxes on the labor supply of married women, assuming that their decision whether to enter the labor market is the marginal one. Like many other studies, this one finds the effect of husband's earnings and the presence of young children to be negative, but wife's earnings and education positive. The negative effect of age found is ascribed to the cohort effect, and possibly also the financial independence of grown children.

Yohalem (1980) See item 1026.
Youssef (1974) See item 1027.
Yusuf and Briggs (1979) See item 1028.
Zabalza (1983) See item 1030.

Chapter 4

OCCUPATIONAL DISTRIBUTION

Though most attention has been focused on the rapid increase in the labor force participation, there has also been a great deal of concern about the fact that most women continue to be employed in predominantly female occupations. Occupational segregation, defined as the percent of women, or men, who would have to change jobs in order to duplicate the distribution of the opposite sex across the standard census occupational categories, has been declining rather slowly, and only in recent years.

The extent to which individual occupations remain segregated is indicated by the fact that of the 503 listed in the 1980 Census, 100 were comprised of more than 95 percent male workers, 21 of more than 90 percent female workers. The far smaller number of female categories is also indicative of the substantial concentration of women in relatively few fields. Further, there is segregation in various other ways.

First, men and women frequently work in different industries as well as occupations. Thus, for instance, a far higher proportion of assemblers is female in the electrical machinery equipment and supply industry than in the motor vehicles industry. Similarly, this is true of school bus drivers as compared to those driving mass transit buses.

Second, even men and women within the same occupation and industry often work in different firms. Many organizations are perfectly segregated in each job category, and in the remainder the amount of segregation tends to be very large. There is also concern whether recent signs of change portend a real trend toward desegregation or merely the feminization of previously male occupations.

Last, there is considerable hierarchical segregation by sex within occupations. A good illustration of this is that among university faculties only one-tenth of full professors, but somewhat more than one-third of assistant professors, as well as slightly more than half of instructors and lecturers, are women. Another example is that while more than one quarter of managers and officials now are women, their representation in top positions continues to be extremely sparse. In the late 1970's among the 500 largest U.S. industrial corporations listed in *Fortune* only one had a woman chief executive and less than 1 percent of the officers and directors listed were women.

Only as we learn more about the full extent of segregation can we hope to determine to what extent each of the following solutions to the high representation of women in low paying jobs is (1) for women to invest more in their "human capital" (acquire more job-related education and skills, particularly by reducing work interruptions and increasing their on-the-job training); (2) for the government to make sure that qualified women have access to male occupations and are fairly treated after entry; (3) for employers to adopt "pay equity," involving equal pay for work of comparable worth.

Much of the research presented in the next two sections, as well as in this one, is related to this complex issue. Progress toward untangling it would be faster if there were more general recognition of the fact that there appears to be a multiplicity of factors contributing to women's inferior status in the labor market, and that, similarly, there is likely to be a variety of approaches that may help to improve it.

339. Albelda, Randy P. "Occupational Segregation by Race and Gender, 1958-1981." ILRR 39, 3 (Apr. 1986): 404-11. (3)

This study disaggregates annual data for 1958 to 1981 by race and sex, and shows that although white women's occupational distribution remained quite stable relative to white men's, nonwhite women's distribution has changed dramatically, particularly compared to white women's. On the other hand the extent of occupational segregation between black women and white men continues to be the greatest of any two groups, while that between black men and white men has also declined substantially. The author shows that education, structural changes in the economy, and economic fluctuations have all played a part in causing these developments.

340. Allison, Elizabeth K. and Pinney Allen. "Male-Female Professionals: A Model of Career Choice." IR 17, 3 (Oct. 1978): 333-37. (3)

A model of entrance into professions is devised to test the hypothesis that both sexes' plans to enter professions are similarly shaped by economic variables. The results for nurses, teachers, chemists and lawyers all showed reasonable results, except for male teachers, a group perhaps not primarily motivated by economic considerations. With respect to the main hypothesis, there are no significant differences in short-run salary elasticities between men and women, and market variables used in this model capture about 25 percent of the changes of entrants of either sex. That women nonetheless enter low-pay professions may be explained by early decisions due to socialization and discriminatory barriers.

341. Almquist, Elizabeth M. "Untangling the Effects of Race and Sex: The Disadvantaged Status of Black Women." SSQ 56, 1 (June 1975): 129-42. (3)

A review of available evidence with respect to employment, earnings, and unemployment, leads the author to conclude that black women are disadvantaged both as blacks and as women. She also believes that the interests of black women coincide to a great extent with those of the feminist movement. This conclusion is supported by findings of Borjas (1983).

342. Almquist, Elizabeth M., Shirley S. Angrist and Richard Michelson. "Women's Career Aspirations and Achievements: College and Seven Years After." SWO 7, 3 (Aug. 1980): 367-84. (3)

This paper tests the hypothesis that for women commitment to an occupational preference in college influences but does not determine their career afterwards because they have to juggle with familial aspirations as well. Thus, only 59 percent of the sample of college graduates worked in their preferred occupation seven years later, though 75 percent of those who had gone to graduate school did. It was also found that college graduates married less often and had children less often than anticipated, but went to graduate school more often. These findings are interesting, but since they are based on a sample of only 58 they must not be regarded as more than suggestive.

Anker and Hein (1985) See item 836.

343. Baron, James N. and William T. Bielby. "Organizational Barriers to Gender Equality: Sex Segregation of Jobs and Opportunities," in Alice S. Rossi, ed. Gender and the Life Course, New York: Aldine Publishing Company, 1985, pp. 233-52. (4)

As reported on in Bielby and Baron (1984) their study of 400 work organizations in California between 1959 and 1979 showed a far larger amount of job segregation by sex than is revealed by national data using broader occupational categories. The most interesting contribution of the paper consists of their suggestions for policies to remedy this situation, based on their observation of the rare instances where there had been significant changes. They note, first, that whoever may be responsible for existing segregation, only management can be expected to reduce it. Second, they believe that pressure applied to a few large firms that already have some women, and could set a good example, would be most effective.

Brown, Moon and Zoloth (1980a) See item 438.

344. Beller, Andrea H. "The Impact of Equal Opportunity Policy on Sex Differentials in Earnings and Occupations." AER 72, 2 (May 1982a): 171-5. (4)

Using cross-section data by state before and after enforcement of EEOC legislation, this study finds mixed results, neutral or even unfavorable for women with only high school education, but favorable for college graduates, among whom new entrants appear to have gained more access to nontraditional jobs. These results are similar to those found by Finis Welch, "Affirmative Action and its Enforcement," AER 71, 2 (May 1981): 127-33, for black men.

345. Beller, Andrea H. "Trends in Occupational Segregation by Sex and Race: 1960-1981" in Barbara F. Reskin, ed., Sex Segregation in the Workplace: Trends, Explanations, and Remedies, Washington, D.C.: National Academy Press, 1984: pp. 11-26. (3)

This comprehensive study suggests that there has been a significant and accelerating decline in occupational segregation during the 1960's and 1970's. Using data from the Current Population Survey, the author calculated that the index of segregation fell from 68.7 in 1960 to 65.9 in 1970 and 61.7 in 1981. She also found evidence that the index was lower, and declined faster for younger cohorts. Some caution in accepting an optimistic view is, however, called for. Occupational segregation is far greater when individual firms and more detailed job categories are examined (Bielby, W. T. and Baron, 1984). Occupations that have become more integrated recently may continue to become female (Reskin, 1984). Further, even if recent rates of decline in the index of segregation did continue, it would nonetheless be a hundred years before the index would reach zero.

346. Beller, Andrea H. "Changes in the Sex Composition of U.S. Occupations, 1960-1981." JHR 20, 2 (Spring 1985): 235-50. (3)

Analysis of data from the 1960 and 1970 Censuses and the Current Population Surveys of 1971 and 1981 shows that occupational sex segregation declined more in the 1970's than it had in the 1960's. Most of the change was caused by the influx of women into traditionally male occupations, particularly those in the managerial category. There was virtually no change, however, in the male crafts occupations.

347. Bergmann, Barbara R. "The Economics of Women's Liberation." <u>ANYAS</u> 208 (Mar. 1973): 154-60. (1,4)

In the feminists' version of a better future there would be no occupational segregation, equal pay for equal work, and equal sharing of unpaid work. Aside from inertia, the main interrelated obstacles to achieving such arrangements are discrimination, inferior job performance by women, women's reluctance to enter "male roles," and the profitability of keeping women in their place. The author concludes that only long-sustained efforts would overcome these barriers. More than 10 years later, many observers would agree.

348. Bielby, William T. and James N. Baron. "A Woman's Place is With Other Women: Sex Segregation within Organizations," in Barbara F. Reskin, ed., <u>Sex Segregation in the Workplace: Trends, Explanations and Remedies</u>, Washington, D.C.: National Academy Press, 1984, pp. 27-55. (3)

This research, based on detailed information for almost 400 California firms with more than 60,000 workers shows a far greater degree of segregation than that found for larger categories by other researchers, such as Beller (1984), Blau, F. D. and Hendricks (1979), and others. Further, there appears to have been no change from 1959 to 1979. Over half of the firms were totally segregated by sex, in the sense that no single job was held by both men and women. Across all firms, the proportion of workers who were in job categories held by both men and women was only 10 percent. The authors also report on mechanisms that help to maintain segregation, including sex-specific allocation of workers sanctioned by collective bargaining, protective legislation in large establishments, and patriarchal behavior of entrepreneurs in small ones.

349. Bielby, William T. and James N. Baron. "Sex Segregation Within Occupations." <u>AER</u> 76, 2 (May 1986): 43-47. (3)

The authors, using a data set described in greater detail in Bielby and Baron (1984), find evidence of pervasive sex discrimination not adequately explained by human capital theory, but consistent with statistical discrimination.

350. Blakemore, Arthur E. and Stuart A. Low. "Sex Differences in Occupational Selection: The Case of College Majors." <u>RES</u> 66, 1 (Feb. 1984): 157-63. (3)

This paper applies the human capital approach to the decision process of students in selecting college majors. The empirical results of the research are consistent with the hypothesis that higher expected fertility is related to selection of occupations less subject to atrophy and obsolescense. The findings are, however, also consistent with the hypothesis that more traditional women are more likely both to plan for larger families and to opt for more traditionally female fields.

351. Blau, Francine D. <u>Equal Pay in the Office</u>. Lexington, MA: D. C. Heath and Co., 1977. (3)

This study of employment patterns of male and female office workers in three large northeastern cities revealed a strong and consistent pattern of sex segregation by establishment among workers employed in the same occupational categories. This evidence is now widely accepted as showing one more form of segregation, not previously recognized. There is, however, little agreement to date on its causes. These findings were also reported in Blau, F. D., "Sex Segregation of Workers by Enterprise in Clerical Occupations," in Richard C. Edwards, Michael Reich, and David M. Gordon, eds., <u>Labor Market Segmentation</u>, Lexington, MA: Lexington Books, 1975, pp. 257-78.

352. Blau, Francine D. and Wallace E. Hendricks. "Occupational Segregation by Sex: Trends and Prospects." <u>JHR</u> 14, 2 (Spring 1979): 197-210. (3)

Using the 183 occupations available in census data for all three decades, it is shown that segregation increased slightly from 72.7 to 73.8 during 1950-1960, mainly because of expansion of female occupations, then decreased somewhat to 70.7 by 1970.

353. Blau, Francine D. and Carol L. Jusenius. "Economists' Approach to Sex Segregation in the Labor Market: An Appraisal." SJWCS 1, 3, (Spring 1976, Part 2): 181-89. (1,3)

This paper is mainly a review of then available work on occupational segregation, but it provides a good deal of evidence that the aggregate supply of female labor is more responsive to wage changes than is the supply of male labor. Reasons for this are that home-making provides a viable alternative to market work for married women, but not for men, and, perhaps, that women may acquire less firm-specific capital than men and hence would be more mobile on that account.

354. Blaxall, Martha and Barbara Reagan, eds. Women and the Workplace. The Implications of Occupational Segregation, Chicago: The University of Chicago Press, 1976. (1,3,4)

This compendium of papers, presented at an interdisciplinary conference, provides a good overview of the causes and results of occupational segregation by sex, as well as a discussion of possible policies that might help to change the situation. Since occupational segregation has declined only modestly over the last decade, these issues remain relevant. Many of the individual essays from this volume are also included in this bibliography.

355. Brito, Patricia K. and Carol L. Jusemius. "Career Aspirations of Young Women: Factors Underlying Choice of a Typically Male or Typically Female Occupation." ASAPP (1978): 50-59. (3)

Human capital theorists such as Polachek (1976) have suggested that women's commitment to the labor force will be related to their choice of a typically male or female occupation. The results of this study are consistent with the hypothesis that for college educated women a short expected work life acts as a barrier to occupations which require post-graduate education. (Or it may be their career aspirations that determine work plans.) For women with high school education or less, however, there seems to be no necessary relationship between labor force commitment and occupational choice.

356. Brown, Randall S., Marilyn M. Moon and Barbara S. Zoloth. "Occupational Attainment and Segregation by Sex." <u>ILRR</u> 33, 4 (July 1980b): 506-17. (3)

The authors use multinomial logit and mutliple discriminant analysis to predict the probability that a person will attain each of several occupational categories, based on the individual's characteristics. Applying to women parameters obtained from a sample of men, they find that their hypothetical results differ substantially when compared to the actual distribution, even after making adjustments for taste differences. Hence they attribute a significant portion of sex segregation to discrimination. With respect to tastes, they assume that women with strong labor force attachment are likely to be as career oriented as men.

Buchele and Aldrich (1985) See item 439.
Bureau of National Affairs (1984) See item 441.

357. Burris, Val and Amy Wharton. "Sex Segregation in the U.S. Labor Force." <u>RRPE</u> 14, 3 (Fall 1982): 43-56. (3)

This paper, like others (Beller, 1984; Blau, F. D. and Hendricks, 1979), shows that there has ben a great deal of stability in sex segregation 1950-1979, but that there has been some decline in professional, technical and managerial occupations. The reason for changes in these "middle class" occupations, as opposed to stability in blue collar jobs, is interpreted in terms of segmented labor markets and differential interests of employers and male employees. The authors conclude by recommending strategies for reducing sex segregation in "working class" occupations.

Cooney (1978) See item 868.

358. Corcoran, Mary E., Greg J. Duncan and Michael Ponza. "Work Experience, Job Segregation and Wages," in Barbara F. Reskin, ed., Sex Segregation in the Workplace. Trends, Explanations, Remedies, Washington, D.C.: National Academy Press, 1984: pp. 171-191. (3)

This paper includes a review of the literature, and reports of the authors' own work using Panel Study of Income Dynamics data, to test the hyotheses that work interruptions cause substantial long run losses of income (Mincer and Ofek 1982) and that women's discontinuous work patterns explain occupational segregation (Polachek 1976). Neither is confirmed. Women reenter at much lower wages than when they left, but catch up rapidly. Cross-section data overestimate long-run losses because they include recent re-entries. As for occupational segregation, the findings of considerable mobility between male and female jobs, similar wage growth and depreciation in both male and female jobs, and the fact that women with discontinuous work careers were no more likely than others to be in female jobs, all suggest that this hypothesis too is seriously flawed. Similar conclusions are reached by England (1982), though a number of other studies show some support for Polachek's theory.

Craig, C., Garnsey and Rubery (1985) See item 869.

359. Datcher, Linda P. "Race/Sex Differences in the Effects of Background on Achievement" in Martha S. Hill, et al., eds. Five Thousand American Families - Patterns of Progress, Vol. 9, Institute of Social Research, University of Michigan, 1981, pp. 359-90. (3)

Though background effects for college attendance used to be greater for men than women, and for whites than blacks, there has been considerable convergence. The difference between young white men and women was found to be insignificant in this study. Similar results were found for total schooling. This investigation also showed that mother's education had a greater effect on daughters than on sons. The study as a whole clearly indicates that a historical, dynamic view of the acquisition of human capital, which recognizes intergenerational links, is the appropriate one.

360. DeFleur, Lois B. "Organizational and Ideological Barriers to Sex Integration of Military Groups." SWO 12, 2 (May 1985): 206-28. (3)

This study relies both on the existing literature about factors affecting sex integration in traditionally all-male fields, and on data from a four-year study at the U.S. Air Force Academy for an analysis of integration in the military. The model developed helps to explain the slow pace of change in incorporating women into the full range of military roles and ranks.

361. de la Vina, Lynda Y. "Female Occupational Distribution: Treiman and Terrell Revisited." SSQ 66, 3 (Sep. 1985): 680-86. (3)

This study applies the Treiman and Terrell (1975) approach to disaggregated 1940-50 data from individual categories. The results show that change in occupations was confined primarily to professionals, managers, clerical and sales workers, service workers and laborers, while there was continuation of the previous structure and even a trend toward further occupational segregation among craftsworkers and operatives.

362. England, Paula. "Assessing Trends in Occupational Sex Segregation, 1900-1976," in Ivar Berg, ed., Sociological Perspectives on Labor Markets, New York: Academic Press, 1981, pp. 273-95. (3)

The author points out that studies relying on cross-section data suggest that occupational segregation contributes substantially to the male-female earnings gap. She goes on to explore the relationship between segregation and income differences over time, using a variety of different methodological approaches. None of them are found fully satisfactory. Difficulties are even found in providing more than an informed guess that there have been small declines in segregation over this century. This paper, accordingly, raises questions about earlier studies that purported to measure changes over many decades.

363. England, Paula. "The Failure of Human Capital Theory to Explain Occupational Sex Segregation." JHR 17, 3 (Summer 1982): 358-70. (3)

The author tests Polachek's (1976) hypothesis that women who expect to interrupt their labor force participation will choose occupations where such interruptions are accompanied by low atrophy rates. She did not find that women were penalized less for time out of the labor force in female than in male occupations. Nor did she find any evidence that women with more continuous employment histories were less likely to be in predominantly female occupations. Similar conclusions are reached by Corcoran, Duncan, G. J. and Ponza (1984). Other studies, however, lend support to Polachek's theory.

364. England, Paula. "Wage Appreciation and Depreciation: A Test of Neoclassical Economic Explanations of Occupatonal Sex Segregation." SF 62, 3 (Mar. 1984): 726-49. (3)

The author uses data from the Panel on Income Dynamics to show that, controlling for education and experience, women in predominantly male occupations have higher earnings than do women in more female occupations. These findings, like those in England (1982), are in conflict with the explanations of occupational segregation suggested by Polachek (1976) and by Zellner (1975), both of whom assert that women have a pecuniary reason to choose occupations traditional for their sex.

365. Falk, William W. and Arthur G. Cosby. "Women and the Status Attainment Process." SSQ 56, 2 (Sept. 1975): 307-14. (3)

A review of major occupational choice theories shows them to be biased toward males, and quite inadequate for females. The authors caution that these theories must be changed to take women's experiences into account if they are to be relevant to this part of the population.

366. Ferber, Marianne A. and Joe L. Spaeth. "Work Characteristics and the Male-Female Earnings Gap." <u>AER</u> 74, 2 (May 1984): 260-64. (3)

This study confirms once again that both human capital and institutional factors affect earnings, but also finds that specific job characteristics, not generally considered, such as control of monetary resources are important determinants of earnings. The results further show that the rewards are not the same for men and women, even in the case of quite specific characteristics, pointing toward the existence of discrimination.

367. Fottler, Myron D. and Trevor Bain. "Sex Differences in Occupational Aspiration." <u>AMJ</u> 23, 1 (Mar. 1980): 144-49. (3)

This paper examines occupational aspirations of a sample of high school graduates. It was found that about twice as high a percentage of males aspired to managerial positions, but females aspired to professional and technical occupations to a somewhat greater extent. Among the remainder, males mainly intended to be craftsmen, operatives and laborers, women planned on clerical and service positions. There was no significant difference for sales occupations. Thus it appears that, for the most part, young men and women continue to be rather traditional in their choice of occupations.

368. Gordon, David M., Richard Edwards and Michael Reich, <u>Segmented Work, Divided Workers: The Historical Transformation of Labor in the United States</u>, Cambridge, England: Cambridge University Press, 1982. (1)

The authors, while subscribing to the institutionalist view of segmented labor markets, argue further that employers as a group benefit from such a strategy. Dividing workers by sex and race prevents them from seeing their common interests and working for a common cause, and would thwart efforts to unionize and obtain a share of power from the capitalists. Radical feminists further add to this explanation (e.g., Hartmann, 1976).

Greenhalgh and Stewart, M. B. (1985) See item 895.

369. Gross, Edward. "Plus Ça Change...? The Sexual Structure of Occupations Over Time." _SP_ 16, 1 (Fall 1968): 198-208. (3)

The author calculated an index of occupational segregation for each Census year from 1900 to 1960. The figures were 66.9 in 1900 and 68.4 in 1960. They varied little during the intervening period, except for very modest declines to 65.7 and 65.6 during the decades which included World War I and World War II respectively. The picture presented of no significant change for more than half a century is no doubt realistic, even though the precise figures are not entirely reliable, in part because of recurrent changes in the Census occupational categories. For more recent studies see, for instance, Beller (1984), Blau, F. D. and Hendricks (1979).

Grossman (1979) See item 229.
Gunderson (1978) See item 614.
Gustman and Steinmeier (1982) See item 486.

370. Halaby, Charles N. "Job-Shift Differences Between Men and Women in the Workplace." _SSR_ 11, 1 (Mar. 1982): 1-29. (3)

This paper uses a career life cycle model of achievement to analyze sex differences in job mobility of management personnel in a large corporation. The results show that male and female job shift regimes are similar in form, but the parameters governing them are significantly different. The author concludes that this shows there are inequities in the rate of return to productive resources, though not in the opportunity to shift.

371. Hartmann, Heidi I. "Capitalism, Patriarchy, and Job Segregation by Sex," in Martha Blaxall and Barbara B. Reagan, eds., _Women and the Workplace: The_

<u>Implications of Occupational Segregation</u>, Chicago: University of Chicago Press, 1976, pp. 137-69. (1)

The author accepts the evidence that there has always been division of labor by sex, but thinks it has not always been hierarchical. This paper investigates the question how the more recent less egalitarian situation came about, and how it was extended to wage labor in the modern period. It is suggested that early on a patriarchal system was established in which men controlled the labor of women and children, and that under capitalism the technique of hierarchical organization was translated into an indirect, impersonal system of control, which enabled men to maintain their superior position. The proposed solution is to abolish not only the hierarchical nature of the division of labor, but the very division of labor between the sexes.

372. Hedges, Janice N. "Women Workers and Manpower Demands in the 1970's." <u>MLR</u> 93, 6 (June 1970): 19-29. (3)

The author concludes that women will have to enter nontraditional occupations to a much greater extent if they are to find jobs in keeping with their abilities. This advice continues to be pertinent more than a decade later, though skilled blue collar trades do not offer good prospects in the 1980's, and probably beyond.

373. Hedges, Janice N. and Sandra E. Bemis. "Sex Stereotyping: Its Decline in Skilled Trades." <u>MLR</u> 97, 5 (May 1974): 14-22. (3)

This paper points to the fact that women in skilled trades about doubled over a bit more than a decade as evidence that the women's movement has been effective in reducing sex stereotyping in these occupations. It is also noted that studies of aptitude reveal no significant barriers to women's entry and that mechanization continues to reduce the need for physical strength. Nonetheless, more than a decade after this article was written, the optimistic predictions of its authors have not proven justified.

374. Hoffman, Saul D. "On-the-Job Training: Differences by Race and Sex." MLR 104, 7 (July 1981): 34-36. (3)

According to Panel Study of Income Dynamics data the jobs of blacks and women, in addition to carrying lower wages and a higher probability of unemployment, also provide less on-the-job training. The average training period for white men was 2.25 years, while it was less than one year for each of the other groups. Even when workers in the same wage bracket were considered, a substantial difference remained. Hence, we may conclude that current earnings differences understate the true gap, for training is also a valuable reward. A longer, more technical report of much the same material is Duncan, G. J. and Hoffman, S. D. (1979).

House (1983) See item 914.

375. Jackson, John H., Timothy J. Keaveny and John A. Fossum. "Sex Differences in Sources of Job Satisfaction." JBE 7, 1 (Summer 1978): 79-96. (3)

Using a large sample of persons in a western state who registered passenger vehicles, the authors found no difference in the overall proportion of males and females satisfied with their jobs. The percentages dissatisfied because of lack of skill utilization or of advancement opportunities was the same for both. These results suggest that components of job satisfaction are similar for men and women. One difference found, however, was that women were slightly more dissatisfied with their pay. In view of the large differences in earnings, the authors argue that what needs to be explained is why women are only slightly more dissatisfied in this respect.

376. Jacobs, Jerry A. "Sex Segregation in American Higher Education." WW 1 (1985): 191-214. (3)

This paper examines sex segregation among persons at various academic degree levels. Using a common measure, which shows the proportion of members of one sex that would have to change fields to duplicate the distribution of the other, it is found that segregation was relatively stable among Ph.D.s, but changed substantially at all other levels. Using a different measure, the probability of intergroup contact, men were increasingly likely to find women to major in the same subject, but not vice versa, showing that women are moving into male fields, but men are staying out of female fields.

Jusenius (1977) See item 503.
Kessler-Harris (1985) See item 104.
Lapidus (1975) See item 932.

377. Lehrer, Evelyn L. and Houston H. Stokes. "Determinants of the Female Occupational Distribution: A Log-Linear Probability Analysis." RES 67, 3 (Aug. 1985): 395-404. (3)

This study examines the skill level and sex composition of occupations, two variables that have been found to be significant influences on female wages. Using data from the National Longitudinal Surveys, Young Women Cohort, it is found that anticipated labor force attachment has a direct impact on the skill level of the worker, but the direct effect of this variable on the sex composition of occupations is not statistically significant. Also, the skill level is positively associated with the probability of being in a male or integrated occupation. Thus the study provides an explanation of the concentration in low-skill female occupations but not for crowding into high-skill female jobs.

378. Leigh, J. Paul. "Sex Differences in Absenteeism." IR 22, 3 (Fall 1983): 349-61. (3)

A model of absenteeism from work is developed, which shows that most of the differences between men and women in this respect are explained by their being in different occupations and having different work-related characteristics. Nonetheless, their reactions to particular characteristics were not always the same. Particularly, women were more likely to miss work because of illness of children, and because of minor health complaints of their own, while men tended to be absent more because of work-related injuries.

379. Leonard, Jonathan S. "Employment and Occupational Advance under Affirmative Action." RES 66, 3 (Aug. 1984b): 377-85. (4)

Disaggregated unemployment data in a new sample of nearly 70,000 establishments from EEO-1 reports and OFCCP records of compliance are used to determine the results of affirmative action in the contractor sector during the late 1970's. The major finding is that it increased minority employment and the demand for minorities in skilled jobs in this sector. The author suggests that the success at this time, contrary to earlier years, was probably due to an increase in the supply of skilled minorities in many fields. He explains the weaker effect on white women as the result of the massive increase in female employment throughout the economy which may have obscured the contractor effect. For both groups, the greatest gains were in growing establishments.

380. Levine, Adeline. "Educational and Occupational Choice: A Synthesis of Literature from Sociology and Psychology." JCR 2, 4 (Mar. 1976): 276-89. (1)

While this is not the main focus of Levine's paper, she points out that many earlier studies of career and educational choices ignored women because they were too complicated, and others tended to view them as either "deviant men" or "deviant women." She argues that more attention needs to be paid to this subject, precisely because it is complex, and that discrimination and fear of discrimination should not be ignored.

381. Lyle, Jerolyn R. and Jane L. Ross. Women in Industry. Lexington, MA: Heath, Lexington Books, 1973. (3)

The main focus of this book is an investigation of the relation between various characteristics of the employing firm and the extent of what the authors consider to be occupational discrimination against women. Their main findings are that among industrial firms there tends to be less discrimination in the larger ones, and that public policy also has some impact. It is frustrating, however, to find that these results are not incorporated into a theoretical framework. It is equally disappointing to find some superficial and unwarranted generalizations, such as the claim that a major reason for the rapid increase in women's labor force participation has been the effort to maintain the purchasing power of households, when in fact the purchasing power of wages has generally been increasing over the long run.

382. Lyon, Larry and Holley Rector-Owen. "Labor Market Mobility Among Young Black and White Women: Longitudinal Models of Occupational Prestige and Income." SSQ 62, 1 (Mar. 1981): 64-78. (3)

Causal models of occupational mobility for black and white young women are developed using National Longitudinal Survey data. They suggest that white women do better because they tend to have numerous advantages as compared to their black counterparts, and that there are only modest levels of discrimination. Their definition of discrimination is, however, very narrow.

383. Lyson, Thomas A. "Race and Sex Segregation in the Occupational Structures of Southern Employers." SSQ 66, 2 (June 1985): 281-95. (3)

Data from the Equal Employment Opportunity Commission are used to examine how establishment characteristics are related to divisions in the work force. The results of this study show that occupational segregation, both by race and by sex, is greatest in establishments with a large proprotion of high-status white collar or skilled blue-collar positions. This suggests that relying only on individual occupational, or industrial characteristics, and ignoring those of the establishment, is inadequate for examining segregation processes.

384. Marini, Margaret M. "Sex Differences in the Process of Occupational Attainment: A Closer Look." SSR 9, 4 (Dec. 1980): 307-61. (3)

Unlike most previous studies of this subject, this one finds significant differences between men and women. At the time of labor market entry the occupational prestige is about the same, but the dispersion is greater for men, and over time their attainment becomes greater. Education is very important for both males and females, but for each the status of the parent of the same sex is more important, and marriage has the opposite effect for men and women.

385. Marini, Margaret M. and Mary C. Brinton. "Sex Typing in Occupational Socialization," in Barbara F. Reskin, Sex Segregation in the Work Place. Trends, Explanations, Remedies. Washington, D.C.: National Academy Press, 1984, pp. 192-232. (1,3)

These authors emphasize pre-market socialization as an important contributor to occupational segregation. A review of the literature provides support for this view. They also talk of differences in abilities and dispositions, but find them to be relatively small and suggest that they may in large part stem from rather than be causes of differences in occupational orientation. One may question the authors' rigid separation between pre-market socialization and the effects of labor market discrimination, for the two are likely to interact.

386. McLaughlin, Steven D. "Occupational Sex Identification and the Assessment of Male and Female Earnings Inequality." ASR 43, 6 (Dec. 1978): 909-21. (3)

Utilizing data from the U.S. Census and the Dictionary of Occupational Titles, this paper presents evidence that the concept of prestige is not likely to be useful in investigating earnings attainment of women as compared to men. Men and women who do quite different work may have the same level of prestige, and some of the task differences are related to earnings. Further, the sex identification of the occupation also appears to influence earnings.

387. Meyer, Peter J. and Patricia L. Maes. "The Reproduction of Occupational Segregation Among Young Women." IR 22, 1 (Winter 1983): 115-24. (3)

Concerned with continued segregation of women in low wage occupations, the authors use data from the 1979 Current Population Survey to investigate the occupational distribution of young women. They find, overall, that the old patterns of segregation persist to a considerable extent even for them. They do find small changes, but unlike Beller (1984), they emphasize continuity. This is a good example how different observers may see the same glass as either half empty or half full.

388. O'Farrell, Brigid and Sharon L. Harlan. "Job Integration Strategies: Today's Programs and Tomorrow's Needs" in Barbara F. Reskin, Sex Segregation in the Workplace. Trends, Explanations, Remedies, Washington, DC: National Academy Press, 1984, pp. 267-91. (4)

The authors examine the experiences of large firms that integrated women into non-traditional jobs. They found government pressure was crucial for progress. Generally external recruitment and training of women for new jobs were combined. But these were not sufficient. Without increasing promotions, many entry jobs would become feminized. To have real integration care is needed to place women into jobs with a potential for upward mobility. To succeed in this, cooperation from top management and, where labor is organized, top union officers appears to be crucial.

389. Palomba, Catherine A. and Neil A. Palomba. "Occupational Segregation and Earnings Differentials by Sex: A Simultaneous Model." RBER 17, 3 (Spring 1982): 45-51. (3)

The authors argue that previous research on occupational segregation has suffered from not treating the female dependent variables in a simultaneous model. Using such a model and Census data from 1960-1970, they conclude that 1) the percent female in an occupation and the sex earnings ratio appear to have been independent as late as 1960, but not in 1970, 2) women have recently been entering occupations where the male-female earnings gap is large, and they suggest this is because of "economic forces," and 3) the larger the proportion of women, the greater the earnings gap. The authors never ask what it is that causes women to face such unfavorable options.

390. Parnes, Herbert S., Carol L. Jusenius, Francine D. Blau Gilbert Nestel, Richard L. Shortlidge, Jr. and Steven H. Sandell. Dual Careers, Vol. 4, Washington, DC: U.S. Department of Labor, Employment and Training Administration, R and D Monograph 21, 1976. (3)

This is a follow-up on Shea et al. (1971) using later data from the National Longitudinal Survey on Young Women. The emphasis in this volume is on life cycle behavior, particularly with respect to education, training and labor force participation, and its effect on occupational attainment.

Parrish (1978) (1986) See items 801, 802.
Pfeffer and Ross, J. (1981) See item 529.

391. Pike, Maureen. "Segregation by Sex, Earnings Differentials and Equal Pay: An Application of a Job Crowding Model to U.K. Data." Appl.E 14 (Oct. 1982): 503-14. (4)

This paper suggests the consequences for male and female earnings and employment that would result if the crowding of women into a relatively narrow range of occupations were to cease. Appropriate assumptions are made, for instance, about labor supply responses. The results suggest that laws enforcing the right of equal access to all occupatons are likely to raise women's wages more than would equal pay within occupations, especially if current occupational distribution is mainly caused by discrimination. It may be objected, however, that this does not mean there is not need for both.

392. Piore, Michael J. "The Dual Labor Market: Theory and Implications," in David M. Gordon, ed., Problems in Political Economy: An Urban Perspective, Lexington, MA: D. C. Heath and Co., 1971, pp. 90-94. (1)

The author argues that stratification in the labor market poses almost insurmountable barriers to individual movement between sectors. He further differs with neoclassical analysis in claiming that workers' income and status do not reflect their productivity in uniform ways, and that in the secondary labor market incomes bear little relationship to productivity.

This theory was developed primarily with reference to problems of race rather than sex, but it nonetheless has received recurrent attention in the literature on the male-female earnings gap. Neoclassical economists tend to deny the existence of a dual labor market. Some feminists dispute its relevance to women.

393. Polachek, Solomon W. "Sex Differences in College Major." ILRR, 31, 4 (July 1978): 498-508. (3)

The author uses two national data sets to analyze sex differences in choice of college major in 1955 and 1973. He concludes that sorting is determined primarily by ability and expected lifetime labor force participation. He ignores the fact that there is no measure of ability which is able to capture the effects of socialization as opposed to inherent traits, and that both choice of field and planned labor force participation are undoubtedly influenced by traditional attitudes about the role of women. Changes in such attitudes over time may explain why, as the author shows, women both planned to spend more time in the labor force, and tended to enter more "male" fields in the later year.

394. Polachek, Solomon W. "Occupational Self-Selection: A Human Capital Approach to Sex Differences in Occupational Structure." RES, 63, 1 (Feb. 1981): 60-69. (1,3)

In this and several other papers ("Occupational Segregation: An Alternative Hypothesis." JCB 5, 1, Winter 1976: 1-12 and "Occupational Segregation Among Women: Theory, Evidence and Prognosis," in Cynthia B. Lloyd, Emily S. Andrews and Curtis L. Gilroy, eds. Women in the Labor Market, NY: Columbia University Press, 1979, pp. 137-57) the author suggests that women who expect their labor force participation to be intermittent find it worthwhile to choose occupations that do not require much investment in human capital and are not subject to much depreciation of human capital during periods of absence from the labor market, even though these occupations have flat earnings profiles. Evidence from empirical studies by other researchers provides only scant support for this hypothesis. For instance, Morgan (1981) did find that jobs with flatter profiles had higher starting wages, but only slightly so. England (1982) did not find that atrophy during work interruptions was less in female than male occupations.

395. Poston, Dudley L. and Gordon C. Johnson. "Industrialization and Professional Differentiation by Sex in the Metropolitan Southwest." SSQ 52, 2 (Sept. 1971): 331-48. (3)

The authors, recognizing that "men's work" in one society is commonly "women's work" in another, do not accept the biological explanation of occupational segregation. Their view, that societal influences play a large part, is confirmed by their findings that there is less professional differentiation in the more industrialized regions of the U.S., where there is presumably more achievement orientation and less stereotyping.

396. Reskin, Barbara F. "Sex Segregation in the Workplace." Gender at Work, Washington, D.C.: Women's Research and Education Institute of the Congressional Caucus for Women's Issues, 1984a, pp. 1-11. (1,3)

This paper provides a concise survey of the main issues related to occupational segregation: recent trends in its magnitude, the consequences of and causes for its existence, factors that would help to accelerate its reduction and, finally, what prospects are for the future in the light of recent developments.

397. Reskin, Barbara F., ed. Sex Segregation in the Workplace. Trends, Explanations, Remedies, Washington, D.C.: National Academy Press, 1984b. (1,3,4)

As stated in the concluding remarks of this volume, the papers in it help us to understand the dimensions of occupational segregation, its causes and its consequences for women. Some consideration was also given to policy intervention. In addition to the essays (almost all of them included individually in this bibliography) there are also thoughtful critical comments in each section. Students of occupational segregation can not afford to miss this book.

398. Reskin, Barbara F. and Heidi I. Hartmann, eds. Women's Work, Men's Work, Sex Segregation on the Job. Washington, D.C.: National Academy Press, 1986. (3,4)

This report is the product of the collective labors of the Committee on Women's Employment and Related Social Issues, consisting of 14 representatives of various social sciences and nonacademic sectors of American society. It reviews the considerable consequences occupational segregation has not only for women, but also for men, families and society, and also makes some recommendations for "ameliorating the waste to the economy, the financial loss to women and their families, and the demeaning of the human spirit that comes from the rigidities inherent in segregating jobs by sex."

399. Roos, Patricia A. "Sex Stratification in the Workplace: Male-Female Differences in Economic Returns to Occupation." SSR 10, 3 (Sept. 1981): 195-224. (3)

Like Rytina (1981) this author shows that earnings tend to be lower in occupations as the proportion of women increases, and that women are paid less than men in the same occupations. She suggests the former is because women are concentrated in low paying occupations, begging the question whether the occupations have low earnings becuase they have a greater concentration of women. Women's lower earnings within occupations are explained in part by the fact that they are less likely to exercise authority. Ferber and Spaeth (1984) also raise the question whether women are rewarded less for authority when they do have it.

400. Roos, Patricia A. and Barbara F. Reskin. "Institutional Forces Contributing to Sex Segregation in the Workplace," in Barbara F. Reskin, Sex Segregation in the Workplace. Trends, Explanations, Remedies, Washington, D.C.: National Academy Press, 1984, pp. 235-60. (3)

Emphasis in explaining segregation here is neither on individuals nor on employers, but on institutions in the labor market which create constraints and barriers that keep women out of non-traditional jobs. Such barriers exist for training programs, hiring and promotion, as well as other aspects of work, as has been documented by a number of studies reviewed in this paper. These studies, however, tend to be of single establishments, or rely on small samples, generally from particular occupations. Hence, there is some question about generalizability.

401. Rosenbaum, James E. "Persistence and Change in Pay Inequalities. Implications for Job Evaluation and Comparable Worth." WW 1 (1985): 115-40. (3,4)

An examination of a large corporation with an ostensibly successful affirmative action program shows that over a 13-year period from 1962 to 1975 women's disadvantages overall were reduced. However, senior women were found not to have shared fully in the gains. Further, college-educated women did particularly well at the entry level, but fared most poorly among those with high tenure. The author concludes that this is primarily because the job structure, substantially stable over this period, served to limit the earnings gains of senior college women. Jobs tended to change little in their relative compensation, even though the firm changed from a job status to a job evaluation system. Thus the results of affirmative action are reassuring in some respects, but caution is required. Particularly, the fact that job evaluation had very little impact on earnings differentials is a matter for concern.

402. Rosenfeld, Rachel A. and Aage B. Sorensen. "Sex Differences in Patterns of Career Mobility." Dem 16, 1 (Feb. 1979): 89-101. (3)

Using 1970 Census data, this study examines the intragenerational occupational mobility between 1965 and 1970 for two cohorts of white men and women. Mobility patterns are separated into a part caused by different occupational origins and destinations, and a part caused by sex-related characteristics. Occupational segregation is found to exert by far the largest influence.

403. Rosenfeld, Rachel A. "Sex Segregation and Sectors: An Analysis of Gender Differences in Returns from Employer Changes." ASR 48, 5 (Oct. 1983). (3)

This research resulted in a variety of interesting findings. Most striking, perhaps, is that workers do move among sex-typical and atypical occupations, with the least likely group to make such a move being married men. The results also show, however, that women do not tend to gain by moving into male occupations. This may be because they move into low-paying occupations, or segregated segments within occupations. Women do gain by moving from more to less competitive sectors, and the probability of such a move is influenced by marital status and labor force attachment.

404. Rytina, Nancy F. "Occupational Segregation and Earnings Differences by Sex." MLR 104, 1 (Jan. 1981): 49-53. (3)

Using cross tabulations from the 1976 Survey of Income and Education of median 1975 annual earnings by occupaton it was shown that the ratio of female to male earnings increased as the proportion of women in the detailed category rose. This relationship was found to hold even when data for year-round full-time workers were examined separately.

405. Schmidt, Peter J. and Robert P. Strauss. "The Prediction of Occupations, Using Multiple Logit Models." IER 16, 2 (June 1975): 471-85. (3Q)

This study analyzed the occupations of persons, taking into account education, experience, race and sex. Both race and sex were found to have a substantial influence on the jobs these people obtained. The authors interpret this as evidence of discrimination, because existing patterns of distribution by occupation cannot be merely explained by differences in education and experience.

406. Semyonov, Moshe and Richard I. Scott. "Industrial Shifts, Female Employment, and Occupational Differentiation: A Dynamic Model for American Cities, 1960-1970." Dem. 20, 2 (May 1983): 163-76. (3)

This study of 70 SMSAs found that between 1960 and 1970 the odds of men joining professional and managerial occupations increased relative to those of women. The authors suggest that this was chiefly because under existing circumstances females entering the labor market were likely to be disproportionately channeled into female occupations. They conclude that traditional modernization theory cannot explain their findings, but that the segmented labor market approach can.

407. Sommers, Dixie. "Occupational Rankings for Men and Women by Earnings." MLR 97, 8 (Aug. 1974): 34-51. (3)

This paper shows earnings, age, schooling, percent employed full year, and percent female by occupational category. The author points out that men earned more than women in every occupation except public kindergarten teachers, that women tend to be more heavily represented in lower-pay occupations, but also that occupations are generally ranked in similar order for both men and women, the rank correlation coefficient being .82.

408. Sorkin, Alan L. "On the Occupational Status of Women, 1870-1970." AJES 32, 3 (July 1973): 235-43. (3)

Using census statistics, the author finds that the relative occupational status of women improved from 1870 to 1950, and particularly during the first 50 years of that period. From 1950 to 1970, however, there was a substantial decline, the relative occupational index falling below that of 1920, mainly because of the far slower growth of female professional and managerial workers, related to the more rapid increase in male educational attainment during these two decades.

409. Spaeth, Joe L. "Differences in the Occupational Achievement Process Between Male and Female College Graduates." SE 50, 3 (July 1977): 206-17. (3)

This study of the college graduating class of 1961 found that women showed greater instability in occupational expectations, reaped lesser returns in occupational status from investments in advanced education, and were less likely to realize their occupational expectations. That the study also found the mean occupational achievement of these young men and women to be the same tells us more about the way sociologists measure such things than about how these people were doing.

Stephan, P. E. and Levin, S. G. (1983) See item 820.
Stevenson (1975) See item 553.
Stewart, M. B. and Greenhalgh (1984) See item 1002.
Strauss and Horvath (1976) See item 554.

410. Streker-Seeborg, Irmtraud, Michael C. Seeborg, and Abera Zegeye. "The Impact of Nontraditional Training on the Occupational Attainment of Women." JHR 19, 4 (Fall 1984): 452-71. (4)

Using a logit model, the authors investigated the effect of nontraditional training under the Comprehensive Employment and Training Act on the occupational attainment of disadvantaged women. They found these women were 29.3 percent less likely than similarly trained men, but 23.8 more likely than women trained in female occupations, to be employed in male occupations. The main difference, however, was that only 6.7 percent of women were trained in such jobs, as opposed to 87.9 percent of men. Women were also paid less in male occupations than men.

411. Strober, Myra H. "Toward a General Theory of Occupational Sex Segregation: The Case of Public School Teaching," in Barbara F. Reskin, ed. Sex Segregation in the Workplace. Trends, Explanations, Remedies. Washington, DC: National Academy Press, 1984, pp. 144-56. (1)

The author rejects the view of economic human capital and sociological status attainment theories which pinpoint women's own behavior as the primary cause of occupational segregation. Her theory suggests that, within constraints, employers--generally men--allow male workers to decide which occupations they will inhabit, and male workers choose those that offer the most attractive economic package. Thus, occupational segregation presumably is the result of a combination of patriarchy and workers' utility maximization, illustrated by historic developments in the teaching profession. While a number of aspects of this theory are problematic, it is useful in contributing new ideas to an ongoing debate.

Szafran (1984) See item 822.

412. Tienda, Marta and Jennifer Glass. "Household Structure and Labor Force Participation of Black, Hispanic, and White Mothers." Dem. 22, 3 (Aug. 1985): 381-94. (3)

This research shows that female heads with minor children are more likely to be in the labor force than married mothers. This was, in part, found to be facilitated by the presence of other adults in female-headed households, often not members of the nuclear family. This solution to the child care problem is, however, only feasible for those who have housing that can accommodate additional persons and have enough skills to ensure them success in the labor market.

413. Treiman, Donald J. and Kermit Terrell. "Women, Work, and Wages--Trends in the Female Occupational Structure Since 1940," in Kenneth Land and Seymour Spilerman, eds., Social Indicator Models, NY: Russell Sage, 1975, pp. 157-202. (3)

The main finding of this 1940 to 1960 study was that basically the occupational structure was similar for both sexes. Generally, men and women in the same occupation had the same characteristics and received the same high or low rewards as compared to persons of the same sex in other occupations. This was true in spite of some differences, such as women working shorter hours and receiving lower pay than men. To a striking extent, however, men and women were distributed differently across jobs, with women being concentrated in jobs that required high skills but were paid badly. These are the facts which, more than two decades later, fuel advocacy of wage equity legislation.

414. Tully, Judy C., Cookie Stephan, and Barbara J. Chance. "The Status and Sex-Typed Dimensions of Occupational Aspirations in Young Adolescents." SSQ 56, 4 (Mar. 1976): 638-49. (3)

This study finds that sex-typing, which is not unrelated to prestige and especially income, has a very strong influence on occupational choice, not influenced by maternal employment, IQ, or grades in school. This is particularly true among white adolescents from high socio-economic status families with a larger number of children. The authors suggest that had they had data on the mother's satisfaction with her job, this variable might have been significant, but they apparently did not consider introducing the mother's occupation.

415. Waite, Linda J. and Sue E. Berryman. "Occupational Desegregation in CETA Programs," in Barbara F. Reskin, Sex Segregation in the Workplace. Trends, Explanations, Remedies. Washington, D.C.: National Academy Press, 1984, pp. 292-307. (4)

Examining CETA's record is considered important as a test case of how much such a program is likely to accomplish, should it be attempted again in the future. The record is not impressive. Of those in CETA jobs, 80 percent of women and 67 percent of men were in the four occupations where unsubsidized workers had the lowest wages, and high unemployment rates. CETA did not alter the percentage of women in lower wage occupations, and their wages were consistently lower than those of men in the same occupation, though the difference was only 10 percent. The authors point out a number of serious issues that would need to be considered if a similar program were to be revived.

416. Waldman, Elizabeth K. and Beverly J. McEaddy. "Where Women Work--An Analysis by Industry and Occupation." MLR 97, 5 (May 1974): 3-13. (3)

Even though women have tended to find jobs disproportionately in the fastest growing industries, primarily service industries, their employment distribution in

1970 was found to bear a striking resemblance to that existing as much earlier as 1940.

Wallace (1976) See item 688.

417. Weisskoff, Francine B. "'Women's Place' in the Labor Market." AER 62, 2 (May 1972): 161-66. (3)

This paper, after acknowledging the substantial rise in women's labor force participation, focuses on occupational segregation, its causes and effects. The author concludes that the elimination of substantial segregation is essential for the achievement of equality, and that "separate but equal" is no more valid for women than for other groups.

418. Williams, Gregory. "The Changing U.S. Labor Force and Occupational Differentiation by Sex." Dem. 16, 1 (Feb. 1979): 73-87. (3)

The degree of occupational differentiation by sex is examined for the period 1900-1970. Using comparable occupations over time, rather than trying to cover all as Gross (1968) did, this author finds a small and irregular but measurable decline in differentiation. He ascribes this not to existing labor force structure, but rather to social and historical factors that have influenced specific occupations in certain decades.

419. Wilson, R. Mark. "An Analysis of Initial Occupational and Educational Choices of Black and White Men and Women." RBER 15, 2 (Winter 1980): 28-65. (3)

This study, using National Longitudinal Survey data, finds that determinants of choice of occupation and education, which are assumed to be made jointly, differ by race as well as by sex. Further research on this subject, preferably with additional variables not available for this study, such as mother's education and occupation, and with more detailed occupational categories, would be very interesting.

420. Zalokar, Nadja. "Generational Differences in Female Occupational Attainment--Have the 1970's Changed Women's Opportunities?" AER 76, 2 (May 1986) 378-81. (3)

Most work on the occupational distribution of women has used data on persons who came of age in the 1940's or 1950's. This paper seeks to determine whether there is evidence of significant changes for younger women by comparing cohorts who were 30-38 in 1967 and in 1982, respectively. Members of the younger group show greater labor force attachment and are more likely to enter more skilled, "less female" jobs, particularly by the time they reach their thirties. The data also show that these young women were more likley to enter more "male" occupations than can be explained by the change in labor force attachment alone, suggesting that it had become easier to enter non-traditional jobs.

Zellner (1972) See item 690.

421. Zellner, Harriett. "The Determinants of Occupational Segregation," in Cynthia B. Lloyd, ed., Sex, Discrimination and the Division of Labor, NY: Columbia University Press, 1975, pp. 125-45. (3)

A model is developed to predict occupational affiliation, but it is not very successful. The author concludes that, among other explanations, it is possible that discrimination plays a role. It is suggested that a good deal of further work needs to be done to develop a satisfactory explanation of occupational segregation. This remains true even today.

Chapter 5

EARNINGS AND THE FEMALE-MALE PAY GAP

When discussing occupational distribution it quickly becomes obvious that this subject is of concern in large part because it is related to men's and women's earnings. The main unresolved issue with respect to both occupations and earnings is to what extent differences in outcomes are explained by differences in human capital, determined by voluntary choice, as opposed to labor market discrimination. Hence it is clear that occupations, earnings, and discrimination are subjects that cannot be considered except in relation to each other. Nonetheless, a separate section is devoted to each, with due recognition that there are substantial overlaps.

The main focus in this section is on work concerned with explaining earnings, and particularly differences in earnings by sex. Most often multiple regressions are used with a measure of earnings as the dependent variable. Characteristics of workers, and frequently direct measures of productivity are included among the independent variables. Models which use extensive measures of human capital, and fairly detailed occupational categories, often succeed in explaining a substantial portion, though not all, of earnings differentials. They may, however, be challenged because they simply take these variables as given.

The situation with respect to human capital is complicated by feedback effects. How much parents invest in a child, how much training and education a young person chooses to get, how much time an individual spends in the labor market, are all likely to be influenced by expected earnings. The division of responsibilities between husband and wife is likely to be influenced by their relative wages. Regrettably, we know very little about the magnitude of these affects. As for occupational categories, it has been argued that they should not be included because they should have no explanatory function beyond the different amounts of human capital they require. But this line of reasoning overlooks such other aspects of jobs as work environment, risk, etc., which would be expected to influence earnings. Thus a number of issues remain unresolved.

The situation is simpler when it comes to a consideration of the actual earnings gap. We have good data that enable us to measure the ratio of weekly as well as annual earnings of female as compared to male workers, and to observe how these figures have changed over time. But even here there are differences in interpretation. Optimists point to the fact that the ratio for annual earnings has risen from 58.9 percent in 1977 to 64.5 percent in 1985, and for weekly earnings from 61.3 percent in 1978 to 68.2 percent early in 1985. Pessimists point out that the ratio for annual earnings was 63.9 percent in 1955 (no weekly data were available then), almost as high as that reached in 1986, and that this country continues to lag behind a number of other advanced industrialized nations, where women workers earn in excess of 80 percent as much as men. This last fact does, however, have its bright side. If other countries have been able to make such progress, there should be hope for the U.S. as well.

422. Abowd, John M. and Mark R. Killingsworth, "Sex, Discrimination, Atrophy, and the Male-Female Wage Differential." _IR_ 22, 3 (Fall 1983): 387-402. (3)

The atrophy hypothesis, tested in this research, claims that individuals may be observationally identical in terms of a particular set of characteristics, but at the same time be different in terms of unmeasured characteristics, because their skills deteriorated during periods when they were out of the labor market. No evidence for this argument was found. The authors conclude this may be the case because in controlling for a large number of variables that reflect characteristics and tastes, these are likely to include factors which influence the continuity or intermittence of labor force participation. The data set used provided unusually comprehensive information about a sample of 2,000 employees of a travel and insurance company.

Ahern and E. L. Scott (1981) See item 723.
Allison (1976) See item 724.
Almquist (1975) See item 341.
Antonello and Coglioni (1977) See item 837.

423. Applebaum, Eileen and Ross Koppel. "The Impact of Work Attitudes Formed Prior to Labor Market Entry on the Process of Early Labor Market Attainment" in Paul J. Andrisani, Eileen Applebaum, Ross Koppel and Robert Miljus, eds. _Work Attitudes and Labor Market Experience_, N.Y.: Praeger Publishers, 1978. (3)

Attitudes were not found to have any effect on the supply of labor of young women 19 to 24 years of age, perhaps showing that at this age career orientation is as likely to keep them in school and out of the labor market as to make them enter the labor market instead of becoming a full-time homemaker. Career commitment is, however, related to lower earnings among those who are employed supporting the human capital hypothesis which suggests young workers with long-run labor force commitment would accept jobs with steeper lifetime earnings profiles.

424. Asher, Martin and Joel Popkin. "The Effect of Gender and Race Differentials on Public-Private Wage Comparisons: A Study of Postal Workers." ILRR 38, 1 (Oct. 1984): 16-25. (3)

A comparison of wages of white men in the postal service and in the private sector show them to be about the same. But the postal service follows a nondiscriminatory wage policy, so that other race-sex groups are paid better, and average wages are higher there than in the remainder of the economy.

425. Barry, Janis. "Women Production Workers: Low Pay and Hazardous Work." AER 75, 2 (May 1985): 262-65. (3)

The author suggests that to the extent women have been in production jobs they have done low-pay and hazardous work. The model used to investigate the hypothesis that women receive lower rewards than similarly qualified men assumes a segmented labor market. The results suggest that men, but not women are compensated for higher risks. On the contrary, women earn less as their work is more hazardous, and this holds in the primary as well as the secondary labor market sector. This may well reflect women's inferior bargaining power.

Bartlett and T. I. Miller (1985) See item 729.
Bartlett and Moser (1974) See item 730.

426. Bassi, Lauri J. "The Effect of CETA on the Postprogram Earnings of Participants." JHR 18, 4 (Fall 1983): 539-56. (4)

A careful examination, which gives particular attention to avoiding selection bias, finds that no one of the various CETA programs was more beneficial to participants than others, but that they all had a positive effect on earnings, and more so for women than men.

Bayer and Astin (1968)(1975) See item 732.

427. Becker, Gary S. "Human Capital, Effort, and the Sexual Division of Labor." JLE 3, 1 (Jan. 1985 Suppl.): S33-S58. (1)

This paper begins with insights one might expect from a seasoned feminist: 1. The evidence suggests that women would earn less, even if their labor force participation were equal to that of men. 2. This is because they do the bulk of housework, even when they work full time. 3. Even a small amount of discrimination can be transformed into a large difference in total outcome. 4. Wives may have to focus on housework because exploited persons are not allowed to participate in activities that undermine their exploitation. After that promising start, the author goes on to set up an elaborate model based on the assumption that women not only spend less time in the labor market, but spend less energy per unit of time on paid work--for which he provides not a shred of evidence--because they continue to do long hours of housework. Bielby, D. B. and Bielby, W. T. (1985) provide evidence suggesting that women actually spend more effort than men on their market work.

428. Behrman, Jere R., Robin C. Sickles and Paul Taubman. "The Impact of Minimum Wages on the Distribution of Earnings for Major Race-Sex Groups: A Dynamic Analysis." AER 74, 4 (Sep. 1983) 766-78. (3)

Though estimates are based on data from truncated earnings distributions and must therefore be viewed with some caution, they indicate that dynamics are important in determining the impact of the minimum wage on earnings distributions. Long-run effects tend to be far larger than short-run effects. A great deal of time appears to be required for labor market adjustments. Hence previous studies focussing on current static effects have not been useful. The results of this study suggest that, in the long run there have been both positive and negative effects for the groups who were supposed to benefit. The authors conclude that the negative effects, especially for the most disadvantaged groups, have been dominant.

429. Bell, Carolyn S. "Comparable Worth: How Do We know It Will Work?" MLR, 108, 12 (Dec. 1985): 5-12. (4)

The author answers the question she poses in the title with a definite "we do not." She claims comparable worth has no basis in law, is difficult to define, and essentially takes us back to a concept of "just price." Nonetheless, she recognizes that there well may be a problem of discrimination and that the proponents of comparable worth have brought this to the attention of the public to a greater extent than was previously the case.

430. Beller, Andrea H. "The Impact of Equal Opportunity Laws on the Male/Female Earnings Differential," in Cynthia Lloyd, Emily S. Andrews and Curtis L. Gilroy, eds., Women in the Labor Market, N.Y.: Columbia University Press, 1979, pp. 304-30. (4)

This paper tests the hypothesis that Title IX was effective in widening curricula opportunities for women, causing more of them to go on to higher education, and therefore had a particularly strong favorable effect on younger cohorts of women. The results of this study confirm the hypothesis.

431. Beller, Andrea H. "The Effect of Economic Conditions on the Success of Equal Employment Opportunity Laws. An Application to the Sex Differentials in Earnings." RES 62, 3 (Aug. 1980): 379-87. (4,3)

But for the worsening of economic conditions, the effectiveness of equal employment opportunity laws in the 1970's would have been greater, according to this author. She concludes that the real earnings cost was greater, and the earnings redistribution smaller because of the high unemployment rate, but that Title VII nonetheless narrowed the sex differential in earnings.

Beller (1982a) See item 344.
Bergmann (1973) See item 347.

432. Bielby, Denise D. and William T. Bielby. "She Works Hard for the Money: Household Responsibilities and the Allocation of Effort." Paper presented at the 1985 Annual Meetings of the American Sociological Association, D.C. (3)

The authors test a recent version of the human capital theory (Becker, G. S. 1985), claiming that an additional reason for women's lower earnings is that they spend less energy on their paid work because of their greater household responsibilities. Using data from the 1977 Quality of Employment Survey, they find that women actually report slightly more effort. They further point out that psychologists have conducted experiments which showed that women tend to underestimate their effort as compared to men.

433. Bloom, David E. and Mark R. Killingsworth. "Pay Discrimination Research and Litigation: The Use of Regression," <u>IR</u> 21, 3 (Fall 1982): 318-39. (2)

The authors recount the history of the use of regressions in litigation, a relatively recent phenomenon, explain its methodology in relatively simple terms, and briefly discuss some of the problems associated with this approach.

434. Borjas, George J. "The Politics of Employment Discrimination in the Federal Bureaucracy." <u>JLawE</u> 25, 2 (Oct. 1982) 271-300. (3)

Recent studies suggest that minorities and women employed by the federal government have substantially lower earnings than "similar" white males, though the difference is somewhat less than that found in the private sector. This study examines differences between various government agencies, and finds they are substantial. The earnings gap is smaller for women and minorities respectively when members of that group are well represented among the constituancy of a particular agency. These findings support a political approach to government behavior, and suggest characteristics of the employer, not just the employee help to determine wages.

435. Borjas, George J. "The Measurement of Race and Gender Wage Differentials: Evidence from the Federal Sector." <u>ILRR</u> 37, 1 (Oct. 1983): 79-91. (3,2)

By focussing on interagency variations in wage differentials in the federal government, the author shows that the use of a simple dummy variable for race or gender tends to produce a downward bias in estimates of the wage differential. The author also finds that differentials by race have a positive correlation to those by gender, and that black females are more negatively affected by their gender than by their race.

436. Bridges, William P. and Richard A. Berk. "Sex, Earnings and the Nature of Work: A Job-Level Analysis of Male-Female Income Differences." SSQ 58, 4 (Mar. 1978): 553-65. (3)

A sample of white-collar workers is used to decompose the earnings gap into components related to differences in employee qualifications, job characteristics, and ways the variables are translated into earnings. All three are found to contribute, the second more than the first, but most of all the third. This study pioneered the use of specific job characteristics.

437. Brown, Gary D. "How Type of Employment Affects Earnings Differences by Sex." MLR 99, 7 (July 1976): 25-30. (3)

The author concludes that in private employment there is a substantial difference between white men and white women in returns to investment in human capital, continuous employment, and experience. He further suggests that it is most likely unequal opportunities for advancement on the job that cause the problem.

438. Brown, Randall S., Marilyn M. Moon and Barbara S. Zoloth. "Incorporating Occupational Attainment in Studies of Male-Female Earnings Differentials," JHR 15, 1 (Winter 1980a): 3-28. (3)

The authors' previous work (Brown, Moon and Zoloth, 1980) showed that if women faced the same structure of occupational determination as men, there would be many more women in managerial and skilled labor jobs and many fewer in clerical and service occupations. Using this occupational distribution, regression estimates of wages as a function of productivity measures show that only 14-17 percent of the differntial is attributable to differences in endowments.

Brown, R. S., Moon and Zoloth (1980b) See item 356.

439. Buchele, Robert and Mark Aldrich. "How Much Difference Would Comparable Worth Make?" IR 24, 2 (Spring 1985): 222-33. (1,3)

Using a model of employment and earnings which specifies that workers' earnings are determined primarily by the requirements or characteristics of their jobs, rather than human capital of the workers themselves, the authors conclude that instituting equal pay for work of comparable worth would virtually eliminate the male-female pay gap. They point out, however, that their sample of young men and women from the National Longitudinal Surveys is not only unrepresentative of older workers, but also tends to be limited to white, full-time workers. Further, it ignores any possible direct effect of human capital variables, as well as the fact job requirements are not always precise. Last, but not least, the study ignores working conditions.

440. Buckley, John E. "Pay Differences Between Men and Women in the Same Job." MLR 94, 11 (Nov. 1971): 36-39. (3)

This is a 1971 follow-up on McNulty's 1967 study, examining all but one of the same occupations. The conclusion is also the same, that sex segregation by firm tends to make a substantial contribution to the male-female earnings gap.

441. Bureau of National Affairs, Inc. "Pay Equity and Comparable Worth," A BNA Special Report, 1984. (3,4)

This report provides a thorough review of various studies and surveys exploring the subject of equal pay for work of comparable value. Included is information on relevant legal developments, actions by various levels of government, and different interest groups, including businesses. The concluding section provides predictions for the future by a number of different persons prominently associated with this controversial issue. A wide variety of views is represented.

442. Burstein, Paul. "Equal Employment Opportunity Legislation and the Income of Women and Nonwhites." ASR 44, 3 (June 1979): 367-91. (4)

This study examines the impact of equal employment opportunity legislation on the earnings of nonwhite men, nonwhite women, and white women, as compared to white men. It is unusual in that it takes into account attitudes toward minorities and women as revealed in relevant questions recurrently asked in national surveys. Unfortunately, changes in these were so highly correlated with changes in education that the author was unable to disentangle them. Nonetheless, the model constructed in this paper works well for nonwhites, but not at all for white women. Thus one conclusion of the study is that there are important differences between race and sex discrimination.

443. Cabral, Robert, Marianne A. Ferber and Carole A. Green. "Men and Women in Fiduciary Institutions: A Study of Sex Differences in Career Development." RES 32, 4 (July 1979): 451-64. (3)

An investigation of three large fiduciary institutions shows that the differential in earnings between male and female employees within detailed occupations are far greater than justified by differences in measured characteristics. This is true even though all jobs are white collar, and, with few exceptions, require no advanced education or specialized training in previous jobs. Further, the size of the earnings differential varies considerably between the three institutions, suggesting capricious discrimination rather than a rational response to unmeasured characteristics.

444. Cain, Glen G. "Welfare Economics of Policies Toward Women." JLE 3, 1 (Jan. 1985, Suppl.): S375-S396. (4)

The rationale for government intervention on behalf of women is examined from the point of view of efficiency, involving issues of market failure and discrimination, and from the point of view of equity, involving the economic well-being of women as compared to men. The author concludes there is no strong case for the former because, in his view neither economic theories nor measures of discrimination demonstrate there would be efficiency gains. He also concludes, however, that a strong case can be made on equity grounds, especially since he finds that, over the life-cycle as a whole, women are poorer than men, according to the customary measures of income. He believes this situation to be chiefly the result of lingering traditional attitudes toward men's and women's roles.

Chapman, B. J. and Harding (1985) See item 858.
Chiplin, Curran and Parsley (1980) See item 860.
Chiplin and Sloane (1976a)(1976b) See items 862 and 863.

445. Chiswick, Barry R. "Immigrant Earnings Pattern by Sex, Race, and Ethnic Groupings." MLR 103, 10 (Oct. 1980): 22-25. (3)

Earnings for immigrant women vary considerably by racial and ethnic group, according to a study based on 1970 data. The author's theory that self-selection causes most immigrants to be highly motivated so that in time they will overtake the native-born is even more relevant for women than for men. While immigrant men initially earn less than those born in the U.S., white immigrant women earn more from the beginning, and those from other ethnic groups earn as much as their U.S.-born counterparts within 5 years. Interestingly, children of immigrant men or women also earn more than those with native-born parents.

446. Coe, Richard D. "Absenteeism from Work" in Greg J. Duncan and James N. Morgan (eds.). Five Thousand American Families--Patterns of Economic Progress, Vol. VI, Ann Arbor: Institute for Social Research, University of Michigan, 1978, pp. 195-230. (3)

Evidence from the Michigan Panel Study of Income Dynamics shows that there are some differences between race-sex groups in absenteeism because of illness of spouse and children, though not much because of their own illness. In some cases women are penalized for these differences, but the effects do not appear to be great. These findings point in the same direction as M. S. Hill's (1978) investigation: that the direct effect of family responsibilities on women's earnings is not likely to be very large.

447. Cohen, Cynthia F. "The Impact on Women of Proposed Changes in the Private Pension System: A Simulation." ILRR 36, 2 (Jan. 1983): 258-70. (4)

This study estimates the effects on pension benefits received by women that would result from some of the changes recommended by the President's Commission on Pension Policy in 1981. First, two simulation models are linked to present barriers to the attainment of benefits by women, such as low levels of coverage in many industries with large numbers of women, requirements for many years of service, the frequent exclusion of part-time workers, etc. The benchmark estimates obtained are then compared with the results when each of the barriers is removed. In three of the five cases significant improvements were found.

448. Cohen, Malcolm S. "Sex Differences in Compensation." JHR 6, 4 (Fall 1971): 434-47. (3)

Relying on data for full-time workers 22 to 64 years old from the University of Michigan 1969 Survey of Working Conditions, this study makes adjustments for age, education, tenure in current job, union membership, absenteeism, a dichotomy for professional and other occupations, and, unlike most other studies, fringe benefits. These adjustments reduce the wage gap from 45 percent to 29 percent of male earnings, even though taking fringe benefits into account tends to increase the differential. Like, for instance, Gwartney and Stroup (1973), Cohen ascribes the remainder of the gap to differences in on-the-job training and women's own job preferences, discounting the possibility of discrimination. For a different view see, for instance, Sawhill (1973).

449. Conte, Michael. "Labor Market Discrimination Against Women," in Greg J. Duncan and James N. Morgan, eds. Five Thousand American Families--Patterns of Economic Progress, Vol. 4, Institute for Social Research, University of Michigan, 1976, pp. 257-84. (3)

Like so many other studies, this one found that male-female earnings differentials could not be fully explained by taking into account such variables as education, experience, etc. The author suggests, but provides no evidence, that some of the remainder is explained by differences, in taste, though he recognizes that discrimination may also play a role, in part through lack of equal access to jobs and promotions. In general, the standard assumptions are uncritically accepted in this research, and the discussion of discrimination is overly simple.

450. Cook, Alice H. "Equal Pay: Where Is It?" IR 14, 2 (May 1975): 158-77. (4)

A brief, but far-ranging review of issues and policies relevant to the goal of bringing about equal pay for women in the United States and other countries.

Corcoran (1978a) See item 206.

451. Corcoran, Mary E. "Work Experience, Work Interruptions, and Wages," in Greg J. Duncan and James N. Morgan, eds. Five Thousand American Families--Patterns of Progress, Vol. 6, Institute for Social Research, University of Michigan, 1978b, pp. 47-103. (3)

This research used Panel Study of Income Dynamics data which are not restricted by age as is true of the National Longitudinal Survey, the only previous data to provide information on work experience. Unlike Mincer and Polachek (1978), Corcoran finds that interruptions have little or no long run effect on earnings, except for women who were out of the labor market directly after leaving school. She also found that white men get substantially greater rewards for experience, mainly because they tend to have considerably longer tenure in their present job, and because they are likely to work full time. Even with all these variables this study accounts for only 36 percent of the gap between white men and women, 27 percent of that between white men and black women. A similar report is found in Lloyd, Andrews, E. S. and Gilroy (1979), pp. 216-45.

452. Corcoran, Mary E. and Paul N. Courant. "Sex Role Socialization and Labor Market Outcomes." AER 75, 2 (May 1985): 275-78. (2,3)

This paper reminds us that the unexplained portion of the male-female earnings gap may be caused by differential socialization as well as labor market discrimination. Socialization of women is likely to influence their choice of occupation, for instance, by making them less confident, providing them with different skills and personality traits, and causing them to internalize traditional sex roles. Socialization and discrimination would be expected to mutually interact in depressing women's earnings. The authors suggest models which allow for such interaction. Such models have the virtue of showing clearly that the effects of discrimination can not be readily separated from the effects of other factors.

453. Corcoran, Mary E., Linda Datcher and Greg J. Duncan. "Information and Influence Networks in Labor Markets," in Greg J. Duncan and James N. Morgan (eds.). Five Thousand American Families--Patterns of Economic Progress, Vol. VIII, Ann Arbor: Institute for Social Research, University of Michigan, 1980, pp. 1-37. (3)

Since other variables do not adequately explain the differences in earnings between white men and the other race-sex groups, this study investigates possible effects of differences in informal information and influence channels used to find work. Not much evidence, however, is found of widespread, long run wage gains from these.

454. Corcoran, Mary E. and Greg J. Duncan. "Work History, Labor Force Attachment and Earnings Differences Between Races and Sexes." JHR 14, 1, (Winter 1979): 3-20. (3)

This article investigates the extent to which differences in work history, on-the-job training, absenteeism, and self-imposed restrictions on work hours and location account for wage differences. The results show that white men tended to have more education and training and less absenteeism than the other race-sex groups, but differences in qualifications explained less than one-third of the gap between white men and black women, one-half between white men and white women and three-fifths between white men and black men.

455. Corcoran, Mary E. and Greg J. Duncan. "Do Women 'Deserve' to Earn Less Than Men?" in Greg J. Duncan et al., Years of Poverty, Years of Plenty. Ann Arbor: Institute for Social Research, 1984, pp. 153-72. (3)

Panel Study of Income Dynamics data are used to investigate whether the female-male earnings gap can be explained by differences in human capital. The conclusion is that this is the case only to a small extent. Only about one-third appears to be attributable to women's greater share in household work. The authors conclude that even far better data would be unlikely to account for the rest. They also suggested that couples could adopt stategies which would enable them to combine family and work roles more efficiently, but believe substantial disparities would remain because of discrimination and differences in socialization.

456. Corcoran, Mary E., Greg J. Duncan and Michael Ponza. "A Longitudinal Analysis of White Women's Wages." JHR 18, 4 (Fall 1983): 497-520. (3)

Like Corcoran (1978), this study again confirms that, contrary to expectations based on human capital theory, interruptions have little effect on women's wages in the long run. Further, wage growth for them is not significantly lower in female than in male occupations. Earnings do increase less, however, among those who work only part time.

Coverman (1983) See item 52.

457. Cox, Donald. "Inequality in the Lifetime Earnings of Women," RES 64, 3, (Aug. 1982): 501-04. (3)

Very little is known about the distribution of women's lifetime earnings, as opposed to current earnings which may be easily obtained from cross-section data. This study uses longitudinal data from Social Security records, and finds that the variation in lifetime earnings of continuous female workers is significantly lower than that derived from cross-section data. Further, it was found that the tendency for lower earnings in early years to be compensated by higher earnings in later life was greater for continuous than discontinuous workers, so that the variation of lifetime earnings is greater among the latter.

458. Cox, Donald. "Panel Estimates of the Effects of Career Interruptions on the Earnings of Women." EI 22, 3 (July 1984): 386-403. (3)

This study uses panel data from Social Security records with up to 23 yearly observations to investigate the effect of intermittent labor force participation on earnings profiles of women. The author can therefore examine the effect of dropping out not only on earnings, afterwards, as for instance Mincer and Ofek (1982) did, but also on earnings before. The latter has been discussed (e.g., Mincer and Polachek, 1974; Sandell and Shapiro, 1978), but not actually observed. The results show that earnings growth is lower in cases where there are future interruptions (but not that they earn more at time of entry). Additionally, it was also found that panel estimates of the earnings effects of experience or time spent out of the labor force are higher than cross-section estimates.

459. Danziger, Sandra K. "Post-program Changes in the Lives of AFDC Supported Work Participants: A Qualitative Assessment." JHR 16, 4 (Fall 1981): 637-48. (4)

Thirty-four recipients of Aid to Families with Dependent Children were interviewed within two years after completing a supported work program. Even though they had not acquired specialized job skills, more than one-third of the sample experienced psychological as well as economic gains. The author concludes that such programs can help to reduce the welfare dependency of families.

460. Danziger, Sheldon. "Do Working Wives Increase Family Inequality?" JHR 15, 3 (Summer 1980): 444-51. (3)

This note, using microeconomic data from the March 1968 and March 1975 Current Population Surveys shows that the earnings of wives have a small equalizing effect on family incomes, to about the same extent in 1967 and in 1974. This was so in spite of the rapid increases in work experience by wives of husbands earning more than average incomes.

461. Dauterine, Jerry W. and Jane E. Jonish. "Wage Differences Among Black and White Career Women." RSE 35, 1 (Apr. 1977): 179-94. (3)

Most attention has been focused on differences in earnings between men and women. This paper focuses on differences among women. Using data for career women, it is shown that human capital and labor market characteristics determine interpersonal variations in wages. They further indicate that differences in endowments and in labor market structure account for most of the discrepancy between black and white women. Thus both supply and demand factors are found to play a part.

462. Daymont, Thomas N. and Paul J. Andrisani. "Job Preferences, College Major and the Gender Gap in Earnings." JHR 19, 3 (Summer 1984): 408-28. (3)

Data from the National Longitudinal Surveys High School Class of 1972 showed that males and females preferred different occupational roles--young men put more emphasis on making money, and the opportunity to achieve leadership roles; young women wanted to be helpful to others, and work with people. They also provided evidence that each group chose different college majors. Analysis indicates that, three years after graduation, between one-third and two-thirds of the earnings gap between them is accounted for by these differences. The problem with this approach is that it accepts the higher rewards for occupations men choose as being non-discriminatory, though that is a controversial issue.

463. DeTray, Dennis N. and David H. Greenberg. "On Estimating Sex Differences in Earnings." SEJ 44, 2 (Oct. 1977): 348-53. (2,3)

In this paper it is argued that the findings of numerous studies that women earn significantly less than men, even when skill-related characteristics are controlled, must be interpreted with considerable care. The authors' main reason for this view is that omitted variables would bias the results. This is true as far as it goes, but assumes first that significant variables are omitted, and further that these would, on balance, bias the results in the direction of overstating rather than understating possible discrimination.

464. Dickinson, Katherine. "Wage Rates of Heads and Wives," in James N. Morgan, Katherine Dickinson, Jonathan Dickinson, Jacob Benns and Greg J. Duncan, eds., Five Thousand American Families--Patterns of Economic Progress, Vol. 1, Institute for Social Research, University of Michigan, 1974, pp. 123-75. (3)

This was the first study to use mental ability as a variable in explaining earnings. Findings show that it influences wage rates primarily via a greater payoff to education. The mechanism was found to be similar for men and women, but females were rewarded far less, not only for education but also for experience and high status occupations. It was further determined that of the many working women in poverty, 55 percent would not have been poor if they had been paid like men.

465. Duncan, Greg J. and Saul D. Hoffman. "On-the-Job Training and Earnings Differences by Race and Sex." RES 61, 4 (Nov. 1979): 594-603. (3)

Direct measures of the effects of training on earnings show that white men receive more than twice as much training as the other race/sex groups, but that all receive proportionate returns to training. An investigation of the determinants for training gives support to both the human capital explanation, but also, especially for women, to the institutionalist view of the process. Data used were from the Panel Study of Income Dynamics. A brief but similar report is Hoffman (1981).

466. Duncan, Greg J. and Saul D. Hoffman. "Dynamics of Wage Changes" in Martha S. Hill, Daniel H. Hill and James N. Morgan, eds., Five Thousand American Families--Patterns of Economic Progress, Vol. 9, Institute for Social Research, University of Michigan, 1981, pp. 45-92. (3)

Unlike cross-sectional data, longitudinal data do not tend to show a smooth curve for lifetime earnings. These findings suggest that factors other than human capital are important in determining earnings. The other major findings of this study were that many more people experience poverty or affluence recurrently than are in either group permanently, and that white men are far more likely to be affluent and far less likely to be poor than minorities and women. More than 10 percent of white men but less than 1 percent of white women and virtually no minorities experienced permanent affluence. Less than 10 percent of white men but 20 percent of black men, one third of white women, and half of black women, were permanently poor.

467. Duncan, R. Paul and Carolyn C. Perruci. "Dual Occupation Families and Migration." ASR 41, 2 (Apr. 1976): 252-61. (3)

This study finds that the husband's occupational prestige and his opportunities for employment elsewhere tend to increase family mobility, but the occupational prestige of the wife and her relative contribution to family income do not. The effect of moving on employed wives tends to be negative, though those who were previously not employed are somewhat more likely to enter the labor market. These conclusions are, on the whole, similar to those reached by Frank (1978).

468. England, Paula, Marilyn Chassie, and Linda McCormack. "Skill Demands and Earnings in Female and Male Occupations." SSR 66, 2 (Jan. 1982): 147-68. (3)

In this study male and female median earnings for full-time, year-round workers are regressed on occupational characteristics, which represent skill demands of the jobs taken from the Dictionary of Occupational Titles. These variables explain 75 percent of the variance in wages. When percent female in the occupation was added, 1 percentage point depressed male wages by $30, female wages, $17. Since, by definition, more women are in female occupations, the net effect of sex composition on wages is to lower women's as compared to men's earnings. It is estimated that 32 percent of the pay gap is explained in this way. Similar results were obtained by Treiman and Hartmann (1981).

469. England, Paula and Steven D. McLaughlin. "Sex Segregation of Jobs and Male-Female Income Differentials," in Rodolfo Alvarez, Kenneth Lutterman and Associates, eds., Discrimination and Organizations, San Francisco: Jossey-Bass, 1979. (3)

The skills required for male and female jobs are to a substantial extent different, but these differences do not help to explain the female-male earnings gap. This is the case because the characteristics generally most rewarded are virtually equally represented in occupations dominated by men and those dominated by women. These issues are explored, with the same results in England, Chassie and McCormack (1982).

470. England, Paula and Bahar Norris. "Comparable Worth: A New Doctrine of Sex Discrimination." SSQ 66, 3 (Sep. 1985): 627-43. (3,4)

Comparable worth discrimination is defined here as a situation that exists when the gender of those doing a job has a net effect on the pay level. This is quite different from the concept of "crowding." Using detailed controls for skill, demands of occupations, this study estimates that 30 percent of the male-female earnings gap is caused by comparable worth discrimination. Aline Quester and Kathleen Utgoff (same issue, pp. 644-49) disagree both with the theoretical formulation and the empirical evidence presented, on the grounds that not all real differences in the occupations are captured, and that competition would not permit such monumental discrimination to persist. England and Norris (pp. 650-53) respond to these criticisms.

471. Farkas, George. "Education, Wage Rates, and the Division of Labor Between Husband and Wife." JMF 41, 3 (Aug. 1976): 473-83. (3)

This paper, relying on data from the Panel Study of Income Dynamics, finds some support for the hypothesis that it is the relative wage rates of husband and wife that determine the division of household labor. However, the net effect of this variable is not very large, and, at least for younger couples, the absolute level of education and the presence of children had a greater effect. The author interprets this to show that behavior is substantially influenced by what is termed the "subculture" to which the family belongs.

472. Featherman, David L. and Robert H. Hauser. "Sexual Inequalities and Socioeconomic Achievement in the U.S., 1962-1973." ASR 41, 3 (June 1976): 462-83. (3)

This paper reports that between 1962 and 1973 occupational and educational achievements of women exceeded those of men, but the ratio of female to male earnings declined slightly. Also, while net returns to education improved more noticeably for women, returns to occupational status have benefited only men. This might lead one to question the usefulness of the way sociologists measure occupational status.

473. Ferber, Marianne A. and Bonnie G. Birnbaum. "Labor Force Participation Patterns and Earnings of Women Clerical Workers." JHR, 16, 3 (Summer 1981): 416-26. (3)

An in-depth case study of women clerical workers at one large institution was conducted to determine the impact on wage rates of years of experience on the one hand, and of periods out of the labor force on the other. Both effects were found to be quite modest. Nor does the timing of interruptions make any difference, except to the extent that valuable experience with current employer is influenced. Overall, however, the effects of individual variables add up, so that there are appreciable differences in earnings. Since the data are from a single institution, they are not necessarily generalizable.

Ferber and Green (1982) See item 749.
Ferber and Kordick (1978) See item 751.
Ferber and Loeb (1973)(1974) See items 752, 753.

474. Ferber, Marianne A. and Helen M. Lowry. "The Sex Differential in Earnings: A Reappraisal." ILRR 29, 3 (Apr. 1976a): 377-87. (3)

A study employing data from the 1970 U.S. Census shows that most of the variance in median earnings of workers in 260 occupations can be explained by the sex composition of the occupation, median years of schooling of workers in the occupation, and the interaction between these two factors. The results suggest that discrimination is likely to be one of the causes of this situation. Paula M. Hudis and David Snyder, ILRR, 32, 3 (Apr. 1979): 378-84, questioned some of the methods employed in this research, but they provide no cause for questioning the basic conclusions.

475. Ferber, Marianne A. and Walter W. McMahon. "Women's Expected Earnings and Their Investment in Higher Education." JHR 14, 3 (Summer 1979): 405-20. (3)

The main purpose of this study was to determine the influence of women's expected earnings on the extent to which they invest in their education, and on their choice of field. It was found that their expectations were unrealistically high, particularly in traditionally male fields. This may help to explain the significant increase in women going on to obtain advanced degrees, and their influx into non-traditional fields, and would, in turn, be expected to lead to further increases in labor force participation. Even so, earnings are likely to fall short of the highly optimistic expectations expressed by these young women.

Ferber and Spaeth (1984) See item 366.

476. Feuille, Peter and David Lewin. "Equal Employment Opportunity Bargaining." IR 20, 3 (Fall 1981): 322-34. (4)

The authors take the view that bargaining is more widely used and is (arguably) more important than litigation as a way of bringing about equal employment opportunity. They go on to examine the process that is used in such cases. This emphasis on bargaining does not mean, however, that public policy is not important in establishing an environment conducive to such efforts, and the threat of enforcement should not be discounted.

477. Filer, Randall K. "Male-Female Wage Differences: The Importance of Compensating Differentials." ILRR 38, 3 (Apr. 1985): 426-37. (3)

An analysis of data from the 1977 Quality of Employment Survey shows that men and women generally hold jobs with substantially different working conditions. The author suggests that men are paid higher wages to compensate for these differences, which in turn contribute significantly to the explanation of the earnings gap. He ignores the problem of the bias injected when the actual rewards for whatever is characteristic of male jobs are higher than for characteristics of female jobs. His conclusion is therefore substantially based on circular reasoning. Similar results were reported in JHR 18, 1 (Winter 1983): 82-99.

Fox (1981)(1985) See items 755, 756.

478. Frank, Robert H. "Why Women Earn Less: The Theory and Estimation of Differential Overqualification." AER 68, 3 (June 1978b): 360-73. (3)

The possibility that wives are paid less than husbands with similar qualifications as a result of following their husband to a particular location is investigated. Evidence that the penalty is greater in smaller labor markets is interpreted as supporting this hypothesis. The author also suggests that differences in male and female productivity related characteristics influence the family decision to give the husband's job precedence rational. Little consideration is given to the possibility that discrimination may play a major role in continuing the vicious circle.

479. Fuchs, Victor R. "Difference in Hourly Earnings Between Men and Women." MLR 94, 5 (May 1971): 9-15. (3)

Beginning with data for nonfarm workers, and adjusting for education, city size, marital status, class of worker and race, the male-female wage gap is reduced from 40 percent to 34 percent of male earnings. After examining evidence on labor force participation, turnover and industry, the author concludes that virtually all of the remainder could be explained by differences in occupation. Not only does this analysis ignore feedback effects, but it also assumes that occupational distribution and earnings differentials between occupations are not themselves influenced by discrimination. Quite a different conclusion is drawn by Sawhill (1973).

480. Fuchs, Victor R. "Women's Earnings: Recent Trends and Long-Run Prospects." MLR 97, 5 (May 1974): 23-26. (3)

The author ascribes the failure of the earnings gap to narrow up to the early 1970's to the large increase in the supply of female labor that had taken place. Such an analysis is, of course, based on the assumption that male and female labor are not close substitutes. This may well be the case, but needs, in turn to be examined. In a similar paper, AER 64, 2 (May 1974): 236-42, emphasis is placed on the inexperience of new entrants, without even considering the possibility that the increased labor force participation is also likely to mean that a larger proportion of women stayed in the labor force without interruption. This is, in fact, what Mallan (1982) found. The author further predicts that in the years ahead women will fare better, as role differentiation diminishes. This does appear to be finally happening in the 1980's, though very slowly.

481. Gleason, Sandra E. "Comparable Worth: Some Questions Still Unanswered." MLR, 108, 12 (Dec. 1985): 17-18. (4)

This paper begins by pointing out that a careful analysis of comparable worth as a national policy has not yet been done, so that many questions remain unanswered. Therefore the author concludes that we know only who will gain or lose, but not by how much. Some would argue that even this conclusion is optimistic.

482. Gold, Michael E. A Dialogue on Comparable Worth. Ithaca, NY: IRR Press, 1983. (4)

This small book touches on most of the pros and cons of the controversial issue of comparable worth, but does so rather superficially. There is little to be learned by someone already reasonably familiar with the subject.

483. Goldfarb, Robert S. and James R. Hasek. "Explaining Male-Female Wage Differentials for the 'Same Job'." JHR 11, 1 (Winter 1976): 98-108. (3)

The authors found that their research does not support the assertion that differences in quit rates explain earnings differences between equally qualified men and women in the same job. This is true when not only quit rates and hiring costs, but differential absenteeism and seniority wage increases are taken into account. The authors point out, however, that their data leave much to be desired, and the analysis could benefit from further elaboration.

Gomez-Mejia and Balkin (1984) See item 763.
Gordon, N. M. and Morton (1976) See item 765.
Gregory, R. G. and Duncan, R. C. (1981) See item 898.

484. Gronau, Reuben. "Wage Comparisons--A Selectivity Bias." JPE 82, 6 (Nov./Dec. 1974): 1119-43. (2)

The author points out that regressions are generally estimated using data on labor force participants. Thus only actual wages are included, while wage offers that were not accepted are excluded, imparting an upward bias to the extent that rejected wages are likely to be lower than those which are accepted. For an alternative view see Lewis (1974).

485. Gunderson, Morley. "Male-Female Wage Differentials and the Impact of Equal Pay Legislation." RES 57, 4 (Nov. 1975): 462-69. (3)

Calculations based on a unique data set enabled the author to determine that male earnings exceeded those of females in positions with identical job descriptions within narrowly defined occupations in the same establishment. The author also concluded that customer, co-worker and employer discrimination all play a part under certain circumstances. Further, no evidence was found that there had been any change since the equal pay legislation was passed. The gap was, however, found to be smaller in firms that were unionized or had an incentive pay system.

Gunderson (1979) See item 901.

486. Gustman, Alan L. and Thomas L. Steinmeier. "The Relation Between Vocational Training in High School and Economic Outcomes." ILRR 36, 1 (Oct. 1982): 73-87. (3)

Using a variety of data sets and methods, the authors find far stronger evidence of positive returns for white females--especially those enrolled in business programs--than for white males. This does not mean, however, that women are paid more than men with equal training, but rather that women without such training are paid less than comparable men.

Haig (1982) See item 903.

487. Halaby, Charles N. "Sexual Inequality in the Workplace: An Employee-Specific Analysis of Pay Differences." SSR 8, 1 (Mar. 1979): 79-104. (3)

This paper extends the work of Malkiel and Malkiel (1973) by examining the differential distribution of men and women across major job classes and hierarchical levels of a firm. The evidence suggests that considerably less of the earnings differential is explained by direct differences in rates of return to human capital, that is to say, wage discrimination, then to unequal distribution across job classes and ranks. These findings are also reported in SF 58, 1 (Sep. 1979): 108-27.

488. Hanoch, Giora and Marjorie Honig. "'True' Age Profiles of Earnings: Adjusting for Censoring and for Period and Cohort Effects." RES 67, 3 (Aug. 1985): 383-94. (3)

Age profiles of white married men and unmarried women ages 40 to 68 are estimated from longitudinal data. After various adjustments are made, male earnings are found to decline later than in other studies--around age 63. Women's employment and earnings increase until the early fifties and begin to decrease in the early sixties. The authors conclude that decline in earnings of both sexes reflects mainly decreases in labor supply beginning in the mid-fifties.

489. Hanushek, Eric A. and John M. Quigley. "Life-Cycle Earning Capacity and the OJT Investment Model." IER 26, 2 (June 1985): 365-85. (3)

The on-the-job training model, never adequately tested before, is carefully examined here. The empirical analysis of patterns of earnings growth of different race, sex and schooling groups provides only scant support for the common specifications of investment patterns and raises questions about the usefulness of the OJT investment model.

490. Harrod, Roy F. "Equal Pay for Men and Women." Economic Essays, London, Macmillan and Co. Ltd., 1952, pp. 42-74. (4)

It is startling to find one of the most eminent economists of his time discussing at length the pros and cons of equal pay for equal work as though there were two sides to the issue. One explanation is that he expected such a law would cause considerable displacement of women from paid occupation. We know now this did not happen, but we also find that the same argument is now used by those who oppose equal pay for work of comparable worth. It should also be noted that the author had a second major concern, namely "the diversion of high-quality women into paid occupations and away from motherhood."

491. Hartmann, Heidi I., ed. Comparable Worth. New Directions for Research, Committee on Women's Employment and Related Social Issues, Washington, DC: National Research Council, 1985. (4,3)

This small book is a sequel to Treiman and Hartmann (1981), providing more information on research relevant to the issue of comparable worth that has already been done, but putting particular emphasis on suggestions for further research. The comprehensive introduction is followed by six papers dealing with various aspects of job evaluation, as well as economic and policy issues related to comparable worth. The paper that stands out particularly is Barbara Bergmann's "The Economic Case for Comparable Worth." She points out that wages influenced by discrimination and other market imperfections cannot be relied upon to lead to an efficient allocation of resources.

492. Henle, Peter and Paul Ryscavage. "The Distribution of Earnings Among Men and Women, 1958-77." MLR 103, 4 (Apr. 1980): 3-10. (3)

While there was a trend toward greater earnings inequality among men, the more unequal distribution among women remained stable during this period. The greater inequality among women is, in part, caused by the low earnings of part-time and part-year workers. Earnings among female full-time, full-year workers are distributed more equally than among comparable males.

493. Hersch, Joni. "Effect of Housework on Earnings of Husbands and Wives: Evidence from Full-Time Piece Rate Workers." SSQ 66, 1 (Mar. 1985): 210-17. (3)

An examination of the effects of a variety of variables on the earnings of 108 married piece rate workers shows that, for the most part they are not the same for husbands and wives. Thus housework has a negative effect on women's earnings, experience has a positive effect. For men, number of children and schooling have a positive effect, age and number of breaks reduce earnings. The main overall conclusion, implied in the author's discussion, is that men's and women's priorities with respect to market and housework continue to be rather different.

494. Hill, Martha S. "Self-Imposed Limit on Work Schedule and Job Location," in Greg J. Duncan and James N. Morgan (eds.). Five Thousand American Families--Patterns of Economic Progress, Vol. VI, Ann Arbor: Institute for Social Research, University of Michigan, 1978, pp. 151-93. (3)

It is usually assumed that married women's tendency to accommodate household demands and husband's career has a substantially negative effect on their earnings. The author finds, however, that evidence from the Michigan Panel Study on Income Dynamics data, provides only scant support for this, because limitations on job location and work hours do not appear to be related to earnings, though geographic mobility is to some extent. Coe (1978) studies the related topic of women's absenteeism from work.

495. Hill, Martha S. "The Wage Effects of Marital Status and Children." JHR 14, 4 (Fall 1979): 19-23. (3)

Research relying on detailed information available from the Panel Study of Income Dynamics finds that, all else equal, marriage has a strong positive effect on men's wages, but no significant effect on women's. These findings, consistent with those of other researchers, may show that married women who opt to remain in the labor market are particularly well motivated, but also that household "responsibilities" do not necessarily have a detrimental effect on work. The situation is different when there are children, which do have a negative effect on mother's earnings. Osterman (1979) obtained similar results. The higher earnings of married men may be caused by greater motivation, or the willingness to pay more to workers whose needs appear greater.

496. Hines, Fred, Luther Tweeten, and Martin Redfern. "Social and Private Rates of Return to Investment in Schooling, by Race-Sex Groups and Regions." JHR 5, 3 (Summer 1970): 318-40. (3)

This study is based on 1959-60 schooling cost estimates and 1959 earnings data from the 1960 Census. Aggregated over all schooling groups, social rates of return were calculated to be 15.1 for white males, 10.2 for other males, 6.4 for white females, and 10.3 for other females. These calculations are, however, based on earnings alone, and totally ignore potential increases in household contributions of more highly educated women. The same is true of Hoffer (1973).

497. Hodson, Randy and Paula England. "Industrial Structure and Sex Differences in Earnings." IR 25, 1 (Winter 1986): 16-32. (3)

In a model which explains 68 percent of the inter-industry variation in male earnings and 91 percent in female earnings, a principal determinant of the male-female gap is found to be the smaller number of hours per week and weeks per year that women work. The authors suggest this may be caused by demand or by supply factors. The other variables found to be important are that women work in industries which are less unionized, and are less capital intensive. The authors conclude that distribution by industry clearly plays a role in causing the lower earnings of women.

498. Hoffer, Stefan N. "Private Rates of Return to Higher Education for Women." RES 55, 4 (Nov. 1973): 482-86. (3)

This study estimates the rate of return to various amounts of education under various assumptions of life-time labor force participation. Rates of return to 4 years of college, and in some instances, 1 to 3 years of college, are found to be higher for women than men. It must be noted, however, that this only means that the increase as compared to high school graduates is greater, not that women college graduates earn more, or even as much as men. On the other hand, any possible increases in the value of home production related to education are ignored in this study, as is true of Hines, Tweeten and Redfern (1970).

499. Horvath, Francis W. "Working Wives Reduce Inequality in Distribution of Family Earnings." MLR 103, 7 (July 1980): 51-53. (3)

Despite increasing numbers of wives from higher income families entering the labor force, data for the late 1970's once again showed that their earnings continued to increase equality of the distribution of income. The combined earnings distribution, whether of all husband-wife families, or those in which both spouses work full time, year round, showed more equality than the husband's earnings distribution.

House (1983) See item 914.

500. Huffman, Wallace E. "The Value of the Productive Time of Farm Wives: Iowa, North Carolina, and Oklahoma." AJAE 58, 5 (Dec. 1976): 836-41. (3)

Farm wives allocate their non-household time between farm work and other market work. Using data from the 1964 Census of Agriculture, this study shows that their farm work contributed significantly to farm output, and that the marginal product of their time spent on such work compared favorably with their market wages.

Izraeli and Gaier (1979) See item 917.

501. Jones, Ethel B. and James E. Long. "Human Capital and Labor Market Employment: Additional Evidence for Women." JHR 14, 2 (Spring 1979): 270-79. (3)

This study, using National Longitudinal Surveys data for young and mature women, shows that human capital theory can help to explain not only wages, but also employment. The probability of working increases both with additional education and work experience. It is further shown that studies which do not have actual but rather potential experience, underestimate the importance of this variable.

502. Joussand, Danielle P. "Can Job Evaluation Systems Help Determine the Comparable Worth of Male and Female Occupations?" JEI 18, 2 (June 1984): 473-82. (4)

The author points out that job evaluations have been widely used for several decades, but that they have been manipulated by employers, and used as an instrument for discrimination. She argues, however, that they could also be used to remedy discrimination if various interest groups were represented in the decision making process.

503. Jusenius, Carol L. "The Influence of Work Experience, Skill Requirement and Occupational Segregation on Women's Earnings." JEB 29, 2 (Winter 1977): 107-15. (3)

This work examines two competing explanations of the earnings gap, the first emphasizing differences in experience, the second focusing on occupational segregation, using the 1972 older cohort of women of the National Longitudinal Surveys. As expected, both are found to be important. The author concludes, therefore, that efforts to reduce segregation are useful. She does not consider the question whether occupational segregation itself may, at least in part, be caused by women's lesser labor force attachment.

Jusenius and Scheffler (1981) See item 779.
Kehrer (1976) See item 782.
Kessler (1983) See item 922.

504. Keyfitz, Nathan. "Equity Between the Sexes: The Pension Problem." JPAM 1, 1 (Fall 1981): 133-35. (4)

The author argues that statistically significant differences in longevity should be taken into account in annuity calculations. His reasons are that equal lifetime rather than equal monthly benefits are fairer, and that equal monthly benefits would mean that women, as a class, would be subsidized by men, as a class. For an opposing view, see John R. Chamberlin, JPAM, 3, 1 (Fall 1983): 126, who favors "unisex" tables for annuity calculations. He argues that this approach will provide equal benefits for men and women with equal longevity, making them equal ex post. This author also suggests that fairness should be extended to individuals, rather than groups, and that therefore differences in average longevity for men and women should not be taken into account. Keyfitz, JPAM, 4, 1 (Fall 1984): 120-21, however, rejects the view that any individual who dies relatively young subsidizes those who live longer, and reiterates his original view, which admittedly involves treating men and women not as individuals, but as members of groups.

505. Kiefer, Nicholas M. "Training Programs and the Employment and Earnings of Black Women," in Cynthia B. Lloyd, Emily S. Andrews and Curtis L. Gilroy, eds., Women in the Labor Market, NY: Columbia University Press, 1979, pp. 289-303. (4)

This study finds that the effects of the Comprehensive Employment and Training Act of 1973 were significant and favorable in terms of employment and earnings. The author warns, however, that in spite of his efforts to eliminate selection bias, his results are not as reliable as would be those from a well-designed experiment.

506. King, Allan G. "Is Occupational Segregation the Cause of the Flatter Experience-Earnings Profiles of Women?" JHR 12, 4 (Fall 1977): 541-49. (3)

Using U.S. Census data for the professions, the author examines the relation between experience-earnings profiles of men and women in different occupations, and finds that the difference between the sexes is to only a minor extent the result of the existing pattern of employment. It is, of course, possible, that the situation among other occupations may be different.

Knight and Sabot (1982) See item 924.
Kottis (1984) See item 925.

507. Koziara, Karen S. "Comparable Worth: Organizational Dilemmas." MLR, 108, 12 (Dec. 1985): 13-16. (4)

This paper explores the political, economic, and social implications of comparable worth for public and private employers and for labor groups. The author believes that decisions to support or oppose it are likely to be made on the basis of what the effect will be on the organization concerned, and suggests that there would be both advantages and problems for employers as well as unions, if comparable worth were to be implemented.

508. Landes, Elizabeth M. "Sex Differences in Wages and Employment: A Test of the Specific Capital Hypothesis." EI 15, 4 (Oct. 1977): 525-38. (3)

Employing 1967 Survey of Economic Opportunity data, the author estimates that at least two-thirds of the male-female earnings differential is accounted for by sex differences in turnover and training. The author herself points out that she made no effort to take account of biases arising from the interaction between discrimination and labor market behavior. This means that the fact women tended to be in jobs with high turnover, possibly because of employer discrimination, is ignored. Further, training is measured by the rate of wage growth experienced by white men. This is debatable, since increases in earnings may, at least in part, be rewards for seniority.

Langwell (1982) See item 785.

509. Lazear, Edward. "Male-Female Wage Differentials: Has the Government Had Any Effect?" in Cynthia B. Lloyd, Emily S. Andrews and Curtis L. Gilroy, eds., Women in the Labor Market, NY: Columbia University Press, 1979, pp. 331-51. (4)

It was found in this study, which employed data from the National Longitudinal Surveys for the years 1968-69 and 1973-74, that there was a substantial narrowing of the male-female wage differential for young cohorts, and that this was mainly the result of an increase in the rate of wage growth for women. The author concludes that government policies designed to improve the market position of minorities and women may well have contributed to this development.

510. Levine, Victor and Peter R. Moock. "Labor Force Experience and Earnings: Women and Children." EER 3, 3 (1984): 183-93. (3)

Unlike most studies which simply count years of experience in the labor force, disregarding the number of hours worked, this variable is introduced here, using data from a survey of parents of school-age children in a suburb of New York City. Contrasting the wages of the women in the sample with the wages of their husbands, it was found that differences in the intensity of prior work experience accounted for about half of the sex-related wage gap.

Livernash (1984) See item 646.

511. Long, James E. and Ethel B. Jones. "Part-Week Work by Married Women." SEJ 46, 3 (Jan. 1980a): 716-25. (3)

Research using data from the National Longitudinal Surveys confirms the hypothesis that part-week workers and their employers have less incentive to invest in their on-the-job training than is the case for full-time workers.

Lyon and Rector-Owen (1981) See item 382.

512. Madden, Janice F. "Economic Rationale for Sex Differences in Education." SEJ 44, 4 (Apr. 1978): 778-97. (3)

Analysis of a subset of the 1969 National Longitudinal Survey of young men and women reveals that women experienced greater gains in occupational status and earnings from high school graduation and greater gains in earnings, but lesser improvement in occupational status from attending college. This explains why women were more likely than men to finish high school, but not why they were less likely to go to college. In fact, their participation in advanced education has been increasing since then. It would be interesting to see an update of this study, which would most likely show that young women with advanced degrees are now entering higher status occupations.

513. Mallan, Lucy B. "Labor Force Participation, Work Experience, and the Pay Gap Between Men and Women." JHR 17, 3 (Summer 1982): 437-48. (3)

The major finding of this study is that the rise in female labor force participation rates from 1956 to 1975 did not depress the overall level of experience. Hence, the author argues, other explanations have to be considered to account for the slight increase in the male-female earnings gap during this period.

514. Maranto, Cheryl L. and Robert C. Rodgers. "Does Work Experience Increase Productivity? A Test of the On-the-Job Training Hypothesis." JHR, 19, 3 (Summer 1984): 341-57. (3)

Much of the research done on the male-female earnings gap assumes that on-the-job training increases productivity and, because men obtain more such training, helps to explain their higher earnings. This paper, using data on wage claims investigations of a state labor department, tests this assumption. Productivity of the investigator is measured as the fraction of wages an employer allegedly owes an employee which is actually collected. Estimates suggest that investigators become significantly more productive for the first six years on the job. This suggests that on-the-job training is valuable, though for how long would surely vary with the type of job.

515. Maxwell, Nan L. and Ronald J. D'Amico. "Employment and Wage Effects of Involuntary Job Separation: Male-Female, Differences." AER 76, 2 (May 1986): 373-77. (3)

Because of rapid technological and other changes, many workers have been displaced. Using National Longitudinal Survey data this study finds that women have greater difficulty recovering their initial labor market position than do men when they lose their job. Female workers tend to be unemployed longer, and experience more wage loss when they do find another job.

McGavin (1983) See item 941.
McLaughlin (1978) See item 386.

516. McNulty, Donald. "Differences in Pay Between Men and Women Workers." <u>MLR</u> 90, 12 (Dec. 1967): 40-43. (3)

This simple tabular analysis of a limited number of office and plant occupations suggests that the earnings gap between men and women in 1966 was considerably smaller within sex integrated firms than between sex segregated firms. This was one of the early findings showing that sex segregation by firm is important. Later studies, such as Blau, F. D. (1977) and Bielby, W. T. and Baron (1984) provided considerably more evidence on this.

517. Meeker, S. E. "Equal Pay, Comparable Work, and Job Evaluation." <u>YLJ</u> 90, 3 (Jan. 1981): 657-80. (4)

This paper concludes that the interpretation the courts have given to Title VII has been excessively narrow. A more reasonable interpretation, it is suggested, should be used to attack wage differentials between largely segregated male and female occupations, even when men and women are not performing substantially equal work. The author, however, also points out that even such a broader policy would only be a partial solution to pay discrimination and occupational segregation.

Megdal and Ransom (1985) See item 794.

518. Mellor, Earl F. "Investigating the Differences in Weekly Earnings of Women and Men." <u>MLR</u> 107, 6 (June 1984): 17-28. (3)

A study using Bureau of Labor Statistics weekly earnings data shows that age and education make a small contribution toward explaining the male-female earnings gap, that occupations are considerably more important, and that hours worked are important even when comparing full-time workers.

Michael (1985) See item 122.

519. Milkovich, George T. "The Male-Female Pay Gap: Need for Reevaluation," <u>MLR</u> 104, 4 (Apr. 1981): 42-44. (3)

The author of this brief note accepts the evidence that discrimination may in part be responsible for the male-female earnings gap, and is concerned why female jobs pay less than male jobs. He therefore considers comparable worth as a way to remedy this situation. Further, he believes it may be possible to develop a taxonomy of work components that would enable us to determine comparable worth. It is rather surprising that he then claims that such a policy might well fail to reduce the earnings gap. No explanation for this conclusion is offered.

520. Mincer, Jacob and Haim Ofek. "Interrupted Work Careers: Depreciation and Restoration of Human Capital." JHR 17, 1 (Winter 1982): 3-24. (3)

This study uses data on married women from the National Longitudinal Surveys to show that real wages are lower at reentry than at the time of labor force withdrawal, and that the decline is greater as the interruption is longer. It is also shown that wages increase rapidly after reentry, but never quite catch up. The authors ascribe the decline and partial restoration to depreciation and "repair" of human capital. Corcoran (1978), on the other hand, suggests that the negative effect of interruptions is primarily due to loss of knowledge of and contacts in the market.

521. Mincer, Jacob and Solomon W. Polachek. "Family Investments in Human Capital: Earnings of Women." JPE 82, 2 (Mar.-Apr. 1974): S76-S108. (2,3)

This was the first study to use longitudinal data to investigate the earnings gap, specifically among white men and women, ages 30 to 44. Further, a two-stage procedure was used to avoid the problems of joint determination of earnings and experience. Nonetheless their most interesting finding, that skills depreciate considerably during interruptions, has been successfully challenged (see Corcoran and G. J. Duncan, 1979; E. B. Jones and J. E. Long, 1979). Question has also been raised about possible inappropriate use of endogenous variables (Sandell and Shapiro, 1978). Thus, such surprising results as a negative relation between wage rate and labor force participation, have not been given general credence, even after Mincer and Polachek defended their model, JHR 13, 1 (Winter 1978): 118-34.

522. Moore, William J., Douglas K. Pearce and R. Mark Wilson. "The Regulation of Occupations and the Earnings of Women." JHR 16, 3 (Summer 1981): 366-83. (3)

In this study the effect of working in a licensed or certified occupation on earnings is investigated using data for mature women from the National Longitudinal Surveys. There is evidence that licensing increases earnings by about 20 percent after controlling for personal characteristics, but that certification has no statistically significant effect.

523. Moran, Robert D. "Reducing Discrimination: Role of the Equal Pay Act." MLR 93, 6 (June 1970): 30-34. (4)

The author points out that the costs of achieving equal pay through government enforcement and litigation are very high. Nonetheless, he concluded that considerable progress was being made at that time. Today we know, however, that the goal of equal pay for equal work is a narrow one, and that even if it were fully achieved this would, by itself, have little effect on the male-female pay gap.

Moroney (1978) See item 952.
Nakamura, A. O. and Nakamura, M. (1985) See item 282.

524. Niemi, Albert W., Jr. "Sexist Differences in Returns to Educational Investment." QREB 15, 1 (Spring 1975): 17-25. (3)

Returns to education for women are found to be about as high or higher as those for men. This does not, however, mean that women and men have equal earnings when they have equal amounts of education, but rather that the gap is at least as large between poorly educated men and women as between well educated ones.

525. Niemi, Albert W., Jr. "Sexist Earnings Differences." AJES 36, 1 (Jan. 1977): 33-40. (3)

This study shows that earnings differentials have been very costly for females as compared to white males, and especially so for those with a college education. This is less true when women's and men's earnings are compared among blacks. The author's explicit aim is only to estimate the differences, not to explain them. In a later note, AJES, 38, 3 (July 1979): 291-92, he points out that this differential was not intended to represent discrimination.

526. Norwood, Janet L. "Perspective on Comparable Worth: An Introduction to the Numbers." MLR 108, 12 (Dec. 1985): 3-4. (4)

In this introduction to a debate on comparable worth the author, who is Commissioner of Labor Statistics, points out that the earnings gap has been gradually narrowing since the late 1970's, and that the differential virtually disappears if occupation and job level is taken into account. She ascribes the fact that women are at lower levels, perhaps somewhat optimistically, to their recent entry, but does recognize that they continue to be concentrated in low-paying occupations.

O'Neill (1984) See item 964.

527. O'Neill, June. "Role Differentiation and the Gender Gap in Wage Rates." WW 1 (1985a): 50-75. (3)

This paper emphasizes the differences of men's and women's roles in the household as the source of the male-female earnings gap, and suggests that "fertility and other factors have given women a strong comparative advantage in performing housework." The author appears to equate women's unique ability to bear children, not a very time consuming activity today when the average number of children is less than two per family, with the very time consuming activity of rearing children, which can presumably be done by men as well. Beyond that, the author also accepts the view that the unexplained portion of the earnings gap is "a measure of our ignorance" rather than necessarily evidence of discrimination, and that competitive forces in any case provide a self-correcting mechanism.

528. O'Neill, June. "The Trend in the Male-Female Wage Gap in the United States." JLE 3, 1 (Jan. 1985b, Suppl.): S91-S116. (3)

This report makes much of the 1977 to 1983 change in the ratio of female to male annual earnings among those employed year-round, full-time from 58.9 percent to 63.6 percent, and emphasizes the even somewhat higher ratio of weekly earnings of 65.6 percent in 1983. While this trend certainly is encouraging, one need not agree with the author's conclusion that therefore government interference is neither necessary nor even desirable.

Pettman (1975) See item 967.

529. Pfeffer, J. and J. Ross. "Unionization and Female Wage and Status Attainment." IR 20, 2 (Spring 1981): 179-85. (3)

The authors found in their earlier research that unionization has a leveling effect on wages and occupational status among men. Using data, once again, from the National Longitudinal Surveys, an extension of their study to include women leads them to conclude that these findings cannot necessarily be generalized. The effect of unionization among women is not only found to be smaller, but is in the opposite direction.

Pike (1982) See item 391.

530. Pike, Maureen. "The Employment Response to Equal Pay Legislation." OEP 37, 2 (June 1985): 304-18. (4)

This study investigates the substitutability of men and women in order to determine the extent to which women's job opportunities are reduced as their relative wages are raised by legislation. Using time series data, it is found that there is strong competition between part-time females and young males, but little effect on employment prospects of full-time women workers.

531. Polachek, Solomon W. "Discontinuous Labor Force Participation and its Effects on Women's Market Earnings," in Cynthia B. Lloyd (ed.), Sex Discrimination and the Division of Labor, NY: Columbia University Press, 1975b, pp. 451-70. (3)

This study was one of the first to suggest that women's discontinuous labor force participation tends to depress women's earnings, and to interpret this in terms of their not only accumulating less valuable experience, but also skills depreciating during their time out of the labor force. The existence of these effects is not in doubt, but our ability to measure their extent is because of the possible existence of feedback effects, and interaction with employer discrimination. Another paper, IER 16, 2 (June 1975): 451-70, covers much of the same ground.

532. Ragan, James F., Jr. and Sharon P. Smith. "The Impact of Differences in Turnover Rates on Male/Female Pay Differentials." JHR 16, 3 (Summer 1981), 343-365. (3)

The authors, employing data from the Public Use Samples of the 1970 Census and from an unpublished Bureau of Labor Statistics sample show that higher quit rates have a negative effect on earnings of men and women, but more so for women, and that higher layoffs have a positive effect on earnings, but less so for women. They further claim that taking differences in turnover into account therefore substantially increases the portion of the male/female earnings gap that is "explained" by human capital and socioeconomic variables. The authors do not seem particularly troubled by the differences in impact they find, nor by the fact that lower earnings of women are likely to be, at least in part, the cause of the higher quit rates.

533. Reid, Clifford E. "The Effect of Residential Location on the Wages of Black Women and White Women." JUE 18, 3 (Nov. 1985): 350-63. (3)

Two waves from the National Longitudinal Survey of women aged 30 to 44 in 1967 and 40 to 54 in 1977 were used to investigate the effect of residential location on wages of black relative to white women. The results show that after controlling for occupation and industry, wages for black female workers appear to be unrelated to residence. Without these controls, central city black women experienced an advantage in 1967, and a disadvantage in 1977. These findings are consistent with other studies made in the 1960's and 1970's. The author suggests the change may be attributed to the likelihood that suburban blacks are better trained and more ambitious, and hence benefitted more from equal opportunity legislation.

534. Remick, Helen, ed. Comparable Worth and Wage Discrimination: Technical Possibilities and Political Realities, Philadelphia: Temple University Press, 1984. (4,3)

This book aims to encourage discussion, research and formation of legal strategies that will further the adoption and implementation of a well designed comparable worth policy. All contributing authors, though they come from different disciplines and have varying views in other respects, share the opinion that wage disparities between male-and female-dominated occupations in large part are based on discrimination. Individual chapters deal with equal worth as part of equal employment policies, occupational segregation, job evaluation methods, and the factors underlying existing salary structures, as well as the legal issues involved in comparable worth.

535. Remus, Wiliam E. and Lane Kelley. "Evidence on Sex Discrimination: In Similar Populations, Men Are Paid Better Than Women." AJES 42, 2 (Apr. 1983): 149-52. (3)

Using a sample of male and female graduates of the Hawaii College of Business, it was found that women earned 81 percent of the salary earned by men. Taking into account ethnicity, type of job, participation rates, and college major did not explain this salary differential. The authors therefore conclude that discrimination is likely to be the cause.

Richman (1984) See item 809.
Robb (1978) See item 975.
Roos (1981) See item 399.
Roos (1983) See item 978.
Rosenbaum (1985) See item 401.
Rosenfeld (1983) See item 403.

536. Rosenfeld, Rachel A. "Job Changing and Occupational Sex Segregation: Sex and Race Comparisons," in Barbara F. Reskin, ed., Sex Segregation in the Workplace. Trends, Explanations, Remedies, Washington, D.C.: National Academy Press, 1984. (3)

Rosenfeld explores why members of each of the four race-sex groups choose, remain in or move from sex-typical or sex-atypical occupations. Very little of this can be explained by personal characteristics, possibly because the data are not sufficiently detailed, or else because external conditions play a major part. Her data also show that a substantial proportion of workers who change jobs move to or from race or sex atypical jobs, but it must be noted that only a relatively small proportion of the workforce tends to move during any year.

Rytina (1981) See item 404.

537. Rytina, Nancy F. "Earnings of Men and Women: A Look at Specific Occupations." MLR 105, 4 (Apr. 1982): 25-31. (3)

This paper provides evidence on the ranking of 250 detailed occupations by earnings, separately for men and/or women. Median earnings for both men and women are shown for only 91 occupations, where substantial numbers of both are represented. Earnings tend to be higher as the proportion of women in the occupation is lower. Further, women, on the average, earn less in all instances where data are available, but the ratio varies from a low of 59.1 for workers in sales, services, and construction, to 93.9 for postal clerks. See also Roos (1981).

538. Rytina, Nancy F. "Comparing Annual and Weekly Earnings from the Current Population Survey." <u>MLR</u> 106, 4 (Apr. 1983): 32-38. (3)

Annual and weekly earnings of men and women in different occupational categories are shown for 1981. Ratios of female to male earnings vary a good deal by occupation but, in a substantial majority of cases, they are higher for weekly earnings. The ratio of female to male weekly earnings is also higher than annual earnings for the labor force as a whole. The former rose from 61 percent in 1978 to 64 percent in 1981, while the latter rose from 59 percent to 60 percent.

539. Sanborn, Henry. "Pay Differences Between Men and Women." <u>ILRR</u> 17, 4 (July 1964): 534-50. (3)

Using 1950 data for annual earnings, standardizing for hours, schooling, race, urban-rural residence, occupation and age, increases the ratio of women's to men's pay from 58 percent to 74 percent. The author further suggests that there is some evidence that part of the remaining differential is accounted for by the greater productivity of male workers, as well as their lower turnover and absenteeism rates. One problem with this study is that it assumes all these factors, including occupational distribution, as given, rather than possibly themselves influenced by discrimination. Sawhill (1973) interpreted similar findings quite differently.

540. Sandell, Steven H. "Women and the Economics of Family Migration." <u>RES</u> 59, 4 (Nov. 1977b): 406-14. (3)

An economic model developed to explain the causes and determine the results of migration is tested using data from the National Longitudinal Survey of Women aged 39 to 49 in 1972. The results show, on the one hand, that the wife's employment is considered in the migration decision, on the other hand, that migration has a positive effect on husband's earnings, but a negative effect on the earnings of wives. This suggests that the wife's job is, after all, only considered of secondary importance.

541. Sandell, Steven H. and Shapiro, David. "The Theory of Human Capital and the Earnings of Women: A Reexamination of the Evidence." JHR 13, 1 (Winter 1978): 103-117. (3)

The authors claim that their improved estimates and more appropriate interpretation show no evidence of greater investment in general training when women reenter the labor force after the birth of the first child, as Mincer and Polachek (1974) suggested. Further, they also estimate the "depreciation" of human capital to be much less during interruptions than the earlier work did. As a result, they explain much less of the male-female earnings gap as caused by differences in human capital.

Sandell (1980) See item 717.

542. Sandell, Steven H. and David Shapiro. "Work Expectations, Human Capital Accumulation, and the Wages of Young Women." JHR 15, 3 (Summer 1980): 335-53. (3)

Using the National Longitudinal Survey data, it is shown that young women who plan to work at age 35 have steeper age-earnings profiles than otherwise similar women who have no such work plans. This is interpreted to show that career plans influence women's decisions which in turn influence their earnings. On the other hand, this study also shows that returns to job tenure do not differ between the two groups.

543. Schlafley, Phyllis, ed. Equal Pay for Unequal Work. A Conference on Comparable Worth. Washington, D.C.: Eagle Forum Education and Legal Defense Fund, 1983. (4,3)

The first three papers are by proponents of comparable worth, but the remainder are by ardent opponents. They consider equal pay for work of comparable worth as either unnecessary, impossible to implement, too costly, destructive of a market economy, or "all of the above." They point out, quite rightly, that not all of the unexplained earnings gap is likely to be caused by discrimination, that the division of labor within the family helps to explain occupational segregation, that job evaluations will not be easy or perfect, and that increasing pay in female occupations will not be costless. They are far less convincing in demonstrating that doing nothing is preferable.

544. Shach-Marquez, Janice. "Earnings Differences Between Men and Women: An Introductory Note." MLR 107, 6 (June 1984): 15-16. (2)

These brief comments contain a useful summary of some of the most serious problems involved in estimating how much of the male-female earnings differential is likely to be caused by discrimination. They serve as an introduction to Mellor (1984) and Sieling (1984).

Shapiro and Stelcner (1981) See item 987.
Siebert and Young (1983) See item 990.

545. Sieling, Mark S. "Staffing Patterns Prominent in Female-Male Earnings Gap." MLR 107, 6 (June 1984): 29-33. (3)

In brief, this paper confirms the fact that earnings differences are rather small between men and women in narrowly-defined jobs, but also reports that relatively few women are found in the higher levels of jobs.

546. Simchak, Morag M. "Equal Pay in the United States." ILR 103, 6 (June 1971): 541-57. (4)

Recent legislation in the United States is reviewed, with special attention to the Equal Pay Act of 1963. The author's optimism, based on a slight narrowing of the earnings gap in 1969, proved to be about a decade premature. It should be noted, however, that she recognized that equal pay for equal work would have limited impact, as long as substantial occupational segregation continues.

547. Simeral, Margaret H. "The Impact of the Public Employment Program on Sex-Related Wage Differentials." ILRR 31, 4 (July 1978): 509-19. (3)

The gross differential between male and female wages was smaller while workers were in the 1971 Public Employment Program than either before or after. The author concluded that even during the program the evaluation of job requirements tended to favor men, but that the wage determination process resulted in more equitable returns to characteristics.

548. Smith, James P. "The Convergence to Racial Equality in Women's Wages," in Cynthia B. Lloyd, Emily S. Andrews and Curtis L. Gilroy, eds., Women in the Labor Market, NY: Columbia University Press, 1979, pp. 173-215. (3)

This is one of the few studies that examines the very rapid closing of the earnings gap between black and white women. Many factors were found to have contributed, including increased similarity in skills and education, the rapid rise in black wages in the South, increased full-time employment of blacks, the substantial decline of domestic service as the primary occupation of black women, as well as affirmative action. It also appears that the recent influx of black women was concentrated among those with relatively higher qualifications, while the opposite was true for white women.

Smith, J. P. and Ward (1984) See item 315.

549. Smith, Sharon P. "Government Wage Differentials by Sex." JHR 11, 2 (Spring 1976): 185-99. (3)

Using a model for estimating the human-capital wage-rate function which does not require detailed information on work history, and data from the 1973 Current Population Survey Tape, this study suggests that women are more highly rewarded in government than in private employment, and increasingly so at a higher level of government.

550. Sorensen, Elaine. "Equal Pay for Comparable Worth: A Policy for Eliminating the Undervaluation of Women's Work." JEI 18, 2 (June 1984): 465-72. (4)

The author argues that firms have not been sex-blind in their determination of female and male wages, but rather have been influenced by social custom. Hence women have been paid less for comparable levels of skill, effort, and responsibility. Proponents of comparable worth argue that perceptions must be changed to correct this situation.

551. Sorensen, Elaine. "Implementing Comparable Worth: A Survey of Recent Job Evaluation Studies." AER 76, 2 (May 1986): 364-67. (4)

Four state-level comparable worth studies, conducted in Iowa, Michigan, Minnesota and Washington are examined, leading the author to conclude that implementing such a policy would eliminate almost half of the male-female earnings gap. She further points out the differences in methodology that have caused other researchers to get different results.

552. Spitze, Glenna D. "The Effect of Family Migration on Wives' Employment: How Long Does It Last?" SSQ 65, 1 (Mar. 1984): 21-36. (3)

Long distance migration is often economically motivated, and generally improves men's employment opportunities. It does, however, often reduce the prospects of married women. Using data from the National Longitudinal Surveys of young and mature women samples, this study shows that such moves do have negative effects on employment status, weeks worked, and earnings, but that they do not last for more than two years. The author does not attribute this to "catching up," but rather to the generally flat earnings profiles of women.

553. Stevenson, Mary H. "Relative Wages and Sex Segregation by Occupation," in Cynthia B. Lloyd, ed., Sex, Discrimination, and the Division of Labor, NY: Columbia University Press, 1975, pp. 175-200. (3)

The empirical work in this paper applies the theoretical framework of the crowding hypothesis (Bergmann 1974) to an examination of occupational categories based on job requirements. The author points out the importance of using groupings that are neither too narrow, nor too broad. The results show both that women are "crowded" into relatively few occupations, and that there is an inverse relationship between occupational concentration and relative wages.

554. Strauss, Robert P. and Francis W. Horvath. "Wage Rate Differences by Race and Sex in the U.S. Labor Market: 1960-1970." Economica, 43, 171 (Aug. 1976): 287-98. (3)

Significant differences in wage rates by race and by sex are found even when industry and occupation are controlled. However, differences within industry and occupation by race diminished over time, those by sex did not, suggesting that it is now mainly adverse employment patterns that reduce earnings of non-whites.

555. Strober, Myra H. and Laura Best. "The Female/Male Salary Differential in Public Schools: Some Lessons from San Francisco 1979." EI 17, 2 (Apr. 1979): 218-36. (1,3)

A theory of sex differences in earnings is developed which emphasizes the role of labor market segmentation. The theory is tested using data for the San Francisco school system in 1979. The evidence shows that sex was a significant determinant for type of school and position of school employees, and that these were more important in determining salaries than human capital variables.

556. Struyk, Raymond J. "Explaining Variations in the Hourly Wage Rates of Urban Minority Group Females." JHR 3, 3 (Summer 1973): 349-64. (3)

Using the usual approach of simultaneity of hours worked and wage rate does not work for urban minority women. The author suggests this is likely to be the case because of their severe family income constraints which make it impossible for them to exercise any choice with respect to work.

Sullerot (1975) See item 1004.

557. Sutter, Larry E. and Herman A. Miller. "Income Differences Between Men and Women." AJS 78, 4 (Jan. 1973): 962-74. (3)

Using evidence from 1967 National Longitudinal Survey data on women aged 30-44 this study concludes that lifetime labor force participation is primarily determined by marital and family status and only secondarily by education. This interpretation, however, ignores the likelihood that education itself influences marital and family status, as well as earnings. Like numerous other studies, this one also shows the relation between labor force participation patterns and earnings.

Swafford (1978) See item 1005.
Swidinsky (1983) See item 1006.
Tahlmann-Antenen (1971) See item 1010.
Takahashi (1975) See item 1011.

558. Treiman, Donald J. "The Work Histories of Women and Men: What We Know and What We Need to Find Out," in Alice S. Rossi, Gender and the Life Course, New York: Aldine Publishing Company, 1985. (3)

This paper suggests that there is much we still do not know about the way differences between men and women in patterns of labor force participation influence their "job trajectories" and earnings over their lifetime. The author points out, for instance, that as of now we do not know whether interruptions reduce women's human capital, as Mincer and Polachek (1974) argue, cause mismatches in jobs when they return to the labor market, as Corcoran, G. J., Duncan and Ponza (1982) suggest, or merely reduce their bargaining power when they have to look for a job while they are not employed, as he suggests.

559. Treiman, Donald J. and Heidi I. Hartmann. Women, Work, and Wages: Equal Pay for Jobs of Equal Value, Washington, DC: National Academy Press, 1981. (4)

A comprehensive and well documented discussion of the reasons why the issue of equal pay for work of comparable worth has come to the fore, and of the problems that might arise if it were to be implemented.

The authors point out various sides of each question, and recognize the promise as well as the difficulties and limitations of this very controversial policy.

560. Tsuchigane, Robert and Norton Dodge. Economic Discrimination Against Women in the U.S., Lexington, MA: D. C. Heath and Company, 1974. (3)

In this work standardized frequency distributions are used. Mean earnings for men with a particular characteristic, say education, are assigned to women with the same characteristic. This procedure is repeated for other characteristics, presumably resulting in an estimate of the earnings differential caused by discrimination alone. There are two difficulties with this approach. First, there is the index number problem. Applying male rewards to female characteristics gives different results than the opposite procedure. Second, there is the possibility of feedback effects, where the existence of discrimination influences worker characteristics.

Tzannatos and Zabalza (1984) See item 1017.
Vansgnes (1971) See item 1019.
Wallace (1976) See item 688.
Weiss and Gronau (1981) See item 337.

561. Wolff, Edward N. "Occupational Earnings Behavior and the Inequality of Earnings by Sex and Race in the United States." RIW 22, 2 (June 1976): 151-66. (3)

This paper, using the 1 in 100 Public Use Samples of the 1960 and 1970 U.S. Population Census, examines differences in earnings between and within occupations by race and by sex. Including part-time workers, men were found to earn more than twice as much as women in both years, and women's earnings were more unequally distributed. Women's occupations were found at the bottom of the earnings scale, but women also earned less within each occupational group except one, and it was the latter that made the greater contribution to the male-female earnings gap.

Chapter 6

DISCRIMINATION

As we have seen, a great deal of work has been done by economists to show that differences between women and men in their own human capital, such as education, training, experience, etc., help to explain existing differences in occupations and earnings. Chapters 2 and 3 encompass publications that shed light on the socialization of individuals that contributes to this situation. Chapters 4 and 5 include much evidence that the resulting disparities in turn contribute to, but do not account for all of the existing occupational segregation or for all of the earnings gap. We now turn specifically to labor market discrimination as a possible additional explanation.

Discrimination may be said to exist when two equally qualified, equally productive workers are not treated equally. An alternative definition, that discrimination exists when two workers who are treated equally are not equally qualified and equally productive has also received some attention.

A number of theories have been developed to suggest why there might be discrimination, whether it is on the basis of sex, race, age, sexual preference, or any other characteristic not directly related to performance in the labor market. One cause for such behavior may be discriminatory tastes on part of employers, customers, or fellow workers. Another possibility is that firms with market power may find it profitable to set lower wage rates for workers who have fewer, or less attractive alternative options. A third theory is that employers without adequate information about the potential productivity of individual workers, tend to judge them by the characteristics of the group they belong to. Last, it has been argued that capitalists benefit from segregating the labor force, and thus keep workers from recognizing their common interest and acting together in concert.

There are a number of variations on these theories. Overcrowding in female occupations, brought about by discrimination against them in other occupations, has been suggested as a cause of lower wages. Institutionalists give a more explicit role to the norms and traditions prevalent in the work place. Radical feminists emphasize the role of traditionally male trade unions as well as male employers in maintaining the power of the "head of the household" in the family. For the most part, these different explanations need not be mutually exclusive, but rather are potentially complementary. To the extent that various types of discrimination interact, there may also be what has been termed "cumulative" discrimination.

In spite of, and perhaps in part because of, the many theories of discrimination, none has gained general acceptance. Most particularly, critics claim that competition should force out firms which discriminate at the expense of efficiency. Such critics also, in some cases, question the very existence of discrimination. They point out that none of the models contain all relevant variables and argue that the extent to which they do not explain all of the existing differences in occupations and earnings, this is merely a measure of our ignorance. Those, on the other hand, who have observed and encountered instances of what they perceive to be discrimination in the real world, and who are familiar with the record of legal convictions and out of court settlements for discrimination in recent decades, are not likely to be so critical of the empirical evidence. They may rather take the view that it is our failure to develop a consistent theoretical framework explaining discrimination that is a measure of our ignorance.

The publications summarized below will enable readers to learn more about the relative merits of the two interpretations. Accepting the existence of discrimination in the long run implies the belief that prejudices may, at times take precedence over profit maximization, and that there is enough market power to make this possible, or even to enable some employers and some workers to benefit from discrimination. Accepting the absence of discrimination implies the belief that there are enough people around who do not discriminate and that the market works well enough so that they can drive out the discriminators.

562. Abowd, John M. and Mark R. Killingsworth. "Sex, Discrimination, Atrophy, and the Male-Female Wage Differential," IR 22, 3 (Fall 1983): 387-402. (3)

The authors use a detailed set of data for a travel and insurance company to test the atrophy hypothesis, defined as the propositon that individuals may be observationally identical in terms of a limited set of measured characteristics at a point in time, but different in important unmeasured characteristics. They find scant support for this "missing variables argument" which is often used to suggest that findings of sex discrimination are likely to have an upward bias.

563. Agarwal, Naresh C. "Pay Discrimination: A Comparative Analysis of Research Evidence and Public Policy in Canada, the United States and Britain." CJWB 18, 2 (Summer 1983): 28-38. (3,4)

This paper provides a very useful review and evaluation of available studies of the extent to which the existing male-female pay gap is explained by discrimination in Canada, Britain and the United States. Equal pay legislation in all three countries is also reviewed. The author concludes that it has not been effective and suggests that broader laws, mandating equal pay for work of equal value, are requried if women and minorities are to make substantial progress in improving their earnings as compared to majority men.

Agarwal and Jain (1978) See item 834.

564. Aigner, Dennis J. and Glen G. Cain. "Statistical Theories of Discrimination in Labor Markets." ILRR 30, 2 (Jan. 1977): 175-87. (1)

The model developed in this paper shows that when blackness itself is considered a negative predictor of ability because the average performance of blacks is lower, each black will be paid less than a white person of equal ability. The same principle of what has come to be called "statistical discrimination" can, of course, apply to women and men.

565. Alexis, Marcus and Marshall H. Medoff. "Becker's Utility Approach to Discrimination: A Review of the Issues." RBPE 12, 4 (Spring 1984): 41-58. (1,3)

The fact that most studies have not confirmed the approach by Becker, G. S. (1957) to discrimination would appear to suggest that existing wage differentials must be generated by a different process. In the absence of better measures, however, such a conclusion cannot be definitive, and many unsettled questions remain.

Allison (1976) See item 724.
Amsden and Moser (1975) See item 726.
Anker and Hein (1985) See item 836.

566. Anonymous. "Academic Freedom and Federal Regulation of University Hiring." HLR 92, 4 (Feb. 1979): 879-97. (4)

The conclusion presented in this article is that the claims of colleges and universities that they are constitutionally protected against government regulation of their hiring and promotion policies are not well founded. Government policy of funding only institutions that comply with federal regulations is judged to be constitutional.

567. Arrow, Kenneth. "Models of Job Discrimination," in Anthony H. Pascal, ed., Racial Discrimination in Economic Life. Lexington, MA: D. C. Heath and Co., 1972: pp. 83-102. (1)

In this paper the neoclassical model of discrimination is extended to include the issue of information costs to the employer who wants to treat workers on the basis of their individual characteristics. If these costs are too high, such an employer may rationally use group averages as a proxy, even in the long run. "The Theory of Discrimination" in Orley Ashenfelter and Albert Rees, ed., Discrimination in Labor Markets, Princeton, NJ: Princeton University Press, 1973, pp. 3-33 is essentially a less technical exposition of the same view. This "perceptual equilibrium model" also introduces a feedback mechanism, where persons who are placed into poorer and lower paying jobs have less incentive to acquire education and skills, and are less likely to become stable employees.

568. Ashenfelter, Orley and Timothy Hannon. "Sex Discrimination and Product Market Competition: The Case of the Banking Industry." <u>QJE</u> 101, 1 (Feb. 1986): 149-73. (3)

This study tests the hypothesis that discrimination will be greater as the degree of market power of the employer increases. The data set, especially constructed, using in part information from the Equal Opportunity Commission, makes possible a detailed examination of the banking industry. The results show a significant negative relationship between market concentration and the relative employment of women in each market, thus confirming the hypothesis. At the same time, no variation between individual firms by market share was discovered.

569. Baldus, David C. and James W. L. Cole. <u>Statistical Proof of Discrimination</u>, NY: McGraw-Hill, 1980. (2)

This book is concerned with the use and interpretation of statistical proofs in discrimination cases. It is, on the one hand, intended to be helpful to lawyers, on the other hand, it tries to give social scientists and statisticians an appreciation of the different functions of quantitative proof, and of "the influence that the law should have over their choices of research design and statistical methodology" when they are working on discrimination cases. The authors also point out that quantitative proof "at best... can provide a presumption by inferring from the general to the particular," and discuss, at considerable length, other problems that frequently arise.

570. Baruch, Grace K. "Maternal Influences Upon College Women's Attitudes Toward Women and Work." <u>DP</u> 6, 1 (Jan. 1972): 32-37. (3)

Alternative hypotheses concerning women's tendency to devalue feminine professional competence were tested using a sample of 86 women college students. The results did not show that male and female competence were differentially evaluated, thus conflicting with Philip A. Goldberg ("Are Women Prejudiced Against Women?" Trans-Action, 5, 5 Apr. 1968: 28-30), whose study was, however, done five years earlier, and used students at a traditionally oriented women's college. Of those who did devalue female competence, most had mothers who did not work, and hence were not exposed to a maternal model of work competence.

Bayer and Astin (1968)(1975) See items 734, 735.

571. Becker, Gary S. The Economics of Discrimination, Chicago: University of Chicago Press, 1957. (1)

This theory, originally developed for race, posits that employers, customers and coworkers may have discriminatory tastes, even when different workers are perfect substitutes in terms of productivity. Employers with such tastes will employ, say, men at higher wages than women, even if it means not maximizing profits. Or, they may pay women less because customers will only buy from them at lower prices, and because male employees have to be compensated for working alongside women.

Critics have suggested, among others: 1. If the majority of employers collude, they may profit from discrimination (Krueger, 1973; Thurow, Lester, Poverty and Discrimination, Washington, D.C.: Brookings Institution, 1969). 2. If discrimination is at the expense of profit maximization, it could presumably not persist in a competitive market (Fujii and Trapani, 1978; Medoff, 1980; Oster, 1975). 3. The theory does not really explain the nature of the process (Shepherd and Levin, S. G., 1973).

572. Beller, Andrea H. "Occupational Segregation by Sex: Determinants and Changes," JHR 17, 3 (Summer 1982b): 371-92. (3,4)

Empirical tests give mixed results for the supply-oriented human capital explanation of occupational segregation, but support the demand-oriented discrimination explanation. Specifically, there is evidence that both Title VII of the Civil Rights Act of 1964 and the federal contract compliance program increased the probability of women workers being employed in male occupations, suggesting that there had been barriers to their entry.

573. Bergmann, Barbara R. "Occupational Segregation, Wages and Profits When Employers Discriminate by Race or Sex." EEJ 1, 2-3 (Apr.-July 1974): 103-10. (1)

While in the model where employers discriminate because of their tastes, segregation of workers is not so much a cause of the earnings differential as a substitute for it, the author here develops a model where it is segregation, and the relegation of women (and minority) workers to a relatively few overcrowded occupations that causes the gap in wages. Further, employers who hire women at low wages will find it profitable to utilize labor intensive methods, causing these workers to be less productive. This "crowding hypothesis" provides a persuasive explanation of the consequences of segregation, but assumes it exists, without explaining its causes. An earlier, somewhat preliminary version of the same theory, applied only to blacks, was proposed in JPE 79, 2 (Mar.-Apr. 1971): 294-313.

574. Bergmann, Barbara R. "Reducing the Pervasiveness of Discrimination," in Eli Ginzberg, ed., Jobs for Americans, Englewood Cliffs, NJ: Prentice-Hall, Inc. 1976. (4)

The author starts from the premise that hierarchical relations among different groups, distinguished by race, sex, religion, etc., are more important in determining the job a person can expect to get than employers' continuing search for talent wherever it might be found. She concludes that only government intervention can change this, and that it would be quite difficult. She also believes, however, that the goals are important enough to be worth the effort.

575. Bergmann, Barbara R. "Discrimination and Unemployment" in Edmond Malinvaud and Jean-Paul Futonssi, Unemploy-

<u>ment in Western Countries</u>, London: Macmillan Press, 1980b, pp. 420-42. (1)

Unlike others, who ascribe higher unemployment rates of minorities and women as compared to white men to their different labor market behavior, a model presented here explains it in terms of labor market segregation, and varying levels in demand deficiency for the individual segments. While the author provides no theoretical explanation for this segmentation, she points to the records of lawsuits brought by workers charging employers and unions with practices denying them access to particular jobs.

576. Bergmann, Barbara R. and William Darity, Jr. "Social Relations, Productivity, and Employer Discrimination." <u>MLR</u> 109, 4 (Apr. 1981): 47-49. (1)

The authors reject the three most common explanations for the hiring of only white males for the best jobs: 1) employer tastes, 2) superior performance of white males, and 3) less variability in qualifications among white males. They focus, instead, on the importance of social relations among people of different race or sex in the workplace, and the connection between productivity and smooth social relations. This explanation helps to make clear why it is so difficult to eliminate discrimination and suggests that more emphasis needs to be placed on educating employees.

577. Bergmann, Barbara and Mary W. Gray. "Economic Models as a Means of Calculating Compensation Claims," in Helen Remick, ed., <u>Comparable Worth and Wage Discrimination</u>, Philadelphia: Temple University Press, 1984. (1,4)

The authors argue that firms practicing sex segregation are inflicting a penalty in the form of lower wages on their employees, but are also taking advantage of the poor labor market alternatives women face as a result of the discriminatory practices of other employers. Assuming one highly paid type of job, and one with lower pay, both of which require the same qualifications, a non-discriminatory firm would hire women for both, but only women would be willing to work in the low-pay job, because men can do better elsewhere. The crucial assumption, implicit in this paper, that the qualifications required for both jobs are the same, or at least comparable, may be satisfied more often than is generally believed, but will surely not hold in all cases.

Bielby, W. T. and Baron (1986) See item 349.
Birdsall and Fox, M. L. (1985) See item 847.

578. Birnbaum, Michael H. "Procedures for the Detection and Correction of Salary Inequities" in Thomas R. Pezzullo and Barbara E. Brittingham, eds., _Salary Equity_, Lexington, MA: D. C. Heath and Co., 1979: 121-44. (2)

The author suggests that the multiple regression approach to measuring discrimination may be misleading. He points out that a regressin of Y on X is not the same as X on Y,and goes on to argue that only if both show women to be at a disadvantage is there evidence of discrimination. His arguments are similar to, and subject to the same challenges as Conway and Roberts (1983). A full discussion of these is available in _JBES_ (Apr. 1984). See also Blau, F. D. and Kahn (1985).

579. Black, Howard R. and Robert L. Pennington. "An Econometric Analysis of Affirmative Action," _RBPE_ 11, 2 (Winter 1981): 267-76. (3,4)

Using multiple regression analysis and data for black and white applicants from D.C. to Fairfax County, it was shown that there exists a significant relation between the percentages of each of these groups, and salary levels based on EEO-4 job categories. The findings of this study lend support to the hypothesis that a vigorous affirmative action program can be effective in reducing the labor market effects of perceived discrimination.

580. Blalock, Hubert M., Jr. _Toward a Theory of Minority-Group Relations_. NY: Wiley, 1967. (1,3)

The theory proposed in this book is essentially that the larger the minority group, the greater is discrimination likely to be. Some evidence to support this view is presented here, as well as by later work (South, Bonjean, Markham and Corder 1982). An alternative, even opposite view is offered by Kanter (1977).

581. Blau, Francine D. "Occupational Segregation and Labor Market Discrimination" in Barbara F. Reskin, ed. Sex Segregation in the Workplace: Trends, Explanations, Remedies, Washington, D.C.: National Academy Press, 1984, pp. 117-43. (1,3)

This is a thorough review of various theories of discrimination and the results and implications of relevant empirical research. The author concludes that labor market discrimination does indeed play a role in producing the lower earnings of women, but that we still lack a widely accepted economic theory of the role of economic segregation, and why it persists in the long run in the face of competition in the labor market.

582. Blau, Francine D. and Lawrence M. Kahn. "The Use of Reverse Regression in Testing for Discrimination." SEJ 52, 4 (Apr. 1985): 1121-26. (2 Q)

In this comment the authors agree with Kamalich and Polachek (1982) that traditional wage regression methods for detecting discrimination may be biased due to errors-in-variables. They show, however, that reverse regression is subject to the same biases, and in any case does not provide enough information to permit a definitive conclusion. They suggest that the best solution is to try to handle the errors-in-variables problem directly through more accurate measurements of performance, use of instrumental variables, and grouped data. This issue is also discussed by Conway and Roberts (1983), and in comments on that paper in JBES, 2, 2 (Apr. 1984).

583. Blinder, Alan S. "Wage Discrimination: Reduced Form and Statistical Estimates." JHR 8, 4 (Fall 1973): 436-55. (2)

In this paper the author developed the method now most widely used for estimating discrimination (see also Oaxaca, 1973). He presents both structural equations, where all independent variables are endogenous and reduced form equations where independent variables are exogenous. His main contribution was to run separate equations for earnings of men and women, then "show" how much of women's lower earnings is caused by outright discrimination, how much because of discrimination in attaining endogenous variables, and how much because of differences in exogenous endowment. One difficulty that remains, however, is the index number problem: Results differ when female coefficients are applied to men rather than vice versa. Another criticism has been suggested by Jones, F. L., "On Decomposing the Wage Gap: A Critical Comment on Blinder's Method." JHR 18, 1 (Winter 1983): 126-30. He points out that Blinder uses a "shift" coefficient, which he considers part of "unexplained" discrimination, and claims his decomposition is unaffected by the choice of omitted category for a set of dummies. Jones, however, demonstrates that the value for the difference in intercepts depends on measurement decisions.

Block and Williams, W. (1981) See item 850.
Bloom and Killingsworth (1982) See item 433.

584. Borjas, George J. and Matthew S. Goldberg. "Biased Screening and Discrimination in the Labor Market." AER 65, 5 (Dec. 1978): 918-22. (1)

The statistical discrimination approach (Phelps, 1972; Aigner and Cain, 1977) is expanded here to show that a firm which uses a screening process that does not provide perfect information of an applicant's productivity may be biased against members of a particular group. In such a case, fewer members of one group may pass a test intended to determine their qualifications, and the predictive power may be less for that group, even though quality is in fact distributed equally across both groups.

585. Boulding, Kenneth E. "Toward a Theory of Discrimination," in Phyllis A. Wallace, ed. Equal Employment Opportunity and the AT&T Case, Cambridge, MA: MIT Press, 1976, pp. 9-15. (1)

Three types of discrimination are discussed. First is the exercise of monopoly power to exclude others from an occupation in order to maintain high earnings. Second is discrimination because of personal prejudice, either for homogeneity, or against others. Third is "role prejudice," the false generalization about appropriate roles for members of particular groups. Frequently these different types of discrimination tend to overlap. The author concludes that they all prevent us from maximizing satisfaction and that "research in prejudice reduction is likely to be one of the most profitable of intellectual activities."

586. Brown, Charles. "The Federal Attack on Labor Market Discrimination: The Mouse that Roared?" in Ronald Ehrenberg, ed., Research in Economics 5, Greenwich, CN: JAI Press, 1982, pp. 33-68. (4)

Evidence of the effects of Title VII, the Civil Rights Act of 1964 and Executive Order 11246 on the economic progress of blacks is evaluated in this paper. Many inconsistencies are found, but cannot readily be explained. One of the most interesting findings is that black women advanced considerably more rapidly than black men during the period since the federal effort began.

587. Brown, Gary D. "Discrimination and Pay Disparities Between White Men and Women." MLR 101, 3 (Mar. 1978): 17-22. (3)

The author suggests that existing differences by sex in pecuniary returns to education and experience may be related to wage, occupational, or employment bias. He further points out that this would be consistent with the theory proposed by Lester Thurow (Poverty and Discrimination, Washington, DC: Brookings Institution, 1969) that the dominant group is expected to maximize a utility function based not only on income, but also on social distance from other groups.

588. Buttler, Richard J. "Estimating Wage Discrimination in the Labor Market." JHR 17, 4 (Fall 1982): 606-21. (2)

Using both a reduced-form earnings function and a structural demand equation the author finds that the two yield quite different results. Since the market analyzed is unique, and the sample size limited, these results should be regarded as only tentative, but they suggest that reduced form earnings functions are inherently unable to tell us anything about market discrimination.

Cabral, Ferber and Green (1979) See item 443.

589. Caplow, Theodore and Reece J. McGee. The Academic Marketplace. NY: Anchor Books, Doubleday, 1965. (3)

The authors who wrote this book in the 1950's, before candor on such issues became inexpedient, freely admit that "women scholars are not taken seriously and cannot look forward to a normal professional career." They suggest this is not because they have low prestige, but rather that they are entirely outside the prestige system in an environment where prestige is considered crucial in furthering progress of the institution. The question arises whether this situation, to a greater or lesser degree persists, though it is no longer acknowledged.

Carazzini (1972) See item 739.

590. Cardwell, Lucy A. and Mark R. Rosenzweig, "Economic Markets, Monopsonistic Discrimination and Sex Differences in Wages." SEJ 46, 4 (Apr. 1980): 1102-17. (1,3)

The authors argue that the usual way of estimating taste discrimination as the part of the earnings gap that cannot be explained by differences in productivity-related characteristics between men and women ignores the possibility that some of the differential may be caused by employers using their market power vis-a-vis women who are more reluctant to move in order to further their own job situation. The empirical evidence in this paper supports the existence of such behavior. This is essentially what Madden (1973) called monopsony discrimination.

Carr (1983) See item 855.
Carvajal and Geithman (1985) See item 856.

591. Chapman, Bruce J. "Affirmative Action for Women: Economic Issues." ABL 11, 1 (Dec. 1984): 30-42. (4)

Research establishes that women receive lower wages than male counterparts with equal qualifications, and that employers tend to systematically overestimate the costs of employing women and exaggerate labor turnover differences between men and women. Therefore, government attempts to influence employers' perceptions of the job potential of women may be seen as both justified and potentially effective. Changing women's own perceptions of their potential may further affect outcomes. Amounts of costs and benefits are not, however, clear.

Chapman, B. J. and Harding (1985) See item 858.

592. Chiplin, Brian. "An Evaluation of Sex Discrimination: Some Problems and a Suggested Reorientation," in Cynthia B. Lloyd, Emily S. Andrews and Curtis L. Gilroy, eds., Women in the Labor Market, NY: Columbia University Press, 1979, pp. 246-71. (2)

The author offers a number of reasons why the residual approach of estimating discrimination should not be regarded as reliable, and should be assumed to have an upward bias. His case for the former is sounder than that for the latter. Further, the shortcomings of the approach should be considered as adequate reason for using it very cautiously, but not for throwing out the baby with the bath.

Chiplin and Sloane (1974)(1976a) See items 861, 864.
Cohen, M. S. (1971) See item 448.
Cole (1979) See item 743.

593. Collat, D. S. "Discrimination in the Coverage of Retirement Plans." YLJ 90, 4 (Mar. 1981): 817-39. (2)

Under the Internal Revenue Code, retirement plans with qualified status generate substantial tax benefits for employees and employers alike. In order to qualify, they must adhere, among others, to requirements for equality of coverage. This paper suggests a single test for this, based on the Gini coefficient, which offers a clear numerical criterion of distribution of benefits.

Conte (1976) See item 449.

594. Conway, Delores and Harry V. Roberts. "Reverse Regression, Fairness and Employment Discrimination." JBES 1, 1 (Jan. 1983): 75-85. (1,2)

In investigating possible discrimination, it is customary to use a regression where salary is the dependent variable, and job qualifications and sex, race, etc. are the independent variables. The authors suggest that there are two distinct aspects of fairness. One is that equally qualified individuals should receive the same pay. The second is that persons receiving the same pay should have equal qualifications. They further argue that the two are not the same, that both deserve attention, and that the latter can be investigated by making salary the independent variable. These issues are discussed at some length in JBES 2, 2 (Apr. 1984). (1,2)

Corcoran (1978) See item 451.
Corcoran and Courant (1985) See item 452.
Corcoran and Duncan, G. J. (1979) (1984) See items 454, 455.
Corcoran, Duncan, G. J. and Ponza (1983) See item 456.

595. Darland, M. G., S. A. Dawkins, J. L. Lavasich, E. L. Scott, M. E. Sherman, and J. A. Whipple. "Application of Multivariate Regression to Studies of Salary Differences Between Men and Women Faculty." Social Statistics Section Proceedings, ASAPP (1973): 120-32. (3)

This study is based on a sample of more than 13,000 faculty surveyed by the Carnegie Commission for whom a great deal of detailed information is provided. Included are such variables as age, marital-parental status, institution, degree, prestige of degree granting institution, field, publications, research support, time spent on teaching and service, as well as a number of interactions. With all these controls, the study nonetheless found unexplained residuals in virtually all fields, which were interpreted as evidence of discrimination.

596. Davis, J. C., C. M. Hubbard and Albert W. Niemi, Jr. "On the Measurement of Discrimination Against Women." AJES 38, 3 (July 1979): 287-92. (2)

This paper basically belabors the obvious by pointing out that estimates of discrimination which are too broadly defined--when earnings differentials are not adjusted for relative productivity--provide a poor guide to policy.

Daymont and Andrisani (1984) See item 462.
DeTray and Greenberg (1977) See item 463.
Duncan, G. J. and Hoffman, S. (1979) See item 465.

597. Edgeworth, Francis Y. "Equal Pay to Men and Women for Equal Work." EJ 32 (Dec. 1922): 431-57. (1)

This is one of the earliest studies to concern itself with unequal pay for men and women. The argument made is that if the labor force is segregated by occupation and unequally distributed, marginal productivity, and hence wages, will be lower in those jobs where supply of workers is relatively large. The author did not go on to consider why supply would be unequal, and does not establish a connection with traditional family roles, which he himself unquestioningly accepts. Much later Bergmann (1974) expanded further upon this theory.

England, Chassie and McCormack (1982) See item 468.
England and Norris (1985) See item 470.
Ferber and Green (1982) See item 749.
Ferber and Kordick (1978) See item 751.
Ferber and Loeb (1973)(1974) See items 752, 753.

598. Ferber, Marianne A. and Anne Westmiller. "Sex and Race Differences in Nonacademic Wages on a University Campus." JHR 11, 3 (Summer 1976): 366-73. (3)

This study set out to test the hypothesis that, when other variables, such as average education and experience with current employer of the workers are taken into account, race and sex do not help to explain wages in different occupations. The results, based on data for the nonacademic work force on a large university campus, do not support this hypothesis, but on the contrary show that sex and race influence the pattern of wage rates. The study has obvious limitations in not having information on many other factors that may legitimately influence earnings.

599. Fidell, L. S. "Empirical Verification of Sex Discrimination in Hiring Practices in Psychology." AP 25, 12 (Dec. 1970): 1094-98. (3)

Descriptions of 10 individuals were sent to 228 graduate departments of psychology. The executive officers of these departments were asked to indicate what position each individual would be qualified for. Persons were reported to be suitable for a higher level job when the respondent believed the candidate to be male rather than female. The most common offers for women were assistant professor, for men associate professor.

600. Finkelstein, Michael O. "The Judicial Reception of Multiple Regression Studies in Race and Sex Discrimination Cases." CLR 80, 4 (May 1980): 737-54. (2)

The paper begins by noting that the use of multiple regression in employment discrimination cases was first suggested as recently as 1975. It has proliferated rapidly since then, and by 1979 a District Judge claimed that such cases had become "contests between college professor statisticians who revel in discoursing about advanced statistical theory." The author goes on to review various controversial issues, including reverse regression (Birnbaum, M. H. 1979; Conway and Roberts, 1983), which he considers unacceptable because it only examines the situation within salary levels, ignoring the manner in which employees reach these levels. In the concluding section he proposes pretrial proceedings to define the data base to be used.

601. Flanders, Dwight P. and Peggy E. Anderson. "Sex Discrimination in Employment: Theory and Practice." ILRR 26, 3 (Apr. 1973): 938-55. (1,3)

The authors test several hypotheses suggested by microeconomic theory to explain the employment patterns of men and women. They conclude that employers appear to think there is a considerable qualitative difference between men and women, but that there is little evidence that women's productivity is low enough to justify existing wage differentials.

602. Follett, Robert and Finis Welch. "Testing for Discrimination in Employment Practices." LCP 46, 4 (Autumn 1983): 171-83. (2)

This paper attempts "to provide an intuitive feel for the logical underpinnings of statistical tests used in EEO litigations." The authors, who have considerable experience with such cases, suggest that differences in statistical litigation are often the product of incomplete and faulty data, as well as careless use of the available evidence. There are, however, also philosophical differences, generally involving questions about which variables to control for, and the choice of norms. Further, the authors question the usual standards for statistical significance when applied to criteria chosen because they are unfavorable to the defendants. Reading their views leaves no doubt about which side these experts usually testify for.

Fuchs (1971) See item 479.

603. Fujii, Edwin T. and John M. Trapani. "On Estimating the Relationship Between Discrimination and Market Structure." SEJ 44, 3 (Jan. 1978): 556-67. (3 Q)

This study tests the hypothesis that managers in industries with market power exercise discretion by discriminating. The model, unlike those used by many previous studies, relies on a fully specified equation. The evidence confirms that demand and supply elasticities are important in explaining discrimination at the industry level. No systematic relationship is found, however, between discrimination and market power. This is discussed further by James H. Medoff, SEJ 46, 4 (Apr. 1980): 1227-34. He argues that the theory proposed by Becker, G. S. (1957) theory implies segregation rather than wage differentials, and goes on to provide evidence that market power is related to employment discrimination.

604. Gastwirth, Joseph L. "Statistical Methods for Analyzing Claims of Employment Discrimination." ILRR 38, 1 (Oct. 1984): 75-86. (2 Q)

Two methods are proposed as more appropriate and often more powerful than the usual ones for testing significance in Equal Employment Opportunity cases involving claims of discrimination in hiring or promotion. Both methods combine one-sample binomial tests and the Mantel-Haenszel procedure. Several illustrations are provided, using data from actual cases.

605. Gaumer, Gary L. "Sex Discrimination and Job Tenure." IR 14, 1 (Feb. 1975): 121-29. (3)

Mancke (1971) argued that women's salaries are lower than those of comparably qualified men because employers believe they will not stay on the job as long as men, and hence will provide a lower rate of return on firm-specific training. This paper provides supporting evidence that this is the case, but also shows that the portion of the wage gap explained by this variable is decidedly small. The author reaches the conclusion that convincing employers of their career aspirations is not likely to have a large pay-off for women.

606. Goldberg, Marilyn P. "The Economic Exploitation of Women," in David M. Gordon, ed., Problems in Political Economy. An Urban Perspective, Lexington, MA: D.C. Heath and Company, 1971, pp. 113-17. (1)

The author, in a radical analysis, likens sexism to racism, arguing that both create a secondary class of workers, permitting low wages and poor working conditions. She further suggests that, though capitalism did not invent the nuclear family, or the notion that women are responsible for home and children, it actively promotes the isolated family unit and women's role in it, and thus facilitates the relegation of women to poorer jobs, and paying them less in comparable jobs.

607. Goldberg, Matthew S. "Discrimination, Nepotism, and Long-Run Wage Differentials." QJE, 97, 2 (May 1982): 307-19. (1)

In this paper the theory proposed by Becker, G. S. (1957) is reformulated from discrimination against a group to nepotism in favor of a preferred group. It is argued that this type of discrimination can persist in the long run. The reason is that firms which discriminate and make lower profits receive utility from their nepotistic behavior, and hence cannot be bought at an advantageous price by non-discriminatory entrepreneurs.

608. Goldberger, Arthur S. "Reverse Regression and Salary Discrimination." JHR 19, 3 (Summer 1984): 293-318. (2 Q)

Reverse regression has been proposed to assess discrimination, because the traditional regression procedure may be biased (Roberts 1980; Conway and Roberts 1983). In this paper it is shown that one of several models tested does justify the use of this novel approach. The author, however, concludes that reverse regression results should not be taken seriously unless accompanied by information needed for thorough testing is included. This subject is discussed further by Goldberger JBES 2, 2 (Apr. 1984): 114-16.

609. Goldstein, Morris and Robert S. Smith. "The Estimated Impact of the Antidiscrimination Program Aimed at Federal Contractors." ILRR 29, 4 (July 1976): 523-43. (4)

This study of the effects of the Office of Federal Contract Compliance during 1970-72 found that government contractors had greater gains in employment shares for black and white males, but greater losses for white females. Similar findings are reported in Hildebrand

(1976). The author ascribes this to the fact that women were not covered by the OFCC affirmative action program.

Goodman and Navarra (1978) See item 764.

610. Gordon, Nancy M. and Thomas E. Morton. "A Low Mobility Model of Wage Discrimination--With Special References to Sex Differentials." JET 7, 3 (Mar. 1974): 241-53. (1)

A model of wage discrimination is developed, relying, like Madden (1973), on market imperfections, and, like Becker, G. S. (1957), on "tastes for discrimination." In this case, it is assumed that men dislike working with women as equals or superiors. The authors conclude that the typical profit-maximizing strategy of a firm then will be to hire both men and women, but not pay them the same.

611. Gordon, Nancy M. and Thomas E. Morton, with Ina Braden, "Faculty Salaries: Is There Discrimination by Sex, Race and Discipline," AER 64, 4 (June 1974): 419-27. (3)

One of the pioneering studies of possible discrimination in academia, based on data for faculty at a large urban university. The results show that women were paid substantially less than men with similar qualifications, but blacks were paid more than whites. Many studies since have confirmed the former, but the more recent studies have generally not addressed the latter.

Gray and Scott, E. L. (1980) See item 768.

612. Green, Carole A. and Marianne A. Ferber. "Employment Discrimination: An Empirical Test of Forward Versus Reverse Regression." JHR 19, 4 (Fall 1984): 557-69. (2 Q)

This paper examines the objections to the usual multiple regression method of estimating discrimination raised by such critics as Birnbaum, M. H. (1979) and Conway and Roberts (1982) and concludes not all are convincing. Further, an empirical test of the Conway-Roberts proposition that reverse rather than forward regression is the proper way to detect salary discrimination is conducted, using the methodology suggested by Goldberger (1984). The conclusion reached is that reverse regression does not provide unbiased estimates in this case.

613. Greer, Charles R. "Returns to Investment in Undergraduate Education by Race and Sex in 1960 and 1970." RBER 12, 2 (Winter 1976-1977): 57-68. (4)

This paper analyzes trends in returns accruing to investment in college education by race and by sex in order to determine whether there have been changes since civil rights legislation was introduced. The study shows that returns for non-white and unmarried females increased relative to those for whites and unmarried males. As might be expected, the largest changes were found for younger cohorts.

614. Gunderson, Morley. "The Influence of the Status and Sex Composition of Occupations on the Male-Female Earnings Gap." ILRR 31, 2 (Jan. 1978): 217-26. (3,1)

The author points out that alternative theories of discrimination tend to lead to different expectations with regard to the contribution occupational distribution makes to the earnings gap. Based on his research he concludes that about half of the gap is caused by direct labor market discrimination, with wage discrimination and occupational segregation having about equal weight.

Gunderson (1979) See item 901.

615. Gwartney, James and Richard Stroup. "Measurement of Employment Discrimination According to Sex." SEJ 39, 4 (Apr. 1973): 575-87. (2)

Using 1960 and 1970 Census data the authors succeed in "explaining" virtually all of the earnings differential between single men and single women, but only at the most one-half of that between married men and married women. They conclude on this basis that it is women's own employment preferences that mainly account for the remaining differential. There are, however, a number of problems that vitiate this study. Among these are the use of the broader concept of income rather than earnings, accepting age as a proxy for experience for women as well as men, and ignoring interactions. Beyond that, it is well known that the most successful women, and the least successful men, are the ones most likely to remain single.

616. Haessel, Walter and John Palmer. "Market Power and Employment Discrimination." JHR 13, 4 (Fall 1978): 545-60. (3)

This paper tests a model which predicts that firms in more highly concentrated industries will be more likely to practice discrimination than other firms. The results generally support this hypothesis for both race and sex. The authors then go on to investigate the implications of equal work - equal pay legislation, and conclude that greater equalization of wages may result in even greater employment discrimination. James H. Medoff, JHR 15, 2 (Spring 1980): 293-95, challenges some of these conclusions. For one, he points out, they assume a perfectly competitive market for labor, with no differences between males and females, whites and non-whites. Second, he argues that a firm hiring a larger number of employees is more likely to exhibit its true discriminatory employment mix.

Haig (1982) See item 903.
Halaby (1979) See item 487.

617. Hamilton, Mary T. "Sex and Income Inequality Among the Employed." AAAPSS 409 (Sept. 1973): 42-52. (3)

An analysis of wages in four narrowly defined occupations -- accountants, tab machine operators, punch press operators, and janitorial workers -- clearly suggests the existence of wage discrimination by sex, and further indicates that the differential is larger than that related to race.

618. Hashimoto, Masao and Leo Kochin. "A Bias in the Statistical Estimation of the Effects of Discrimination." EI 18, 3 (July 1980): 978-86. (2 Q)

The authors point out, much like Conway and Roberts (1983) that a least squares estimate of the effect of discrimination using a dummy, say for sex or race, is likely to be exaggerated if the data used contain measurement errors. They further claim that using grouped data may be preferable, but admit it has shortcomings. Their approach thus raises questions as well. Avoiding, or minimizing measurement errors may be preferable.

619. Hersch, Joni and Joe A. Stone. "'New and Improved' Estimates of Qualification Discrimination." SEJ 52, 2 (Oct. 1985): 484-91. (2 Q)

Conway and Roberts (1982), Kamalich and Polachek (1982) and others have suggested a "reverse" test for discrimination, concerned with qualifications of people with equal wages, instead of the usual approach of examining wages of workers with equal qualifications. The two approaches would yield the same result only if there were no sources of error in the relationships. The authors suggest that a method which treats multiple qualifications as jointly dependent variables is an improvement on earlier work. Their results show discrimination against women in terms of pay, against men in terms of qualifications. This approach raises some of the same questions discussed in Blau, F. D. and Kahn (1985), Goldberger (1984), and Green and Ferber (1984).

620. Hildebrand, George A. "A Symposium. Evaluating the Impact of Affirmative Action: A Look at the Federal Contract Compliance Program." ILRR 29, 4 (July 1976): 485-586. (4)

This special volume is composed of papers and comments presented at a conference co-sponsored by the New York State School of Industrial and Labor Relations at Cornell University and the U.S. Department of Labor in May 1975. As one commentator points out, the basic problems in attempting this evaluation of Affirmative Action are those of making causal inferences from an uncontrolled experiment. In so far as any general conclusions may be drawn they are that enforcement was not very effective, but probably did help to improve the situation for black men, at least in blue collar occupations. The fact that this was, at least at that time, apparently at the expense of women, rather than white men, as was also found by Goldstein, M. and Smith, R. S. (1976), is not that surprising, given that the program emphasized only race, not sex, up to 1972.

621. Hill, Martha S. "Authority at Work: How Men and Women Differ," in Greg J. Duncan and James N. Morgan (eds.), Five Thousand American Families--Patterns of Progress, Vol. VIII, Ann Arbor: Institute for Social Research, University of Michigan, 1980, pp. 107-46. (3)

This paper focuses on differences between male and female workers in the attainment of authority. The fact that education has about three times as much effect on men accounts for much of the difference in the authority they have as compared to women.

622. Hirsch, Barry T. and Karen Leppel. "Sex Discrimination in Faculty Salaries: Evidence from a Historically Women's University." AER 72, 4 (Sept. 1982): 829-36. (3)

Like other research on salaries in academia, this study of what was historically a state university for women finds that female faculty are paid less than equally qualified males. In this case, however, the lower pay is entirely caused by the market, and women are not treated significantly differently than men once they are at this institution. The authors point out that the results are consistent either with the hypothesis that this university discriminates in favor of women (though they do not explain why the predominantly male faculty would put up with this) or that other institutions discriminate against women.

Hoffman, E. P. (1976) See item 774.
Holmes, R. A. (1976) See item 912.

623. Hunter, John E. and Frank L. Schmidt. "Ability Tests: Economic Benefits Versus the Issue of Fairness." IR 21, 3 (Fall 1982): 293-308. (4)

The authors claim, on the basis of extensive empirical research, that ability tests can be useful predictors of job performance, and that decreased use of such devices has led to declines in productivity. They further argue that research shows tests are both valid for and fair to minority applicants. A more balanced appraisal might be that some tests are fair and useful, but that others may not be. Therefore, the real issue is not whether tests should be used, but to make every effort that they not be abused.

624. Jain, Helen C. and Peter J. Sloane. "Race, Sex and Minority Group Discrimination Legislation in North America and Britain." IRJ 9, 2 (Summer 1978): 38-55. (4)

This article describes, in some detail, the various types of legislation introduced in Britain, Canada and the U.S.A. to reduce discrimination by race and by sex. Enforcement and results are also examined and critically evaluated.

625. Jain, Helen C. and Peter J. Sloane. "Minority Workers, The Structure of Labour Markets and Anti-Discrimination Legislation." IJSE 7, 3 (1980): 95-121. (3,4)

A review of various studies highlights the significance of internal labor markets, which facilitate the use of race or sex as a cheap screening device. This leads to poorer jobs for minorities and women, and helps to explain the large portion of the earnings gap not accounted for by differences in human capital. The authors further raise the question whether some of the criteria used for hiring and promotion by employers are acceptable requirements for the job or amount to indirect discrimination. The last part of the paper suggests a variety of policies that would improve the situation of minorities and women, including improved placement, greater investment in education and training, and requiring government preference in employment and expenditures.

626. Jain, Helen C. and Peter J. Sloane. Equal Employment Issues, NY: Praeger, 1981. (1,3,4)

This book includes a thorough examination of the theory of and evidence for discrimination in the labor market. There is also a review of relevant legislation in the U.S., Canada and Great Britain. It appears that these laws have not resulted in much progress for women in terms of the earnings gap as of the time this book was written. Only in Great Britain did it narrow, and the authors ascribe this to income policies. They further conclude that not too much should be expected from equal opportunity legislation, because attitudes of employers and unions change only slowly, and labor market policies alone are in any case inadequate. These views take little account of possible feedback effects, which may be important, particularly in the long run.

Johnson, G. E. and Stafford (1974)(1975)
See items 777, 778.

627. Johnson, John D., Jr. and Charles L. Knapp. "Sex Discrimination by Law: A Study in Judicial Perspective." NYUR 46, 4 (Oct. 1971): 675-741. (3)

A review of a century of the judiciary shows a great deal of sex discrimination, defined by the authors as preoccupation with group characteristics. They conclude that the courts have a better record on cases of discrimination involving race than on those involving sex.

628. Johnson, William G. and James Lambrinas. "Wage Discrimination Against Handicapped Men and Women." JHR 20, 2 (Spring 1985): 264-77. (3)

After appropriate correction for selectivity bias, this study indicates that almost one-third of the wage differential between handicapped and other men, and one-half of that between women can be attributed to discrimination. The authors further conclude that handicapped women are also subjected to sex discrimination.

629. Kamalich, Richard F. and Solomon W. Polachek. "Discrimination: Fact or Fiction? An Examination Using An Alternative Approach." SEJ 49, 2 (Oct. 1982): 450-61. (2 Q)

The authors show that traditional methods for estimating the extent of wage discrimination may be biased if the observed qualifications of workers are imperfect measures of their real productivity. They suggest that using reverse regression, where qualifications are the dependent variable, and wage the independent variable, is the solution to this problem. This analysis is similar to that of Birnbaum, M. H. (1979), Conway and Roberts (1983) and others. For alternative views see Blau, F. D. and Kahn (1985) and an extended discussion in the JBES (Apr. 1985).

630. Kanter, Rosabeth. Men and Women of the Corporation, NY: Basic Books, Inc., 1977. (1,3)

This pathbreaking book provided an analysis of the particular difficulties identifiable "outsiders" encounter when they are such a small proportion of an otherwise homogeneous group as to be "tokens," and how the situation changes as their ratio increases so that they become a minority, and eventually a subgroup. Few would question the insights about problems of tokens, but there has been considerable controversy about the effects of increasing numbers. The majority may feel increasingly threatened, and hence become more antagonistic as the proportion of "others" grows (Blalock 1967; South, Bonjean, Markham and Corder 1982). Another contribution of Kanter's book is an interesting discussion of the peculiar aspects of secretarial work.

631. Kapsalis, Constantine. "A New Measure of Wage Discrimination." EL 9, 3 (1982): 287-93. (2)

This author, like Conway and Roberts (1983), Kamalich and Polachek (1982), and others, points out that the conventional method of measuring wage discrimination tends to have an upward bias. He also suggests the alternative approach of comparing male and female characteristics within the same wage bracket, but concedes that further statistical analysis of this method is required. Goldberger (1984) and Blau, F. D. and

Kahn (1985) have provided some of this. Also David E. Hojman, EL 14, 1 (1984): 87-91 argues that comparing male and female characteristics within the same wage bracket creates a downward bias because it excludes the wage regression constant term.

Katz (1973) See item 781.

632. Kelley, Maryellen. "Discrimination in Seniority Systems: A Case Study," ILRR 36, 1 (Oct. 1982): 40-55. (3,4)

This paper uses a case study to examine what constitutes illegally discriminatory treatment in a seniority system in light of the 1977 U.S. Supreme Court decision in Teamsters vs. U.S., which determined that seniority systems that have a disparate impact on women and black workers are not necessarily illegal. The author obtained data from published sources and internal union documents for one particular system, and concluded that she was able to show that this system did illegally discriminate against both white women and black workers. She suggests her approach could be applied more generally.

Kessler-Harris (1985) See item 104.
Koch and Chizmar (1976) See item 784.
Kottis (1984) See item 925.

633. Krueger, Anne O. "The Economics of Discrimination." JPE 71, 5 (Oct. 1963): 481-86. (1 Q)

The model developed shows that, under certain conditions, a majority group may gain economically if it discriminates against a minority and that this is true not only for workers.

634. Kryger, Barbara R. and Richard Shukiar. "Sexual Discrimination in the Use of Letters of Recommendation: A Case of Reverse Discrimination." JAP, 63, 3 (June 1978): 309-14. (3)

Letters of recommendation were sent to 128 male personnel managers, some favorable, some unfavorable. An analysis of variance was computed on 75 usable responses and showed that female applicants were perceived to have more initiative and responsibility as well as greater ability to learn quickly than male applicants. They were preferred in terms of proceeding with the interview as well. The authors make little of the fact that women were also more likely to be considered for a position lower than the one they applied for and that, in any case, the willingness to interview may have more to do with eagerness to consider women candidates than to hire them.

635. Krzystofiak, Frank and Jerry Newman. "Evaluating Employment Outcomes: Availability Models and Measures." IR 21, 3 (Fall 1982): 277-92. (4)

This paper points out that during the 1970's the availability of protected groups increasingly became the accepted standard by which an employer's hiring and promotion behavior was judged. Nonetheless, the authors assert, after careful consideration of the issues, availability remains an ambiguous construct.

Landau (1984) See item 931.
Landes (1977) See item 508.
Larsen (1971) See item 935.

636. Larwood, Laurie, Barbara Gutek and Urs E. Gattiker. "Perspectives on Institutional Discrimination." GOS 9, 3 (Sept. 1984): 333-52. (1)

Three theoretical perspectives, economic, sociological, and psychological, are examined. The authors contend that a fourth perspective, one that analyzes the decision processes of the rational manager concerned with the opinions of powerful others, is also needed for a full understanding of organizational discrimination. They further suggest that this approach has significant implications for finding ways to end discrimination.

637. Ledvinka, James and Hugh J. Watson. "Processing of Discrimination Charges by EEOC." JBR 3, 2 (Apr. 1975): 149-56. (4)

The U.S. Equal Employment Opportunity Commission is the principal enforcement agency for equal employment law. This paper examines the agency's procedure for handling discrimination charges, and provides evidence of the growing work load that caused problems and impeded fair and effective enforcement of the law.

638. Leonard, Jonathan S. "Antidiscrimination or Reverse Discrimination: The Impact of Changing Demographics, Title VII, and Affirmative Action." JHR 19, 2 (Spring 1984a): 145-74. (3)

This study shows no evidence that the productivity of women or minorities fell as compared to that of men as their employment increased in recent decades, pointing to the conclusion that there have been no efficiency costs brought about by policies intended to reduce discrimination. Evidence is also found that Title VII was successful in improving the position of minorities.

639. Leonard, Jonathan S. "The Impact of Affirmative Action on Employment." JLE 2, 4 (Oct. 1984c): 439-63. (4)

When employment data for more than 68,000 establishments are examined between 1974 and 1980, it is found that both minority and female workers have increased more rapidly at firms subject to affirmative action. Compliance reviews also were found to be effective. Similar findings are reported in Leonard (1985 JLE).

640. Leonard, Jonathan S. "What Promises Are Worth: The Impact of Affirmative Action Goals." JHR 20, 1 (Winter 1985a): 3-20. (4)

This study, a follow-up to Leonard (JLE 1984), finds that while goals tend to be inflated and are generally not fulfilled, establishments that promise to employ more women and minorities actually employ more in subsequent years. This provides further evidence that affirmative action has been effective, even though detailed enforcement tools have not always been useful.

641. Leonard, Jonathan S. "Affirmative Action as Earnings Redistribution: The Targeting of Compliance Reviews." JLE 3, 3 (July 1985b): 363-84. (4)

The author suggests that affirmative action may be used to reduce discrimination, or to redistribute jobs and earnings. In his view, different strategies would be pursued in each of these. Since he found that firms with very low proportions of women and minorities were not more likely to be targetted for review than others, but that this was the case for establishments with a high ratio of white-collar workers, he concludes that the goal was probably earnings redistribution. Alternatively one might conclude that it is only white-collar workers who have succeeded in gaining enough influence to achieve reduced discrimination.

642. Levin, Sharon G. "Profit Maximization and Discrimination." IOR 4, 2 (1976): 108-16. (3)

This study tests a carefully specified form of the taste discrimination hypothesis suggested by Becker, G. S. (1957) and finds that firms with relatively greater potential discretionary resources appear to engage in more discrimination. This result tends to support the possible long-run existence of taste discrimination. So does the fact that more discrimination is also found in manager controlled firms than in those controlled by owners, because the former would be expected to be less interested in profit maximization.

643. Levinson, Richard. "Sex Discrimination and Employment Practices: An Experiment with Unconventional Job Inquiries," SP 22, 4 (Apr. 1975): 533-43. (3)

In this study men and women made phone calls in response to job advertisements. Among women, 28 percent of those who inquired about traditionally male jobs, and among men 44 percent of those who inquired about traditionally female jobs were told they would not like the job, or would not be good at it.

644. Lewis, H. Gregg. "Comments on Selectivity Biases in Wages Comparisons." JPE 82, 6 (Nov./Dec. 1974): 1145-55. (2 Q)

The author expresses reservations regarding Gronau's (1974) assumption that the wage offer distribution would have a dispersion large enough so that the observed distribution would differ substantially from the total distribution. He explains that when market forces have brought about an equilibrium, this would not be the case. Those of us who do not share the "true faith" that markets generally are in equilibrium cannot be expected to agree with him.

645. Lianos, Theodore P. "A Note on Discrimination in the Labor Market." SEJ 43, 2 (Oct. 1976): 1177-80. (1)

The author develops a variant of the "taste discrimination" proposed by Becker, G. S. (1957). He assumes that, say, at least some firms will hire only women when no men are available at the going wage rate. In such a case, employers would fail to maximize profits, women would be paid less than men, and total unemployment would be higher.

646. Livernash, Robert E., ed. Comparable Worth: Issues and Alternatives, Washington, DC: Equal Employment Opportunity Council, 1980 (Second edition, 1984). (4)

This book consists of a series of papers which forcefully and, on the whole, competently point out all possible, and some very unlikely problems that would be involved in instituting the policy of equal pay for work of comparable worth. Solutions to these problems are generally not considered, nor are alternative ways of achieving pay equity. All of this gives the editor's professed dedication to nondiscrimination a hollow ring. This impression is reinforced by such platitudes as "Nondiscrimination in pay practices is an objective shared by employers, employees, and society generally." If that were true, who would there be left to do any discriminating?

647. Lobue, Marie. "Adjustment to Labor Productivity: An Application to the Economics of Discrimination." SEJ 50, 1 (July 1983): 151-59. (1)

A model is developed which assumes that the employer is faced with greater uncertainty when choosing workers from an unfamiliar than from a familiar group. The analysis shows that even without a taste for discrimination a wage differential will exist under these conditions. The author suggests that this explains why studies assuming perfect information have produced inconsistent results. This is essentially a variation on the models of statistical discrimination developed much earlier, by Phelps (1972), Aigner and Cain (1977).

648. Long, James E. "Employment Discrimination in the Federal Sector." JHR 11, 1 (Winter 1976): 86-97. (3)

According to this research, based on micro data from the 1970 Census, employment and earnings in the Federal Civil Service varied by race and sex after adjustments were made for differences in characteristics related to productivity. Thus, employment opportunities did not appear to be equal even there.

649. Luksetich, William A. "Market Power and Sex Discrimination in White-Collar Employment." RSE 37, 2 (Oct. 1979): 211-214. (3)

This study investigates the relationship between market structure and employment opportunities for women and minorities. A positive effect of concentration on upper level white-collar positions is found for non-whites, but not for women. It may be that equal opportunity enforcement, at least for non-whites, was stricter in larger firms.

650. Lundberg, Shelly J. and Richard Startz. "Private Discrimination and Social Intervention in Competitive Labor Markets." AER 73, 3 (June 1983): 340-47. (1)

In this paper a model of statistical discrimination is presented where the agents are maximizing competitive firms which act upon all available information, and maximizing workers who decide on human capital investments in terms of known wage schedules. It is further assumed that firms are able to assess the productivity of members of one group more reliably than for those of another group. The authors show that the allocation of resources achieved in this labor market can be improved by prohibiting discrimination based on group membership. This conclusion is also consistent with the model of Borjas and Goldberg, M. (1978).

651. Madden, Janice F. The Economics of Discrimination, Lexington, MA: D. C. Heath and Co., 1973. (1)

The main contribution of this work is to develop a theory of discrimination based on a monopsony model, where the employer has market power as a buyer of labor. In this case, if the supply of female labor is less elastic, or less responsive to wage changes, than is male labor, the employer will maximize profits by paying lower wages to women. Such a situation may well exist in particular local labor markets, to the extent that women tend to be less willing to move to further their career, and may have fewer alternative career options. On the other hand, as Blau, F. D. and Jusenius (1976) point out, the aggregate supply of female labor seems to be more elastic than male supply.

652. Madden, Janice F. "Discrimination -- A Manifestation of Male Market Power?" in Cynthia B. Lloyd, ed., Sex Discrimination and the Division of Labor, NY: Columbia University Press, 1975, pp. 146-74. (1)

In this paper Madden compares the model of "taste discrimination" (Becker, G. S. 1957) with her own model of "monopsony discrimination" (Madden 1973), with special emphasis on the different policy implications of each. For one, in the former, equal pay requirements without effective laws against discrimination in hiring, would lead to sex segregation by firm.

653. Madden, Janice F. "A Spatial Theory of Sex Discrimination." JRS 17, 3 (Dec. 1977): 369-80. (1)

This paper presents what is essentially a special case of the theory developed in Madden (1973). This model reconciles the existence of employer discrimination with the traditional assumption that they will seek to maximize profits. Assuming that women are less responsive to wage changes, employers will find it worthwhile to pay them lower wages than those paid to equally qualified men. Two conditions need to be satisfied for this to be the case: 1. Women must be less mobile than men among spatially separated firms. 2. Market goods must not be easily substituted for household produced goods. Work by other researchers suggests these conditions are generally not likely to be satisfied (Blau, F. D. and Jusenius, 1976).

654. Madden, Janice F. "The Persistence of Pay Differentials: The Economics of Sex Discrimination." WW 1 (1985): 76-114. (1,3)

After a careful review of the literature, this author concludes that no statistical studies have been able to explain most, let alone all, of the sex-wage differential by productivity, and that there is no concensus about analytical models having demonstrated convincingly that sex discrimination in the labor market can persist. Hence both proponents and opponents of government intervention in the labor market can find support for their views that women are paid less because they are women, or because they are less productive. Madden emphasizes that both factors may play a role, and are likely to interact.

Maki (1983) See item 939.

655. Mancke, Richard B. "Lower Pay for Women: A Case of Economic Discrimination?" IR 10, 3 (Oct. 1971): 316-26. (3)

A theory of sex-wage differentials is developed and tested, which maintains that they are caused by the expectation of the employers that women will not stay on the job as long as men and hence are less willing to provide firm-specific training for them. Gaumer (1975) confirms this relationship, but also shows that its effect is rather modest. Another problem with this theory is that it may well represent a case of self-fulfilling prophecy: women are not hired for jobs providing for upward mobility, so they have little reason to stay. Blau, F. D. and Kahn (1981) provide evidence women's turnover in similar jobs is not very different from men's. Strober, IR, 11, 2 (May 1972): 279-84, argues that incorrect perceptions by employers amount to prejudice and result in discrimination, and that women should not have to make extraordinary efforts to persuade employers to give them the same opportunities men get automatically.

656. Mayo, James M., Jr. "Job Attainment in Planning: Women Versus Men." WO 12, 2 (May 1985): 147-65. (3)

This study shows that the failure of women to be fully integrated into professional practice is caused by women's lesser qualifications. At the same time, it is not clear whether women have equal opportunity to acquire these qualifications.

657. McCabe, George P., Jr. "The Interpretation of Regression Analysis. Results in Sex and Race Discrimination Problems." AS 34, 4 (Nov. 1980): 212-215. (2)

Like a number of other authors, this one points out that misspecification of regressions is likely to lead to erroneous results. He further suggests that careful examination of residuals can help, and that any subjective processes involved should be carefully examined for bias. He concludes, however, that "No statistician or other scientist should ever put himself/herself in a position of trying to prove or disprove discrimination." If such rigid standards were applied to all problems, statisticians would be immobilized.

658. Medoff, Marshall H. "The Equal Rights Amendment: An Empirical Analysis of Sex Discrimination." EI 18, 3 (July 1980): 367-79. (3)

An analysis using 1970 Census data showed that the unexplained residual of the earnings gap between men and women was greater in the states that had ratified ERA. This comparison did not, however, adjust for differences in occupations, and used a single regression for men and women. Janet C. Hunt, EI 21, 1 (Jan. 1983): 140-45 found using separate regressions for men and women, and adjusting for a variety of regional differences, that there is less discrimination in ERA-ratifying states.

Meeker (1981) See item 517.
Metzker (1980) See item 945.

659. Milkovich, George T. and Renae Broderick. "Pay Discrimination: Legal Issues and Implications for Research." IR 21, 3 (Fall 1982): 309-17. (4)

This paper examines the evolving definition of pay discrimination and delineates questions for future research. Special emphasis is placed on the importance of finding better ways to define and measure the relative value of jobs in a nondiscriminatory manner.

Miller, P. W. and Volker (1984) See item 948.

660. Moore, Robert L. "Employer Discrimination: Evidence from Self-Employed Workers." RES 65, 3 (Aug. 1983): 496-501. (3)

This study is based on the premise that if employer discrimination is an important factor in bringing about lower earnings for minorities and women, the self-employed among these groups should do better than those employed by others. The data show that this is not the case. What is overlooked is the possibility that there may be discrimination by customers, lenders, and workers, all of whom may prefer to deal with, or work for, white men. It may also be that discrimination by employers takes the form of not hiring women and minorities, who would then crowd into the self-employed sector, and depress earnings there.

661. Moore, William J. "The Impact of Children and Discrimination on the Hourly Wage of Black and White Wives." QREB 17, 3 (Autumn 1977): 43-64. (3)

Using a human capital model, the author estimates that the number of children has a significant though small negative effect on the earnings of married women, other things being equal. The effect appears to be greater for white than for black wives.

Moore, W. J. and Newman (1977) See item 796.

662. Mount, Randall I. and Richard E. Bennett. "Economic and Social Factors in Income Inequality: Race and Sex Discrimination and Status as Elements in Wage Differentials." AJES 34, 2 (Apr. 1975): 161-74. (3 Q)

Using several econometric techniques, the authors show that including sex as a variable, when education, occupation, class of worker, industry, race, marital status, hours and weeks worked, as well as age are already accounted for, represents a significant improvement in explanatory power. It must be noted, however, that their data do not include years of experience or length of tenure in the job.

663. Munts, Raymond and David C. Rice. "Women Workers: Protection or Equality?" ILRR 24, 1 (Oct. 1970): 3-13. (4)

The authors argue against the position of the Equal Employment Opportunities Commission that prohibiting women from certain occupations or limiting their hours of work "tends to discriminate rather than protect." They suggest that it is a mistake to trust the free market to adequately protect workers. One may well agree with that, but believe that the proper solution is to mandate safe, decent working conditions for all employees, and to require hours short enough so that both men and women have time and energy to devote to their families.

664. Oaxaca, Ronald. "Male-Female Wage Differentials in Urban Labor Markets." IER 14, 3 (Oct. 1973a): 693-709. (2)

Similar to the procedure suggested by Blinder (1973), and subject to the same limitations.

665. Oaxaca, Ronald. "Sex Discrimination in Wages," in Orley Ashenfelter and Albert Rees, eds., Discrimination in Labor Markets, Princeton, NJ: Princeton University Press, 1973b. (3)

One of the many estimates of the extent to which the earnings gap can be explained by measured differences in male and female worker characteristics, this study leaves 80 percent of the wage differential between men and women unexplained. Among the reasons for this large proportion is the fact that occupations are not included, which may be reasonable, and the absence of information on actual work experience, which is unfortunate.

666. Olson, Craig A. and Brian E. Becker. "Sex Discrimination in the Promotion Process." ILRR 36, 4 (July 1983): 624-41. (3)

Using data from the Quality of Employment Panel, this study investigates gender differences in the incidence of and returns to promotions. The results indicate that, after controlling for differences in job level and individual ability, women are less likely to be promoted than men, though they are equally rewarded when they are advanced to a higher position.

O'Neill (1984) See item 964.

667. Oster, Sylvia M. "Industry Differences in the Level of Discrimination Against Women." QJE 89, 2 (May 1975): 215-29. (1,3)

The author first examines whether discrimination is related to the degree of monopoly power of the employer, but finds little support for this explanation how behavior contrary to profit-maximization might persist. She therefore rejects the Becker, G. S. (1957) hypothesis that employers discriminate because of their own preferences, and goes on to demonstrate that employer behavior is likely to be a rational response when other workers prefer not to work with women, at least in many kinds of jobs.

Osterman (1981) See item 799.

668. Osterman, Paul. "Sex Discrimination in Professional Employment: A Case Study." ILRR 32, 4 (July 1979): 451-64. (3)

This study uses data on over 700 professional employees in a metropolitan publishing firm to examine sex discrimination. The results show that men receive substantially larger earnings when they are married and have children. The author concludes this is neither because of differences in labor supply, nor because of statistical discrimination, but rather because managers believe these men "deserve more." Lawrence M. Kahn, ILRR, 34, 2 (January 1981): 273-75, shows that Osterman's findings are consistent with statistical discrimination, which Osterman concedes. Even so, he does not agree with Kahn's conclusion.

669. Osterman, Paul. "Affirmative Action and Opportunity: A Study of Female Quit Rates." RES 64, 4 (Nov. 1982): 604-12. (4)

This paper demonstrates that enforcement activities of the Federal Contract Compliance Program reduced quitting among female workers. It is argued, though not proven, that this is because of improved opportunities. To the extent this is true it suggests the importance of feedback effects on women's labor market behavior, and the possibility that improving their opportunities would lead to increased productivity.

670. Parcel, Toby L. and Charles W. Mueller. Ascription and Labor Markets. Race and Sex Differences in Earnings, NY: Academic Press, 1983. (1,3)

This book critically explores existing explanations of earnings differentials by race and by sex, and offers a good deal of empirical evidence to support the authors' views. The first of their main conclusions is that differentiation of labor markets along regional, industrial, and occupational lines is most useful for the analysis of inequality. A second important conclusion is that discrimination among males is mainly a function of differential access to resources, though there are also differences in returns. Sex discrimination among whites, on the other hand, is mainly a matter of differences in the efficiency of the use of resources.

671. Pezzullo, Thomas R. and Barbara E. Brittingham. Salary Equity, Lexington, MA: Lexington Books, D.C. Heath and Co., 1979. (2)

Many of the papers included in this volume, concerned with the issues involved in the extension of the Equal Pay Act to college and university faculty, give evidence of inadequate familiarity with their subject. The book might, nonetheless, be useful to readers who want an introduction to this issue, but some of the articles included are at a level of sophistication which makes them inaccessible to anyone without substantial statistical training. Thus, much of what is offered is already known to the expert, and the untutored reader will be left floundering.

672. Phelps, Edmund S. "The Statistical Theory of Racism and Sexism." AER 62, 4 (Sept. 1972): 659-61. (1)

This very brief paper was the first to present the statistical discrimination theory. Briefly stated, it is that "the employer who seeks to maximize profit will discriminate against blacks or women if he believes them to be less qualified, reliable, long-term, etc." This view has since then received wide currency, and has also been further refined and embellished, e.g., Aigner and Cain (1977); Arrow (1973).

673. Polachek, Solomon W. "Potential Biases in Measuring Male-Female Discrimination." JHR 10, 2 (Winter 1975a): 205-29. (2,3)

This paper purports to show both theoretically and empirically that being married and having children have opposite effects on husbands and wives throughout the duration of the marriage. The usual explanation for this is that having the responsibility of being the breadwinner will spur a man on to greater efforts in the labor market, while household responsibilities detract from those of a woman. The possibility that marital and parental status may be used as the basis for statistical discrimination by employers is ignored.

674. Polachek, Solomon W. "Simultaneous Equations Models of Sex Discrimination," in John R. Moroney, ed., Income Inequality: Trends in International Comparisons, Lexington, MA: D. C. Heath, 1979, pp. 115-34. (1)

The author begins by pointing out that much disagreement continues to exist about the extent to which demand and supply factors contribute to different labor market outcomes for women and men. This is important, because each results in different policy implications. The model developed in this paper leads the author to conclude "that numerous human capital variables differ not only by sex but by marital status, and family size within sex groups." He also finds that "even when adjusted for the possibility of reverse causality, human capital variables maintained their importance." None of this, as the author admits, proves that discrimination on the demand side does not also play a role.

675. Polhemus, Craig E. "'Good Faith,' Discrimination and Back Pay." MLR 98, 10 (Oct. 1975): 57-60. (4)

In Albermarle Paper Co. v. Moody and Halifax Local N. 425, United Papermakers and Paperworkers (1975) the Supreme Court decided that good faith attempts to obey the law are not in themselves sufficient to shield an employer from liability to compensate workers who have suffered continuing effects of past discrimination. Back pay may be mandated.

676. Ragan, James F., Jr. and Sharon P. Smith. "Statistical Discrimination as Applied to Quit Behavior." QREB 22, 3 (Autumn 1982): 104-12. (3)

This study, using unpublished data provided by the U.S. Bureau of Labor Statistics, finds evidence that earnings of individuals are related to the past quit behavior of the group of which that person is a member. This is interpreted to confirm statistical discrimination -- the individual being judged by the characteristics of the group.

Reagan (1975) See item 804.
Reagan and Maynard (1974) See item 805.
Reskin (1976)(1979) See items 806, 808.
Robb (1978) See item 975.

677. Roemer, John E. "Divide and Conquer: Microfoundations of a Marxian Theory of Wage Discrimination." BJE 10, 2 (Autumn 1979): 695-705. (1)

The author develops a bargaining model of wage determination, as opposed to a competitive model, and uses it to demonstrate that there are discriminatory equilibria where both white and black workers are worse off, and employers are better off than would be the case if workers were unified. He further argues, that because of the bargaining structure, such a situation can persist. Presumably a similar model could be developed to explain discrimination between men and women.

678. Rosenblum, Marc. "Evolving EEO Decision Law and Applied IR Research." IR 21, 3 (Fall 1982): 340-51. (4)

This paper discusses the evolution of the Supreme Court's interpretation of EEO law with respect to equal treatment versus equal impact. Given that many unresolved questions remain, in spite of the increasing use of more sophisticated quantitative techniques, the author believes that more contributions of industrial relations researchers could be very helpful.

679. Saltzstein, Grace H. "Personnel Directors and Female Employment Representation: A New Addition to Models of Equal Employment Opportunity to Policy?" SSQ 64, 4 (Dec. 1983): 983, 734-46. (3)

The independent influence of hiring agents' attitudes on employment outcomes is assessed, using data on female employment in 20 Texas cities over a five-year period. Several individual characteristics of personnel directors were found to have important influence on employment policies.

Sanborn (1964) See item 539.

680. Sawhill, Isabel V. "The Economics of Discrimination Against Women: Some New Findings." JHR 8, 3 (Summer 1973): 383-96. (3)

Employing data from the 1967 Current Population Survey, and adjusting for race, region, education, age, weeks worked per year, and full time vs. part time work, this study found that women's earnings increased from 46 percent to merely 56 percent of those of men. Using a proxy for labor force experience only increased the ratio by one more percentage point. Unlike Cohen, M. S. (1971), Fuchs (1971), Gwartney and Stroup (1973), Sanborn (1964), and others, Sawhill concludes that discrimination, both directly and indirectly via influencing women's aspirations and occupations, is likely to account for most of the remaining gap.

Shepherd and Levin (1973) See item 816.

681. Shoben, Elaine W. "The Use of Statistics to Prove Intentional Employment Discrimination." LCP 46, 4 (Autumn 1983): 219-45. (2)

One highly controversial question today is whether only purposeful discrimination is statutorily prohibited. Recognizing that this is increasingly the accepted view, the author argues that this does not necessarily preclude the use of statistics, especially if the concept of intent is broadly construed. For example, adoption of a requirement whose exclusionary effect on a particular group is virtually certain to occur might be so interpreted. She nonetheless recognizes that these new standards make statistical proof more difficult and concludes by urging that intent should not be required when analyzing the results of subjective interviews under Title VII.

682. Shorey, John. "Employment Discrimination and the Employer Tastes Model." <u>SJPE</u> 31, 2 (June 1984): 157-75. (1)

"Taste" discrimination (Becker, G. S. 1957) in the primary sector of a segmented labor market is analyzed in this paper. The conclusion is that it can persist because it increases the employer's profits and provides protection for the workers. According to this model unions play an important role. Therefore, the author suggests that the workers who are discriminated against must become more active in the unions if they are to improve their situation. He also points out that government may need to support separate representation for disadvantaged workers if there is to be any progress.

683. Siebert, W. S. and Peter J. Sloane. "The Measurement of Sex and Marital Status Discrimination at the Workplace." <u>Economica</u>, 48, 190 (May 1981): 125-41. (2,3)

Earnings functions estimated from personnel records data are used to measure discrimination within establishments, including a financial institution, a government department, and a light engineering firm. The approach is based on the premise that the most appropriate comparison to make for purposes of isolating discrimination is between single men and single women, because there will be the least difference in unmeasured motivational influences. This ignores evidence that it is married men and single women who tend to be most successful, and raises question about their findings that one firm discriminated by sex, another against single people, and a third against married women and single men.

4. South, Scott J., Charles M. Bonjean, William T. Markham and Judy Corder. "Social Structure and Intergroup Interaction: Men and Women of the Federal Bureaucracy." ASR 47, 5 (Oct. 1982): 587-99. (3)

Contrary to Kanter (1977), this research suggests that the greater the proportion of women in a work unit, the less frequently they tend to interact with men, and the less support they tend to receive from men. This is consistent with the hypothesis that members of the majority feel increasingly threatened as the proportion of "others" rises.

685. Steinberg, Ronnie and Lois Haignere. "Separate But Equivalent: Equal Pay for Work of Comparable Worth." Gender at Work, Washington, D.C.: Women's Research and Education Institute of the Congressional Caucus for Women's Issues, 1984, pp. 13-26. (4,2)

A brief, useful summary of the history and current status of "comparable worth," with special emphasis on methodological issues.

686. Stiglitz, Joseph. "Approaches to the Economics of Discrimination." AER 63, 2 (May 1973): 287-95. (1)

The author develops several possible models of wage discrimination to determine under what circumstances it would be possible for groups with identical economic characteristics to receive different wages in a market equilibrium. They essentially involve taking into account the consequences of discriminatory preferences and recognizing the existence of market imperfections. Which of the models is appropriate has strong implications for the desirability of alternative policies.

Sullerot (1975) See item 1004.
Tsuchigane and Dodge (1974) See item 560.
Turnbull and Williams (1974) See item 1016.
Vetter (1981) See item 826.

687. Wallace, Phyllis A. "Employment Discrimination: Some Policy Implications," in Orley Ashefelter and Albert Rees, eds. Discrimination in Labor Markets, Princeton, NJ: Princeton University Press,1973, pp. 155-75. (4)

This paper assesses the status of equal employment opportunity at the time and concludes that progress had been slow because it was "difficult for small agencies with limited resources to deal effectively with powerful coalitions of employers, unions, bureaucrats, congressmen and others." The paper concludes by suggesting possible alternative strategies.

688. Wallace, Phyllis A., ed. Equal Employment Opportunity and the AT&T Case. Cambridge, MA: The MIT Press, 1976. (3,4)

All the chapters in this book except Boulding (1976) are based on information collected in connection with the AT&T case, which was settled in 1973 when the company signed a consent degree with the EEOC involving a remedial wage adjustment of 38 million dollars. The various essays deal with the consequences of institutionalized employment discrimination in this company, at the time the largest employer in the country. They are, however, also concerned with the questions how and to what extent equity can be achieved in the workplace and how the effects of past discrimination can be mitigated without imposing undue burdens on others.

689. Wallace, Phyllis and Annette M. LaMond, eds. Women, Minorities and Employment Discrimination, Lexington, MA: Lexington Books, D. C. Heath and Co., 1977. (3)

This book is a compendium of papers originally written for a series of workshops held at MIT in 1974, focusing on equal employment opportunities. The authors represent several disciplines and various points of view. The chapters provide both an overview of research that had been done up to that time, and suggestions for further investigations that should prove useful.

Zabalza and Tzannatos (1985) See item 1031.

690. Zellner, Harriet. "Discrimination Against Women, Occupational Segregation, and the Relative Wage." AER 62, 2 (May 1972): 157-60. (1)

Occupational segregation is examined as the mechanism of discrimination. It is assumed that discrimination takes the form of a preference for males over equally qualified females in masculine occupations, thus increasing the supply of women to "feminine" occupations, and reducing their earnings in both sectors. If discrimination is based on erroneous perceptions of women, their influx would be expected to help to remedy it. If, on the other hand, it is a matter of taste, as suggested by Becker, G. S. (1957) no such benign effect may be expected.

Chapter 7

UNEMPLOYMENT

Having, so far, focused on labor force participation, occupations and earnings, it would be easy to gain the impression that the only issue for a woman is what kind of work to do--housework or market work, and what kind of market work. In reality there has been a significant minority of men and women ranging from over 3 percent to over 9 percent over the last 40 years who wanted to work for pay but have not been able to find employment. They are officially classified as unemployed. This includes everyone not currently working for pay but looking for work, or temporarily laid off from a job to which they expect to return.

During the last decade particularly, the rate of unemployment has been at levels unusually high for the post World War II period. The question why this country has had, and has tolerated, such a situation is an important subject which is, however, beyond the scope of this volume. Two issues are of particular concern here: (1) why, during most years, the unemployment rate in this country and in most, though not all others, has been higher for women than for men; and (2) whether unemployment of women is a matter of equal concern as joblessness of men.

Just as there has been an ongoing debate about occupational segregation and women's lower earnings, so there has been disagreement about the causes for their relatively high unemployment rates. The literature on this subject is not very extensive, but the works summarized below do provide some evidence on the extent to which such factors as women's lesser labor force attachment and greater commitment to homemaking increases the likelihood that they will be unemployed and reduces the severity of problems associated with not being able to find a job. At the same time, further exploration of these topics is needed, especially as conditions are changing both with respect to women's commitment to market work, and the dependence not only of single women but of families on women's earnings.

One question that has received a good bit of attention is what the effect of the general unemployment rate is likely to be on women's labor force participation. On the one hand, inability to find a job is expected to cause some to become "discouraged workers," to stop actively looking for work. On the other hand, when husbands lose their jobs, wives may become "additional workers" to tide the family over. There is, of course, reason to believe that both these effects will operate to some extent, but there is much disagreement which is likely to dominate. It may well be that the answer differs from time to time, and place to place.

Almquist (1975) See item 341.

691. Barnes, William F. and Ethel B. Jones. "Women's Increasing Unemployment: A Cyclical Interpretation." QREB 15, 2 (Summer 1975): 61-69. (3)

Increases in women's unemployment rates as compared to those of men during the preceding years are investigated. When examined as a function of the cycle, and of changes in the definition of unemployment, the authors conclude there has been no secular change in the relationship. Other studies, such as Ferber and Lowry (1976) and B. T. Niemi (1976) reached the opposite conclusion.

692. Barrett, Nancy S. and Richard D. Morgenstern. "Why Do Blacks and Women Have High Unemployment Rates?" JHR 9, 4 (Fall 1974): 452-65. (3)

Relying on data drawn primarily from the Work Experience Surveys this study suggests that high job turnover is the main cause of high unemployment rates among blacks and young people of both races, as well as persons with low skills. Women, on the other hand, and particularly white women of childbearing age, are found to be at a disadvantage because they are unemployed longer between jobs.

693. Barth, Peter S. "Unemployment and Labor Force Participation." SEJ 34, 3 (Jan. 1968): 375-82. (3Q)

Unlike Alban and Jackson, M. (1976) and Strand and Dernburg (1964), this study found no evidence for an additional worker effect for women. Unlike Blau, F. D. (1978) these researchers also discovered very little evidence for any discouraged worker effect for women, though some effect was found for men. This is surprising in view of the fact that the proportion of discouraged workers tends to be considerably higher among women.

Bergmann (1980b) See item 575.

694. Blau, Francine D. "The Impact of the Unemployment Rate on Labor Force Entrants and Exits," in Isabel V. Sawhill, ed., Women's Changing Roles at Home and on the Job, National Commission on Manpower Policy Special Report No. 26, Washington, D.C.: 1978. (3)

The evidence shows that the discouraged worker effect dominates for white women. They are increasingly unlikely to be in the labor market as the unemployment rate increases. Among black women the additional worker effect is dominant as more of them enter the work force to compensate for the loss of earnings of other family members. In both instances the main effect is on entries rather than exits. In other words, women do not tend to move in and out, but merely adjust the timing of entry.

695. Blau, Francine D. and Lawrence M. Kahn. "Causes and Consequences of Layoffs." EI 19, 2 (Apr. 1981): 270-96. (3)

Women are found to be considerably less prone to layoffs than men with similar characteristics, but blacks considerably more so than comparably qualified whites. White men are more likely to be reemployed than members of either of the other groups, but are also more likely to experience long-run unfavorable effects on their earnings as a result of unemployment.

Chakrabarti (1977). See item 857.

696. DeBoer, Larry and Michael C. Seeborg. "The Female-Male Unemployment Differential: Effects of Changes in Industry Employment." MLR 107, 11 (Nov. 1984), 8-15. (3)

For the first time since 1947, the unemployment rate of men exceeded that of women in 1982. The reason was the heavy concentration of men in the industries that were hard-hit by the most serious recession since the 1930's. The authors also predict that, because of the expected growth of various industries, unemployment may continue to be lower for women than for men in the future. This is, however, less likely to be true during prosperous times.

697. Ferber, Marianne A. and Helen M. Lowry. "Women: The New Reserve Army of the Unemployed." SJWCS 1, 3 (Spring 1976b, Part 2): 213-32. (3)

This study confirms that to some extent women's behavior contributed to their high unemployment rates as compared to men during the period 1948-72. It is also suggested, however, that their higher turnover rate, their tendency to spend less time on job search, their lesser willingness to adjust domicile to job, and their inclination to crowd into a few female occupations may, at least in part, be a rational response to existing discrimination. This paper also emphasized the widening gap between the unemployment of women on men, but as DeBoer and Seeborg (1984) point out, the situation was reversed in 1982-83. They ascribe this to changes in industrial structure, but ignore the greater cyclical swings in men's unemployment.

698. Finegan, T. Aldrich. "Discouraged Workers and Economic Fluctuations." ILRR 35, 1 (Oct. 1981): 88-102. (3)

It is well known that most discouraged workers are women. This study indicates that the number of persons discouraged for job-market reasons has shown substantial cyclical swings, though the number who are discouraged for personal reasons does not. Hence the findings shed light on the social costs of a slack economy. The author further points out that procyclical swings in the size of the labor force are far larger than can be accounted for by discouraged workers alone, and that many individuals not counted in this category enter when unemployment is low.

699. Finn, Michael G. "Understanding the Higher Unemployment Rate of Women Scientists and Engineers." AER 73, 5 (Dec. 1983): 1137-40. (3)

Unemployment rates among scientists and engineers in the late 1970's, while quite low overall, were almost twice as high for women as for men. The difference can be explained by women being considerably more likely to put restrictions on their job search, and, to a lesser extent, by the larger proportion of women among recent graduates who have a higher unemployment rate than older cohorts.

700. Johnson, Janet L. "Sex Differentials in Unemployment Rates: A Case for No Concern." JPE 91, 2 (Apr. 1983a): 293-303. (2)

The author argues that the unemployment rate for women is overstated because the number of unemployed is related only to those in the labor force, not to the whole population, and because homemakers who are looking for work are counted as unemployed, while workers looking for another job are not. This whole line of reasoning is based on three highly debatable implicit assumptions. The first is that all women not in the labor market are homemakers. The second is that homemaking is a genuine though unpaid form of employment. The third, and most controversial, is that only women but not men have the alternatives of being a homemaker. The casual treatment of women's unemployment is all the more surprising in view of the author's (1983b) conclusion that most unemployment is involuntary.

701. Johnson, Janet L. "Unemployment as a Household Supply Decision." QREB 23, 2 (Summer 1983b): 71-88. (3)

A model is developed which takes into account the spouse's labor market opportunities, and considers the behavior of husbands and wives separately. The model is tested at two different points in the business cycle, with respect to both becoming unemployed, and duration of unemployment. The fact that neither unemployment insurance nor employment opportunities of the spouse have any significant effect is interpreted to show that most nonemployment is involuntary at all stages of the cycle.

702. Jones, Ethel B. Determinants of Female Reentrant Unemployment. Kalamazoo, MI: W. E. Upjohn Institute for Employment Research, 1983. (3)

This study involved the use of two samples of reentrants constructed from National Longitudinal Survey data for 1973, aged 20-28 years and 35-49 years respectively. Contrary to the frequently held view that reentrants generally experience a period of unemployment, this was found to be true for only one out of three. The model constructed to examine the determinants of reentrant unemployment emphasized availability of labor market information, the acceptance wage of the woman, her prior search plans, and labor market conditions. The independent variables important for mature women were education, experience and previous plans. For younger women the same variables were significant plus migration, number of children at home, and race.

703. Jones, Ethel B. and James E. Long. "Part-Week Work and Women's Unemployment." RES 63, 1 (Feb. 1981): 70-76. (3)

Contrary to expectations, the authors find that the probability and duration of unemployment are not different between part-week and full-week workers, once employee and labor market characteristics are taken into account.

Joshi (1981) See item 919.

704. Klein, Deborah P. "Trends in Employment and Unemployment in Families." MLR 106, 12 (Dec. 1983): 21-25. (3)

Not surprisingly, data show that multi-earner families have extra protection against financial reversals. The most interesting finding of this paper is, however, that during the recession of the early 1980's employment of married women declined less than that of married men. The author ascribes this to the fact that men tend to work in industries which are more cyclically sensitive. Further, heavily blue-collar industries were particularly hard-hit during this recession.

705. Kleinman, Samuel. "A Note on Racial Differences in the Added-Worker/Discouraged-Worker Controversy." AE 291 (Spring 1976): 74-75. (3)

The author addresses the puzzling fact that the labor force participation of white women tends to decline with increasing unemployment, while this is not true for black women, which tends to remain the same, or even increases. Blau, F. D. (1978) also found such differences. Kleinman suggests that because blacks have less investment in human capital and experience more unemployment they are under greater pressure to increase labor force participation. Hence there is a stronger income effect working in favor of the added-worker and a weaker substitution effect discouraging workers in black families. One might reach the same conclusion if black earnings are lower because of discrimination rather than because they have acquired less human capital.

706. Kreps, Juanita and Robert L. Clark. Sex, Age and Work: The Changing Composition of the Labor Force. Baltimore, MD: Johns Hopkins University Press, 1975. (4)

This book, written at a time of high unemployment, addresses the questions to what extent this has been caused, or at least aggravated, by changes in the composition of the work force, and what the implications are for the future. In the concluding section some suggestions are offered for ways to investigate the existing problems. Clearly, the issues addressed are still relevant a decade later.

707. Lillydahl, Jane H. and Larry D. Singell. "The Spatial Variation in Unemployment and Labor Force Participation Rates of Male and Female Workers." RS, 19, 5 (Oct. 1985): 459-69. (3)

This paper begins by reviewing the theoretical explanations for differences in work and residential choices of men and women. Using data from five metropolitan areas, the authors go on to investigate male and female unemployment and participation rates separately, and find spatial patterns to be significantly different for each of the two groups. For instance, greater distance from work increases unemployment and decreases labor force participation for women, but has the opposite effect for men.

708. Lingle, R. Christopher and Ethel B. Jones. "Women's Increasing Unemployment: A Cross-Sectional Analysis." AER 68, 2 (May 1978): 84-89. (3)

Cross-section data from the 1960 and 1970 Censuses are used to investigate why the unemployment rate of women in the post WWII period was higher, and increasingly so, than for men. The authors emphasize the extent to which cyclical swings in women's unemployment are smaller, but also point out that when women drop out of the labor force during times of recession this introduces costly discontinuity in their labor force participation.

Lundberg (1985) See item 267.

709. Lynch, Gerald J. and Thomas Hydak. "Cyclical and Noncyclical Unemployment Differences among Demographic Groups." GC 15, 1 (Jan. 1984): 9-17. (3)

First, this paper examines whether the "full employment unemployment rate" has changed over time for men and women, blacks and whites, adults and teens. The conclusion is that it has risen for all teens and all women, and that, therefore, the "natural rate" for the population as a whole has increased. The authors give no thought to the possibility that these groups have absorbed unemployment instead of the others, as is suggested by Bergmann (1980b). Second, the impact of minimum wages and unemployment compensation on the full-employment unemployment rate of each group is examined. Unemployment compensation appeared to have little effect, but minimum wage was found to have a substantial effect on black teens.

710. Marston, Stephen T. "Employment Instability and High Unemployment Rates." BPEA 1 (1976): 169-203. (3)

This author argues that the high unemployment rates for non-whites, teenagers and women result mainly from excessive job losses and quits, not from difficulties in finding jobs. He further claims that these high rates are not only associated with the type of jobs, but with the characteristics of workers. The author does not consider the fact that it is in part the outflows which make it easier for those looking for a job to find one, which tends to reduce the effect job entrants have on unemployment.

Maxwell and D'Amico (1976) See item 515.
Mincer (1966) See item 276.

711. Mooney, Joseph D. "Urban Poverty and Labor Force Participation." AER 57, 1 (Mar. 1967): 104-119. (3)

The main conclusions of this paper are that the responsiveness of poor, and especially non-white married women with husbands present to changes in the unemployment rate is considerably greater than that of their nonpoor and their white counterparts. The author interprets this as showing the greater willingness of the former to take advantage of favorable conditions to bring the family out of poverty. Glen G. Cain and Jacob Mincer, AER, 59, 1 (March 1969): 185-94 argue that the conclusions of this study are incorrect, chiefly because the author uses cross-section data to interpret changes over time, but also because his findings about differences between the populations are inconclusive. Mooney responds by pointing out that he admitted shortcomings in his original paper, but defends his basic results and their policy implications.

712. Morgenstern, Richard D. and Nancy S. Barrett. "The Retrospective Bias in the Unemployment Reporting by Sex, Race and Age." JASA 69, 346 (June 1974): 355-57. (2)

Comparing a survey taken during the relevant week and one conducted a year later, there appears to be a relative understatement of unemployment among women and youths. It is suggested that the cause for this may be the somewhat ambiguous social role of these two groups.

713. Niemi, Beth T. "The Female-Male Differential in Unemployment Rates." ILRR 27, 3 (Apr. 1974): 331-50. (3)

This study tests the effect of three factors often cited to explain the fact that the rate of unemployment is higher for women than for men: (1) the high rate of movement into and out of the labor market; (2) lower occupational and less economically purposeful geographic mobility; (3) lack of specific training. Only the first is found to be of substantial importance. The third is offset by the fact that women are employed in more cyclically stable industries.

714. Niemi, Beth T. "Geographic Immobility and Labor Force Mobility: A Study of Female Unemployment," in Cynthia B. Lloyd (ed.) Sex, Discrimination and the Division of Labor, NY: Columbia University Press, 1975, pp. 61-89. (3)

The author sets out to explain the generally higher unemployment rate of women as compared to men, as well as the widening of the gap during the post WWII period. She concludes that women's status as secondary workers was an important factor, causing them to have relatively little specific training, and a low rate of intra-labor force mobility. Contrary to many other writers, she ascribes considerably less significance to women's tendency to have high labor force turnover. By hindsight, now that the gap has narrowed, and even reversed in 1982-83, we may well conclude that the author did not put sufficient emphasis on the industrial structure of the economy.

715. Papps, Ivy. "Equal Pay and Female Unemployment." EA U.S.) 1, 1 (Oct. 1980). (3)

The author argues that women tend to be less productive than men, even in the same job. Hence, she concludes that if forced to pay equal wages, employers will prefer to hire men, and women will experience higher unemployment rates. This argument has been used for a long time, but there is no evidence of this in countries where the earnings gap has been decreasing rapidly.

716. Rea, Samuel A., Jr. "Unemployment and the Supply of Labor." JHR 9, 2 (Spring 1974): 279-89. (3)

This paper uses data from the March 1967 Current Population Survey to integrate reported unemployment into a model of labor supply. Based on the assumption that the individual faces a fixed wage rate, the model estimates that about half of the time not spent in employment is leisure time for married women, but, at the other extreme, none is leisure time for husbands whose wives are not in the labor force. (Obviously, the author chooses to ignore any distinction between leisure and housework.) The results also suggest that there is only a slight additional worker effect.

717. Sandell, Steven H. "Is the Unemployment Rate of Women Too Low? A Direct Test of Economic Theory of Job Search." RES 62, 4 (Nov. 1980): 634-38. (3)

The regression analysis using National Longitudinal Surveys data gives support to the hypothesis that women with a higher reservation wage experience a longer period of unemployment but obtain higher paying jobs. It was also determined that women who were dismissed had longer unemployment spells than those who quit. No difference, however, was found by race after controlling for other factors. The author concludes that women should be encouraged to take a longer time for job search, in order to raise their earnings.

718. Stevens, Lonnie K., Charles Register and Paul Grimes. "Race and the Discouraged Female Worker: A Question of Labor Force Attachment." RBPE 14, 1 (Summer 1985): 89-97. (3)

An econometric model is used to examine the extent of labor force attachment of men and women over the business cycle. For women, as a group, the results show a considerably greater tendency to drop out of the labor force during recessions, but this is not true for minority females. This confirms the general impression that minority women increasingly play the same role in society as men.

719. Strand, Kenneth and Thomas Dernburg. "Cyclical Variations in Civilian Labor Force Participation." RES 46, 4 (Nov. 1964): 378-91. (3)

This paper found both substantial discouraged worker and additional worker effects on women as the unemployment rate increased. The study was, however, criticized for faulty specification, primarily on the grounds that the basic equation exploits an identity. Barth (1968), avoiding these problems, obtained different results.

720. Vickery, Clair. "The Impact of Turnover on Group Unemployment Rates." RES 59, 4 (Nov. 1977b): 415-26. (3)

The effect of voluntary turnover on the unemployment rate of black and white men and women is examined. The author concludes that as much as 75 to 80 percent of the difference in the unemployment rates of white women as compared to white men, and 30 to 60 percent of the difference between black men and women can be explained in this way. She does add the caveat that a reduction in the voluntary turnover rate might increase the duration of spells of unemployment. This point is more fully developed by Bergmann (1980b).

721. Vickery, Clair, Barbara R. Bergmann, and Katherine Swartz. "Unemployment Rate Targets and Anti-Inflation Policy as More Women Enter the Workforce." <u>AER</u> 68, 2 (May 1978): 90-98. (4)

The authors argue that because occupational segregation is the primary reason women tend to experience higher unemployment rates, higher turnover rates for women should not be used to justify upward revisions of unemployment targets as female labor force participation increases. They further suggest that reducing occupational segregation would tend to reduce the amount of inflationary pressure associated with any given level of unemployment.

Werneke (1978) See item 1022.

Chapter 8

WOMEN IN INDIVIDUAL OCCUPATIONS

Though some issues are the same or similar for women in the labor market throughout the economy, in other respects the conditions and problems encountered differ considerably in various sectors. Hence it is not surprising that a good deal of work has focused on workers in particular occupations and industries.

There are reasons why some segments have received more attention than others. Clerical, or so-called pink-collar jobs, stand out because for a long time they have been by far the largest source of employment for women. Women's professions have come in for their share of interest because their members are relatively well educated, visible, and are becoming increasingly vocal. Women in academia, particularly, have been the subject of a disproportionate amount of research, in part for the same reasons, and partly because research is done primarily by members of this group. The existence of a well-established hierarchy within faculties and ready availability of data are additional contributing factors. Women managers and executives, another small but growing minority, with a good deal of visibility and potentially a lot of influence, are also receiving attention.

Work on other occupations is far sparser. This is particularly unfortunate because there are important problems that deserve investigation. For instance, the male-female earnings gap is larger among sales workers than in any other major occupational category. While women are very heavily represented among service workers, some of the detailed occupations in this group, such as police officers and firefighters continue to be among the most highly segregated. Women have made very little progress in integrating any of the skilled blue collar occupations. The same is true of agriculture, forestry and fishing. There would be almost no women in this sector, if it were not for migrant farm workers. They are, along with domestic service employees, among the most poorly paid and lowest status workers in our economy. They are also largely female, and predominantly nonwhite. It is hoped that these segments of the work force will receive more attention in the future.

722. Abbott, Edith. Women in Industry. New York: D. Appleton and Company, 1909. (3)

An extensive history of women's employment in industry in the United States from the Colonial period onward, with special emphasis on five branches that employed large numbers of women. The main aim of this book was to show that women always played an important role in industrial production, and that these workers did not receive adequate attention from the women's movement at the turn of the century.

723. Ahern, Nancy C. and Elizabeth L. Scott. Career Outcomes in a Matched Sample of Men and Women Ph.D.s, Washington, DC: National Academy Press, 1981. (3)

A detailed analysis of men and women Ph.D.'s, matched by age, experience and field, showed that there were differences between them in both rank and earnings. Other findings were that only 10 percent of women with young children dropped out, and that women not married, and those without children, fared no better than mothers, Young women were slightly more likely to have moved, and were somewhat more likely to be at prestigious institutions than their male peers, and considerably more so than older women. It remains to be seen how these young women will progress in their careers over time.

724. Allison, Elizabeth K. "Sex-Linked Earnings Differentials in the Beauty Industry." JHR 11, 3 (Summer 1976): 383-90. (3)

This case study concludes that about two-thirds of the earnings differential within this occupation can be plausibly associated with differences between men and women in productivity. Interviews further suggested four reasons for these differences: (1) most women expected to work only until the birth of their first child, though, as the author points out, this was not realistic; (2) apprenticeships that led to higher-level jobs were not open to older women when they decided to remain in the labor market; (3) there may have been discrimination in obtaining apprenticeships; and (4) nonpecuniary considerations may be more important for women.

725. Allison, Elizabeth K. and Pinney Allen. "Male-Female Professionals: A Model of Career Choice." IR 17, 3 (Oct. 1978): 333-37. (3)

Estimates of male and female supply responses to changes in salaries in two female professions (nursing and teaching) and two male professions (chemistry and law) are found to be roughly equal for both sexes. Two possible explanations are offered why women nonetheless tend to be in low-pay occupations. One is that basic career decisions are made at a very early age and cannot readily be reversed later. Secondly, it may be discrimination that keeps women out of highly paid jobs.

726. Amsden, Alice H. and Colette Moser. "Job Search and Affirmative Action," AER 65, 2 (May 1975): 83-91. (3)

This study examined the job market for male and female economists 1973-74, utilizing data collected by the American Economic Association and the Committee on the Status of Women in the Economics Profession. The main findings were that there appeared to be no consistent differences between the opportunities for interviews and job offers of equally qualified men and women, but that women already employed continued to perceive problems of discrimination against women. This perception was shared by only a small proportion of men.

727. Bailyn, Lotte. "Family Constraints on Women's Work." ANYAS 208 (Mar. 15, 1973): 82-90. (3)

This paper deals with women who are married to highly educated men, because the author thinks that among these is likely to be the greatest amount of "wasted talent." She believes the main constraints on these women come from their "family responsibilities." She also points out, however, that those who are themselves highly educated are increasingly likely to be in the labor force, and suggests we can learn from the fact that those who have been most successful were employed, at least part time, even while they had preschool children.

728. Baran, Barbara and Suzanne Teegarden. "Women's Labor in the Office of the Future: Changes in the Occupational Structure of the Insurance Industry" in Lourdes Beneria, ed. Women and Structural Transformation: The Crisis of Work and Family Life, New Brunswick, NJ: Rutgers University Press, 1985. (3)

A thorough investigation of a major property/casualty company and some more general research of the insurance industry, as a whole, leads the authors to very gloomy conclusions. Minority women, now mainly in low-level clerical jobs are likely to lose their jobs as firms move to white suburbs, and as more of the work is automated. Skilled, and especially white clerical workers are expected to find jobs, but not opportunities for upward mobility. Only college-educated women will probably fill increasingly larger proportions of professional and managerial jobs, but they may find that these categories have become de-skilled and resegregated.

729. Bartlett, Robin L. and Timothy I. Miller. "Executive Compensation: Female Executives and Networking." AER 75, 2 (May 1985): 266-701. (3)

This study attempts to determine the influence of professional contacts on careers of women and concludes that among top female executives networking is as important as human capital investments.

730. Bartlett, Robin L. and Colette H. Moser. "Women at Work: Female Segregation and Sex Concentration in the Work Force." NJEB 13, 4 (Autumn 1974): 74-91. (3,4)

The purpose of this study is to provide additional insight into factors contributing to the earnings gap by examining the status of female clerical workers. From 1962 to 1972 the earnings of women as compared to men in this occupation declined, as did those of female clerical workers compared to other female workers. This appears to be related to growing female concentration, and increasing sex segregation within the clerical occupational category. The authors suggest that young women should be encouraged to enter other occupations.

Bartol, K. M. and Bartol, R. A. (1975) See item 839.

731. Basil, Douglas C. Women in Management, NY: Dunellen, 1972. (3)

In response to concern about women as an unused resource, the author attempted to learn about the reasons for their sparse representation among managers. For this purpose a survey was conducted of about 2,000 firms and governmental units. Questionnaires were sent to the highest ranking male and female executive in each, inquiring about the representation of women in managerial positions, followed by questions about male and female attitudes toward them. In all, 214 males and 102 females responded. The results showed an extremely small proportion of women, especially in private firms, and at upper levels of management. Some favorable and some unfavorable attitudes toward women managers were found among both men and women, but the latter were somewhat more likely to have positive views. Similar findings from another survey are reported by Schwartz (1971).

732. Bayer, Alan E. and Helen S. Astin. "Sex Differences in Academic Rank and Salary Among Doctorates in Teaching." JHR 3, 2 (Spring 1968): 191-200. (3)

Information obtained on about 2,700 recent science doctorates and technical personnel showed that beginning academic rank was unrelated to sex, as was promotion in the natural sciences. On the other hand, in the social sciences women were promoted more slowly, and salary differentials unfavorable to women existed in all fields, at all ranks. Thus the authors conclude that women are at a disadvantage in salary, but much less so in rank. At least two serious questions must, however, be raised. First, no distinction is made for quality within the categories of "Colleges" and "Universities." Second, the sample of women in various categories is very small, in one case only 17.

733. Bayer, Alan E. and Helen S. Astin, "Sex Differentials in the Academic Reward System," Science, 188 (May 23, 1975): 796-802. (3)

American Council on Education data for 1972-73 show that academic men and women differ in educational background, field, professional activities, work setting, and related characteristics which influence rewards. Even after all these were taken into account, however, there was clear evidence of discrimination in salaries and, to an extent, in promotions. The authors concede that there may be still other unmeasured characteristics, but point out that the variables used may be proxies for these, that some may not favor men, and that others may simply reflect the cumulative effect of sex discrimination. Their conclusions are similar to those of numerous studies investigating individual institutions.

734. Bell, Carolyn S. "Economics, Sex and Gender." SSQ 55, 3 (Dec. 1974b): 615-31. (1)

The thrust of this paper is summarized succinctly in its opening sentence and closing paragraph. "Who speaks for economics? Men do." "Both economic analysis and economic policy dealing with individuals, either in their roles as providers or consumers, have been evolved primarily by men. Insofar as economic analysis has developed policy solutions, it has, to quote Representative Martha Griffiths, 'met the social concerns of the nation as defined by men. It has not met the social concerns of the nation as defined by women, or as defined by men and women....' We have, then, a sexually neutral economics: its gender is indubitably male." More than 10 years later this complaint is only somewhat less timely.

735. Binkin, Martin and Shirley J. Bach, Women and the Military, Washington, D.C.: The Brookings Institution, 1979. (3)

A thoughtful review of the situation of women in the military confirms the authors' judgment that the character and composition of this institution mirrors the attitudes of society at large. Women's presence in the armed forces, even though they comprise only a very small percentage, is indicative of progress, but substantial continued inequality shows the strength of tradition. There is a useful appendix briefly discussing the situation in other countries.

Birdsall and M. L. Fox (1985) See item 847.
Blitz (1975) See item 849.

736. Blitz, Rudolph C. and Chin H. Ow. "A Cross-Sectional Analysis of Women's Participation in the Professions." JPE 81, 1 (Jan.-Feb. 1973): 131-44. (3)

Using demand and supply equations the authors attempt to explain differences in women's participation in the professions by state. Industrial structure, level of women's education, availability of domestic help, and ratio of male to female professional income all turned out to be significant as explanatory variables. Per capita income was not. The authors conjecture that this is because they have only aggregate data.

737. Bognano, M. F., J. S. Hixson and J. R. Jeffers. "The Short-Run Supply of Nurse's Time." JHR 9, 1 (Winter 1974): 80-94. (3)

This study finds that the main determinant of the labor force participation of married professional nurses, when demographic factors are held constant, is their husband's earnings, while their own wage rate has no significant effect. It is also shown that within the existing range of observations, there is a positive though small response to their own wage rate in amount of time supplied. The author concludes that in the short run policies such as providing child care and retraining would increase supply more than would higher wages, but recognizes that increased pay might attract more young people into the profession in the long run.

Boulier and Pineda (1975) See item 852.

738. Busch, Paul and Ronald F. Bush. "Women Contrasted to Men in the Industrial Sales Force: Job Satisfaction, Values, Role Clarity, Performance and Propensity to Leave." JMR 15, 3 (Aug. 1978): 438-48. (3)

This study investigates differences between females and males in the industrial sales force. Women and men are compared on various aspects of job satisfaction, on importance of job components, on performance, role clarity and propensity to leave the organizations. The only differences found were that women had lower role clarity and a higher propensity to leave. The authors also make a number of useful suggestions for reducing these disparities. Jackson, J. H., Keaveny and Fossum (1978) also showed that, on the whole, men and women were quite similar with respect to job satisfaction.

739. Carleton, Bette N. "The Status of Women in Accounting." MA 55, 3 (Sept. 1973): 59-62. (3)

This paper reports on the experiences of some of the women who have been entering accounting, a previously predominantly male field. It appears, on the whole, that they are being accepted, albeit at times grudgingly.

740. Cartter, Alan M. and Wayne E. Ruhter. The Disappearance of Sex Discrimination in First Job Placement of New Ph.D.'s, Los Angeles, CA: Higher Education Research Institute, 1975. (3)

On the basis of their investigation the authors conclude that women do at least as well as men in terms of the rank of the institution where they receive their first job. They do not, however, examine information on the quality of the candidate, or on the type of appointment and salary obtained.

741. Centra, John A. Women, Marriage and the Doctorate. Princeton, NJ: Educational Testing Service, 1974. (3)

This survey of 3,658 men and women who received Ph.D.'s in 1950, 1960 or 1968 provides a wealth of data on their professional and family lives. The author concludes that the women who combine homemaking and career frequently find that both suffer. Though he points out that not all women experience such problems, he tends to emphasize negative aspects and fails to adequately note the evidence of trends toward a substantial decline in differences in behavior and outcomes for women and men over the two decades examined in this work.

Chiplin (1981) See item 859.

742. Cole, Jonathan R. Fair Science: Women in the Scientific Community. N.Y.: Free Press, 1979. (4)

This author begins by acknowledging that until recently inequality between men and women was accepted as natural, and that the few women scientists there were, were largely treated as invisible, including those who made significant contributions. After examining, at great length, the current situation, however, he concludes that "to an extraordinary degree the scientific community distributes its resources and rewards in an equitable fashion." He does not explain what caused this dramatic turnabout, and the evidence supporting his view of the present is by no means entirely convincing. A good deal of it amounts to showing that those who decide on the rewards are also the ones who judge whether those who receive them are worthy.

743. Cook, Alice H. "Women and American Trade Unions." AAAPSS 375 (Jan. 1968): 124-32. (3)

This is one of the few papers devoted to the subject of women workers and trade unions. The attitude of unions toward protective legislation for women and equal opportunity legislation is singled out for particular attention, as are special clauses concerning women in union contracts and the participation of women in the political life of unions. The author's pessimistic and well-documented conclusion was that little had changed over 20 years.

744. Corazzini, Arthur J. "Equality of Employment Opportunity in the Federal White Collar Civil Service." JHR 7, 4 (Fall 1972): 424-45. (3)

Basing this study on data collected by the U.S. Civil Service Commission, the author adjusted for age, education, pre-government experience, supervisory responsibility, formal training, occupational group, and marital-parental status, and was able to raise the ratio of women's to men's earnings from 69 percent to 80 percent, even without an adequate control for work experience. The relatively small remaining gap is not surprising since first, we are dealing with a single sector of the economy and second, there is general agreement that women tend to do better in the government than in the private sector.

745. Daly, Patricia A. "Unpaid Family Workers: Long-Term Decline Continues." MLR 105, 10 (Oct. 1982): 3-5. (3)

From 1950 to 1981, while the labor force increased substantially, the number of unpaid family workers declined to less than half. Most of these workers have been in agriculture, and a large proportion of them have been women.

Davidson and Cooper (1985) See item 872.
Deere (1982) See item 873.

746. Dewey, Lucretia M. "Women in Labor Unions." MLR 94, 2 (Feb. 1971): 42-48. (3)

Since the late 1950's, while the number of women in unions had increased, in absolute terms, and relative to men, it had not kept pace with the increase in women entering the labor force. Further, they continued to be seriously underrepresented among union officers. Since this paper was written, the proportion of union members who are women has increased, though there has been no corresponding increase among officers, and there has been some progress in unions addressing "women's issues."

747. Dexter, Carolyn R. "Women and the Exercise of Power in Organizations: From Ascribed to Achieved Status." WW 1 (1985): 239-58. (3)

The author explains women's underrepresentation among managers in large part as the result of conflicts between women's socialization to ascribed status and the achieved status demands for executives.

748. Ferber, Marianne A. and Helen M. Berg. "Men and Women Graduate Students: Who Succeeds and Why?" JHE 54, 6 (Nov.-Dec. 1983): 629-48. (3)

Among graduate students at the University of Illinois at Urbana-Champaign, the 44 percent who were women were very similar to their male colleagues in many ways, including satisfaction and perceived problems with graduate school, and in very few of them leaving without a degree. They were, however, more likely to pursue terminal master's degrees as opposed to doctor's degrees, were particularly overrepresented in education and underrepresented in the sciences, and were less confident of their ability to handle their work even though their credentials were at least as good. Both men and women students most often established close professional relationships with faculty of the same sex. Since such close relationships proved to be strongly related to successful completion of their program, the small number of faculty women puts women students at a clear disadvantage, particularly in traditionally male fields. On the other hand, women did better than men in education.

Ferber and Birnbaum, B. G. (1981) See item 473.

749. Ferber, Marianne A. and Carole A. Green. "Traditional or Reverse Sex Discrimination? A Case Study of a Large Public University." ILRR 35, 4 (July 1982): 550-64. (3)

This study assesses the extent and causes of sex discrimination in academic positions at a large public university, using detailed career information for all individuals hired for full-time faculty positions 1975-1979. Women were found to receive $2,000 less per year, all else equal, and were also less likely to be hired for tenure-track positions. These results suggest affirmative action had not been entirely successful as yet with respect to faculty employment.

750. Ferber, Marianne A. and Joan A. Huber. "Husbands, Wives and Careers." JMF 41, 2 (May 1979): 315-25. (3)

This research, based on a large national sample of individuals who received their Ph.D.s either between 1958 and 1963 or between 1967 and 1972, showed that having a Ph.D. spouse tended to have a negative effect on the labor force participation of wives, and on offices held and articles published by husbands. There was, however, no direct effect on earnings of husbands, or of wives who were in the labor force.

751. Ferber, Marianne A. and Betty Kordick. "Sex Differentials in the Earnings of Ph.D.'s." ILRR 31, 2 (Jan. 1978): 227-38. (3)

Using a survey of two cohorts of men and women who received Ph.D.s in the years 1958-63 and 1967-72, the authors found that most of the earnings differentials between the sexes could not be explained by women's career interruptions or their lesser willingness to accumulate human capital. Further, their results conflicted with the hypothesis proposed by Johnson, G. E. and Stafford, F. P. (1974) that the earnings gap would narrow once women permanently reentered the labor force. Hence it appears that women's own behavior is not primarily responsible for their lower earnings among Ph.D.s.

752. Ferber, Marianne A. and Jane W. Loeb. "Performance, Rewards and Perceptions of Sex Discrimination of Male and Female Faculty Members." AJS 78, 4 (Jan. 1973): 995-1002. (3)

A study based on a survey of male and female faculty at a large, research oriented university showed the following: (1) wives, with or without children, are no less productive than single women, yet appear to experience less success in academia, (2) marital and, for men, parental status may enter reward decisions, perhaps because of perceptions of financial needs, (3) neither men nor women appear to be less productive, or receive lower rewards, in the relatively female fields, (4) women are more inclined to think there is sex discrimination than men do.

753. Ferber, Marianne A. and Jane W. Loeb. "Professors, Performance and Rewards." IR, 13, 1 (Feb. 1974): 69-77. (3)

Questionnaire data from a sample of full-time university faculty were used to investigate the influence of productivity, longevity, and perceived financial needs on salaries. The main conclusions were that productivity appears to influence rank far more than salary within rank and that tenure in the job influences salaries of men far more than those of women. It was also discovered that being married to another faculty member tends to depress the earnings of both men and women, perhaps because of the lesser mobility of such couples.

754. Ferber, Marianne A., Jane W. Loeb and Helen M. Lowry. "The Economic Status of Women Faculty: A Reappraisal." JHR 13, 3 (Summer 1978): 385-40. (3)

This study, conducted at a large, research-oriented institution, finds support for the hypothesis that performance is, at least in part, a function of rewards. The results also show that quality of faculty, as measured by number of publications, has improved since the introduction of affirmative action. Further, no evidence was found that faculty wives are more highly rewarded than other women. These results suggest that concern about a possibly harmful impact of affirmative action on universities is misplaced.

Ferber and Westmiller (1976) See item 598.
Fidell (1970) See item 599.
Finn (1983) See item 699.

755. Fox, Mary F. "Sex, Salary and Achievement: Reward-Dualism in Academia." SE 54, 2 (Apr. 1981): 71-84. (3)

Achievement is the main determinant of salary for both men and women, but women's returns are lower. Women's earnings also vary less with differences in race, citizenship or university location, but more according to credentials. Thus, the author concludes that standards are not entirely universalistic and that returns to achievement are modified by a dual reward structure.

756. Fox, Mary F. "Location, Sex Typing, and Salary Among Academics." WO 12, 2 (May 1985): 186-205. (3)

This study finds that intra-university location by type and size of unit is more important in determining the salary of men than of women, even though some similar patterns emerge for both sexes.

757. Fraker, Susan. "Why Women Aren't Getting to the Top." F 109, 8 (Apr. 1984): 40-45. (3,4)

This paper begins by noting that "No women are on the fast track to the chief executive's job in any Fortune 500 corporation," even though women have been moving into management for a number of years. The author concludes that the reasons for this are rather elusive, but may well include inadequate support from senior management, unwillingness to permit managers to work part-time or take off a few months during times of peak family demands, and, perhaps most important, the failure to consider success in attracting and developing competent women managers as an important criterion in judging an executive's performance.

758. France, Judith E. and Michael C. Seeborg. "Labor Market Performance of Female CETA Participants." EF 10, 1 (Summer 1979): 55-64. (4)

This study found that CETA vocational education in Indiana did not seem to be moving economically disadvantaged women into male occupations in significant numbers. Further, those few who obtained training in non-traditional occupations experienced greater difficulties in finding jobs than did the others. On the other hand those who did find jobs had somewhat higher earnings than their traditional counterparts. Because the sample was small and geographically restricted, the results cannot necessarily be generalized.

759. Frank, Robert H. "Family Location Constraints and the Geographic Distribution of Female Professionals." JPE 86, 1 (Feb. 1978a): 117-30. (3,4)

Because a far smaller proportion of professional men than professional women live in two-career families, the problems of location are more serious for the latter group. For this reason, in the absence of discrimination, female professionals would be expected to be more heavily concentrated in urban areas. The author concludes that it is therefore unfair to expect employers in small labor markets to hire women in proportion to their availability in the country as a whole. He does not point out that, by the same token, employers in large urban areas should be expected to hire a larger proportion of women.

760. Ginzberg, Ely and Alice Yohalem, eds. Corporate Lib: Women's Challenge to Management, Baltimore, MD: Johns Hopkins Press, 1973. (3,4)

This compendium of papers presented at a conference sponsored by the Graduate School of Business at Columbia University, anticipated major changes in the role of women in management over the following decade. Attention is divided between the concerns of women who want to make progress and those of the gatekeepers who are in a position to facilitate or inhibit it, while recognizing that both sides operate within the cultural and economic setting of total society. Taken as a whole, the book provides a good balance in its emphasis on what needs to be done by employers, by government, and by women themselves to enable women not only to attain management positions, but to reach the middle and top levels.

761. Goldman, Nancy. "The Changing Role of Women in the Armed Forces." AJS 78, 4 (Jan. 1973): 892-911. (3)

The author studies the role of women in the armed forces, the epitome of a male-dominated establishment, as a limiting case of the changing role of women in occupational and bureaucratic structures. A gradual increase in numbers, and a slow but continuing expansion of assignment is projected on the basis of the evidence. There is, on the one hand, the commitment of the government to bringing about equality, on the other hand a lack of opportunity for women to do the things men do by excluding them from training for combat.

762. Goldstein, Elyse. "Effect of Same-Sex and Cross-Sex Role Models on the Subsequent Academic Productivity of Scholars," <u>AP</u> 34, 5 (May 1979): 407-10. (3)

Publication rates of Ph.D.'s who had dissertation advisors of their own sex were found to be greater than of those who had advisors of the opposite sex.

763. Gomez-Mejia, Luis R. and David B. Balkin. "A Union Impacts on Secretarial Earnings: A Public Sector Case." <u>IR</u> 23, 1 (Winter 1984): 97-102. (4)

Using a sample of 40 city governments, the researchers find that, at least in the public sector, secretarial unions may well have a positive effect on earnings of their members. For an entrant, the increase appeared to be about 14 percent. This helps to explain the increase in unionization of this type of employees.

764. Goodman, Janet S. and Virginia Novarra. "The Sex Discrimination Act 1975--File and Forget." <u>PR</u> 7, 1 (Winter 1978): 14-18. (4)

The authors conclude that in the United States EEO law, though initially ineffective, evolved in the course of the 1970's into a rather useful instrument, and that the same is likely to be true with respect to the legislation introduced in 1975. They were probably correct about this, but overlooked the possibility that such progress could also be reversed by an unsympathetic administration and the judges appointed by such an administration.

765. Gordon, Francine E. and Myra H. Strober. "Initial Observations on a Pioneer Cohort: 1974 Women MBAs." <u>SMR</u> 19, 2 (Winter 1978): 15-23. (3)

Some differences were found among male and female MBAs in this sample. Women had less mathematics and science training, received less counseling, and aspired to lower salaries. In other respects the two groups were quite similar.

766. Gordon, Nancy M. and Thomas E. Morton. "The Staff Salary Structure at a Large Urban University." JHR 11, 3 (Summer 1976): 374-82. (3)

This paper uses data on full-time non-faculty employees of a large, urban university to examine the male-female wage differential, controlling for age, education, marital status, years at the university, and job. Even though this institution had an exceptionally large number of job titles, women staff members earned significantly less than men in the same category. Estimates vary from 7 to 17 percent, depending which one of three approaches is used.

Gordon, N. M., Morton and Braden (1974) See item 611.

767. Gramm, Wendy L. "The Labor Force Decision of Married Female Teachers: A Discriminant Analysis Approach." RES 55, 3 (Aug. 1973): 341-48. (3)

Discriminant analysis is used because there are three possible types of labor force status: full-time work, part-time work, or no paid work. Explanatory variables -- wage of husband, full-time wage of wife, part-time wage of wife, household assets, household age, and age of children -- make it possible to distinguish between all three outcomes. The author therefore concludes that women working full-time should not be lumped with those who work part-time. Armando J. Baqueiro, James J. Breen, David E. Mead and Donald E. Wise, RES 58, 2 (May 1976): 241-44 criticizes the way the research was carried out and Gramm responds.

768. Gray, Mary W. and Elizabeth L. Scott. "A Statistical Remedy for Statistically Identified Discrimination." A 66, 4 (May 1980): 174-81. (2,4)

It is argued here that when a statistical study shows that women as a group are rewarded less than men, "flagging" those women who are paid less than predicted by the male reward structure is not an acceptable remedy. Since women as a group were presumably discriminated against, this may be equally true for those who are relatively well paid. The authors therefore suggest that all women should have their salary adjusted. One problem is that this approach tacitly accepts the importance of unmeasured characteristics and hence opens the door to the argument that these may also justify the higher earnings of men.

769. Grossman, Allyson S. "Women in Domestic Work: Yesterday and Today." <u>MLR</u> 103, 8 (Aug. 1980): 17-21. (3)

A century ago, half of all wage-earning women were private household workers. In 1979 fewer than 3 percent were so employed. This change has been particularly important for black women who have been heavily overrepresented in this occupation. Among the relatively few domestic workers today, blacks tend to be middle-aged cleaners or servants, whites are likely to be young babysitters.

770. Gurin, Patricia and Carolyn Gaylord. "Educational and Occupational Goals of Men and Women at Black Colleges." <u>MLR</u> 99, 6 (June 1976): 10-16. (3)

Surveys at schools that have been historically black show that women have lower educational expectations and aspire to jobs with lower prestige and ability requirements than men. The author is not concerned about the possibility that prestige and skill requirements rankings may be influenced by the extent to which an occupation is male or female.

Hamilton (1973) See item 617.

771. Hamovitch, William and Richard D. Morgenstern. "Children and the Productivity of Academic Women." <u>JHE</u> 48, 6 (Nov./Dec. 1977): 633-45. (3)

Data collected by the Carnegie-American Council on Education show that, other things held constant, women faculty publish somewhat less than men, but there is no evidence that children have any influence on number of publications or on the probability of becoming "outstanding." Like others, the authors fail to consider the possibility of a positive self-selection for those mothers who remain in the labor market.

772. Hanson, R. J. and R. J. F. Spitze. "Increasing Incomes of Farm Families Through Dual Employment." AFR 35 (Oct. 1974): 59-64. (3)

This analysis extends that of previous studies which showed the increasing dependence of farm families upon off-farm employment by investigating in more detail husband's and wife's employment. New evidence is provided from 1971 Illinois data. Last, the importance of dual employment in providing staying power to part-time farmers is discussed.

773. Harlan, Sharon L. "Federal Job Training Policy and Economically Disadvantaged Women." WW 1 (1985): 282-310. (4)

The author critically examines women's opportunity for enrollment, participation in different types of training, and occupational sex segregation as related to the 1982 Job Training Partnership Act and its predecessor, the Comprehensive Employment and Training Act. This is followed by a critique of the studies that have addressed the question whether women benefitted from these programs.

Hirsch and Leppel (1982) See item 622.

774. Hoffman, Emily P. "Faculty Salaries: Is There Discrimination by Sex, Race and Discipline? Additional Evidence." AER 66, 1 (Mar. 1976): 196-98. (3)

Using data from one large institution, it is shown that the estimate of discrimination in earnings is considerably larger when rank is not introduced as an independent variable. This would be expected, since rank is determined by the same people, in much the same way, as is salary.

775. Holmstrom, Lynda L. The Two-Career Family. Cambridge, MA: Schenkman, 1972. (3)

An in-depth study of 20 career couples led the author to conclude that the main problems they faced were related to the inflexibility of occupations, the isolation of the modern family, and the existing definition of masculinity as superiority. Some specific findings otherwise were that husbands tended to be supportive and to participate more in housework than those in traditional families. Nonetheless, these couples were far from egalitarian. The concluding section of the book is devoted to a discussion of various ways to improve this situation.

776. Jewell, Donald O. Women and Management: An Expanding Role, Atlanta, GA: School of Business Administration, Georgia State University, 1977. (3)

This book begins with several chapters containing background information on the changing role of women in the labor market, then goes on to provide short papers which offer a variety of individual views and experiences specifically related to careers of women executives. The essays are, for the most part, written on a popular level.

777. Johnson, George E. and Frank P. Stafford. "The Earnings and Promotion of Women Faculty." AER 64, 6 (Dec. 1974): 888-903. (3)

An investigation of various aspects of the status of female relative to male faculty in six disciplines, using data from the NSF register for 1970, shows that women's salaries are 4 to 11 percent lower at the start, and 13 to 23 percent lower 15 years later. The authors conclude that these results would be expected in the absence of labor market discrimination because of career interruptions and part-time work. These conclusions have been challenged by other researchers, notably Myra H. Strober and Aline O. Quester, AER 67, 2 (Mar. 1977): 207-13. They point out that Johnson and Stafford do not explain the initial differential, fail to show that women work in less research-oriented institutions by choice, and ignore feedback effects of lower rewards, to mention only some of the most obvious problems. Stephen Farber, AER, 67, 2 (Mar. 1977): 199-206 finds that using longitudinal data, he cannot confirm either that older women catch up in earnings or that, all else equal, they are more likely to be promoted than men with comparable characteristics.

778. Johnson, George E. and Frank P. Stafford. "Women and the Academic Labor Market" in Cynthia B. Lloyd, ed. Sex, Discrimination and the Division of Labor, NY: Columbia University Press, 1975, pp. 201-19. (3)

This paper is very similar to Johnson and Stafford (1974), and, for the most part, reaches the same conclusions. There is, however, one important change. The authors examine the possibility that discrimination might also help to explain the existing differences in men's and women's status in academia, and conclude that they cannot disprove this possibility.

779. Jusenius, Carol L. and Richard M. Scheffler. "Earnings Differentials Among Academic Economists: Empirical Evidence on Race and Sex." JEB 33, 2 (Winter 1981): 88-96. (3)

This study, relying on data from the National Academy of Sciences 1973 Survey, finds that variables affecting earnings differed by race and sex, and that among older cohorts substantial earnings differences still existed between men and women, whites and non-whites. For black males this was true even at the start of their careers. This study included some useful variables not taken into account by earlier researchers, but can be faulted for also including rank, a variable itself potentially subject to bias. Most serious, however, was not including productivity.

780. Kahne, Hilda. "Women in the Professions: Career Considerations and Job Placement Techniques." JEI 5, 3 (Sept. 1971): 28-45. (3)

This paper focuses on aspects of social structures and attitudes as important determinants of career choice and job placement. Issues of concern to professional women are examined, in the hope of improving the understanding of ways in which they are disadvantaged, and what might be done about it.

781. Katz, David A. "Faculty Salaries, Promotions, and Productivity at a Large University." AER 63, 3 (June 1973): 469-77. (3)

This study is based on information for the faculty of one large, research oriented institution. A great deal of detailed information similar to that used by Darland (1973) and Ferber and Loeb (1974) was used, but the analysis was based on a single regression, with sex as a dummy variable. In view of extensive findings showing that the salary structure for men and women tends to be quite different, this approach must be regarded as unsatisfactory.

782. Kehrer, Barbara H. "Factors Affecting the Incomes of Men and Women Physicians: an Exploratory Analysis." JHR 11, 4 (Fall 1976): 526-45. (3)

Data from the American Medical Association's 1973 Eighth Periodic Survey of Physicians are used to investigate earnings differences between male and female doctors. The study shows that women tend to possess less favorable characteristics, but that only about one-quarter of the difference in hourly net income was attributable to that, the remainder being caused by differences in the income structure. The author is not prepared to ascribe this to discrimination. However, her interpretation that women tend to obtain higher marginal returns to particular characteristics can equally be viewed as women being penalized more for not having them. An update (Langwell, 1982) reaches rather different conclusions.

783. Kilson, Marion. "Black Women in the Professions, 1890-1970." MLR 100, 5 (May 1977): 38-41. (3)

Not only have women in general had a higher representation in the professions than in the labor force, but this is also specifically true for black women. More than half of black professionals have been women since 1940 (though this has only been true of all women since 1986). In both groups, however, by far the largest numbers have been in the female professions: nurses, librarians, social workers, and teachers.

784. Koch, James V. and John F. Chizmar, Jr. "Sex Discrimination and Affirmative Action in Faculty Salaries." EI 14, 2 (Apr. 1976): 16-23. (3)

The main finding of this research (also reported in The Economics of Affirmative Action, Lexington, MA: Lexington Books, 1976) was that faculty women at the university the authors investigated were underpaid relative to men before an equity adjustment was made, but overpaid afterwards. One variable included was "evaluation of peers," which the researchers claim may capture various characteristics for which no data were available. The obvious possibility that this variable may also capture the discrimination which caused women to be underpaid in the first place is never considered.

785. Langwell, Kathryn M. "Factors Affecting the Incomes of Men and Women Physicians: Further Explorations." JHR 17, 2 (Spring 1982): 261-75. (3)

This paper updates and reexamines the work of Kehrer (1976) using a later set of data, from the American Medical Association Twelfth Periodic Survey of Physicians. The author concludes, mainly on the basis of women having fewer office visits by patients per hour, that their lower productivity probably explains much of the earnings differential. She does point out that this measure does not take into account such other activities as hospital, emergency rooms, or home calls, nor the quality of office visits, but then ignores all this in drawing her conclusions.

786. LeGrande, L. H. "Women in Labor Organizations: Their Ranks are Increasing." MLR 101, 8 (Aug. 1978): 8-14. (3)

During the decades 1956 to 1976 fully 17 million women entered the labor force. While only 6 percent of these joined labor unions, more joined associations. They were also more likely to become officers in the latter than in the former.

Leon and Bednarzik (1978) See item 253.

787. Lester, Richard A. Antibias Regulations of Universities: Faculty Problems and Their Solutions, NY: McGraw-Hill, 1974. (4)

The author views the existing system of appointing faculty as so nearly perfect that any interference must be looked upon askance. Recognizing the very low representation of minorities and women, he does propose efforts to train more graduate students from these groups, and suggests goals for new hires, but apparently sees no need for monitoring what happens to them afterwards. Given the author's belief that "the best available person" is always chosen, and that hiring and promotion procedures "conform to the principle of equal opportunity," it is perhaps more surprising that he wants any supervision at all, rather than that he does not want more of it.

788. Levin, Michael. "Women as Soldiers--The Record So Far." PI 21 (August 1984): 31-43. (3)

Since the end of conscription in 1973 the military has accepted larger numbers of women, and has been more likely to place them in nontraditional jobs, though they continue to be excluded from combat assignments. The tone of this paper is well illustrated by the author's declaration that the armed forces have, otherwise, made every effort to live up to their promise of equal opportunity, and by his nostalgia for the days when "the ultimate test for female service was whether it freed men to fight." Needless to say, he concludes that full integration of women into the military would be a disaster.

789. Link, Charles R., and Russell F. Settle. "Labor Supply Responses of Licensed Practical Nurses: A Partial Solution to a Nurse Shortage?" JEB 37, 1 (Feb. 1985): 49-57. (4)

The authors suggest that what they term the "perennial shortage of registered nurses" can be alleviated by substituting licensed practical nurses. They determine that this is feasible, because the supply of practical nurses is very responsive to higher wages. It is interesting, of course, that they do not bother to investigate whether higher wages for registered nurses would also remedy the shortage, as is very likely the case, at least in the long run.

790. Lundeen, Ardelle A. and Annette L. Clawson. "The Conduct of the Survey on the Opportunities for and Status of Women in Agricultural Economics," and Lee, Linda K. "A Comparison of the Rank and Salary of Male and Female Agricultural Economists." AJAE 63, 5 (Dec. 1981): 1010-24. (3)

The Executive Board of the American Agricultural Economics Association appointed a committee to investigate the status of women in their profession. A survey was conducted to get the necessary information. About 5 percent of the practitioners at that time were women. It was found that a smaller proportion of them were in academia; they were less likely to have a Ph.D., and had about the same number of publications. Their salaries, as compared to men, were lower than would be expected in terms of their qualifications. There were differences found in the characteristics and motivation of men and women who entered the profession. Women were more likely to be single, and those who had families were more likely to have them after completing their education. They tended to have husbands with equal or higher education and income. As students, they more often had female role models, and were more inclined to take general economics courses. In their work they were as specialized as their male colleagues, but were more often in human and less often in business-oriented specialities. A larger proportion of women than men entered this field because of intellectual challenge.

791. Malkiel, Burton G. and Judith A. Malkiel. "Male-Female Pay Differentials in Professional Employment." AER 63, 4 (Sept. 1973): 693-705. (3)

This case study of one private institution has unusually good data on many variables, including education, field of study, experience, absenteeism, publications and marital status. Adjusting for all of these raises women's earnings as compared to men's (depending on the weighting) to between 75 and 89 percent. Most of the remainder is accounted for by job level which, like Sawhill (1973), they ascribe to discrimination in occupational assignment.

792. Malveaux, Julianne. "The Economic Interests of Black and White Women: Are They Similar?" RBPE 14, 1 (Summer 1985): 5-27. (3)

This article examines the question whether the interests of black and white women are similar in the context of differences in the occupations of the two groups, and of the feminization of poverty. The author concludes that in many, though not all ways, their concerns differ, because only white men have the resources to be oppressors. There is no reason to question that black men and women, to some extent, share a common agenda. But one might like to see greater recognition of the extent;this is also true of black and white women.

793. McDowell, John M. "Obsolescence of Knowledge and Career Publications Profiles: Some Evidence of Differences Among Fields in Costs of Interrupted Careers." AER 72, 4 (Sept. 1982): 752-68. (3)

The author begins from the premise that the relatively small proportion of women who get Ph.D.'s as compared to those who finish college, and the strong negative correlation between advanced education of women and fertility shows that academic careers are not compatible with family objectives for women. He further suggests that this is particularly true in fields characterized by rapid technological turnover, where learning efforts have to be sustained throughout a scholar's career. It does not occur to the author that when knowledge becomes rapidly obsolete, a late start, and interruptions would be less of a handicap. Nor, of course, does he consider that husbands and wives might share family responsibilities.

794. Megdal, Sharon B. and Michael R. Ransom. "Longitudinal Changes at a Large Public University: What Response to Equal Pay Legislation?" AER 75, 2 (May 1985): 271-74. (3)

Using data for the University of Arizona for 1972, 1977 and 1982 concerning career-type teaching faculty and including information on salary, rank, tenure, department, highest degree and sex, it was found that women were paid less than men with the same measured characteristics. Unlike earlier studies, however, they found that for women who were present over the entire period, the gap has not increased. This leads to the surprising conclusion that most of the differential arises at the time of hire. The authors suggest this may be because women are of lower quality than men, or because there is discrimination, but provide no evidence for either.

795. Mitchell, Janet B. "Why Do Women Physicians Work Fewer Hours Than Men Physicians?" I 21, 4 (Winter 1984): 361-68. (3)

Women physicians work significantly fewer hours than men. This study based on national survey data for office-based private practice physicians found that this does not appear to be related to child care, as is generally assumed. Further, the results suggest that higher earnings would not cause women physicians to work more. Instead, shorter hours for women, but not men, appear to be related to high family incomes.

796. Moore, William J. and Robert J. Newman. "An Analysis of the Quality Differentials in Male-Female Academic Placements." EI 15, 3 (July 1977): 413-34. (3)

Using data from the 1969 and 1974 Handbook of the American Economic Association, this study found that males had a 22.2 percent advantage in placement quality over women between 1960 and 1974. The authors further concluded that most of this differential could be attributed to some form of discrimination. Thus, their findings are in conflict with Johnson, G. E. and Stafford (1974), and support the views of Strober and Quester (1976).

797. Mueller, Marnie W. "Economic Determinants of Volunteer Work by Women," SJWCS 1, 2 (Winter 1975): 325-38. (3)

This work is based on a sample of 311 women who had done graduate or professional work at Columbia University between 1941 and 1951. While this group is clearly not representative of the population, it is women with this level of education and income, and in this age group who are most active in volunteer work.

The evidence is interpreted to show that they do it in substantial part to build and maintain their human capital and to aid in their job search. For a less positive view of volunteer work as a way to a successful career see Francine D. Blau, "Comment," SJWCS 2, 1 (Autumn 1976): 251-54.

798. Orth, Charles D. and Frederick Jacobs. "Women in Management: Pattern for Change." HBR 49, 4 (July-Aug. 1971): 139-47. (4)

The authors believe that despite the fears harbored by many male managers, more women hired for management positions would benefit business. They therefore urge corporate leaders to institute programs that would further this aim, including making an occupational census, gathering data on former women employees, revising recruiting procedures and expanding training opportunities for women.

799. Osterman, Paul. "Sex Discrimination in Professional Employment: A Case Study: Reply." ILRR 32, 4 (Jan. 1981): 451-64. (3)

The author, who finds that marriage has a positive effect on men's earnings, subscribes to the interpretation that the additional responsibilities increase their motivation. But his hypothesis that marriage would have the opposite effect on women is not supported, quite likely because there is a positive self-selection among married women who choose to maintain their professional career. Like Hill, M. S. (1979), Osterman, however, finds that children do have a negative effect on mothers' earnings.

800. Parrish, John B. "Employment of Women Chemists in Industrial Laboratories." Science, 148, 3670 (Apr. 30, 1965): 367-36. (3)

It was found that women constituted 22 percent of the professional personnel in 65 chemical and pharmaceutical laboratories. The majority had only B.S. degrees, and managers thought they were more capable than most men at that level, because high ability males tend to go on to graduate work. On the other hand, women had higher turnover rates than men, though this was less true of those with B.S. and Ph.D. degrees than of those with M.S. degrees.

801. Parrish, John B. "Women and Minorities as a Professional Resource: A Study of Progress and Change." QREB 18, 3 (Autumn 1978): 55-66. (3)

Data are provided to document the progress women and minorities, and particularly minority women are making in obtaining professional training. The author does not, however, adequately emphasize that they continue to be quite unequally represented across various fields.

802. Parrish, John B. "Are Women Taking Over the Professions?" Ch 28, 6 (Jan./Feb. 1986): 54-58. (3)

"If present trends continue -- as there is every reason to believe -- by the end of the 1980's women will constitute a majority of newly trained professionals in many fields." Hence, the author concludes we are "feminizing our professional resources." It is, nonetheless, the case that women continue to be very unequally distributed throughout the professions, even among new graduates. Notably, they have made least progress in some of the most highly paid fields, such as engineering. Hence, it would be appropriate to temper the author's optimism somewhat.

803. Randall, Donna M. "Women in Toxic Work Environments: A Case Study and Examination of Political Impact." WW 1 (1985): 259-81. (3)

The author examines the complex issues involved in the growing tendency for the chemical industry, as well as other manufacturing industries, to exclude fertile women from employment that might injure a fetus. She points out that reproductive risks exist for men as well, and argues that the government should be concerned with adequate protection for all workers.

804. Reagan, Barbara B. "Two Supply Curves for Economists: Implications of Mobility and Career Attachment of Women." AER 65, 2 (May 1975): 100-107. (3)

The author uses data provided by the Committee on the Status of Women in the Economics Profession of the American Economic Association to test her hypothesis that employers continue to perceive differences in the employability of women and men, and that women economists are less responsive to changes in wage rates, making it worthwhile for employers to pay them less than they pay men with comparable qualifications. She concludes that the results of her study give tentative support to both hypotheses.

805. Reagan, Barbara B. and Betty J. Maynard. "Sex Discrimination in Universities: An Approach Through Internal Labor Market Analysis." AAUPB 60, 1 (Spring 1974): 13-21. (3)

A study at Southern Methodist University showed that 75 percent of women faculty had salaries markedly below those of men with comparable academic credentials and productivity. The authors suggest that the main reasons for this are (1) an unconsciously narrow perception of women's roles, and (2) the peculiar relationship of many women to the external labor market, apparently because of family ties. The authors also discuss the differences in relation between the internal and external labor markets by field.

806. Reskin, Barbara F. "Sex Differences in Status Attainment in Science: The Case of the Postdoctoral Fellowship." ASR 41 (Aug. 1976): 597-612. (3)

This research examines the status-attainment process of 450 male and female chemists, focusing on postdoctoral fellowships because they are thought to be important in furthering professional careers. The results show sex interactions for both the determinants and effects of the award and prestige of these fellowships. This is the case even after marital status is taken into account, though the effect of merely receiving any fellowship on productivity is the same for both men and women. The author concludes that these findings raise serious questions about objective, sex-neutral standards in science.

807. Reskin, Barbara F. "Scientific Productivity, Sex, and Location in the Institution of Science." AJS 83, 4 (Mar. 1978): 1235-43. (3)

Among the main findings of this study, based on a population of 229 female and 221 male chemists who had obtained their degrees at U.S. universities between 1955 and 1961, were that women published somewhat less than men and that their patterns of publication were less stable over time. It was also discovered that women's productivity was more responsive to prestigious postdoctoral fellowships, employment in tenure track university positions and collegial recognition.

808. Reskin, Barbara F. and Lowell L. Hargens. "Scientific Advancement of Male and Female Chemists," in Rodolfo Alvarez and Kenneth G. Lutterman and Assoc., eds., Discrimination in Organizations, San Francisco, CA: Jossey-Bass, 1979, pp. 100-22. (3)

The authors test the hypothesis that institutional discrimination in an organization will result in processes of cumulative advantage being weaker, and links between positional outcomes and those between early and later positions also being less strong. In this study such differences were found between male and female chemists.

809. Richman, Bill D. "Faculty Salaries at a Small University: Does Sex Matter?" QJBE 23, 2 (Spring 1984): 47-57. (3)

Like studies of larger, research-oriented institutions, this investigation of a small liberal and applied arts university found an unexplained salary differential, though it is smaller. The author leaves open the question whether this differential is the result of discrimination or of human capital attributes of faculty that are not adequately modeled.

810. Rosen, Benson and Thomas H. Jerdee. "Sex Stereotyping in the Executive Suite." HBR (Mar.-Apr. 1974a): 45-58. (3)

The authors find a considerable lag between managerial policy and its implementation with regard to the acceptance of women in management positions, because of the persistence of social and psychological barriers. There is both greater concern about the careers of men, and greater scepticism about the abilities of women. Further, managers see no need for organizations to change, but want women to adjust to the existing situation. The authors, on the other hand, feel that it is up to managers to give up old biases and encourage women and men equally if progress is to be made.

811. Rosen, Benson and Thomas H. Jerdee. "Effects of Applicant's Sex and Difficulty of Job on Evaluations of Candidates for Managerial Positions." JAP 59, 4 (Aug. 1974b): 511-12. (3)

Using 235 undergraduate business students as subjects, this study confirmed that sex role stereotypes influence evaluations of applicants and selection decisions. Male applicants were accepted more frequently than equally qualified female applicants, and were evaluated more favorably, particularly so for "demanding" managerial positions.

812. Rosen, Benson and Thomas H. Jerdee. "Perceived Sex Differences in Managerially Relevant Characteristics." SR 4, 6 (Dec. 1978): 837-43. (3)

A national sample of 884 male managers rated females lower on 1) aptitudes, skills and knowledge, 2) motivation and job interest, 3) temperament, 4) work habits and attitudes. Further, this was true in a variety of jobs, organizations, and industries. The authors conclude:"Perhaps the best way to combat these perceptions is with more accurate information about the actual behavioral characteristics of male and female employees."

813. Rossi, Alice S. and Ann Calderwood. Academic Women on the Move. New York: Russell Sage Foundation, 1973. (3,4)

This book consists of papers which examined the problems and the prospects of women in academia at the time when their underrepresentation, isolation, and generally disadvantaged position was just beginning to receive attention. Conditions have, for the most part, improved since then for both women students and women faculty, but much of the information provided may still be useful to those concerned with safeguarding the gains and with making further progress.

Rytina (1982) See item 537.

814. Schwartz, Eleanor B. The Sex Barrier in Business, Atlanta, GA: Bureau of Business and Economic Research, Georgia State University, 1971 (3)

The first section of this book consists of a brief history of the role of women in the U.S., followed by a history of legislation relevant to women's position in the labor market, including a fascinating summary of the debate about the inclusion of "sex" in Title VII of the Civil Rights Act. The last section focuses on women in management, including the results of a survey of 900 managers, one-third of them female. The findings, like those of Basil (1972) are that there are very few women executives, especially at high levels. Attitudes toward them are mixed, and this is true for both men and women, though the views of the latter tend to be more positive.

815. Searleman, Alan, et al. "Are the Fruits of Research Available to All? The Effects of Sex and Academic Rank on Reprint-Sending Behavior." SR 9, 11 (Nov. 1983): 1091-1100. (3)

Reprints were requested from 1,200 authors of psychological articles by men and women of varying academic rank. Neither sex nor rank of requester had any significant effect, except that males received responses significantly faster. Male authors were somewhat more likely to honor requests than female authors. Ranking of institution of authors and requesters was not included in this study and might help to explain the differences that were found.

Shaw (1983) See item 309.

816. Shepherd, William G. and Sharon G. Levin. "Managerial Discrimination in Large Firms." RES 55, 4 (Nov. 1973): 412-22. (3)

An effort to find determinants of the extent to which women and blacks are employed in managerial jobs is essentially unsuccessful. In the main, the study shows that except for a few "women's industries," management of large firms is a distinctly white male preserve.

817. Sigelman, Lee. "The Curious Case of Women in State and Local Government." SSQ 56, 4 (Mar. 1976): 591-604. (3)

Women in all states are represented in state and local government at least in proportion to their representation in the labor force, but are disproportionately relegated to lower-level jobs. It is also reported, however, that they are most successful in reaching higher-level positions where there are the highest ratios of women. The most surprising finding of this study is that female employment in the public sector is higher in both quantity and quality in more traditional areas. There is some evidence that this may be in part because minorities do so poorly there.

Silverstone and Ward (1980) See item 992.

818. Sloan, Frank A. and Somchai Richupan. "Short-run Supply Responses of Professional Nurses: A Microanalysis." JHR 10, 2 (Spring 1975): 241-57. (3,4)

This research, based on data from the Public Use Sample of the 1960 Census, addresses the questions whether hospitals exercise monopsony power with respect to nurses, and whether the supply of nurses is responsive to changing wages. The results suggest a substantial response to hourly wages, as well as to the wage of their spouse for married nurses.

819. Stead, Bette A. Women in Management, Englewood Cliffs, NJ: Prentice-Hall, 1978. (3)

This readable book consists of a large number of short papers covering topics from stereotyping and other barriers that continue to stand in the way of women's entry into and progress within management, to discussions of how women function in management positions and ways of implementing equal opportunity for women. There is little emphasis on research and analysis, but a wealth of interesting anecdotal evidence.

820. Stephan, Paula E. and Sharon G. Levin. "Sex Segregation in Education: The Case of Doctorate Recipients." JBE 12, 2 (Winter 1983): 67-94. (3)

This investigation of sex segregation in Ph.D. fields confirms the need for an interdisciplinary approach to this subject. The authors found that differences in cognitive patterns, availability of financial support, the degree to which research can be done individually, as well as the extent of discrimination encountered all played a part in determining the proportion of women in a particular field.

821. Strober, Myra H. "Women Economists' Career Aspirations, Education and Training." AER 65, 2 (May 1975a): 92-99. (3,4)

The author examines how women decide to become economists, so that ways may be found that will encourage more of them to enter this predominantly male field. She makes the following tentative suggestions: (1) Professionals might arrange to meet with female high school students, (2) efforts should be made to interest more college women to take economics courses, (3) more financial aid might be provided to graduate students so they will not have to drop out to support their families.

Strober and Best (1979) See item 555.

822. Szafran, Robert F. Universities and Women Faculty. Why Some Organizations Discriminate More Than Others. N.Y.: Praeger Publishers, 1984. (3)

The author examines hiring, promotion, and salary practices of different universities. He concludes that they tend to discriminate against women, and that this is particularly true of the most affluent. The second conclusion is suspect, because he fails to recognize that highly ranked institutions tend to hire only highly ranked candidates from highly ranked institutions. Also, his estimates of salary discrimination are likely to be seriously flawed because he uses rank and tenure as independent variables, not taking into account that these variables themselves may be tainted by discrimination.

823. Theodore, Athena, ed. The Professional Woman. Cambridge, MA: Schenkman Publishing Company, Inc., 1971. (3)

This book is composed of a large number of relatively brief essays concerned with various aspects of the socialization, career choices, labor force behavior and family commitments of career women. Some of them are out of date by now, but many of the problems addressed continue to exist today.

824. Tolles, H. Arnold and Emmanuel Melichar. "Studies of the Structure of Economists' Salaries and Income." AER 58, 4, Part 2 (Dec. 1968). (3)

This examination of earnings of male and female economists ignores the possible differences in reward structure for the two groups, which were invariably found in later studies of the same issue.

825. Tucker, Sharon. "Careers of Men and Women MBA's 1950-1980." WO 12, 2 (May 1985): 166-85.

This study, relying upon a qualitative analysis of intensive interviews of male and female MBA recipients, concludes that women's salaries and authority were below those of men, and that they most often felt blocked from further advancement. It was also found that women rarely held positions with business firms. The author offers a number of different explanations for this, ranging from employer discrimination and lack of peer support to lesser organizational commitment by women.

Turnbull and Williams, G. (1974) See item 1016.

826. Vetter, Betty M. "Women Scientists and Engineers: Trends in Participation." Science, 214, 4527 (18 Dec. 1981):L 1313-21. (3)

The proportion of doctorates in science and engineering awarded to women increased from 7 percent in 1965 to 23 percent in 1980. At the same time, the proportion unemployed continued to be higher among women, and their starting salaries lower. Further, the disparity in earnings tended to increase with degree levels and with years of experience.

827. Wallace, Phyllis A., ed. Women in the Workplace, Boston, MA: Auburn House Publishing Company, 1982. (3,4)

This book includes chapters on women in different occupational groups, from managers to white collar and blue collar workers, and how they have been affected by affirmative action. It appears that they have only made limited progress. Among clerical and blue collar workers a great deal of sex segregation continues, and virtually none of the women are promoted to management. More young women are hired for entry level management jobs, but very few of them progress much further. One explanation suggested for this is that corporations have been unwilling to reduce requirements for very strong work commitment during the years when demands for childrearing are also high. Another explanation offered is discrimination.

Wallace, Datcher and Malveaux (1980) See item 334.

828. Wasserman, Elga, Arie Y. Lewin and Linda H. Bleiweis, eds. Women in Academia: Evolving Policies Toward Equal Opportunities, NY: Praeger, 1975. (3,4)

This volume is based on a conference held to bring together university women, university administrators, and representatives of the executive branch of government and enable them to become familiar with affirmative action legislation. The book contains chapters on the drafting and implementation of effective affirmative action plans suggestions, how to set hiring goals and remedy salary inequities, and case studies of efforts to increase participation of women in academic life. All are written by persons sympathetic to the goal of equal opportunity in institutions of higher education.

829. Wells, D. Colin. "Some Questions Concerning the Higher Education of Women." _AJS_ 14, 6 (May 1909): 731-39. (3)

The author discusses the then recent trend toward educating women beyond "the grammar grades." His conclusions, no doubt relatively enlightened for that time, were that a happy outcome was to be expected, but that (1) women's intellectuality may become uncomfortable for men; (2) public life may become excessively emotional and even hysterical; (3) women may be corrupted in competing with men for positions of material advantage, and thus degraded.

830. Wertheimer, B. M. and A. M. Nelson. _Trade Union Women: A Study of Their Participation in New York City Locals_. NY: Praeger Publishers, 1975. (3)

This book reports on a study of the participation of women in New York City labor union locals. Its purpose was to learn more about the reasons for women's failure to move into leadership positions in these organizations in spite of the largely female membership in many of them. Among the explanations a survey of union members discovered were the attitudes of men towards women's roles in unions, as well as women's lack of confidence and inability to visualize themselves as leaders rather than helpers. Women, however, also thought that if they had more education they would be able to take on more responsible positions.

831. Willacy, Hazel M. and Harvey J. Hilaski. "Working Women in Urban Poverty Neighborhoods." MLR 93, 6 (June 1970): 35-8. (3)

This paper emphasizes the extent to which women in urban poverty neighborhoods, regardless of race, are handicapped in their job search, and that the problems of non-white women are especially serious. The effects of their environment on labor force participation rates, occupational distribution, unemployment rates, and family composition are shown.

832. Wolfson, Theresa. The Woman Worker and the Trade Unions. NY: International Publishers, 1926. (3)

This book, concerned with the issue of the under-representation of women in labor unions, is included not because of its profundity, but rather because it is representative of the frequent absence of careful thought on women's issues -- even, as in this instance, by a female author. We are, on the one hand, told that "The labour movement in the United States is becoming increasingly conscious of the ever-growing group of women workers as possible competitors in the economic world," and is therefore interested in bringing them into the unions. On the other hand, there is the claim that union leaders are frustrated because they have not had much success in organizing women. Could it be that women workers were not interested in being organized for the benefit of men?

Zabalza (1979) See item 1029.

Chapter 9

WOMEN THROUGHOUT THE WORLD

It is beyond the scope of this bibliography to encompass the literature published in and about other countries, and especially that not written in English. It will, however, enhance the value of this book to cover enough such works to provide some idea of the status of women in the rest of the world. A good many items that make a contribution to our understanding of particular issues have been crossreferenced in the appropriate chapters; others that are useful in comparing the economic status of women in different countries are listed in the General section.

Information about similarities and differences in the role of women in various parts of the world is not only interesting in its own right, but also sheds light on the controversial question to what extent this role is determined by society rather than nature. If there is great variation in the status of women, even in countries at the same stage of economic development, as cultures, ideologies and religions differ, there is little reason to believe that biology is destiny. Furthermore, we may be able to learn from countries which have succeeded in making more progress toward equality between men and women than has the U.S.

Among the relatively few authors who have examined these issues there has often been a tendency to emphasize the similarity in the problems of women, and to point out, perhaps somewhat defensively, that they have not achieved equality with men anywhere. There are serious problems with these generalizations. First, they are often based on a sample of countries that are relatively similar in other respects. Broad conclusions based on a relatively homogeneous group of countries must clearly be viewed with considerable caution. Second, the contention that women everywhere appear to have an inferior economic status, though true, ignores the substantial differences in the extent of that inferiority. A good example is the fact that among full-time, year round workers in all countries for which data are available, women earn less than men; but in Japan the ratio is less than 60 percent, while it is close to 90 percent in Sweden. Or again, while there appears to be occupational segregation by sex in all countries, the degree to which it exists varies widely.

This is not to suggest that one should go to the opposite extreme of noting only the differences, and overlooking the similarities in the problems that women throughout the world tend to share. It is, for instance, noteworthy that women in all known societies are the chief tenders of home, hearth and children, and are very much underrepresented among executives and managers--whether of governments, large enterprises, or, for the most part, even small businesses and farms.

The sparse selection of works in English, readily available to the American reader, does not do justice to the broad scope of this subject. It does, however, give at least some indication of its breadth and diversity. It is to be hoped that improvement in the quality and comparability of data published by various countries, and further work by researchers, in this country and elsewhere, will make it possible to learn more about the as yet unresolved questions.

833. Abbott, Joan. "The Employment of Women and the Reduction of Fertility: Implications for Development." <u>WD</u> 2, 2 (Feb. 1974): 23-26. (4)

A general but rather superficial overview which concludes that more women working for pay will not take away jobs from men because they tend to work in different sectors. It is also suggested that increasing labor force participation of women will encourage economic development, and help to reduce fertility.

Adler and Hawrylyshyn (1978) See item 31.
Agarwal (1983) See item 563.

834. Agarwal, Naresh C. and Helen C. Jain. "Pay Discrimination Against Women in Canada: Issues and Policies." <u>ILR</u> 117, 2 (Mar.-Apr. 1978): 169-77. (3,4)

A review of existing research shows continued pay discrimination against women in Canada in spite of laws prohibiting it since the early 1960's. The authors attribute this to the following shortcomings in the laws: 1) The definition is restricted to pay only and does not cover fringe benefits. 2) Equal work is interpreted narrowly and does not cover work of equal value. 3) No guidelines are provided for assessing the value of work. 4) The law is restricted to equality within a single establishment, a definition narrower than a single employer. 5) Enforcement procedures have been lax.

835. Anker, Richard. "Female Labour Force Participation in Developing Countries: A Critique of Current Definitions and Data Collection Methods." <u>ILR</u> 122, 6 (Nov.-Dec. 1983): 709-23. (2)

Various alternative definitions of labor force participation are discussed, ranging from considering only paid labor, to including all productive work. Methods of collecting data are also discussed. Preliminary results from a survey carried out in rural India are used to show the effect of employing the different concepts.

836. Anker, Richard and Catherine Hein. "Why Third World Urban Employers Usually Prefer Men." ILR 124, 1 (Jan.-Feb. 1985): 73-90. (3)

In nonagricultural Third World employment women are outnumbered by men 3 to 1. Further, they are concentrated in a relatively few industries. Data from Cyprus, Ghana, India, Mauritius, Nigeria and Sri Lanka confirm a general employer reluctance to hire women, in part because of stereotypes concerning women. These views are serious barriers to women's entry to many jobs, but cause them to be preferred for a few others. The beliefs underlying the sex-typing of jobs are not always supported by facts. Protective legislation creates additional barriers. Like many others, the authors fail to note that there may well be a vicious circle involving discriminatory perceptions and women's behavior.

837. Antonello, Paola and Giorgio Goglioni. "Wages, Salaries and Female Employment in U.K. Manufacturing." EurER 9, 2 (May 1977): 209-20. (3)

A cross-section study of 116 manufacturing sectors shows that the proportion of women in each industry can be explained by the type of work involved. They tend to work part-time and to do less heavy, less dangerous and less skilled work. This helps to explain women's lower wages. It must be recognized, however, that not only women themselves, but employers and unions play a part in this allocation of male and female workers. Further, it is also the case that women are paid less even when they do the same work.

838. Barrett, Nancy S. "Have Swedish Women Achieved Equality?" Ch 16, 5 (Nov.-Dec. 1973): 14-20. (3)

The brief summary of this paper says "Five years ago Sweden announced a bold effort to help women obtain equality in the labor market by changing occupational roles. So far tradition has proved stronger than policy." In many respects this is true even more than 10 years after it was written. The author ascribes this largely to the fact that women's traditional role is part of the family system on which society is based, and implies that the Swedish experiment has been a failure. Many would quarrel with that interpretation. First, 5 or even 50 years is a short time in the long span of history. Second, Sweden has experienced an enormous increase in women's labor force participation, and a substantial decline in the earnings gap.

839. Bartol, Kathryn M. and Robert A. Bartol. "Women in Managerial and Professional Positions: The United States and the Soviet Union," ILRR 28, 4 (July 1975): 524-34. (3)

There are obvious problems in finding appropriate comparisons between a state socialist and private enterprise economy. Overall, the evidence suggests that women in the USSR have not achieved equality, but have made more progress in attaining professional positions than in the U.S.A. This difference is likely to be meaningful, even though the term "professional" tends to be more loosely construed in the Soviet Union, and women's labor force participation in general is higher there. The difference in managerial positions held by women is smaller, but not negligible. The authors also note, however, that such progress has been at the expense of women having far less leisure than men.

840. Behrman, Jere R. and Barbara L. Wolfe. "Labor Force Participation and Earnings Determinants for Women in the Special Conditions of Developing Countries," JDE 15 (1984): 259-88. (3)

This study explores special labor market conditions in one developing country, Nicaragua. The main findings are: (1) presence of small children is less of a deterrence to labor force participation than in economically advanced countries, presumably in part because of the prevalence of extended families, in part because of urgent need; (2) education, at least beyond primary school, and experience, have a substantial effect on occupation and earnings, (3) other human capital factors, especially nutrition, have some impact as well. These findings are quite similar to those of Kelley, A. C. and deSilva (1980) for Brazil, and Concepcion (1974) for rural areas in some Asian countries.

841. Benatia, Farouk. "Some Ideas About Women's Work in Algeria." ISSJ 32, 3 (1980): 464-78. (1)

The author begins from the proposition that women's emancipation is desirable, and goes on to argue that only gainful employment will accomplish this. His assumption that neither women nor men, both of whom often continue to hold traditional views, would notice the change or resist it seems rather optimistic.

Beneria (1979) See item 40.

842. Beneria, Lourdes. "Conceptualizing the Labor Force: The Underestimation of Women's Economic Activities." JDS 17, 3 (Apr. 1981): 10-28. (1,2)

The main issue emphasized by the author is that household production should be viewed as an economic activity, and that individuals engaged in such work should be regarded as productive. Thus economic activity would be defined in terms of contributing to human welfare rather than in terms of economic growth and accumulation. A second, and rather different point brought out in this paper is that concepts of labor force participation vary between countries. Therefore comparisons among available statistics can be misleading.

843. Ben-Porath, Yoram and Reuben Gronau. "Jewish Mother Goes to Work: Trends in the Labor Force Participation of Women in Israel, 1955-1980." JLE 3, 1 (Jan. 1985, Suppl.): S310-S327. (3)

The labor force participation of Jewish women in Israel increased between 1955 and 1980, but most rapidly in the 1970's, and mainly among married women with children. The rise in participation is chiefly ascribed to increasing years of education of women, even though the earnings gap among highly educated women and men actually increased during the last decade. This decline in relative wages is explained by the continued occupational segregation.

844. Berent, Jercy. "Some Demographic Aspects of Female Employment in Eastern Europe and the USSR." ILR 101, 2 (Feb. 1970): 175-92. (3,4)

Like many other authors, this one sees a conflict between the high labor force participation of women in the USSR and Eastern Europe and their needed contribution to the future growth of the labor force. He expects pro-natalist measures, already introduced in some countries, to become more common.

845. Berliner, Joseph S. "Education, Labor Force Participation and Fertility in the USSR." JCE 7, 2 (June 1983): 131-57. (3)

An investigation using Soviet Census data finds that in the USSR the effect of education on fertility is positive for women, negative for men in urban areas. This is the opposite of the situation in the U.S. Interestingly, the effect of female education works mainly indirectly through changing labor force participation, which, beyond some point, appears to decline with higher earnings. These findings are consistent with those of Ofer and Vinakur (1983).

846. Bilsborrow, Richard E. "Effects of Economic Dependency on Labor Force Participation Rates in Less Developed Countries." OEP 29, 1 (Mar. 1977): 61-83. (3)

The hypothesis that a high ratio of dependent children to adults increases labor force participation in less developed countries is tested using aggregate data for 34 countries, and is found wanting. In fact, female labor force participation, and hence total participation is lower as the dependency ratio rises. Perhaps those who expected the opposite were tacitly thinking of men only.

847. Birdsall, Nancy and M. Louise Fox. "Why Males Earn More: Location and Training of Brazilian Schoolteachers." EDCC 33, 3 (Apr. 1985): 533-56. (3)

Female teachers in Brazil earn only half as much as male teachers, but at least 74 percent of this gap can be explained by differences in personal characteristics, mobility, and geographic location, while there is evidence only of a small amount of discrimination. The reason for that may be the highly institutional setting, where it is perhaps surprising that women are discriminated against at all. It may also be that women get less training at least in part because of real or perceived barriers to higher level jobs, rather than only for reasons of personal preference.

848. Biryukova, A. P. "Special Protective Legislation for Equality of Opportunity for Women Workers in the USSR." ILR 119, 1 (Jan.-Feb. 1980): 51-65. (4)

The first sentence sets the tone of this paper. "It is being increasingly recognized that, while motherhood remains their most vital social function, women also have an essential contribution to make through active participation in public life." In fact, a case can be made that women's public role was widely recognized during and immediately after the revolution, and their role as mothers has been increasingly emphasized since. It is hardly a mark of progress that protective legislation is not justified only in terms of physiological and psychological differences between the sexes, but by women's "double burden," and far less attention is given to the possibility of men sharing homemaking responsibilities.

849. Blitz, Rudolph C. "An International Comparison of Women's Participation in the Professions." JDA 9, 4 (July 1975): 499-510. (3)

The author concludes that there is some evidence that economic development coincides with the proportion of women in the labor force increasing, but also recognizes that the percentages are very widely dispersed in less developed economies. By contrast, the proportion of women among professionals (architects, dentists, engineers, lawyers and physicians) are greater in the top tier of developing countries than in western advanced industrialized nations. Both labor force participation and representation of women in the professions is notably higher in the Soviet-type countries than in any of the other groups.

850. Block, Walter and Walter Williams. "Male-Female Earnings Differentials: A Critical Reappraisal." JLR 2, 2 (Fall 1981): 385-87. (3)

The authors of this note argue that in attributing 58.9 percent of the earnings gap standardized for occupation and industry, and 75.4 percent of the unstandardized earnings gap to discrimination, Robb (1978) overlooked the possibility that marriage has the opposite effect on the productivity of men and women, and that some of the earnings differential may be explained by variables not included in her study. Further, they suggest that employers may give preferential treatment to men over women not because of tastes for discrimination, but because of inadequate information. There is justification for raising these issues, but no evidence is provided to what extent they are of substantive importance.

851. Boserup, Ester. Women's Role in Economic Development, N.Y.: St. Martin's Press, 1970. (1,3)

This pioneering work provides an in-depth examination of the role of women in underdeveloped agricultural economies and of the changes that take place with modernization of agriculture, urbanization, and industrialization. The author emphasizes the extent to which these developments, especially as encouraged by representatives from more advanced economies, have often been detrimental to the status of women.

852. Boulier, Bryan L. and Portia Pineda. "Male-Female Wage Differentials in a Philippine Government Agency." PEJ 14, 4 (1975): 436-448. (3)

Using the same model as Malkiel and Malkiel (1973), the earnings gap is investigated for regular male and female employees with at least one year of college in a single government agency. Only a small portion of the differential is explained by differences in measurable personal characteristics. The main reason for their lower earnings appears to be that women tend to have lower level jobs than men with similar characteristics.

853. Canlas, Dante B. and Mohd Razak. "Education and the Labor Force Participation of Married Women: West Malaysia, 1970. PEJ 18, 2 1979): 163-79. (3)

Cross section analysis is carried out to test the hypothesis that in poor families, there is target-setting behavior, while among the wealthy, women tend to optimize. The results of the study bear this out, because years of schooling have a different effect on the labor force participation of married women above or below a certain threshold income. In terms of policy, the important conclusion is that increasing education short of reaching that threshold will not increase labor force participation.

854. Carliner, Geoffrey, Christopher Robinson and Nigel Tomes. "Female Labour Supply and Fertility in Canada." CJE 13, 1 (Feb. 1980) 46-64. (3)

Labor supply and fertility are estimated simultaneously on the basis of 1971 Canadian Census data. More highly educated and urban women are found to have fewer children and supply more labor, everything else equal. Catholics have more children, but supply as much labor as non-Catholics.

855. Carr, Shirley G. E. "Sex-Based Discrimination in Employment: Problems and Progress in Canada." ILR 122, 6 (Nov.-Dec. 1983): 761-70. (4)

A brief summary review of Canadian legislation and institutional arrangements aimed at achieving greater equality for women in the labor market.

856. Carvajal, Manuel J. and David T. Geithman. "Income, Human Capital and Sex Discrimination: Some Evidence from Costa Rica, 1963 and 1973." JED 10, 1 (July 1985): 89-115. (3)

The authors point out that the lower earnings of women as compared to men are especially serious in poor countries where even men's incomes are low. They therefore choose one of the less developed countries to investigate whether human capital factors are able to explain all of the earnings gap. They find this is not the case for Costa Rica, and conclude that their results largely support the existence of sex discrimination for that country. There is also evidence provided, however, that discrimination appears to have diminished between 1963 and 1973.

857. Chakrabarti, Kumar. "The Causes of Women's Unemployment in India." EA 22, 5 (May 1977): 177-83. (3)

The large and growing unemployment rate in the 1970's is attributed to the large influx of women job seekers while demand did not increase correspondingly. The author suggests that the fault lies mainly in a defective development process, because many of the new jobs that are being created require skills most women do not have. The author also believes, however, that direct discrimination plays a part.

858. Chapman, Bruce J. and J. Ross Harding. "Sex Differences in Earnings: An Analysis of Malaysian Wage Data." JDS 21, 3 (Apr. 1985): 362-76. (3)

A conventional human capital earnings function is applied to Malaysian wage data in order to examine sex differences in earnings. In the main, the relationships found are similar to those in more economically advanced countries. The results of the study suggest that the major part of the earnings gap is caused by occupational distribution.

859. Chiplin, Brian. "An Alternative Approach to the Measurement of Sex Discrimination: An Illustration from University Entrance." EJ 91, 364 (Dec. 1981): 988-97. (3Q)

The author is critical of the usual approach of using earnings functions and interpreting the differences in these functions for men and women as evidence of discrimination. Not only is the correct specification of the functions crucial, but the question may be raised whether the earnings criteria of the employer are reasonable. Further, the estimated earnings function is influenced by supply as well as demand. The author is able to disentangle demand and supply in the case of admission of students to an economics department, and finds no evidence of discrimination. It is, however, quite a leap of faith to the conclusion that this has direct implications for the labor market.

860. Chiplin, Brian, M. M. Curran and C. J. Parsley. "Relative Female Earnings in G. B. and the Impact of Legislation" in Peter J. Sloane (ed.), Women and Low Pay, Macmillan, London, 1980, pp. 57-126. (3,4)

On the basis of their research, the authors conclude that in Great Britain between 1966 and 1976 the flat rate increases in women's wages brought about by income policies did far more to reduce the male-female earnings gap than equal pay and equal opportunity legislation. There are, however, some problems with their model estimating the latter. For one, they introduce a time trend, without even raising the question whether it might have been caused by the legislation which was, in fact, introduced during this period. It is entirely possible that income policy and anti-discrimination laws both played a part.

861. Chiplin, Brian and Peter J. Sloane. "Sexual Discrimination in the Labor Market." BJIR 12, 3 (Nov. 1974): 371-402. (3)

The authors define discrimination (like Becker, G. S. 1957) as employers, and employees, deriving satisfaction from various types of exclusion and wage differentials. They conclude on the basis of their investigation that the effect on women's earnings is primarily through unequal wages, rather than unequal occupational and industrial distribution. Equal pay legislation would therefore appear to be useful. The authors warn that unemployment of women and further crowding into female jobs may result unless all real differences between male and female workers are taken into account. They fail to warn, however, that in reality it may be unwarranted perceptions and irrelevant differences that may be taken into account and perpetuate discrimination.

862. Chiplin, Brian and Peter J. Sloane. "Male-Female Earnings Differences: A Further Analysis." BJIR 14, 1 (Mar. 1976a): 77-81. (3)

In this brief note the authors report that even using new data on detailed occupational categories, they find that unequal pay is far more important than unequal occupational distribution in causing the earnings gap. They suggest that employment of women in low-pay establishments is one reason, and that the categories used are still too broad to take into account job grades and incremental pay systems.

863. Chiplin, Brian and Peter J. Sloane. "Personal Characteristics and Sex Differentials in Professional Employment," EJ 86, 344 (Dec. 1976b): 729-45. (3)

This study of separate earnings functions of male and female employees in a large firm in Great Britain finds that, controlling for a wide variety of worker characteristics, much of the pay gap between men and women can be explained by differences in endowments if male rewards are used for females. When, however, female rewards are used for males, the extent of discrimination is far greater. No explanation is offered by the authors, but a plausible interpretation is that though women would gain from higher qualifications if they were rewarded as men are, they would gain little from acquiring more human capital as long as they are rewarded as women. Also, though more than half of the difference between men and women in reaching higher level jobs can be explained, women who were promoted tended to be assigned to less responsible posts at lower salaries.

864. Chiplin, Brian and Peter J. Sloane. Sex Discrimination in the Labor Market, London: Macmillan Press, Ltd., 1976c. (1,3,4)

A comprehensive review of theories of discrimination and a thorough evaluation of empirical work in the U.S. and Great Britain make this small book very useful to anyone with a reasonable background in economics and statistics. Its acknowledged limitation is that the authors accept the paradigm of profit maximization and cost minimization, while giving scant attention to alternatives. Needless to say, their own original contributions incorporated in this volume are formulated within the same framework.

865. Ciancanelli, Penelope. "Exchange, Reproduction and Sex Subordination Among the Kikuyu of East Africa." RRPE 12, 2 (Summer 1980): 25-36. (3)

This paper argues that among the Kikuyu of East Africa trade in slaves and ivory played a significant role in the emergence of a division of labor based on female cultivators and male self-defense, and the emergence of polygynous households composed of several female cultivators and one male "defender." One problem with this reasoning is that many differences in male and female behavior are simply assumed, and are then used to explain other differences.

866. Colombino, Ugu and Bianca De Stavola. "A Model of Female Labor Supply in Italy Using Cohort Data." JLE 3, 1 (Jan. 1985, Suppl. S275-S292. (3)

Using two versions of a behavioral model of female labor force participation in Italy, the flat female participation profile over time appears to be caused by counter-balancing economic effects, such as a strong positive effect of women's own wages, and an at least equally strong negative effect of men's wages. With the recent rise in women's earning power, however, some work-disincentive effects, such as age and presence of young children, appear to be less strong.

867. Concepcion, Mercedes B. "Female Labor Force Participation and Fertility," ILR 109, 5-6 (May-June 1974): 503-17. (3)

Data from a number of Asian countries show the expected negative relation between women's labor force participation and fertility in urban, but not in rural areas. The author suggests that the nature of rural society is such that there is no conflict between paid work and having children. Similar conclusions were drawn by Behrman and Wolfe (1984) for Nicaragua, and Kelley, A. C. and deSilva (1974) for Brazil.

868. Cooney, Rosemary S. "A Comparative Study of Work Opportunities for Women." IR 17, 1 (Feb. 1978): 64-74. (3)

The author uses data spanning most of this century for the U.S. and European countries, to test the hypothesis that the growth in industrial/occupational structure has favored not only increased female participation in nonagricultural work, but also declining occupational segregation and an improvement in relative earnings. She finds that this appears to be the case in the long run, but there is little evidence for such a relationship in the short run.

869. Craig, Christina, Elizabeth Garnsey and Jill Rubery. "Labour Market Segmentation and Women's Employment: A Case Study from the United Kingdom." ILR, 124, 3 (May-June 1985): 267-80. (1)

The authors argue that it is not labor market imperfections neoclassical economists talk about, or differences in market productivity that explain pay inequality, but rather systematic and inherent social and economic processes which differentiate the labor force and segment the labor market.

870. Darling, Martha. The Role of Women in the Economy: A Summary Based on Ten National Reports, Washington, DC: OECP, 1975. (3)

This small book offers information on women's labor force participation, unemployment, education, occupations, earnings, and household work, as well as a brief summary of relevant legislation in 10 advanced industrial countries. As the author herself points out, this volume is an overview report, not an in-depth definitive work, and the data presented are not always comparable. Within these limitations, however, it is quite successful in comparing the status of women in the countries included in the survey.

871. Dauffenbach, Robert C. and Ali M. El-Hun. "Married Female Labor Force Participation in a Less Developed Country." JED 5, 1 (July 1980): 45-65. (3)

The authors note that, though no cause/effect relationship has been established, few countries have achieved economic growth without coincident rise in labor force participation of women. Yet little research has been done on determinants of labor force participation of married women in less developed countries. This investigation of the situation in

Libya found that age, education and children tend to have a positive effect, while income has a negative effect. These results lead to the conclusion that increasing education for women is a crucial strategy for a country that wants to encourge their entry into the labor market.

872. Davidson, Marilyn and Cary Cooper. "Women Managers: Work, Stress and Marriage." IJSE 12, 2 (1985): 17-25. (3)

Evidence is presented that women managers are subject to even more pressures than their male counterparts. The authors attribute this mainly to prejudice and discrimination. They also point out, however, that the women who break into middle or senior management positions have learned to cope with the situation, and that their management styles are not substantially different from those of men.

873. Deere, Carmen D. "The Division of Labor by Sex in Agriculture: A Peruvian Case Study." EDCC 30, 4 (July 1982): 795-811. (3)

This case study, to an extent, confirms Boserup's (1970) hypothesis about sexual division of labor and type of cultivation. Where plow agriculture is practiced, men are the primary workers. Nonetheless women also participate in this essentially familial agriculture, especially among the poorer peasants. Where farming ceases to be the main source of income, it also ceases to be predominantly male, and women become virtually equal participants. Among wealthy peasants, on the other hand, women play a very small role in agriculture and hired labor is common.

874. Denti, Ettore. "Sex-Age Patterns of Labour Force Participation By Urban and Rural Populations." ILR 98, 6 (Dec. 1968): 525-50. (3)

This study relies on data from 40 countries in Africa, North and South America, Asia and Europe. National differences in statistical reporting are especially serious for the female labor force, particularly in rural areas of less developed countries.

Nonetheless, there is also evidence of greater real variation in female than male activity rates, influenced by social and cultural as well as economic factors.

875. Devaud, Marcelle and Martine Levy. "Women's Employment in France: Protection or Equality?" ILR 119, 6 (Nov./Dec. 1980): 739-54. (4)

When women, mainly from rural areas, were drawn into the industrial labor force during the second half of the 19th century, conditions were such that there was a perceived need for protective legislation. The position most commonly accepted in France now is that protection should be restricted to the relatively brief periods involving maternity, that is to say pregnancy and child birth. Otherwise there is emphasis on equality, including participation of both parents in child rearing.

876. Devi, D. Radha and M. Ravindra. "Women's Work in India." ISSJ 35, 4 (1983): 683-701. (3)

The proportion of women in paid employment in India is very low, but those who are, tend to have very stable labor force attachment. Most of these workers are, nonetheless, in low-pay, low-status occupations. In fact, 80 percent are in agriculture, only 16 percent in the modern sector. Beyond that, the author notes that the existence of wage discrimination against women is widely noted in all types of employment.

877. DeVries, Margaret G. "Women, Jobs, and Development." FD 8, 4 (Dec. 1971): 2-9. (3)

This is a brief discussion, on a general and popular level, of the role of employment of women in developing countries, given increasing concern with economic progress, underemployment, and a high birth rate.

878. Dixon, Ruth B. "Women in Agriculture: Counting the Labor Force in Developing Countries." PDR 8, 3 (Sep. 1982): 539-66. (2)

The author argues that the undercounting of women (and children) in the labor force leads to serious errors of fact, and possibly to mistaken policies by excluding women from technical assistance of all types. The worst offenders are population censuses. Censuses of agriculture conducted under FAO sponsorship provide considerably higher estimates.

879. D'Onafrio-Flores, Pamela and Sheila M. Pfaflin, eds. Scientific-Technological Change and the Role of Women in Development, Boulder, CO: Westview Press, for the United Nations Institute for Training and Research, 1982. (3)

The papers in this book share the view that women have been and are integrated in economic development, but are excluded from the mainstream of economic and political decision making. They further show that modernization of agriculture often causes women to lose control of their cash-earning positions, both as sellers of products and as paid workers. This is especially so since the men who introduce new methods in developing countries often tend to ignore women. One of the recommendations that emerges is that women should play a more active part in international agencies.

880. Due, Jean M. and Jean T. Peterson. "Women in Agricultural Development." IR 27, 1 (Winter 1985): 22-24. (3)

This paper emphasizes the need to know the sex roles in a particular culture if economic aid is to be helpful in bringing about progress. The authors also point out, however, that these roles can change with economic development.

881. Due, Jean M. and Rebecca Summary. "Constraints to Women and Development in Africa." JMAS 20, 1 (Mar. 1982): 155-66. (3)

It was found that women have far less access to education as compared to men in underdeveloped countries. Similarly they have little access to modern credit institutions.

882. Durand, John D. <u>The Labor Force in Economic Development</u>, Princeton, NJ: Princeton University Press, 1975. (3)

In brief, the author's conclusions are that activity rates of the youngest and oldest females will tend to decline, though less than those of men in the same age groups, but that labor force participation for intermediate age women may go up or down with industrialization, depending on such factors as cultural setting. He rejects the cross-sectional evidence of a U-shaped pattern, where labor force participation would first decline and then rise as economies advance. He concedes that social changes may eventually bring about an upturn of female employment as developing countries continue to progress, but ignores economic development as a possible factor contributing to this.

883. Elizaga, Juan C. "The Participation of Women in the Labour Force of Latin America: Fertility and Other Factors." <u>ILR</u> 109, 5-6 (May-June 1974): 519-38. (3)

Labor force participation of women was found to be very low in Latin America, and had changed little between 1950 and 1970. Data on urban areas for a number of countries show that education and modernization of the economy are more important influences on women taking paid jobs than fertility. These findings may seem surprising, but are consistent with those of other studies of developing countries, where extended families reduce the problems of child care.

884. Eyland, E. A., C. A. Mason and H. M. Lapsley. "Determinants of Female Employment." <u>ER</u> 58, 161 (Mar. 1982): 11-17. (3)

This study, using data from a survey of over one thousand women aged between 20 and 60, all living in a middle class suburb of Sydney, finds that age, marital status, level of education and, where relevant, age of youngest child, are the personal characteristics that are significant determinants of labor force participation.

885. Finch, Janet. "Work, the Family and the Home: A More Egalitarian Future?" IJSE 12, 2 (1985): 26-35. (3)

The author reviews the varied evidence which shows that domestic responsibilities in Great Britain continue to be very unequally distributed between women and men. She also concludes that this is not likely to change substantially without equally substantial social and economic changes.

Fogarty, Rapoport, R. and Rapoport, R. N. See item 8.

886. Franz, Wolfgang. "An Economic Analysis of Female Work Participation and Fertility: Theory and Evidence for the Federal Republic of Germany." JLE 3, 1 (Jan. 1985, Suppl.): S218-S234. (3)

Because trends in labor force participation rates differ among various groups of females--specifically, they declined sharply for young single women, but increased substantially for married women--it is necessary to consider them separately. Wage and income elasticities were also estimated and the expected results were obtained.

887. Franz, Wolfgang and S. Kawasaki. "Labor Supply of Married Women in the Federal Republic of Germany: Theory and Empirical Results from a New Estimation Procedure." EE 6, 2 (1981): 129-43. (1,3 Q)

Using an intrafamily life cycle model and individual census data, both participation and hours of work of married women are estimated. Information on all potentially important variables was not available, but it was possible to use a method to eliminate selectivity bias. Such factors as education, income of husband and presence of young children had the expected effect. The findings with respect to the positive impact of women's own wage were similar to Heckman (1980) for the U.S., but in conflict with the findings of Nakamura, M., Nakamura, A. O. and Cullen (1979) for Canada.

888. Galenson, Marjorie. Women and Work: An International Comparison, ILR Paperback No. 13, N.Y. State School of Industrial and Labor Relations, Cornell University, 1973. (3)

This slim volume constituted one of the earliest examinations of the relative status of women in different countries. We can certainly learn from such comparisons, even when they all too often exclude the Third World. This book can be faulted, however, for putting all the emphasis on the fact that women are less than equal in all the countries, rather than giving due recognition to the differences in the extent to which this is the case. The author also too readily accepts that women "restrict themselves to the conventional women's work--whether from preference, timidity, or ignorance...."

889. Glucklich, Pauline and Margery Povall. "Equal Opportunities: A Case for Action in Default of the Law." PM 11, 1 (Jan. 1979): 28-32. (4)

The authors believe that both in Great Britain and in the U.S. the impact of legislation to outlaw sex discrimination was minimal. They urge, however, that personnel policies to reduce discrimination should be adopted, in part to make further legislation unnecessary, in part because this will lead to more effective use of human resources. Hence the conclusion is reached that personnel specialists have an important role to play in this respect.

890. Gomori, Edith. "Special Protective Legislation and Equality of Employment Opportunity for Women in Hungary." ILR 119, 1 (Jan.-Feb. 1980): 67-77. (4)

The author argues that equality of rights for women needs to be supplemented by special rights and even privileges, in part because of their biological and physical characteristics and their special responsibilities as mothers, in part to compensate for the discrimination they suffered for so long. This appears to be the official government ideology. Feminists may well applaud the view that compensation for past disadvantages is in order, but many would look askance at the tacit acceptance of the traditional role of the mother.

891. Gordon, Ian and Ian Molho. "Women in the Labour Markets of the London Region: A Model of Dependence and Constraint." US 22, 5 (Oct. 1985): 367-86. (3)

This paper relies on a simultaneous equations model of labor and housing market relationships in the London Metropolitan region to investigate characteristics of female labor markets in a spatial context. The results show not only restricted commuting fields for women, but also that the residential location of married women tended to be determined by access to male, not female, employment opportunities. It was further found that limited access to home ownership restricted the residential mobility of women who were not married. Even so, female unemployment was not very sensitive to local demand for labor, because married women tended to drop out of the labor force, and single women moved.

892. Gottfried, Heidi and David Fasenfest. "Gender and Class Formation: Female Clerical Workers." RRPE 16, 1 (Spring 1984): 89-103. (1)

The authors argue that the usual Marxist analyses of class relations essentially ignore the condition of women workers under a dual system of domination by capitalism and patriarchy. For one, such investigations tend to use unionization and strike activity as a yardstick of class activity, while women have been in occupations that have traditionally not been viewed as suitable areas for unionization because of conditions beyond the control of the women themselves.

893. Greenhalgh, Christine A. "A Labour Supply Function for Married Women in Great Britain." Economica, 44, 155 (Aug. 1977): 249-65. (3)

Wage and income elasticities were estimated using cross-section data for British towns. Results are similar to those found in U.S. studies. The author also points out that increases in labor force participation in Britain were greater between 1951 and 1971 than indicated on the basis of cross-section estimates. She interprets this as suggesting a shift in preferences toward paid work.

894. Greenhalgh, Christine A. "Participation and Hours of Work for Married Women in Great Britain." OEP 32, 2 (July 1980): 296-318. (3)

Supply responses of married women are examined using British data from a survey of families in 1971. Problems in making such estimates are discussed, but the fact that the results, both for responses to women's own wages and to other family income, are reasonably close to U.S. estimates in such studies as Ashenfelter and Heckman (1974) is taken as evidence that they are fairly reliable, and can be used in projecting responses to policy changes.

895. Greenhalgh, Christine A. and Mark B. Stewart. "The Occupational Status and Mobility of British Men and Women." OEP 37, 1 (Mar. 1985): 40-71. (3)

The main findings of this study are that the occupational status and mobility of men and women in Great Britain differ significantly, with men experiencing greater upward mobility and achieving higher occupational status. Single women, however, do somewhat better than married or divorced women.

896. Greenhalgh, S. "Sexual Stratification: The Other Side of 'Growth with Equity' in East Asia." PDR 11, 2 (June 1985): 265-314. (1)

Asian societies have had strong sexual and generational hierarchies, and great emphasis on intergenerational obligations. Current reliance of these economies on exports produced by cheap female labor continues in this tradition, not only in Taiwan, but in the other industrializing countries in that region. The author believes that such exploitation of daughters by their families is likely to decline as income rises, but expects sons to continue to do better.

897. Gregory, Paul R. "Fertility and Labor Force Participation in the Soviet Union and Eastern Europe." RES 64, 1 (Feb. 1982): 18-31. (3)

The author first points out that both Western and socialist theories accept the importance of opportunity cost. He goes on to show that in fact, both East and West, children have a negative effect on labor force participation, high wages have a positive effect, and a lesser differential between male and female wages reduces fertility. One major difference, however, is that in Eastern countries education has a positive effect on fertility.

898. Gregory, R. G. and R. C. Duncan. "Segmented Labor Market Theories and the Australian Experience of Equal Pay for Women." JPKE 3, 3 (Spring 1981) 403-28. (3)

This paper analyzes the impact of the large increases in the wages of women as compared to those of men in Australia between 1969 and 1975. The effect on women's employment is found to be surprisingly small. The authors assume this is so because of the large degree of occupational segregation. The effect on income redistribution in favor of women, on the other hand, was found to have been substantial.

899. Gregory, R. G., P. McMahon and B. Whittingham. "Women in the Australian Labor Force: Trends, Causes and Consequences." JLE 3, 1 (Jan. 1985, Suppl.): S293-S309. (3)

Between 1966 and 1982 women increased their share of the work force by 15 percent, while their average earnings rose 30 percent as compared to men. As a result, women's share of the wage bill went up from 18 percent to 28 percent. As in other countries most of the influx into the labor force consisted of married women, and fully 90 percent of the increase was attributable to part-time employment. Unlike the situation in other countries, wage coefficients were generally not found to be significant, presumably because the wage rate is administratively set and has not played a market clearing role. Nor do the higher wages appear to have resulted in a higher quality labor force. It does not seem to have occurred to the authors that the rigid job segregation which they believe has protected women's jobs may also be an obstacle to upgrading women workers.

900. Gronau, Reuben. "The Allocation of Time of Israeli Women." JPE 84, 4 (August 1976, Part 2): S201-20. (3)

Schooling is found to be an important determinant of labor force participation of Israeli women, even beyond the effect it has on wages. Highly educated women for the most part substitute market work for housework, rather than for leisure. One suspects this may be related to the availability of inexpensive help. Even so, preschool children reduce both the mother's market work and her leisure, regardless of amount of schooling. The author concludes by making some interesting comparisons with the U.S. For one, though female labor force participation is lower in Israel, it is higher when education is held constant.

901. Gunderson, Morley. "Decomposition of the Male/Female Earnings Differential: Canada 1970," CJE 12, 3 (Aug. 1979): 479-85. (3)

Using the usual method for decomposition, and 1971 Canadian Census data, the author estimates that only about 40 percent of the earnings gap is explained by differences in endowments. Since this is substantially true even for women who are likely to have work histories similar to those of men, such as single women, the remainder of the gap is ascribed to discrimination.

902. Gustafsson, Siv and Roger Jacobsson. "Trends in Female Labor Force Participation in Sweden." JLE 3, 1 (Jan. 1985, Suppl.): S256-S274. (3)

As in studies for several other countries (e.g., Smith, J. P. and Ward, M. P., 1985, for the U.S.) the rapid increase in the labor force participation rate of Swedish women was found to be chiefly attributable to increases in female real wages. In Sweden, these have risen rapidly even relative to the earnings of men, and the introduction of compulsory separate taxation in 1971 further reduced the difference in male and female after-tax earnings.

903. Haig, B. D. "Sex Discrimination in the Reward for Skills and Experience in the Australian Labor Force." ER 58, 161 (Mar. 1982): 1-10. (3)

Human capital equations are estimated for males and females in Australia, which express earnings as the product of endowments and the return on these endowments. The main explanation for the difference in earnings is the far lower return to qualifications for women than for men. This is in part because of occupational segregation, but is also true within occupations.

904. Haig, B. D. and Margaret Wood. "A Simulation Study of Married Women in the Australian Work Force, 1961-72." AEP 15, 27 (Dec. 1976): 171-85. (3)

The authors found relatively small cyclical movements of female discouraged workers which were outweighed by changes in the numbers of additional workers. They further found that the total pool of cyclical and structural discouraged workers was not large, though there appeared to have been an upward trend between 1971 and 1975. W. J. Merrilees, AEP 17, 31 (Dec. 1978), however, claimed that Haig and Wood counted only those discouraged workers who volunteered the relevant information, and that their methods had other problems as well. His own estimates of discouraged workers were considerably higher, and were in line with those of U.S. studies. Haig and Wood, AEP 17, 31 (Dec. 1978): 368-70 defend their results.

905. Hartog, Jan and Jules Theeuwes. "The Emergence of the Working Wife in Holland." JLE 3, 1 (Jan. 1985, Suppl.): S235-55. (3)

The increase in the labor force participation rate of married women in Holland from virtually zero in 1945 to almost one-fourth in 1975 is investigated using a model based on cross-section data. The rather high own-wage elasticity found suggests that Dutch wives should be expected to catch up increasingly with considerably higher labor force participation rates of married women in other comparable industrialized countries.

906. Heer, David M. and Nadia H. Youssef. "Female Status Among Soviet Central Asian Nationalities: The Melding of Islam and Marxism and Its Implication for

Population Increase." PS 31, 1 (Mar. 1977): 155-73. (1)

There is clearly a potential conflict between Marxist emphasis on the rights of women and traditional Islamic ideology confining them to the role of wife and mother. The authors test the hypothesis that in terms of amount of education relative to men, non-agricultural labor force participation, and child dependency, Islamic women in the USSR would lag behind other Soviet women, but do better than Islamic women elsewhere. This was found to be the case with respect to education and labor force participation, but not for child dependency.

907. Heggade, O. D. "Development of Women Entrepreneurship in India--Problems and Prospects." EA 26, 1 (Jan.-Mar. 1981): 39-50. (4)

The author proposes that women might turn to entrepreneurship as a solution for India's high female unemployment and underemployment rates. S/he also recognizes, however, that serious obstacles of a social, cultural, economic and institutional nature exist in the way of this solution.

908. Hein, Catherine. "Jobs for the Girls: Export Manufacturing in Mauritius." ILR 123, 2 (Mar.-Apr. 1984): 251-65. (3)

The author finds that in Mauritius, unlike most other developing countries, industrialization is considerably expanding the employment opportunities for women. She believes that one reason for this is the lower minimum wage for female workers, and another is women's docility, and suggests that both of these are related to the low social and economic status of women. Their employment also has negative aspects, for hard work and poor nutrition combine to cause serious problems of physical fatigue.

909. Heitlinger, Alena. Women and State Socialism. Sex Inequality in the Soviet Union and Czechoslovakia, McGill-Queen's University Press, Montreal, 1979. (1,3)

The four parts of this book deal with (1) three theoretical perspectives on the social relationships between men and women, (2) the relationship between socialist and feminist movements, (3) and (4) the effects of the state socialist transformation of women's roles in the U.S.S.R. and in Czechoslovakia. On the basis of the available evidence the author concludes that the following factors help to account for the failure of these countries to implement their policy of liberating women: First, resources have been scarce, and growth, especially of heavy industry, had a higher priority than providing goods and services for consumers. Second, the traditional family structure remained unaltered. Last, but not least, the prevalence of sexist cultural norms and the failure to understand that they must be changed proved to be a barrier to progress.

910. Henry, Frances and Pamela Wilson. "The Status of Women in Caribbean Societies: An Overview of Their Social, Economic and Sexual Roles." <u>SES</u> 24, 2 (June 1975): 165-198. (3)

This is an overview of the status of women not only in economic, but in social, sexual and religious spheres. Not surprisingly, there are differences in different countries, but the authors conclude that women always play a subservient role, and nonetheless are often perceived as successful manipulators. This paper makes no comparison with societies outside the Caribbean. Gloomy as this picture is, there is much evidence that women's status compared to that of men is considerably worse in many other parts of the world, particularly with respect to labor force participation.

911. Hill, M. Anne. "Female Labor Force Participation in Developing and Developed Countries - Consideration of the Informal Sector." <u>RES</u> 65, 3 (Aug. 1983): 459-68. (3)

While many models assume that the only choice is "to work, or not to work," there is also the choice to work in the formal or the informal sector. This issue is particularly important in many developing countries. Using a mathematical logit technique, it is determined that women in Japan treat these two sectors as distinct.

912. Holmes, R. A. "Male-Female Earnings Differentials in Canada." JHR 11, 1 (Winter 1976): 109-17. (3)

Using data from the Canadian Survey of Consumer Finances for 1967, which includes workers employed part time or full time, the results show that the gross female-male earnings ratio varies from 35 to 40 percent for the lower education levels, to 60 to 65 percent for the highly educated. When various worker characteristics are introduced, they account for about one-fourth of the gross differential. The author discusses the pros and cons of ascribing the remainder of the gap to discrimination, and the possibility that societal discrimination may also influence the characteristics which "explain" part of the earnings gap.

913. Horna, Jarmila L. A. "Current Literature on the Position and Roles of Women in Czechoslovakia." CSP 20, 1 (Mar. 1978): 78-90. (3)

Sources for this paper are publications by sociologists and demographers, mainly Czechoslovak, Soviet and Polish, as well as statistical data provided by ministries, labor unions and planning institutes. The blind optimism of the early years after the revolution has been replaced by greater realism, the author concludes. She also points out that even now women's organizations are expected to mobilize women for building socialism, and have little opportunity to mobilize for real equality of women, in society or in the home.

914. House, William J. "Occupational Segregation and Discriminatory Pay: The Position of Women in the Cyprus Labour Market." ILR 122, 1 (Feb. 1983): 75-93. (3)

At the time of this study Cyprus had no equal pay or equal opportunity legislation of any sort. There was evidence that women were at a serious disadvantage both with respect to occupational structure and earnings. The author concludes that more research about the reasons for this situation is needed, but also suggests that legislation will be needed if it is to improve.

915. Humphrey, John. "The Growth of Female Employment in Brazilian Manufacturing Industry in the 1970's." JDS 20, 4 (July 1984): 224-47. (3)

Contrary to some predictions, female employment in Brazilian manufacturing grew rapidly during the 1970's, aided by the labor shortage that accompanied the high growth rate. Women's share of the labor force rose across all sectors, causing structural modifications, including a rigid sexual division of labor within industry. This clearly has disadvantages for women, but also makes it unlikely that they will lose their jobs to men when the tight labor market eases.

916. Iglesias, Feliciano H. and Michelle Riboud. Trends in Labor Force Participation of Spanish Women: An Interpretive Essay." JLE 3, 1 (Jan. 1985, Suppl.): S201-S217. (3)

A model based on cross-section data overpredicts the long-term increase in labor force participation of Spanish married women. A specification which uses average labor force experience as an endogenous variable corrects this problem. The improved model also suggests an increasing effect of education on participation, as was found for French women by Riboud (1985).

917. Izraeli, Dafna N. and Kalman Gaier. "Sex and Interoccupational Wage Differences in Israel." IR 18, 2 (Spring 1979): 227-32. (3)

An examination of the evidence shows that in Israel earnings in male occupations are considerably higher than in female occupations, but that this is not true of non-segregated occupations. Further, men tend to earn more in male than in female occupations, but this is not consistently true for women. The author concludes that in Israel, as elsewhere, occupational segregation contributes to the earnings gap.

Jain and Sloane (1978) (1980) (1981)
See items 624, 625, 626.

918. Jonung, C. "Sexual Equality in the Swedish Labor Market." MLR 101, 10 (Oct. 1978): 31-35. (3,4)

This paper reports on the policies instituted in Sweden, the country most devoted to establishing equality between men and women both in the labor market and in the household. On the whole, there has been greater success in making it possible for women to combine market work with household work than in bringing about substantially more sharing of household work between men and women.

919. Joshi, Heather E. "Secondary Workers in the Employment Cycle: Great Britain 1961-74." Economica, 48, 189 (Feb. 1981): 29-44. (3)

An investigation of employment fluctuations shows that these were greater for women with young children and for male pensioners, groups that would be expected to include more discouraged workers than the remainder of the population. For women as a whole, however, employment showed no more instability than for men.

920. Joshi, Heather E., Richard Layard and Susan J. Owen. "Why are More Women Working in Britain?" JLE 3, 1 (Jan. 1985, Suppl.): S147-76. (3)

The answer to the question for Britain, as for the U.S. (see, for instance, Smith, J. P. and Ward, M. P., 1985) is rising real wages. In that country, however, there was also a 15 percent rise in the pay of women relative to men, which, according to the authors, did not cause a decline in relative demand for female employees. A contributing factor may be that employment discrimination was outlawed during the same period. More important probably was that female-intensive sectors of the economy, including government, expanded, and that the ratio of female to male employment in these sectors increased quite sharply.

921. Kelley, Allen C. and Lea M. deSilva. "The Choice of Family Size and the Compatibility of Female Workforce Participation in the Low Income Setting." RE 31, 6 (Nov. 1980): 1081-1101. (3)

This study investigates family size and the labor force participation of women in an underdeveloped country, using data for a region in Brazil. Some interesting differences were found as compared with advanced countries. Children have little deterrent effect on mothers' labor force participation, because extended families are common. Education substantially reduces both number of children born and the number that die, with primary education having most of the effect. Education also increases labor force participation, but this effect comes mainly with higher education. The findings with respect to fertility and labor force participation are consistent with those of Behrman and Wolfe (1984) for Nicaragua and Concepcion (1974) for some Asian countries.

922. Kessler, Sid. "Comparability." OBE 45, 1 (Feb. 1983): 85-104. (3,4)

This paper examines the role of comparable worth in pay determination, especially in the public service sector. The history and present status of the concept in Great Britain is presented. The author concludes that wages in the real world, as opposed to economists' models, are not and cannot be determined by supply and demand alone. Hence he argues that appropriate institutional interference is warranted.

923. Khodaja, Sonad. "Women's Work as Viewed in Present-Day Algerian Society." ILR 121, 4 (July-Aug. 1982): 481-87. (3)

The author stresses that Algeria is only beginning a transition from a traditional society, where the patriarchal extended family is the unit of production, to an industrialized society, where women may become independent workers. The importance of a change in attitudes, as well as legislation, as necessary for further progress is emphasized.

924. Knight, J. B. and R. H. Sabot. "Labor Market Discrimination in a Poor Urban Economy." JDS 19, 1 (Oct. 1982): 67-87. (3)

A study in Tanzania, based on a survey of manufacturing employees found that, like in other countries, men earn more than women. But unlike elsewhere, virtually all of the differential can be explained by differences in economic characteristics. Male and female workers with the same characteristics are paid about the same. On the other hand, only a small part of the black-white differential in earnings could be accounted for.

925. Kottis, Athena P. "Female-Male Earnings Differentials in the Founder Countries of the European Economic Community: An Econometric Investigation." DE 132, 2 (June 1984): 204-23. (3)

The results of this research indicate that in all of the countries except for the Netherlands women earn less than would be expected in terms of their work-related characteristics. It should be noted, however, that information on such variables as work experience and job tenure are not included.

926. Krebs, Edith. "Women Workers and the Trade Unions in Austria: An Interim Report." ILR 112, 4 (Oct. 1975): 265-78. (3)

After a brief description of overall trends in women's employment, occupations, and earnings in Austria, this paper focuses on the position of women in the trade unions, and the position of trade unions on women's issues. The author finds that, even though representation of women in trade unions is high as compared to other countries, they are poorly represented among officers. Union efforts to promote better conditions for women are therefore credited largely to the efforts of male trade unionists.

927. Kumiansky, Anna. "Soviet Fertility, Labor Force Participation and Marital Instability." JCE 7, 2 (June 1983): 114-30. (3)

Chronic labor shortages and concern with a low birthrate have brought about a great interest in the USSR in the relation between labor force participation and fertility. In this paper a simultaneous equations model based on neo-classical theory of household behavior is used to investigate this issue. The results suggest that methods to increase fertility, such as outlawing abortion, would greatly reduce labor force participation, and that greater labor force participation would reduce fertility even more. Provision of more child care would raise both, but not very much, while higher levels of education for women would actually be expected to reduce both. The author does not consider the possibility of a substantial change in sharing household work, perhaps because it appears unlikely at this time.

928. Kurian, George and Ratna Ghosh, eds. Women in the Family and the Economy: An International Comparative Survey. Westport, CT: Greenwood Press, 1981. (3,4)

This extensive collection of essays deals with many aspects of women's lives, from family, social and religious environment to fertility, employment and occupational choice in a large number of developed and developing countries. Though the individual chapters are brief, they are in general of very high quality.

929. Kynch, Jacely and Amartya Sen. "Indian Women: Well-Being and Survival." CJE 7, 3-4 (Dec. 1983): 363-80. (3)

This paper is concerned with the decline in the female-male ratio in the population of India during this century. Substantial sex-bias is found in malnutrition, hospitalization and morbidity, as well as mortality.

930. Kyriazis, Natalie and J. Henripin. "Women's Employment and Fertility in Quebec." PS 36, 3 (Nov. 1982): 431-40. (3)

The data used were obtained from the Quebec survey of fertility conducted by the Centre de Sontage de l'Universite de Montreal. The traditionally high fertility has been declining, and economic factors are found to play an important role. Most interesting is that no reciprocal relationship between employment and fertility is discovered, though fertility does influence the amount of time worked since marriage. The author plausibly concludes that these Catholic women continue to place great importance on their traditional role as mothers.

931. Landau, C. E. "Recent Legislation and Case Law in the EEC on Sex Equality in Employment." ILR 123, 1 (Jan.-Feb. 1984): 53-70. (4)

This article takes stock of recent progress under EEC and national legislation towards "equal pay for work of equal value," and towards equality of opportunity and treatment in all other respects related to work. The author concludes that, on the whole, legislation and case law are in advance of realities in the labor market, but that there is also room for further improvement in the legal field.

932. Lapidus, Gail W. "USSR Women at Work: Changing Patterns." IR 14, 2 (May 1975): 178-95. (3)

Though women in the USSR are more heavily represented both in heavy, unskilled labor and in scientific and technical occupations than in the industrialized Western countries, men predominate in skilled labor and managerial positions. The author ascribes the remaining segregation to differences in aspirations, in turn caused by the continuing constraints imposed upon women by their role in the family, not greatly alleviated by the economic decisions of the political hierarchy.

933. Lapidus, Gail W. Women in Soviet Society: Equality, Development and Social Change. L.A.: U. of Calif. Press, 1978. (1,3,4)

This thorough study of the development of the position of women from pre-revolutionary days to the 1970's explicitly aims to avoid the usual approach of judging the progress of women by the standards of the libertarian and individualistic concerns of nineteenth century Marxism or feminism. The author takes the view that the real aims of the regime has been to facilitate the seizure and consolidation of power and to enhance its economic and political capacity. Readers will learn a great deal about women in the USSR, but their appreciation of the author's interpretation will crucially depend on the extent to which they share the above point of view.

934. Lapidus, Gail W., ed. Women, Work and Family in the Soviet Union. PE 24, 5-6-7 (Sept.-Oct.-Nov. 1981). (3)

An introduction by the editor provides a broad overview both of the position of women in the Soviet Union, and the perceptions of the situation by various social scientists in that country. The remainder of the volume consists of three major segments concerned with levels and patterns of women's employment, its impact on the family, and policies that influence the situation. Each segment consists of a number of brief papers, all translated from the Russian. In general, they tend to expound the official point of view.

935. Larsen, C. A. "Equal Pay for Women in the United Kingdom." ILR 103, 1 (Jan. 1971): 1-11. (4)

After a detailed examination of the Equal Pay Act of 1970 which required employers in the United Kingdom to remove all discrimination by 1975, the author considers its implications. S/he concludes that so far from increasing women's unemployment, equal pay will widen women's opportunities, because employers are less likely to consider them inferior when they are no longer cheaper. At the same time, she expects problems to remain with respect to opportunities for training of women, and with respect to their own motivation.

936. Layard, Richard, M. Barton and Anton Zabalza. "Married Women's Participation and Hours." Economica, 47, 185 (Feb. 1980): 51-77. (3)

Like other studies, this one finds a positive effect of women's own wages, and a negative effect of husband's wages on wive's labor force participation. Age of the youngest child is the most powerful single factor. All these variables, however, explain no more than one-third of the post World War II growth of labor force participation in England. Husband's employment status is also important, but surprisingly wives of unemployed husbands are substantially less likely to be in the labor force. The same was found to be true in Australia (Soherer, 1978) apparently because of unemployment insurance provisions.

937. Leijon, Anna G. "Sexual Equality in the Labor Market: Some Experiences and Views of the Nordic Countries." ILR 42, 1 (Aug.-Sept. 1975): 109-24. (3)

The drive toward equality for women began earlier, and has gone further in the Scandinavian countries than elsewhere. Sweden, particularly, has gone so far as to fail to ratify ILO Conventions because of being protective of women, and hence discriminatory. Even so, occupational segregation remains extensive, and family responsibilities continue to be quite unequally divided.

938. Leppel, Karen. "The Relations Among Child Quality, Family Structure and the Value of Mother's Time in Malaysia." MER 27, 2 (Oct. 1982): 61-70. (3)

This study was intended to test a model of relationships between "child quality," as measured by educational attainment, and the value of a woman's time in Malaysia, using data of the Malaysian Family Life Survey collected in 1976-77. The results indicate that the size and age composition of the household influence a woman's asking wage. Data deficiencies were, however, serious, and precluded any conclusions about child quality.

939. Maki, Dennis R. "Unions as 'Gatekeepers' of Occupational Sex Discrimination: Canadian Evidence." ApplE 15, 4 (Aug. 1983) 469-77. (3)

Using data on union membership from Statistics Canada, the author did not find any positive evidence of discrimination against women by unions. There is a considerably smaller proportion of female than of male workers in labor unions, which might be caused by discrimination, but could also be brought about by differences in tastes for unionism.

940. Mason, Karen O. and V. T. Palan. "Female Employment and Fertility in Peninsular Malaysia: The Maternal Role Incompatability Hypothesis Reconsidered." Dem. 18, 4 (Nov. 1981): 549-75. (3)

Analysis of the 1974 Malaysian Fertility and Family Survey shows a negative relationship between women's work and fertility only when there is a serious conflict between working and caring for children. The simple hypothesis of conflict between children and work therefore seems less appropriate for the case of Malaysia than a more complex one that takes into account the structure of the household's socioeconomic opportunities, which may be traditional or modern, with varying roles of children and other family members.

941. McGavin, P. A. "Equal Pay for Women: A Reassessment of the Australian Experience." AEP 22, 40 (June 1983): 48-59. (3)

Unlike Gregory, R. G. and Duncan, R. C. (1981) this author uses hours of work and concludes that the effect of the full implementation of equal pay in 1975 was to reduce the proportion of the labor force that was female compared to what it would have been in the absence of this policy. He points especially to the increase of part time women workers in the private sector, and the increased employment of women in the government sector. Gregory and Duncan respond by pointing out that women's wages already increased by 30 percent between 1969 and 1975, when there was growth in female relative to male employment. Hence, changes after 75 may well be caused by changing occupation mix.

942. McMahon, Patrick J. "An International Comparison of Labor Force Participation, 1977-84." MLR 109, 5 (May 1986): 3-12. (3)

This paper compares labor force participation of various demographic groups in Australia, Canada, West Germany, Japan, Sweden and the U.S. There were considerable differences among them, but there was a consistent pattern of declines in the labor force participation of men, and increases for women.

943. McNabb, Robert. "The Labor Force Participation of Married Women." MSESS 3 (Sept. 1977): 221-35. (3)

This paper examines the reasons for the increased labor force participation of women in Great Britain, with particular emphasis on regional variations. The most important explanatory variables found were women's wages and industrial structure. Testing for the impact of economic conditions, a stronger discouraged worker than added worker effect was found, consistent with later findings by Layard and Zabalza (1980), and those of Soherer (1978) for Australia. The presence of children also appeared to influence the labor force participation decision, but this varied considerably according to their age.

944. Meissner, Martin, Elizabeth W. Humphreys, Scott M. Meis and William J. Scheu. "No Exit for Wives: Sexual Divison of Labour and the Cumulation of Household Demands." CRSA 12, 4 (Nov. 1975): 424-39. (3)

An investigation of the sexual division of labor of several hundred families in Greater Vancouver, Canada, showed that husbands tend to remain insensitive to the cumulation of demands on wives' time of household, employment, and young children.

945. Metzker, Maria. "Overt and Disguised Discrimination Against Women in Collective Agreements: Findings of an Austrian Survey." ILR 119, 2 (Mar.-Apr. 1980): 243-53. (3)

This survey of the situation in Austria examines all areas in which there was differentiation between men and women in collective bargaining agreements in force in March 1978, focusing on the extent to which the classification of occupations into particular wage groups was based on sex-specific criteria. A variety of possible sources of discrimination was discovered. The paper concludes with a brief discussion of anti-discrimination legislation that had recently been introduced.

946. Miller, Barbara D. "Female Labor Participation and Female Seclusion in Rural India: A Regional View." EDCC 30, 4 (July 1982): 777-94. (3)

This investigation of various regions in India gives scant support to the hypothesis that female labor force participation is related to natural ecology. A clearer relationship is found between the pattern of women's participation in the labor force and variations in seclusion, as for instance, represented by their appearance in marriage processions. Even here, however, there are notable "patches of discord."

947. Miller, Paul W. and Paul A. Volker. "A Cross-Section Analysis of the Labor Force Participation of Married Women in Australia." ER 59, 164 (Mar. 1983): 28-42. (3)

This paper models labor force participation of married women in Australia using cross-section data from the 1976 Census. In general, expected wage, husband's income, rural/urban residence and fertility had the same effects found in other industrialized countries. One interesting difference was that little evidence of a discouraged worker effect was found. This might be because the variable used to determine its existence was unemployment among men, rather than unemployment among women, but that has been standard practice in other studies as well. The authors also note that immigrant women were more likely to be in the labor force than native females.

948. Miller, Paul W. and Paul A. Volker. "The Screening Hypothesis: An Application of the Wiles Test." EI, 22, 1 (Jan. 1984): 121-27. (2)

This paper tests the screening hypothesis of Peter Wiles, which states that only if trained individuals earn more in jobs for which their training is directly relevant than in other positions does human capital explain the differential in returns. Using data from a census of recent economics and science graduates from Australian universities, the researchers find this to be the case only for male science graduates. This also suggests that female graduates are less likely to obtain jobs where their particular skills are utilized.

949. Mincer, Jacob. "Inter-Country Comparisons of Labor Force Trends and of Related Developments: An Overview," in Richard Leyard and Jacob Mincer, eds., Growth of Women's Labor Force: Causes and Consequences 3, 1 (Jan. 1985, Suppl.) S1-S32. (1,3)

This is the introduction to a volume of essays, each of which deals with the economic status of women in 12 industrialized countries (all of them included in this bibliography). It provides an overview and critique of the data and empirical research they offer, as well as the theories on which they rely. The authors adhere to neoclassical theory, with emphasis on the importance of human capital, but there is much information that should be useful to readers, whether or not they hold the same views.

950. Moock, Peter R. "The Efficiency of Women as Farm Managers: Kenya." AJAE 58, 5 (Dec. 1976): 831-35. (3)

This study compares the extent to which men and women in Kenya are able to acquire knowledge how best to combine inputs in the production of maize on small-size farms. It appears that education has a more positive impact on women, which the author believes may be because only the less capable among educated men remain in this sector. Men, on the other hand, benefit more from contact with extension programs. The reason suggested for this is that women are not offered as much help, a view widely shared by experts in this field.

951. Morgenstern, Felice. "Women Workers and the Courts." ILR 98, 10 (Oct. 1975): 15-27. (4)

The author suggests that the trend of judicial decisions concerning the problems of women in the labor market and in society at large may be a useful indicator of women's changing status. She provides a brief summary of key decisions during recent years in a number of countries. While she admits that any general conclusion on such a broad topic is bound to be problematic, she believes that the general pattern is encouraging.

952. Moroney, John R. "Do Women Earn Less Under Capitalism?" in John R. Moroney, ed., Income Inequality, Lexington, MA: Lexington Books, 1978, pp. 141-60. (3)

The evidence offered in this paper shows that the male-female earnings gap is not smaller in Czechoslovkia, Hungary and Poland than in many West European countries. The author also makes much of the fact that the gap is larger in English speaking countries, but as it happens the situation has changed radically since this observation was made. This is true in Great Britian and, particularly, in Australia.

953. Moskoff, William. "Women and Work in Israel and the Islamic Middle East." QREB 22, 4 (Winter 1982): 89-104. (3)

The author concludes that the labor force participation of Moslem women is extremely low because the social and cultural forces of Islam impinge on their role as workers. Israeli women have a far greater participation rate, but a great deal of occupational segregation exists there as well. This is true even in the kibutzim which have historically had an egalitarian ideology.

954. Myrdal, Alva and Viola Klein. Women's Two Roles: Home and Work, London: Routledge and Kegan Paul, Ltd., Second Edition, 1968. (3)

This book, first published in 1956, is a survey of the position of women in France, Great Britain, Sweden and the United States. The main emphasis of the work, now widely regarded as a classic, is on the revolutionary change of women's entry into the labor market, and the failure of society to achieve a complementary reorganization "such as would make this development beneficial to all concerned." The authors, however, conclude on an optimistic note, suggesting that these changes are coming, albeit slowly.

955. Nakamura, Alice and Masao Nakamura. "A Comparison of the Labor Force Behavior of Married Women in the

United States and Canada, with Special Attention to the Impact of Income Taxes." Economet. 49, 2 (Mar. 1981): 451-89. (3,4)

The probability of working, hours of work, and wage rate are estimated for U.S. and Canadian wives. An important difference between the two is that Canadian couples must file separate tax returns. Because of the interdependence of hours of work and the marginal tax rate an iterative process is employed. Unlike most other studies, the results here point toward wives working fewer hours as the wage rate increases.

956. Nakanishi, Tamako. "Equality or Protection? Protective Legislation for Women in Japan." ILR 122, 5 (Sept.-Oct. 1983): 609-21. (4)

In 1977 the Japanese government published a 10-year National Plan of Action for the Promotion of Measures relating to Women and expressed its determination to bring about a climate more favorable to their progress in the labor market. A committee was also established to review protective legislation, and to recommend changes in line with the most recent scientific findings. The author believes that measures not only to safeguard health and safety, but to alleviate the heavier family responsibilities of women are justified. As is so often the case, family arrangements are simply accepted as a given.

957. Nash, Edmund. "The Status of Women in the U.S.S.R." MLR 93, 6 (June 1970): 39-44. (3)

A brief, but useful survey which points out that women in the USSR not only have an extremely high labor force participation rate, but also have achieved a very respectable representation among professionals and technicians, and generally are quite satisfied with their working conditions. On the other hand, the author also reports on the substantial double burden of Soviet women, who continue to do most of the housework. What the author fails to report is that women are seriously underrepresented in the higher levels of most occupations, and that such evidence as exists suggests that there is a substantial male-female earnings gap. For a report that emphasizes these gloomier aspects, see, for instance, Lapidus (1978).

958. Nasr, Julinda A., Nabil F. Khoury and Henry T. Azzam, eds. Women, Employment and Development in the Arab World, NY: Mouton Publishers, 1985. (3,4)

This book provides information on women's labor force participation in Arab countries, with special emphasis on Lebanon, the Yemen Arab Republic, the Gulf States and Jordan. A survey of sex-role orientation among university students shows women to be considerably less traditional than men. Some chapters contain policy recommendations for making more progress toward integrating Arab women in economic development, and suggestions for urgently needed research. This is a useful source of information about the set of countries where women continue to play the smallest role in the paid labor force.

959. Nielsen, Ruth. "Special Protective Legislation for Women in the Nordic Countries." ILR 119, 1 (Jan.-Feb. 1980): 39-49. (4)

In the Nordic countries, where women have achieved a relatively high degree of equality, the use of special protective legislation reached its peak as early as the first quarter of this century, and has virtually disappeared since. The author nonetheless examines the pros and cons of special protection, and concludes by agreeing with what she perceives to be the general consensus that, under present conditions, traditional sex-role stereotypes are no justification for such policies.

960. Novikova, E. E., V. S. Iazykova, and Z. A. Iankova. "Women's Work and the Family." PE 24, 5-6-7 (Sept.-Oct.-Nov. 1981): 165-90. (3)

A rather dull discussion of the official Soviet view of women and work, typified by considering "dual" roles of women, without raising the possibility that men with families might also have dual responsibilities. Further, while noting that there is "reason to express our gratitude to our mothers, wives, and sisters for their selfless work," housework is nonetheless referred to as "nonproductive."

961. OECD, <u>The Integration of Women into the Economy</u>. Paris, 1985. (3)

This book provides a wealth of information on the economic status of women in the advanced industrialized countries, as well as an overview of the position of girls and women in the educational system, the treatment of women in social security, taxation, and other government policies related to women.

962. Ofer, Gur and Aaron Vinakur. "The Labor Force Participation of Married Women in the Soviet Union: A Household Cross-Section Analysis." <u>JCE</u> 7, 2 (June 1983): 158-76. (3)

The main findings of a study using data obtained from emigrants is that the high labor force participation of Soviet women is in part explained by relatively high wages, large amounts of schooling, low-family income, and small numbers of children, but that ideology and social pressure also play a role. At the same time, there is evidence that the supply of labor is eventually backward bending, that is to say, as wage rate increases to a high level, hours worked decline. These findings are consistent with those of Berliner (1983).

963. Officer, L. H. and P. R. Anderson. "Labour Force Participation in Canada." <u>Can JE</u> 2, 2 (May 1969): 278-87. (3)

Labor force participation in Canada is examined using quarterly data for 1950 to 1967. It was found that during periods of high unemployment the discouraged worker effect predominated for female teenagers, but the additional worker effect was greater for adult women. Over the long run, higher income caused young women to stay in school longer. But greater acceptance of employment for women and decreasing birth rates were associated with higher labor force participation, so that they can no longer be merely regarded as secondary workers.

964. O'Neill, June A. "Earnings Differentials: Empirical Evidence and Causes" in Gunther Schmid and Renate Weitzel, eds. Sex Discrimination and Equal Opportunity: The Labor Market and Employment Policy, NY: St. Martin's Press, 1984, pp. 69-91 (3)

This paper provides a good deal of information about changes in the male-female earnings gap in five industrialized countries, and shows that the other four have made considerably more progress in reducing the differential than has the U.S. Even so the author clings to the view that the unexplained portion of it is "a measure of our ignorance" and need not create a presumption that there is discrimination. If, however, it were true that the explanation for much of the gap in the U.S. is that women and men "evaluate job characteristics differently because of differences in their roles in the home," why would this not be equally true elsewhere?

965. Palmer, Ingrid. "Rural Women and the Basic-Needs Approach to Development." ILR 115, 1 (Jan.-Feb. 1977): 97-107. (3)

The author points out that present methods of introducing commercial crops and technological improvement in agriculture often increase women's work, but also reduce their rights to participate in the returns. Hence she believes that "the basic needs approach" concerned with supply and demand for essentials through more remunerative and higher-productivity employment would be preferable. There must, however, be concern not only with the needs of the family unit, but with production relations and access to assets of men and women as well.

966. Pavlatova, Jarmila. "The Woman in the Work Process." CED 8 (May 1978): 56-65. (1,3)

This is a report of the Presidium of the Central Committee of the Communist Party of Czechoslovakia. Hence it is not surprising to find the view that the establishment of a Marxist-Leninist society is both necessary and sufficient for achieving equality for women. Some data are provided, showing substantial improvement in women's education, a very high degree of labor force participation, and a relatively small degree of occupational segregation. No information on hierarchical segregation within occupations, or on earnings, is offered. Nor is there any mention of division of household work. For a quite different view see Scott, H. (1974).

967. Pettman, Barrie O., ed. Equal Pay for Women. Progress and Problems in Seven Countries. Bradford, England: MCB Books, 1975. (3)

The rather uneven papers in this book focus on the effect government policies in six advanced industrialized countries have had on the male-female earnings gap in each of them.

968. Pittin, Renee. "Documentation and Analysis of the Invisible Work of Invisible Women: A Nigerian Case Study." ILR 123, 4 (July-Aug. 1984): 473-90. (3)

The author argues that the use of male-biased instruments and techniques substantially undervalues women's work in Third World countries. This is true even of their income producing activities, as shown in this case study of secluded women in a Northern Nigerian city.

969. Powell, Dorian L. "Female Labour Force Participation and Fertility: An Exploratory Study of Jamaican Women." SES 25, 3 (Sep. 1976): 234-58. (3)

The most striking finding of this study is that both labor force participation and fertility of Jamaican women are very high. This suggests compatibility of their role in the labor market and in the family, as appears frequently to be the case in developing countries. Nonetheless, women with four or more children were less likely to be employed. It was also found that unions other than marriage, common in this country, tend to be less stable than marriages, and are even less likely to inhibit labor force participation.

970. Powell, Dorian L. "The Role of Women in the Caribbean." SES 33, 2 (June 1984): 97-122. (3)

The author shows that Caribbean women have always operated in roles which spanned the private and public domain. On the one hand, their role as mother (though not necessarily as wife) was always of great importance. On the other hand, many have been major or even sole providers for their families. Not only have they engaged in many activities in what is termed the "informal sector," but they also have had a very high labor force participation rate, only slightly below that of men. At the same time, educational opportunities for women are only beginning to improve, and their role in politics is very limited. No information on earnings is provided.

971. Ram, Rati. "Market Opportunities, Intrafamily Resource Allocation and Sex-Specific Survival Rates: An Intercountry Extension." AER 74, 5 (Dec. 1984): 1080-86. (3)

This study extends that of Rosenzweig and Schultz (1982) by using a larger sample and considering overall male-female survival rates. It confirms their findings that the partial effect of higher labor force participation rates of women is to shift allocation of family resources toward them so as to generate higher female survival rates and longer female life-spans. The author then argues that it is not selfishness, but rationality that induces allocation in the direction that provides a higher economic payoff, but apparently forgets that you have to be alive in order to share in the payoff that is being rationally maximized.

972. Ratner, Ronnie S., ed. Equal Employment Policy for Women. Strategies for Implementation in the United States, Canada and Western Europe, Philadelphia: Temple University Press, 1980. (4)

The editor provides a good idea of the scope of this volume when she says that its chapters deal with a wide array of issues ranging from mandating equal employment policy through legislation and collective agreements to implementing it through administrative agency regulations, court decisions, conciliation and arbitration.

The authors explore as well the relationship between equal employment policy, other labor market policies and social policies such as day care programs, family allowances, maternal and parental leave policies, and social services for the aged. Finally, they consider family-related incentives implicit in tax policy and social security benefits. While inevitably somewhat uneven, and not uniform in coverage, this is an interesting and informative book.

973. Renaud, Paul S. A. and Jacques J. Siegers. "Income and Substitution Effects in Family Labour Supply," DE 132, 3 (1984): 350-66. (3)

Using data for married couples in the Netherlands and a model similar to that developed in Leuthold (1978) it is found that income effects are negative, but significant only for wives, and that wives' labor supply is also more sensitive to wage changes than is that of husbands.

974. Riboud, Michelle. "An Analysis of Women's Labor Force Participation in France: Cross-Section Estimates and Time-Series Evidence," JLE 3, 1 (Jan. 1985, Suppl.): S177-S200. (3)

Historic trends in women's labor force participation in France are overpredicted by a model based on cross-section data, which measures the effects of wives' wages, husbands' earnings, families' unearned income, and number of children. A different specification (following Mincer and Polachek, 1974) using the fraction of lifetime after leaving school spent in the labor force, gives an accurate prediction. This model also shows that the positive effect of education on labor force participation increased. Similar results were obtained for Spain by Iglesias and Riboud (1985).

975. Robb, Roberta E. "Earnings Differentials Between Males and Females in Ontario, 1971." CJE 11, 2 (May 1978): 350-59. (3)

Separate earnings functions were estimated for men and women, and the differential was decomposed by the Blinder (1973) method, for all males and females, and for males and single females 30 years of age and over. In both cases the unexplained portion was lower in a regression standardized for occupation and industry. This supports other U.S. and Canadian studies showing that part of the earnings gap is caused by occupational segregation. The other interesting finding is that while the unexplained differential is smaller for single women, the pattern is essentially the same as for all women. Block and Williams, W. (1981) raise questions about the author's conclusion that the unexplained differential is likely to represent discrimination.

976. Robertson, Matthew and Ann S. Roy. "Fertility, Labor Force Participation and the Relative Income Hypothesis: An Empirical Test of the Easterlin-Wachter Model on the basis of Canadian Experience." AJES 41, 4 (Oct. 1982): 339-50. (3)

This research uses Canadian data to test the Easterlin-Wachter hypothesis that fertility and labor force participation depend on the level of actual family income relative to the desired level of income. The hypothesis is, however, modified by using incomes of other age groups, rather than of parents to determine the desired income level. The authors claim the results support the hypothesis, for the baby boom led to a decline in income of young adults relative to older cohorts, and young women's labor force participation increased. But do they really expect that young women will be more likely to stay home when wages for them, as well as their husbands, will be higher?

977. Robinson, Chris and Nigel Tomes. "More on the Labour Supply of Canadian Women." CJE 18, 1 (Jan. 1985): 156-63. (3)

The authors, using a different data set, confirm the findings of Nakamura, A. O. and Nakamura, M. (1981), that, contrary to the general consensus, women, like men, tend to supply a smaller quantity of labor at a higher wage rate.

978. Roos, Patricia A. "Marriage and Women's Occupational Attainment in Cross-Cultural Perspective." ASR 48, 6 (Dec. 1983): 852-64. (3)

This paper examines differences in labor force behavior and occupational attainment between ever married and never married women in 12 industrialized countries in order to test the hypothesis that gender differences in domestic responsibilities explain occupational segregation. The study offers some evidence that never married women are more similar to men than women who are or have been married, but the differences between them do not, for the most part, translate into differences in occupational prestige and wage rates, and the outcome is rather similar for the two groups of women.

979. Rosenzweig, Mark R. and T. Paul Schultz. "Market Opportunities, Genetic Endowments, and Intrafamily Resource Distribution: Child Survival in Rural India." AER 72, 4 (Sept. 1982): 803-15. (3)

Using data from rural India, the authors show that, contrary to the implication of theories which suggest that parents will allocate investment to children so as to equalize the opportunity of individuals with different endowments, parents reinforce differences associated with the sex of their children. Boys, who are expected to be more economically productive, receive a larger share of family resources, as shown by their higher rate of survival. As might be expected, this disparity is greatest among the poorest families.

980. Ruggie, Mary. The State and Working Women. A Comparative Study of Britain and Sweden. Princeton, NJ: Princeton University Press, 1984. (4)

The author focuses on the role of the government in mediating the relationship between social forces and women's position. Specifically, she argues that the liberal-welfare approach in Britain has been far less successful in achieving greater equality for women than the societal corporate model in Sweden, where goals are determined by bargaining among the leading partners in the government coalition of state, labor and capital.

981. Safilios-Rothschild, Constantina. "The Influence of the Wife's Degree of Work Commitment Upon Some Aspects of Family Organization and Dynamics." JMF 32, 4 (Nov. 1970b): 681-91. (3)

This study, based on data for 896 Greek women collected in 1966-67, shows that employed women with high work commitment are generally more satisfied with their marriage, and perceive their relationship with their husbands as more egalitarian than do those with low work commitment. This is so even though husbands actually participate more in household work, when wives belong to the latter group.

982. Schmid, Gunther and Renate Weitzel. Sex Discrimination and Equal Opportunity: The Labor Market and Employment Policy, NY: St. Martin's Press, 1984. (3,4)

Most of the papers in this book examine the changing economic status of women in West Germany, Sweden, the United Kingdom and the United States. With the exception of the useful summary chapter by Schmid, the comparisons for the most part emphasize similarities, generally failing to explore reasons for existing differences. Thus we do not learn why women's unemployment rate is lower than men's in the U.K., why the earnings gap is so much smaller in Sweden than in other countries, why women are overrepresented in agriculture in Germany, and very much underrepresented in the U.S. One chapter deals with the problems of evaluating the success of various systems, which are real enough. But one may question one of the author's main recommendations, to shift from a focus on individuals to viewing them as members of households, especially today when families so often break up.

983. Schultz, T. Paul. "Changing World Prices, Women's Wages, and the Fertility Transition: Sweden, 1860-1910." JPE 93, 6 (Dec. 1985): 1126-54. (3)

A thorough investigation shows that changes in demand which increased women's wages compared to those of men explained one-quarter of the decline in fertility during this period.

984. Scott, Hilda. Does Socialism Liberate Women? Experiences from Eastern Europe. Boston: Beacon Press, 1974. (3,1)

In brief, the answer to the question in the title is "no." After a rather thorough examination of the situation in Czechoslovakia (there is far less information about other countries), the author reaches the conclusion that socialist ideology has made important contributions to the economic and social progress of women, but that there has been no transformation of private housekeeping into a social industry. Nor have any of the countries developed a plan for changing this situation. Though this book has a great deal of interesting information it could have been improved by including a systematic presentation of relevant data.

985. Seear, B. N. Reentry of Women to the Labor Market After an Interruption of Employment, Paris: Organization for Economic Cooperation and Development, 1971. (3)

This survey examines the problems of women involved in reentry to the labor market in all the countries belonging to the OECD. There is concern about the costs and benefits not only for the women involved, but also for the economies in which they live. Finally, there are suggestions for making reentry easier.

986. Seguret, Marie-Clair. "Women and Working Conditions: Prospects for Improvement?" ILR 122, 3 (May-June 1983): 295-311. (3)

Beginning with standard observations that a large a proportion of the world's labor force is female, but that women continue to fare poorly in the labor force, both because of the type of jobs they have, and because of their "family responsibilities," the author goes on to make recommendations for bringing about improvements. They are no more novel or profound than her analysis of the existing problems.

987. Shapiro, David M. and Morton Stelcner. "Male-Female Earnings Differentials and the Role of Language in Canada, Ontario and Quebec." CJE 14, 2 (May 1981): 341-48. (3)

This study suggests that the unexplained portion of the male-female earnings gap was somewhat smaller for Quebec than for Ontario, or for Canada as a whole. Evidence was also found that the gap was smaller in the public than in the private sector. Nonetheless, the wage determination process was found to be similar in all instances. With respect to language, bilingualism did not appear to command a premium for either sex, though Quebec linguistic origins are significant in determining male earnings.

988. Shimada, Haruo and Yoshio Higuchi. "An Analysis of Trends in Female Labor Force Pariticipation in Japan." JLE 3, 1 (Jan. 1985, Suppl.): S355-S374. (3)

The labor force participation of women has been declining from the post World War II period of industrialization through the 1970's. This drop is entirely due to a reduction among agricultural households, where the participation rate had been extremely high, while that in other households has been steadily increasing. Labor supply equations for these paid employees estimated from time-series data show the expected negative income and positive wage elasticities. Cross-section analysis gives similarly reasonable results.

989. Shorey, John. "An Analysis of Sex Differences in Quits." OEP 35, 2 (July 1983): 213-27. (3)

This study shows that, all else equal, men are more likely than women to quit their jobs. Overall, quit rates are, however, higher for women because of their lower wages and inferior labor market opportunities. Women were also found to be more likely to quit and leave the labor force, while men are more likely to leave for another job. In general, these results for Britain are very similar to those found by Blau, F. D. and Kahn (1981) for the U.S.

990. Siebert, W. S. and A. Young, "Sex and Family Status Differentials in Professional Earnings: The Case of Librarians." SJPE 30, 1 (Feb. 1983): 18-41. (3)

Data collected by mail survey in Britain are interpreted to show that family role factors determine motivation and earnings, while sex discrimination plays an insignificant part. Nonetheless, married men receive higher earnings than measured productivity can explain. The authors claim this may be because of unmeasured motivational effects, but discrimination in favor of this group is clearly an alternative explanation.

991. Siegers, Jacques J. and R. Zandanel. "A Simultaneous Analysis of the Labour Force Participation of Married Women and the Presence of Young Children in the Family." DE 129, 3 (1981): 382-93. (3Q)

Like many other studies in industrialized countries, this one finds a strong negative relationship between presence of young children and the labor force participation of mothers, in this case in the Netherlands. Using a sophisticated econometric procedure the authors find evidence that causality runs from labor force participation of married women to the presence of young children in the family.

992. Silverstone, Rosalie and Audrey Ward, eds. Careers of Professional Women, London: Croom Helm Ltd., 1980. (3)

The problems of women in seven different professions--accountancy, architecture, dentistry, medicine, nursing, physiotherapy and teaching--are discussed in light of the widespread pattern of career interruptions, but also long-term commitment to the labor market. Career choices, and strategies for coping with family and career under existing constraints, as well as career outcomes, are discussed.

993. Sloane, Peter J., ed. Women and Low Pay, London: The Macmillan Press, Ltd., 1980. (3,4)

The papers in this book, dealing primarily with developments in Great Britain, but also Canada and the U.S., take note of the low earnings of women, and their disproportionate representation among the poor. They go on to examine the reasons for this, attempting to determine to what extent it is women's lower qualifications, their lower occupational achievement with the same qualifications, or lower earnings in similar jobs that account for this. Chiplin, Curran and Parsley particularly focus on policies that may have contributed to the significant decline in the male-female earnings gap in the 1970s in Great Britain.

994. Smith, Stanley K. "Determinants of Female Labor Force Participation and Family Size in Mexico City." EDCC 30, 1 (Oct. 1981): 129-52. (3)

This study of Mexican women uses a one period, static model which views utility as a function of "child services," market goods and services, and leisure. The results show that the wife's potential wage has a significant negative effect on work in the traditional sector (which can be combined with child care), a significant positive effect on work in the modern sector (not compatible with child care), and a significant negative effect on family size. One reason for these relationships is that wages are higher in the modern sector, particularly for women with relatively high levels of skills, so that the opportunity cost of time spent with children is the difference between wages in the two sectors.

995. Soherer, P. A. "The Perverse Additional Worker Effect in Australia." AEP 17, 31 (Dec. 1978): 261-75. (3)

In Australia, as in Great Britain (Layard and Zabalza, 1980; McNabb, 1977), wives of unemployed men are less likely to be in the labor force than those whose husbands are working, while the opposite is true in the U.S. The author suggests this is probably the case because in Australia a family on unemployment insurance is subject to a means test and finds that its benefits are virtually reduced by the total amount of the wife's earnings. It should be noted that their behavior shows that wives in both countries still tend to be secondary wage earners.

996. Sonin, M. "Socioeconomic Problems of Female Employment." PE 24, 5-6-7 (Sept.-Oct.-Nov. 1981): 22-32. (3)

The author propounds the official Soviet line that since the revolution women have achieved de facto as well as de jure equality. If this were truly the case, there would hardly be any need, more than 60 years later, to address "socioeconomic problems of female employment" or to emphasize the need for raising the skills of female workers.

997. Sorrentino, Constance. "International Comparisons of LFP 1960-81." MLR 106, 2 (Feb. 1983): 23-36. (3)

Data for nine advanced industrialized economies show significant differences in the trend of male and female labor force participation over the two decades concerned. The former declined in all cases, the latter increased in five countries throughout the whole period, and in all but one during the latter half. We are also shown the differences in age structure of employment between men and women, and at different times for women.

998. Standing, Guy. "Education and Female Participation in the Labour Force." ILR 114, 3 (Nov.-Dec. 1976): 281-97. (3)

Surprisingly, the author, unlike many others, does not find the evidence convincing that there a consistent association between education for women and their higher labor force participation in developing countries. Even more surprisingly, while recognizing a number of reasons why a positive relationship should exist, he argues that there might be offsetting forces, though he admits they "are less easy to demonstrate." The two conclusions that seem more solidly based are that as long as women's labor force participation is low, it will be argued that scarce resources should be allocated to a greater extent to educating men, and that there is a tendency to ignore the benefits of education for nonmarket activities.

999. Standing, Guy. Labour Force Participation and Development. Geneva International Labour Office, 1981. (3)

This monograph is primarily concerned with low-income industrializing economies, and mainly focuses on the labor force participation rate of women. The author warns that due caution must be exercised in applying evidence from the more advanced countries, where most research has been done to date, and also points out that other methodological problems exist. The analysis of the determinants of labor force participation examines, in addition to economic growth, changing patterns of fertility, growing need for cash income, the structure of employment and unemployment, rural-urban migration and the spread of education. Like Durand (1975) he emphasizes that women's labor force participation often tends to decline in the early stages of development.

1000. Steel, William F. "Female and Small-Scale Employment under Modernization in Ghana." EDCC 30, 1 (Oct. 1981): 153-67. (3)

This paper examines developments in Ghana and finds no support for Boserup's (1970) thesis that industrialization in its early stages tends to diminish female employment opportunities in agricultural and small-scale production, and presumably causes a decline in women's labor force participation. On the contrary, women in Ghana were successfully absorbed in the growing manufacturing industries throughout the 1960's. This may illustrate Durand's (1975) point that the effect of development on female employment will vary in different socities.

1001. Stelcner, Morton and Jan Breslaw. "Income Taxes and the Labor Supply of Married Women in Quebec." SEJ 51, 4 (Apr. 1985): 1053-72. (3,4)

Using a variety of estimation techniques the authors find that wives rationally perceive the effects of a very progressive and high income tax. A positive relation between labor force participation and own wage, and a negative relation between labor force participation and the tax rate are found.

1002. Stewart, Mark B. and Christine A. Greenhalgh. "Work History Patterns and the Occupational Attainment of Women." EJ 94, 375 (Sept. 1984): 493-519. (3)

This study of British women workers shows a substantial downward effect of interruptions of work experience on later economic position. Work history patterns were found to differ systematically with age, education, marital status, as well as initial occupation.

1003. Stokes, C. Shannon and Yen-Sheng Hsieh. "Female Employment and Reproductive Behavior in Taiwan." Dem. 20, 3 (Aug. 1983): 313-31. (3)

Unlike many studies which take fertility as given and consider women's labor force participation the dependent variable, the causal connection here is assumed to be the other way around. Clearly, there is some justification for both approaches. In any case, the relationship between female employment and fertility preferences or behavior is found to be very weak in this national sample of Taiwanese women, and this is true even for women who work in the modern sector. This is typical of other non-western societies as well (e.g., Behrman and Wolfe, 1984; Concepcion, 1974; Kelley, A. C. and deSilva, 1980).

1004. Sullerot, Evelyne. "Equality of Remuneration for Men and Women in the Member States of the EEC." ILR 112, 2-3 (Aug.-Sept. 1975): 87-108. (3,4)

The author points out, first of all, how difficult it is to compare the earnings of men and women and shows the problems this creates for the equal pay legislation that has been introduced in the EEC countries. She also points out, however, that progress has been made.

1005. Swafford, Michael. "Sex Differences in Soviet Earnings." ASR 43, 5 (Oct. 1978): 657-73. (3)

Virtually no data are published in the USSR that shed light directly on the earnings of women as compared to men. This study, relying on unpublished data for the capital of Armenia, found that women's earnings were about 65 percent of men's earnings. The author suggests there is evidence this may be representative for the country. Estimates of other researchers have been somewhat higher.

1006. Swidinsky, Robert. "Working Wives, Income Distribution and Poverty." CPP 9, 1 (Mar. 1983): 71-80. (3)

This paper examines the impact of working wives on income distribution and poverty in Canada in 1977. The evidence from 13,140 husband-wife family units suggests that the effect was to reduce income inequality only slightly, and to lower the incidence of poverty by no more than about 28 percent. The author's conjecture that "most of the increased participation probably occurred among families whose income was already above the poverty line" is plausible, but the conclusion that improved labor market opportunities for women will do little to combat poverty ignores the importance of female-headed households.

1007. Szabady, Egon. "Gainful Occupation and Motherhood Position of Women in Hungary." Pop R 13, 1-2 (Jan.-Dec. 1969): 59-67. (3)

The author begins by suggesting that "In Hungary today, the central problem of the position of women is the conflict between the continuation of their gainful occupation and the fulfillment of their family tasks." His opinion is that women have been fully "emancipated," and that attention should now be turned toward helping them with their double burden. As long as this limited view of emancipation, and of housework as women's responsibility continues, one may expect the male establishment to continue to be generous with words but stingy with resources that would really help to solve the problem.

1008. Szalai, Alexander, ed. The Use of Time. The Hague: Mouton, 1972. (3)

While one would hope that this book is by now out of date, to the extent that the allocation of time may have changed since the early 1970's, there is no more recent work that even approximates its international coverage, and careful presentation of findings. Further, such evidence as is available here and there shows that changes in the division of time between men and women have been far from dramatic.

1009. Szinavacz, Maxmilliane E. "Role Allocation, Family Structure and Female Employment." JMF 39, 4 (Nov. 1977): 781-91. (3)

This study takes into account not only employment of the wife, but the closeness of her contacts with kin and interaction with them as determinants of task allocation and decision-making within the family. Based on data on 1370 Austrian blue-collar workers, the results suggest that the wife's reliance upon relatives is related to a high degree of role segregation between spouses even when she is in the labor market. Therefore, the author concludes that the wife's employment does not necessarily lead to egalitarian relationships.

1010. Tahlmann-Antenen, Helene. "Equal Pay: The Position in Switzerland." ILR 104, 4 (Oct. 1971): 275-88. (3)

Switzerland did not ratify the ILO Equal Remuneration Convention of 1951. The author examines the obstacles that have stood in the way of such action. She also makes suggestions how women might achieve equality without such legislation, but in a country which is opposed to equal pay laws it seems rather unrealistic to assume that they will implement the policies she suggests for achieving equality in the home, the educational system and the labor market.

1011. Takahashi, Nabuko. "Women's Employment in Japan in a Period of Rapid Technological Change." ILR 98 6 (Dec. 1968): 493-510. (3)

The author concludes that the extensive redistribution of women's employment, in both quantity and nature, between 1955 and 1965 was realized with relatively little trouble. Women's total labor force participation increased, while there was a very large shift from agriculture and mining to other sectors. The transition was facilitated by thoughtful cooperation between employers and labor unions, and by the high growth rate of the economy. In view of what we know about the status of women in Japan today, the optimism of this report seems unwarranted.

1012. Takahashi, Nabuko. "Women's Wages in Japan and the Question of Equal Pay." ILR 111, 1 (Jan. 1975): 51-68. (3)

As is true elsewhere, the introduction of "equal pay" legislation has done little to close the male-female earnings gap in Japan. The author provides evidence that the large existing differential in earnings is caused by the behavior both of the employers and of the women workers themselves. She further believes that societal attitudes continue to play a large part, and governmental policies to improve the situation have not been effective.

1013. Taylor, Debbie, ed. Women: A World Report. London, Methuen London Ltd., 1985. (3)

This book proclaims the ambitious goal of attempting "to capture the essence of the position of women at the end of the decade [for women] and set it down as a benchmark against which the future can be measured." It would be overly optimistic to assume that any single volume can live up to such a high purpose, but this work, mainly by telling the story of individual women throughout the world, offers a good many insights that will help to supplement the more orthodox and usually far more general work of social scientists.

1014. Treiman, Donald J. and Patricia A. Roos. "Sex and Earnings in Industrial Society: A Nine-Nation Comparison." AJS 89, 3 (Nov. 1983): 612-44. (3)

Several hypotheses that might explain the substantial differences in male-female earnings found in nine countries are tested: Scant evidence is found that women's deficiency in human capital, their greater household responsibilities, or their concentration in low paying jobs contribute much to the earnings gap. The authors conclude that the main cause may be "deeply entrenched in institutional arrangements that limit women's opportunities and achievements." We might have gained more useful insights if the authors had also examined the rather substantial differences between countries in the size of the earnings gap and in their institutions.

1015. Turchaninova, Svetlana. "Trends in Women's Employment in the USSR." ILR 112, 4 (Oct. 1975): 253-64. (3)

The author not only proclaims that "full equality for women in every field of economic, social and political activity is one of the basic principles of the Soviet State," but also points to the high labor force participation of women, and their representation in high status occupations as evidence of success. The only "outstanding problems" mentioned are the need to "give women more leisure and expand their vocational training," and to improve occupational safety. For a very different view, which empahsizes women's failure to reach the top, the male-female earnings gap, and the large burden of housekeeping Soviet women face, see, for instance Lapidus (1978).

1016. Turnbull, P. and G. Williams. "Sex Differentials in Teacher's Pay." JRSS Series A, 137, Part 2 (1974): 245-58. (3)

Earnings differences between teachers who were single women, married women and men in Great Britain were examined. Though most of the differential between married women and men was accounted for when length of service was taken into account, a significant unexplained gap remained. Moreover, the position of married women teachers deteriorated slightly between 1963 and 1971. Single women were found to do better than married women, but not as well as male teachers.

1017. Tzannatos, P. Zafivis and Zabalza Anton. "The Anatomy of the Rise of British Female Relative Wages in the 1970's: Evidence From the New Earnings Survey." BJIR 22, 2 (July 1984): 177-94. (3)

This paper examines the sudden and rapid rise of female relative to male wages in the 1970's in Great Britain, and finds that it was very uniform across all sub-groups studied, except for white collar employees in the public sector. The authors conclude this was neither caused by compositional effects, nor by any significant deterioration of male earnings, but that the machinery of pay determination adopted may have contributed substantially in the implementation of equal pay legislation.

1018. United Nations, The Economic Role of Women in the ECE Region, New York, 1980. (3)

A study compiled by the Economic Commission for Europe that provides a good deal of information on labor force participation, occupational distribution, pay differentials, and education of women as compared to men for European countries, East and West, as well as Canada and the U.S. While in a rapidly changing world the data provided inevitably are somewhat at variance with the current situation, the generally thoughtful discussion and evaluation of the various factors that interact in determining the economic role of women, duly emphasizing differences as well as similarities among various countries, continues to make this a useful reference work.

1019. Vansgnes, Kari. "Equal Pay in Norway." ILR 103, 4 (Apr. 1971): 379-92. (4)

Since pay rates in Norway are generally fixed by means of collective bargaining, government worked toward equal pay for women by promoting its implementation in that manner. In 1961 the major organizations of employers and of workers agreed to this goal, and the male-female earnings gap declined appreciably after that. Not surprisingly, however, women continue to have lower wages than men to some extent, in part because of occupational segregation, in part because of less continuous employment.

1020. Verma, Prakash C. "Trend Analysis of Women's Employment in India in the Organized Sector 1962-1973." EA 20, 11 (Nov. 1975): 441-45. (3)

Employment of women in the organized sector (defined as public sector establishments and all those non-agricultural establishments in the private sector employing 10 or more workers) was found to have increased slightly more than that of men in all states in India between 1962 and 1973. The rate of increase had been higher in the public sector, though the total number employed was greater in the private sector.

Ward, K. B. and Pampel (1985) See item 335.
Weller (1968) See item 171.

1021. Weller, Robert H. "Role Conflict and Fertilty." SES 18, 3 (Sep. 1969): 263-72. (3)

The author reports that no negative relation was found in Puerto Rico between women's labor force participation and fertility. This is consistent with the findings of other studies for developing countries, such as Behrman and Wolfe (1984), Concepcion (1974), and Kelley, A. C. and deSilva (1980), and supports the author's view that women there do not experience role conflict as women in industrialized countries do. He concludes that employment, per se, cannot be counted on to reduce the nubmer of children, especially not low pay, flexible jobs, such as domestic service.

1022. Werneke, Diane. "The Economic Slowdown and Women's Employment Opportunities." ILR 117, 1 (Jan.-Feb. 1978): 37-52. (3)

An analysis of the effects of a recent recession in Belgium, France, Sweden and the United Kingdom shows that it had a very negative effect on women's already weak economic position. The author ascribes this to the concentration of female workers in a narrow range of low-skill jobs, particularly vulnerable to an economic downturn, as well as their lack of seniority and lack of access to training.

1023. Winegarden, C. R. "Women's Fertility, Market Work and Marital Status: A Test of the New Household Economics with International Data." Economica, 51, 204 (Nov. 1984): 447-56. (3)

A model is constructed which uses data from a number of European countries to show that higher real wages for women reduce their propensity to marry and to bear children. Higher wages for men have the opposite effect. These results are in accord with the predictions of the "new household economics."

1024. Wolchik, Sharon L. "Elite Strategy Toward Women in Czechoslovakia: Liberation or Mobilization?" SCC 14, 2-3 (Summer/Autumn 1981): 123-34. (3)

The author concludes that, in spite of the historically less subservient position of women in Czechoslovakia, as compared to many other countries, and the relatively positive attitude of the population toward greater equality for women, official policies, with respect to women's issues, are essentially the same as in the USSR. Women are chiefly viewed as a resource for building a socialist society, and their equality has remained a secondary issue. Unequal division of labor in the home has not been challenged and with growing concern about the low birth rate emphasis on motherhood has grown.

1025. Wolfe, Barbara L. and Jere R. Behrman. "Who Is Schooled in Developing Countries? The Roles of Income, Parental Schooling, Sex, Residence, and Family Size." EER 3, 3 (1984): 231-45. (3)

This paper reports that, contrary to the usual situation in developing nations, girls receive more education than boys in rural areas of Nicaragua. At the same time, the authors also found a preference for male children among a substantial minority of mothers. Both these findings are ascribed to the higher productivity of boys which, on the one hand, raise the opportunity cost of their schooling, on the other hand, lead to higher expected returns from them.

1026. Yohalem, Alice M., ed. Women Returning to Work. Policies and Progress in Five Countries. Totowa, NJ: Allanheld, Osmun and Co. Publisher, Inc., 1980. (3)

This book focuses on problems associated with late entry and reentry of women into the labor market in five advanced industrialized countries, a major phenomenon in recent years in all of them. Each chapter discusses the reasons for this development in one country, describes its various aspects, and finally, offers information about various policies that have been used or might be used to facilitate the process.

1027. Youssef, Nadia H. Women and Work in Developing Societies, Westport, CT: Greenwood Press, 1974. (3)

The author sets out to show that the participation of women in the nonagricultural labor force is not simply a function of economic development. She demonstrates this by contrasting women's participation in economic activities in a group of Latin American and Middle Eastern countries, roughly similar in terms of industrial and occupational structures, and suggests that it is differences in women's education and family arrangements, and their interaction with the existing social organization that explains the substantial disparities in women's status in the two regions. It should be noted, however, that labor force participation of women is low in Latin America compared to the rest of the world. This bears out Denti's (1968) conclusion that female activity rates are influenced by social and cultural, not merely economic conditions.

1028. Yusuf, Farhat and D. K. Briggs. "Female Participation in the Labor Force of Selected Latin American Countries." PDR 18, 3 (Autumn 1979): 215-29. (3)

An examination of data from 17 Latin American countries showed that female education, fertility and urbanization were the three variables most strongly related to women's labor force participation. Of these, the proportion of 15 to 19 year olds receiving a secondary education turned out to be particularly important, accounting for more than two-thirds of the variation. The authors fail to consider the possibility, however, that the same attitudes that encourage more education for women may also be conducive to encouraging them to enter the labor force.

1029. Zabalza, Anton. "The Determinants of Teacher Supply." REStud. 46, 1 (Jan. 1979): 131-47. (3)

This study shows that a specification for labor supply which includes both starting salary and the rate of increase produces better results than when only starting or average salary is used. The evidence also indicates that men are quite responsive to career prospects but women are influenced to a far greater extent by immediate earnings. Nonetheless, prospective earnings profiles are relevant for both men and women.

1030. Zabalza, Anton. "The CES Utility Function, Non-Linear Budget Constraints and Labour Supply: Results on Female Participation and Hours." EJ 93, 370 (June 1983): 312-30. (2,3,Q)

This paper presents an estimation procedure that, among other things, takes into account the tax system and distinguishes between those who do, and do not, pay taxes. The results obtained for British wives suggest that earlier, less sophisticated models may have underestimated the responsiveness of women's labor supply to economic factors.

1031. Zabalza, Anton and P. Zafivis Tzannatos. "The Effect of Britain's Anti-Discriminatory Legislation on Relative Pay and Employment" EJ 95, 379 (Sept. 1985): 679-99. (4)

Contrary to others, such as Chiplin, Curran and Parsley (1980), these authors take the view that the 15 percent increase in pay of women as compared to men is not explained by shifts in female employment from low to high paid sectors, but rather by increases in pay within sectors. It is further argued that this was not the result of incomes policies, but rather of anti-discrimination legislation. Whatever the reasons for the substantial narrowing of the earnings gap, the authors show that it was achieved without any unfavorable effect on women's employment.

AUTHOR INDEX

SUBJECT INDEX